CYLINDER SEALS

A Documentary Essay on the Art and Religion of the Ancient Near East

by

H. FRANKFORT, M.A., Ph.D.

Research Professor of Oriental Archaeology in the Oriental Institute, the University of Chicago; Extraordinary Professor in the History and Archaeology of the Ancient Near East in the University of Amsterdam; Correspondent of the Royal Netherlands Academy of Sciences

LONDON
MACMILLAN AND CO.
1939

Republished in 1965 by Gregg Press Limited
1 Westmead, Farnborough, Hants., England

Printed in England

TO THE MEMORY
OF
HUMFRY PAYNE

TABLE OF CONTENTS

CHAPTER III. THE SUBJECTS OF THE EARLY DYNASTIC SEALS

SECTION III

THE SEALS OF THE SARGONID AGE

CHAPTER I. DEVELOPMENT AND SCOPE OF THE SARGONID STYLE

CHAPTER II. THE SUBJECTS OF THE SARGONID SEALS

SECTION V

THE SEALS FROM THE KASSITE TO THE PERSIAN PERIOD

SECTION VI

THE DERIVATIVE STYLES OF THE ANCIENT NEAR EAST

PREFACE

THE CYLINDER SEALS of Mesopotamia constitute her most original contribution to art. They reflect, moreover, several aspects of her civilisation of which detailed knowledge from other sources is scanty. Her neighbours adapted her form of seal, and it is estimated that over 10,000 cylinder seals are known. The purpose of this book is to reduce that vast accumulation to a comprehensible order, and to determine what conclusions we are entitled to draw from the documentary evidence which these seals supply.

No abstract principle of classification will serve the purpose. It is essential to disentangle the sequence through which the various styles of glyptic art flowered in and around Mesopotamia. Hitherto the most conspicuous and hardy growths have alone been recognised, and even these remained unrelated and therefore full of unexplained peculiarities, while the numerous hybrids altogether defied understanding. In the absence of sufficient stratigraphical evidence for a detailed historical account other criteria have sometimes been sought. Attempts were made to study the seals according to their subject-matter, or to isolate certain groups of common origin. But many subjects remained in use, though altered in appearance, through long periods, or were revived after temporary eclipse. Identical motives possessed widely different significance at various times. Neither scene nor symbol can be interpreted irrespective of the age to which the seal belongs. And a local classification is no more satisfactory because the glyptic art of all the regions of the Near East is to a large extent dependent upon that of Mesopotamia and only explicable by reference to that cultural centre. The best method is still the one followed by that pioneer in our field, Joachim Ménant, namely to trace the historical perspective which is inherent in the material.

The need of makeshifts has in any case diminished of recent years, since the large quantity of seals found in regularly conducted excavations has established their date beyond question. Together with the inscribed seals of certain rulers and officials these stratified seals and impressions supply the framework for the classification of the thousands of cylinders in public and private collections of which the provenance is unknown. Special research devoted to selected periods or groups will lead to yet greater precision, but only the seals of the first millennium B.C. remain surrounded by that vagueness which results from the absence of modern stratigraphical data. Even in Syria such are now being found. Until these are available a certain amount of definition may be achieved by studying Syrian seals in conjunction with successive Mesopotamian types upon which the Syrian groups depend. Although we cannot hope to reach finality by an indirect method, it will appear that the approach is by no means unprofitable.

Complete uncertainty still prevails on the subject of signets or stamp-seals. The simplicity—even crudeness—of their designs makes dating more hazardous; stratigraphical evidence is of the scantiest, and since their repertoire and distribution differ from those of the cylinders, and since they are in all respects of far less importance, they have been excluded from our present survey.

This book displaces neither the catalogues of the various collections nor the publications of excavators. The collections contain many excellent and interesting pieces which we have not reproduced, since our concern here is with the typical and not with the exceptional. And only a complete series of seals as found together in the same layer of an excavated site can give an impression of the range of quality and the variety of design prevailing at any one period. But both types of publication can be used with profit only after a previous study of the subject. This is obvious in the case of the catalogues of collections in which nothing, not even the genuineness of the objects, can be taken for granted. And among the seals found in excavations there is always a considerable number found outside the proper context, for the engraved stones were both indestructible and valuable, and therefore remained in use as heirlooms or were reused—as they are to-day—when accidentally discovered. It is therefore a mistake to rely blindly on stratigraphical data in dealing with individual seals, though the application of such data to large quantities is ultimately the basis of our knowledge.

I have attempted to choose the illustrations in such a way that they may enable the investigator, in conjunction with the text, to determine the age of the vast majority of cylinder seals. The student of religion and the philologist will find in our discussion of the seal designs as well-defined an iconography as can be established by a collation of all the pictorial variants of each theme and figure. For a more complete understanding of these we depend upon their own ability to find textual references which may substantiate, elaborate or supersede our interpretations. This book should supply them with the basis for a much needed confrontation of pictorial and written evidence.

The average quality of the seals here illustrated is somewhat higher than that of a normal series found during excavation. But in poorly executed work the features which are characteristic of their age are apt to be blurred together with the rest of the design. They are therefore often difficult to date and liable to cause confusion; they are best dealt with by determining from which of the more competent productions they are likely to be derived. Thus we are once more led to the conclusion that the style of the seal designs is the surest guide to their age and therefore to their interpretation.

With unexpected frequency I have encountered the objection that stylistic criteria are subjective. As to that, no more can be admitted beyond the fact that the ability to see with precision and to note all that can be seen varies with the observer, while training counts for much. I shall have failed if the demonstrations which follow do not develop the capacity, in the reader unaccustomed to such matters, for observing stylistic features, as well as convince him of their objective existence and significance.

The stylistic development, then, of the most characteristic pictorial expression of the Babylonians, forms the continuous narrative of this book. It is periodically interrupted by chapters discussing the subjects of the seals of each period. It is prefaced by a chapter disposing of some subsidiary matter and followed by a discussion of cylinder seals found outside Mesopotamia. The individual seals are referred to by letters and numbers explained on p. xx. A Chronological Index will be found at the end of the book.

Polemics have been reduced to a minimum. My indebtedness to the work of predecessors—Ménant, Ward, Weber, Delaporte, Contenau and von der Osten—is obvious and far-reaching. It would not have served any useful purpose to discuss differences of opinion, often caused by acquaintance with material which was not available when they were writing.

Although this book does not bear the imprint of the University of Chicago Press, it is intimately related to the field work of the Oriental Institute in Iraq, which I have directed for seven years. Not only have many of the general problems concerning us been solved as a result of those excavations, but the work has produced the largest collection of accurately stratified seals which has ever come to light. These seals, almost a thousand in number, will be published in a volume entitled *Cylinder Seals from the Diyala Region*, which is being prepared for the press simultaneously with this book. I am indebted to the Director of the Oriental Institute, Dr John A. Wilson, for the permission to illustrate some unpublished cylinders found in the excavations of the Oriental Institute.

Three members of the Iraq Expedition have generously given of their spare time to assist me. Mrs Rigmor Jacobsen granted me the benefit of her unrivalled skill in making the most of each seal by preparing impressions and photographs, not only of those found in our own excavations but also of a number of seals from other sites, such as Ur and Kish, which are now in the

Museum at Baghdad, and of cylinders bought by the Iraq Museum and the Allard Pierson Museum in Amsterdam. Miss G. Rachel Levy prepared the drawings for Pls. IV*g–l*; XI *a*, *h*; and text-figs. 1, 3, 7–12, 14, 15, 25, 40, 43, 81; and Miss Mary A. Chubb those of text-figs. 13, 30, 63, 64, 65, 69, 70; and both gave me substantial assistance in preparing the book for the press.

Finally, I want to express my gratitude to those persons and institutions, enumerated on pp. xvii–xix, who allowed me to reproduce certain seals and often supplied photographs so as to ensure the best possible reproductions of the objects in their care.

ACKNOWLEDGMENTS

The Author wishes to acknowledge his gratitude to the heads of institutions, individual scholars and publishers by whose courtesy the following illustrations are included.

Dr John A. Wilson, Director of the Oriental Institute, the University of Chicago: Plates I*d–n*; II*a, l*; VI*a, d–j*; VII*b, c, e, f, h–k*; IX*a–e, h*; X*a, e–g*; XIV*a, c, j*; XV*l, m*; XVI*e, h*; XVIII*f*; XIX*e*; XX*a, c*; XXI*b, d, ef*; XXIII*c, j*; XXIV*b, f*; XXV*b, e*; XXVI*a–c, l*; XXVII*c, g, k*; XXX*b, g*; XXXVIII*a, f, g, j, l*; XXXIX*b, f, h*; XL*b, f*; XLI*d*; XLIII*a, e, g*. Text-figures 27, 29, 34, 35, 108.

The Trustees of the British Museum and Keeper of Assyrian and Egyptian Antiquities: Plates V*g, j*; VI*b*; VIII*b*; XII*a*; XVII*a, h*; XVIII*a*; XIX*a*; XXII*e, f*; XXIV*c*; XXV*c, d*; XXVII*a, i*; XXVIII*a, j*; XXX*k, m*; XXXI*a*; XXXII*f, g, i*; XXXIII*a, d, e*; XXXIV*e, i*; XXXV*a, d, g, h, k*; XXXVI*b*; XXXVII*d*; XL*m*; XLI*a*; XLIII*l*; XLIV*i*; XLV*i*; XLVI*h, i, o, p, q*. Text-figures 13, 100, 101.

The Visitors and Keeper of the Ashmolean Museum: Plates I*c*; X*h*; XIV*f*; XV*g*; XXI*i*; XXIII*g*; XXXVIII*c, e, h, i, k*; XXXIX*c, d, e*; XLI*f*; XLII*l*; XLIV*b, f, k, n*; XLVI*v*.

The Director of the Vorderasiatische Abteilung der Staatlichen Museen, Berlin: Plates I*b*; III*a*; V*e*; VIII*j*; IX*c*; XV*n*; XVII*g, j*; XVIII*a*; XX*d*; XXII*h*; XXIII*f*; XXV*f*; XXIX*e, k*; XXX*c, f, i, l*; XXXI*c*; XXXII*c, d*; XXXIII*b, c, j*; XXXIV*a, b, f, g, h*; XXXVI*a, l*; XXXVII*b, c, k*; XXXIX*a*; XL*a*; XLII*e, n*; XLIV*m*. Text-figures 50–59, 64, 72–78.

The Director of the Museum of Fine Arts, Boston: Plates II*h, n*; XXV*g*; XXVI*j*; XXVII*b*; XXIX*f*; XXXII*b*; XXXVII*a, f, n*; XLI*r*; XLII*c*; XLIII*n, o*; XLV*g, j*. Text-figure 30.

The Director of Antiquities, Baghdad: Plates II*g*; III*b*; VII*a*; IX*i*; X*b*; XIX*f*; XXIX*m*; XXXII*a*; XXXVII*g*.

The Director of Antiquities, Jerusalem: Plates XLI*o, p*; XLIII*c, d*; XLIV*o, r, s, t*; XLV*a, h*; XLVI*r*.

The Director of the Musée Guimet: Plates XXII*i*; XXVII*h*; XXXIV*j*; XXXV*l*.

The Carnegie Institution of Washington: Text-figures 36, 41, 66, 67, 68, 85, 86, 88, 89.

Dr Ernest A. Mackay and the Field Museum of Natural History at Chicago: Plates VIII*a, e, g, i*; XIV*d*; XV*b, g*.

The Director of the Royal Dutch Cabinet of Medals, The Hague: Plates XII*b*; XXIV*d*; XXVI*e*; XXXIX*g*. Text-figure 42.

The Pierpont Morgan Library: Plates IV*h*; VII*g*; XI*a*; XXII*a*; XXIII*d, e*; XXV*h*; XXVII*e*; XXVIII*n*; XXXI*h*; XLIV*k*.

The Director of the Aegyptische Abteilung der Staatlichen Museen, Berlin: Plate XLVI*a, b, c, e, j, k*.

The Director, The German Archaeological Institute, Athens: Plate XLII *o*.

The Director, Skulpturgalerie, Dresden: Plate V *c*.

The Director, Staatlicher Münzsammlung, München: Plate XIII *b*.

The Curator of the Beyrouth Museum: Plate XLI *m*, *n*.

M. Louis Delaporte: Plates II *b*, *e*, *j*, *k*, *o*; IV *g*, *i*, *j*, *k*, *l*; V *a*, *b*, *f*, *h*; VII *d*; VIII *c*, *f*, *h*, *k*; X *d*; XIV *e*; XV *d*; XVI *g*; XVII *d*; XVIII *g*, *h*, *i*, *j*; XIX *b*; XX *b*, *f*, *g*; XXI *a*, *g*, *h*; XXII *b*, *d*, *g*; XXIII *i*; XXIV *e*; XXVIII *b–i*, *k*, *m*; XXIX *i*; XXX *d*, *e*, *h*; XXXI *b*, *d*, *g*, *j*; XXXIII *f*, *i*, *k*; XXXIV *c*; XXXV *f*, *i*; XXXVI *h*, *k*; XXXVII *m*; XXXIX *i*, *k–n*, *q*, *r*; XL *d*, *e*, *i*, *j*, *o*; XLI *b*, *c*, *e*, *g*, *h*, *l*; XLII *b*, *d*, *i*; XLIII *b*, *i*, *k*; XLIV *a*, *c*, *g*, *j*; XLVI *d*, *l*, *m*, *n*. Text-figures 7, 8, 12, 14, 25, 31, 32, 37, 38, 39, 71, 82, 83, 84, 92.

Sir Leonard C. Woolley: Plates VIII *d*; XII *c*; XIII *c–h*; XIV *b*, *g*, *i*; XV *a*, *b*, *d*; XVI *a*, *b*, *d*; XVII *i*; XVIII *b*, *d*, *k*; XIX *d*, *e*; XX *h*, *k*, *i*; XXII *j*; XXIII *h*.

Dr H. H. von der Osten: Plates VI *c*; X *b*; XV *j*; XVII *b*, *e*; XXIV *b*; XXV *a*; XXVI *h*; XXVII *d*, *j*, *m*; XXVIII *d*; XXIX *g*, *h*; XXX *j*; XXXII *e*; XXXIII *h*; XXXV *e*; XXXVI *e*, *f*, *j*; XXXVII *c*, *l*; XXXIX *p*; XL *c*; XLI *i*, *j*, *k*; XLII *g*, *h*, *m*; XLIII *a*; XLIV *d*, *l*, *q*. Text-figures 3, 65.

Dr C. W. McEwan: Plates I *d*, *e*; XXXVIII *a*, *f*, *g*, *j*, *l*; XXXIX *b*, *f*, *h*; XL *b*, *f*; XLI *d*; XLIII *a*, *e*, *g*.

Dr E. Heinrich: Plate XI *a–g*, *i–n*. Text-figures 24, 26.

Prof. A. Nöldeke and Dr E. Heinrich: Plates III *e*; IV *a–f*, *m*. Text-figures 2, 4, 5, 6.

Dr G. Contenau: Text-figures 33, 79, 80.

Sir Arthur Evans: Text-figures 103–107.

Dr K. Bittel and Dr H. Güterbock: Text-figures 90, 91.

Prof. Claude F. A. Schaeffer: Plates XLV *b*, *d*, *e*, *f*, *k*, *m*, *n*; XLVI *s*.

Mr Louis Speleers: Plates XXIV *a*; XXVI *g*; XXVIII *l*; XXIX *a*, *l*; XL *l*.

Prof. Léon Legrain: Plates IX *f*, *g*; XXIII *b*; XXV *i*; XXIX *d*. Text-figures 9, 10, 11, 15, 16, 17, 18, 19, 28.

Dr Erich F. Schmidt: Text-figures 69, 70.

Dr E. F. Weidner and Dr D. Opitz: Plate XXII *k*. Text-figures 60–62.

Mr G. D. Hornblower: Plates XLIV *u*; XLVI *t*, *u*.

Prof. Sir William M. Flinders Petrie: Plate XLVI *f*, *g*. Text-figures 93–99.

Prof. Robert H. Pfeiffer: Plates II *m*; XXX *a*; XLII *a*. Text-figures 44–49.

Monsieur R. Ghirshman: Plates XXXVIII *b*, *d*; XLIII *j*.

Mrs E. Douglas van Buren: Plate XLIV *e*.

Prof. E. A. Speiser: Plate III *e*.

The late Mr J. L. Starkey: Plate XLIII *f*, *h*.

Mr M. E. L. Mallowan: Plate XLIII *m*.

Dr Julius Jordan: Plate III *f*.

Dr Hetty Goldman: Plate XLV *c*.

Messieurs Ernest Leroux et Cie, Paris:

From *Mémoires de la Délégation en Perse*: Plate IV*g, i, j, k, l*.

From *Collection De Clercq. Catalogue*, Vol. I, *Cylindres Orientaux*: Plates XIII*a*; XVI*c*; XVII*c*; XXII*c*; XXV*j*; XXVI*d*; XXVII*f, l*; XXXI*e, f, k*; XXXVI*g*; XXXVII*i, j, m*; XXXIX*o*; XL*n*; XLI*q*; XLII*f*; XLIV*p*.

From Focillon, *L'art des sculpteurs romans*, Pl. XLI: Plate XLVII*a*.

Messrs Bernard Quaritch Ltd., London:

From *Catalogue of the Collection of Antique Art formed by James, Ninth Earl of Southesk*, edited by his daughter Lady Helena Carnegie: Plates XVII*f*; XXIV*h*; XXVI*i, k*; XXIX*b, j*; XXXI*i, l*; XXXIII*g*; XXXV*b, c, j*; XXXVI*c, i*; XXXVII*h*; XLII*j, k*.

Yale University Press:

From *Historical, Religious and Economic Texts*, by James B. Nies and Clarence E. Keiser, Vol. II, Pl. 76*e*: Plates I*a*; V*d*.

The Clarendon Press, Oxford:

From *Necrocorinthia*, by Humfry Payne, Text-figures 12, 22*a*, 22*b*, 28 and Pl. III, 3: Text-figures 110–114.

Prof. J. Droop and the Liverpool University Press:

From *The Vaulted Tombs of Messara*: Text-figure 102.

Editions G. Van der Oest, Brussels:

From Godard, *Les Bronzes du Luristan*: Text-figure 115.

Messieurs Hachette, Paris:

From Perrot et Chipier, *Histoire de l'Art dans l'Antiquité*, III, 772: Text-figure 109.

From Pottier, *Vases antiques du Louvre*, Pl. 45, No. E. 627: Plate XLVII*a*.

Messrs Velhagen und Klasing, Leipzig:

From H. Hahne, *Das Vorgeschichtliche Europa*, Seite 109, abb. 131: Text-figure 116.

The Editor:

Bulletin Archéologique du Comité des Travaux historiques et scientifiques, 1906, p. 272.

Verlag Brückmann A. G., Munich:

From Bernheimer, *Romanische Tierplastik und Ursprünge ihrer motive*, Abb. 31, 75, 100, 134: Plate XLVII*d, e, g, h*.

LIST OF ABBREVIATIONS

(a) SEAL IDENTIFICATIONS

A+no.	=L. Delaporte, *Catalogue des Cylindres Orientaux* (*Musée du Louvre*), II: Acquisitions.
D+no. E+no. G+no. K+no. S+no. T+no.	=*Ibid.* I: Fouilles et Missions.
P+no.	=Palestine Museum.
Qa+no. Qb+no. Qc+no. Qd+no. Qe+no.	=*Catalogue of the Collection of Antique Art formed by James, Ninth Earl of Southesk*, edited by his daughter Lady Helena Carnegie (London, Bernard Quaritch, 1908).
Ag.+no.	=Object found by the Iraq Expedition of the Oriental Institute of the University of Chicago at *Tell Agrab*.
As.+no.	=*Ibid.* at *Tell Asmar*.
Ish.+no.	=*Ibid.* at *Ishchali*.
Kh.+no.	=*Ibid.* at *Khafaje*.
a+no. b+no.	=Object found by the Syrian Expedition of the Oriental Institute of the University of Chicago at *Chatal Huyuk*.
x+no. y+no. z+no.	=*Ibid.* at *Tell Judeideh*.
B.M.	=British Museum.
I.M.	=Iraq Museum.
V.A.+no.	=Object in the Vorderasiatische Abteilung der Staatlichen Museen, Berlin.
V.A.T.+no.	=Tablet in the Vorderasiatische Abteilung der Staatlichen Museen, Berlin.

(b) PUBLICATIONS AND COLLECTIONS

A.f.O.	=*Archiv für Orientforschung*.
A.J.	=*Antiquaries Journal*.
A.J.A.	=*American Journal of Archaeology*.
A.J.S.L.	=*American Journal of Semitic Languages*.
A.P.M.	=Allard Pierson Museum, Amsterdam.
Bernheimer	=Richard Bernheimer, *Romanische Tierplastik und die Ursprünge ihrer Motive* (F. Brückmann, Munich).
B.N.	=L. Delaporte, *Catalogue des Cylindres Orientaux de la Bibliothèque Nationale* (Ernest Leroux, Paris, 1910).
Boston	=Boston Museum of Fine Arts (cylinders not published elsewhere).
Brett	=H. H. Von der Osten, *Ancient Oriental Seals in the Collection of Mrs Agnes Baldwin Brett* (Oriental Institute Publications, XXXVII, Chicago, 1936).

Brussels = L. Speleers, *Catalogue des intailles et empreintes orientales des Musées Royaux du Cinquantenaire* (Brussels, 1917).

C.B.S. = (*see* Philadelphia).

Chicago = Museum of the Oriental Institute, the University of Chicago.

De Clercq = *Catalogue méthodique et raisonné de la Collection De Clercq*, I (Ernest Leroux, Paris, 1890).

H.S. = D. G. Hogarth, *Hittite Seals* (Oxford, 1920).

J.A.O.S. = *Journal of the American Oriental Society.*

J.E.A. = *Journal of Egyptian Archaeology.*

Kish, A Cemetery = Ernest Mackay, Report on the excavation of the "A" Cemetery at Kish, Mesopotamia. (Field Museum of Natural History, Anthropology Memoirs I, Chicago, 1925, 1929.)

(Unpublished seals are indicated by museum numbers.)

La Haye (*or* The Hague) = Joachim Ménant, *Catalogue des Cylindres Orientaux du Cabinet Royal des Médailles* (The Hague, 1878).

Mâle = Emile Mâle, *L'Art religieux du XIIe siècle en France.*

M.D.P. = Jacque de Morgan and others, *Mémoires de la Délégation en Perse* (Ernest Leroux, Paris, 1898).

Ménant = (*see* La Haye above).

Musée Guimet = L. Delaporte, *Cylindres Orientaux* (Annales du Musée Guimet, XXXIII; Ernest Leroux, Paris, 1909).

Newell = H. H. Von der Osten, *Ancient Oriental Seals in the Collection of Mr Edward T. Newell* (Oriental Institute Publications, XXII, Chicago, 1934).

O.I.P. = *Oriental Institute Publications.*

Philadelphia = Léon Legrain, *The Culture of the Babylonians from their Seals in the Collection of the University Museum* (Publications of the University Museum: *Babylonian Publications* XIV, XV).

P.S.B.A. = *Proceedings of the Society of Biblical Archaeology.*

R.A. = *Revue d'Assyriologie.*

Rowe = Alan Rowe, *A Catalogue of Egyptian Scarabs, Scaraboids, Seals and Amulets in the Palestine Archaeological Museum* (Cairo, 1936).

T.G. = *Tepe Ghiyan.*

Ur = C. Leonard Woolley, *The Royal Cemetery* (Ur Excavations, II, Pls. 192–215).

U.V.B. = (*Erster, etc.*) *Vorläufiger Bericht über die von der Notgemeinschaft der deutschen Wissenschaft in Uruk-Warka unternommenen Ausgrabungen*, in *Abhandlungen der Preussischen Akademie der Wissenschaften*, Phil.-Hist.-Klasse, 1930, etc.

Ward = W. H. Ward, *The Seal Cylinders of Western Asia* (Publication No. 100 of the Carnegie Institution of Washington, Washington, 1910).

Ward-Morgan = W. H. Ward, *Cylinders and other Oriental Seals in the Library of J. Pierpont Morgan* (New York, 1909).

(Photographs of some seals in this collection were obtained through the kind assistance of the Curator of Near Eastern Antiquities in the Metropolitan Museum, New York.)

Weber = Otto Weber, *Altorientalische Siegelbilder* (*Der Alte Orient*, XVII–XVIII, Leipzig, 1920).

Z.A. = *Zeitschrift für Assyriologie.*

LIST OF ABBREVIATIONS

[illegible]

LIST OF PLATES

(N.B. The plates will be found at the end of the volume)

Plate no.	Description	Publication or Identification	Reference in text
VI.	*Earlier half of the Jemdet Nasr Period*		310
a.	The sacred herd	Kh. VII/260	27, 30, 31, 33, 41, 146
b.	Imdugud and wild animals	B.M. 113875	32
c.	Game, monster and tree on mountain	Brett, 16	32, 33, 58, 307
d.	Mountain goats and brook	Kh. VI/416	4, 34
e.	Geometric design	Kh. V/156	4, 39, 42, 229
f.	Geometric design	Kh. VI/356	4, 35, 39, 42, 229
g.	Geometric design	Kh. V/95	4, 39, 42, 229
h.	Geometric design	Kh. VI/360	4, 39, 42, 229
i.	Geometric design	Kh. VI/413	4, 39, 229
j.	Disintegration of representational design	Kh. VI/346	4, 34, 39, 42, 229
VII.	*Jemdet Nasr Period*		
a.	Lion and bull	I.M. 13653	6, 27, 31
b.	Temple and geometrical pattern	Kh. VII/128	31, 35, 229, 293
c.	Fishes and plants	Kh. III/1078	31
d.	Temple and herd with Mother-Goddess symbol, with an Early Dynastic design added in later times	A–27	31, 33, 229
e.	Geometrical design	Kh. VI/388	35, 229
f.	Spouted vases and temple	Kh. VII/282	33, 34, 37, 229
g.	Temple, herd, spouted vases and stream	Pierpont Morgan Library	31, 33, 35, 37, 229
h.	Temple, herd and filling designs	Part of Kh. VI/159	31, 33, 34, 35, 229
i.	Temple and herd	Kh. VI/165	31, 33, 35, 229
j.	Birds	Ag. 35/514	35, 229
k.	Temple, bird and vases	Kh. VI/174	33, 35, 37, 229
VIII.	*Jemdet Nasr Period*		
a.	Fishes and geometrical design	Mackay, *Jemdet Nasr*, Pl. 73, No. 6	35, 227, 229, 293
b.	Scorpions	I.M. 9282	35, 293
c.	Squatting women on couches and vases	A–112	4, 36, 37, 229, 293, 294
d.	Squatting women on couches, goat and other designs	*A.J.* x, 46*d*	4, 36, 37, 75, 229, 293, 294
e.	Standing women	*Jemdet Nasr*, Pl. 73, No. 24	4, 36, 37, 229, 293
f.	Squatting women and "spider" design	A–113	3, 36, 37, 229, 293, 294
g.	File of goats	*Jemdet Nasr*, Pl. 73, No. 19	4, 36, 293
h.	Goats, amphorae and "ladder" design	B.N. 504	4, 33, 34, 36, 293

N.B. The impressions are reproduced approximately natural size except the following:

Enlarged. XIX *c, e*; XXI *g*; XXII *e, f*; XXIII *b, e, h*; XXIV *g*; XXV *e, f, g*; XXVI *f, g, h, j*; XXVII *a, b, i*; XXVIII *c, d, g, k, m, n*; XXIX *a*; XXXI *a*; XXXIII *e*; XXXV *k*; XXXVII *b, c, g, j, k, l, m*; XLI *a, e, f, g, i, p*; XLII *c, e*; XLIII *b, l*; XLV *c, j*.

Reduced. II; V; VI; VII; XI; XIV *j*; XVIII *a, k*; XXIV *c*; XXXII; XXXIII *f, i, k*; XXXVIII *a, e*; XXXIX *a, b*; XLV *a, k*; XLVI *g*.

TEXT-FIGURES

PRELIMINARIES

§ I. ORIGIN AND USE

THE ORIGIN of the cylinder seal precedes the invention of writing. The earliest clay tablets found in Mesopotamia bear impressions of engraved cylinders (§§ 5–7). Some of these documents represent a quite elementary stage in which only numbers—the most important and most easily confused element in each transaction—were inscribed to assist memory. Then almost immediately writing-signs were added to the numerals.[1]

When the early picture-writing became conventionalised, a special technique of handling the stylus reduced the individual signs to groups of wedge-shaped impressions qualified by the name of "cuneiform". The contracts, letters, receipts and other documents thus written were legalised by the personal seal impressions of parties and witnesses [Pl. II *m* (end of volume)] who rolled their cylinders over the still moist clay. This method of sealing was peculiar to Mesopotamia. It is true that cylinder seals were used in Egypt during the Third Millennium B.C. (§ 45, p. 292), and at various times in Syria, Palestine and Anatolia, but only in periods of strong Babylonian influence. Normally the *cachet*, the stamp-seal, prevailed in those regions. It penetrated into Mesopotamia in the First Millennium B.C., though as rare exceptions stamp-seals occur at all periods.[2] But in Assyrian times it rapidly increased in popularity, and by the seventh century B.C. had become predominant, finally ousting the cylinder in Persian times. Since the earliest tablets with seal impressions belong to the Fourth Millennium B.C., the history of cylinder seals covers a period of well over three thousand years.

In the early stages of its existence, however, the sealing of documents was not the exclusive, nor even the most usual function of the cylinder seal. The thousands of Early Dynastic tablets from Fara and Telloh bear no seal

[1] See for these earliest tablets: A. Falkenstein, *Archaische Texte aus Uruk* (Berlin, 1936).

[2] Thus we found in one season at Tell Asmar, among 200 Akkadian cylinders, two stamp-seals. See *Oriental Institute Communications*, No. 16, Figs. 27, 32. There is no proof that the pendants of varying shape (animal, lion's head, dome) which are mostly found in the Jemdet Nasr and Early Dynastic periods were ever used as seals, though they often bear on their bases designs made with drill-holes which could be impressed. The impressions of stamp-seals found at Arpachiya and Nineveh (*Iraq*, II, Pl. IX and pp. 98 ff.) are of an entirely different nature, and agree with the "Tell Halaf" pottery found at those sites in showing that that part of the country bore at first stronger affinities with North Syria than with Southern Mesopotamia.

impressions at all. It was for the safeguarding of possessions or merchandise that the cylinder seal was most commonly used during the Third Millennium B.C. Small and valuable objects were packed in jars; a piece of cloth or animal skin was then stretched across the opening and bound with string round the neck, and over this fastening, surrounding the neck of the vase between lip and shoulder, moist clay was laid, over which the cylinder seal was rolled in all directions (Text-fig. 1). It was, of course, impossible to tamper with the contents of the jar without breaking the sealing.

Impressions of the seal of Lugalanda, a ruler of Lagash, show on the inside marks of basket-work, and are supposed to have secured baskets containing the (unsealed) tablets found in such profusion beside the sealings. Bales of goods packed in mats were tied with rope and the knot was again

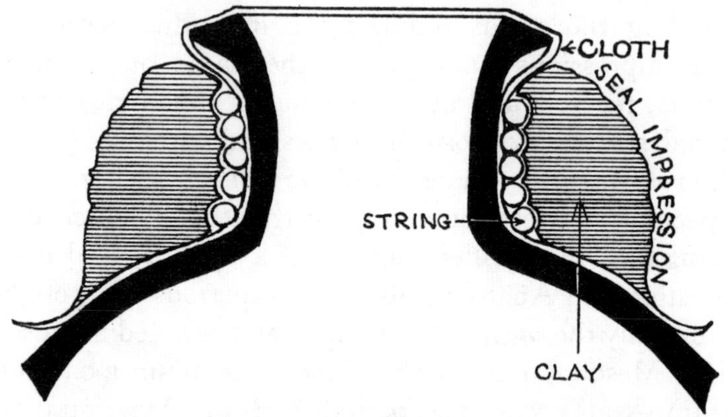

Text-fig. 1. Section of the sealed neck of a storage jar.

covered by a lump of clay to take the impression of the cylinder. Similar sealed lumps were used as labels, which when perforated and tied to the wares enabled the rightful owner to be identified.

It is this use, as a mark of ownership, which explains the curious shape of the cylinder seal. For it is pre-eminently suited to cover varying surfaces with a distinctive design. The legalising of written documents by seal impressions is merely a secondary use of the cylinder, understandable since the seal design proved personal ownership.

It is remarkable that the cylinder seal was adopted in Egypt in proto-Dynastic times, almost certainly in imitation of Mesopotamia, and in any case in its original application, for jar sealings. But in the Nile valley the use of papyrus as writing material eventually brought with it a change-over to the more practical form of the signet or stamp-seal, while the retention of clay as the basis of script in Mesopotamia may well account for the parallel retention of the cylinder seal, although the stamp-seal, impracticable for the safeguarding of goods, would serve as well or better for the legalisation of written material.

Yet another application of the cylinder seal as mark of ownership or as trademark is found in Western Asia. The cylinder is sometimes rolled over the shoulder of a jar before the baking, when the clay is still soft—a usage of such obvious efficacy that one wonders at the rarity of its occurrence (Pl. II *o*). It is known at Susa, in the Khabur region, at Byblos, and at Megiddo in Palestine, but not in Mesopotamia proper. Most instances seem to belong to the Early Dynastic period.[1] An interesting modern parallel is supplied by the wooden *roulette* employed by the natives of Nigeria to impress the designs on pots.[2] In Western Asia this usage remains isolated and without consequence, and it throws no light on the origin of the cylinder seal.

Occasionally this curious device has been thought to imitate marked arrow-shafts[3] or joints of reeds,[4] but these speculations, besides being gratuitous, do not account for the facts. The form of the cylinder seal is adequately explained by the function which it was meant to fulfil, namely to impress a distinctive mark on a soft material of varying extent, the clay with which packages and store-jars were secured and which, subsequently, became the vehicle of writing.

In this book we shall be mainly concerned with the seal designs, which can only be reproduced in impressions. It is not generally realised that very different impressions can be produced with the same cylinder, and our judgment of the quality, especially as regards composition, can be affected by irregularities which do not occur on the original cylinder at all. Our Pl. XXXVII *n* should be compared with another impression of the same seal[5] which has been made on a softer material with a more slanting thrust. The wheel of the chariot in our illustration is higher than it is wide, but in the older impression it is oval-shaped with long axis horizontal, and also the horses have longer bodies. The result is that these animals appear much less spirited than in our figure but, on the other hand, the dragon, which appears

[1] See for a full discussion of this group see § 35 (p. 227).

[2] *Man*, June, 1934, No. 107, Pl. F. These objects are now in the British Museum. The designs are zigzags, drawn either parallel or so as to form lozenges, and they are almost identical with those found on some long seals of glazed steatite of the Jemdet Nasr Period.

[3] Hilprecht, *The Babylonian Expedition*, Vol. I, Part II, p. 36.

[4] C. W. King, *Handbook of Engraved Gems*, p. 3; and H. R. Hall, *Ancient History of the Near East*, p. 89.

[5] J. D. Beazley, *The Lewes House Collection of Ancient Gems* (Oxford, 1920), Pl. I, No. 8.

in a more oblique position, seems to have gained thereby a more aggressive, and therefore fiercer, effect.

§ 2. MATERIAL, TECHNIQUE OF CUTTING, SHAPE

The *material* used for the cylinder seals varies greatly at times and cannot therefore be accepted as a trustworthy guide to their age. It is true that during certain periods some materials were especially popular, but these did not exclude the use of others even then. Nevertheless, the existence of such fashions and preferences invests the material of the cylinder with some value as a secondary indication of its date of production. Thus we find that in the Uruk period white or pink marble was common (Pl. I *a*, *b*) and its use persisted into the Jemdet Nasr epoch, which furthermore favoured various coloured limestones, among which a light grey kind is especially distinctive. The short, squat seals used towards the end of the period were almost all made of red, grey or green limestone (Pls. I *j*; VIII *c–i*); the tall, slender seals with geometric patterns (Pls. I *h*, *i*, *n*; VI *d–j*) were almost invariably of faience or glazed steatite.

In the First Early Dynastic period the thin seals of the "Brocade" style were usually cut from black, blue or green limestone, or dark serpentine (Pls. II *a*; IX *a–e*).

The Second Early Dynastic period used semi-translucent white or green serpentine, aragonite, calcite or shell core; the semi-translucent stones remained usual for small cylinders showing ritual scenes or the "herdsman" motive in the Third Early Dynastic period (Pl. XV *h*, *k*), while the friezes of fighting animals then commonly occur on seals cut from the core of large shells brought from the Persian Gulf[1] (Pl. II *b*); the same motive appears also on smaller seals of lapis lazuli. Occasionally cylinders of gold or silver, either solid or made of foil covering a bitumen core, are found at this level.

In Sargonid times the greatest variety of stones prevails; the hardest materials, such as jasper and even rock crystal, were used, while the soft shell cores became rare and were discontinued before the end of the period.

The cylinders of the Third Dynasty of Ur present in the matter of material as in other respects a complete contrast with those of Akkadian times. Haematite cylinders now far outnumbered all other materials, and this remained the case until the end of the Dynasty of Hammurabi (Pl. II *d*), though occasionally lapis lazuli was used—as before—for exceptional and valuable seals. In Syria haematite remained the most usual material for

[1] Univalves of the genera Trito and Melo. See Heuzey, *Catalogue des Antiquités Chaldéennes*, p. 383.

seals (Pl. II *j*) until glazed pottery or faience gained the upper hand in Mitannian times (Pl. II *i*) and continued predominant.

In Babylonia the Kassites favoured chalcedony or agate, and this predilection was shared by the Assyrians and neo-Babylonians (Pl. II *e*, *f*, *k*), but other stones, especially semi-translucent varieties like carnelian, were freely used. Lapis lazuli was imitated in Assyrian glass frit, but real glass was very rarely used for seals; volcanic glass (obsidian) was occasionally used in the Second Millennium B.C. Blue chalcedony was comparatively common in Persian times.

In discussing the *technique* of the seal-cutters, it should be remembered that no cylinder seal antedates the use of metal in Mesopotamia. Until Assyrian times, when iron came into use, all cylinder seals were cut, drilled through and decorated by means of copper tools, which, in the case of hard stones, were probably fed with emery powder. The actual instruments have been found at Tell Asmar, in private houses dating to the Dynasty of Sargon of Akkad. They were packed, together with some completed and some unfinished cylinder seals, beads and strips of copper and silver, into a small pot which evidently contained the stock-in-trade of a jeweller or travelling craftsman.[1] There were several gravers and small-edged chisels, and one piece which is best explained as the borer belonging to a bow-drill. It had a spatula-shaped cutting-edge and its stem was square in section, so that it could be firmly stuck in the wooden shaft to which the bow-string imparted the revolving motion; the same instrument is still used with astonishing efficiency by the craftsmen of the bazaars.

The axial perforation was not drilled through in one direction, but holes were made at both ends, to meet sometimes at an obtuse angle inside the cylinder, a circumstance which must have frayed many a string.

Small cutting disks of various sizes, and also tubes with a circular cutting-edge, were used in conjunction with the bow-drill from Kassite times onwards; they were used most frequently in the Mitannian seals from Northern Mesopotamia and Syria; but a few instances of the First Babylonian Dynasty are known where the rotating disk, and perhaps the tube, were used.[2] The tube cut circles (Pl. XXXI *a*, *d*; XLIII) or, when applied at an angle, crescents. The disks were used to execute the usual intricate designs which, however, were reduced in the process to groups of straight lines, thus becoming simpler than those cut freehand with a graver. The elaboration of technique brought with it an impoverishment of quality. The

[1] *Oriental Institute Communications*, No. 16, p. 47.

[2] A–366; A–456. The tubular drill seems to have been in Bibliothèque Nationale, 230, which is on a line with our Pls. XXX *h*, XXXI *e*.

lines cut with a disk are recognisable by their shape: they are wider, and often deeper, in the middle than at the ends.

It is generally assumed that in Assyrian times an appliance not unlike the potter's wheel was introduced, worked by foot and keeping the cutting tools in rapid rotation, but since the same result could be achieved with the bow-drill, it seems difficult to be positive on this point. Some cylinders, decorated not by *intaglio*, but in relief, are apparently Armenian imitations of Mesopotamian cylinder seals. Their date is difficult to establish.[1] Other cylinders with relief are not connected with seals at all, but are decorated tubes used by joiners or cabinet-makers.[2]

Peculiar *shapes* are found in the Uruk and Jemdet Nasr periods, when axial perforation had not yet become the rule, and various arrangements for suspension were cut in one piece with the actual cylinder.[3] This was surmounted either by a loop (Pl. I *a*, *e*, *g*) or a conical piece connected loop and cylinder.[4] When cylinders of these early periods resemble those of later times in the possession of an axial perforation for suspension, this is no proof that they were worn in the same way. Metal parts taking the place of the stone-cut loop have often been lost. Thus we see in Pl. I *b* a seal mounted on a copper rod which is fixed to the figure of a ram cast in copper and horizontally pierced for suspension.[5] Several seals with this device are known, and at times, when it has been lost, there are signs of its original position on the top of the cylinder (Pl. I *g*). A simpler arrangement consists of a short dowel and a loop of stone resembling that which is cut in one piece with the cylinder (Pl. I *a*). These loose pieces were fixed into the cylinder, which was only partially perforated, by means of some adhesive substance.

In contrast with later usage, axial perforation is not general among the earliest seals. Sometimes the cylinders are without any perforation at all (Pl. VII *a*). Again, a curious type of perforation is adopted, to be discarded in later times. On the top of the cylinder two holes were drilled obliquely towards the axis so that they met some way below the top surface in a hairpin bend, and a string for suspension could be drawn through them (Pl. I *c*). This "loop-bore"[6] has not yet been observed in Mesopotamian

[1] Sidney Smith, *Early History of Assyria*, pp. 329 f. and Pl. XX *a* and Fig. 22.

[2] Weber, Nos. 3, 231; Woolley, *Royal Cemetery*, Pl. 197, N. 56.

[3] Seals of the Jemdet Nasr period crowned with a loop cut from the stone are V.A. 612; *Jemdet Nasr*, Pl. 73, Nos. 30, 31; Louvre, S. 311 and several from Khafaje.

[4] Louvre, A. 116; Newell, 690.

[5] Similarly, Louvre, A. 25, where the reclining figure of a bull is cut from the stone in one piece. Also Heinrich, *Kleinfunde*, Pls. 17 *a* (=our Pl. III *e*), *b*; 18 *b*, *d*.

[6] Hogarth, *Hittite Seals*, 18.

excavations, though it occurs on one seal in the Baghdad Museum.[1] In Syria it is common with seals which show designs in the Jemdet Nasr style.[2]

Cylinders were worn vertically as a rule, either strung as a pendant to a necklace or, in some cases, to a wristband. In Early Dynastic times they were sometimes stuck on tall pins with which cloaks were fastened[3] (Pl. II *l*). The best pieces were mounted on metal wire and set between caps of copper, silver or gold (Pl. II *j*). In Kassite times these caps sometimes overlapped the edge of the cylinder with triangles covered with gold *granulé*, and this costly mounting was imitated by the seal-cutters in stone, as late as Assyrian times (Pl. XXXII *a*, *c*, *i*). A seal edged by incised triangles covered with dots would give an impression very similar to that of a gold-capped seal of the sort just described.

No cylinder has ever been found mounted on a swivel. In Egypt, however, a cylinder mounted in a frame which was worn round the neck served as the hieroglyph with which the title "treasurer" was written in the Old Kingdom —see Cover and Title-page.[4]

The *shape* of the cylinder proper is also subject to variations, but what we have said with regard to the material applies again. Though particular models are preferred at certain times, there are always so many exceptions that a date can but rarely be assigned to a seal on the exclusive evidence of its shape. It is true, however, that in a general way the Uruk period can be said to use large broad cylinders to accommodate the fine and elaborate designs in which it excels. The Jemdet Nasr period shows the greatest variety (Pl. I *c*–*n*). The squat seals, sometimes so concave as to approach hour-glass shape, are as characteristic of the age as are the tall, slender seals of glazed steatite with geometrical designs. Their height measures 2 to 3 times their diameter. The tallest of all belong to the Brocade style of the First Early Dynastic period (Pl. II *a*). Subsequently, however, there is much less difference of proportion and the large majority of cylinders are about 1½ times as high as they are wide, a shape already found with the others of the Uruk and Jemdet Nasr periods. The size of the cylinders conforming approximately to this proportion still varies considerably in Early Dynastic times, small rolls of semi-translucent stone occurring together with large examples

[1] Iraq Museum, No. 2806.

[2] Hogarth, *Hittite Seals*, 18; and our Pl. XXXVIII *c*, *f*; several unpublished seals in the National Museum, Aleppo.

[3] In Shubad's grave were found three cylinders attached to gold pins with lapis heads. Woolley, *Royal Cemetery*, pp. 243, 247.

[4] After *Zeitschrift für aegyptische Sprache*, XXXV, 106.

cut from shell-core or limestone. In Sargonid times the cylinder often shows a slight concavity (Pl. II *h*); and there is still a considerable variety in size (Pl. II *c*, *g*, *h*). Occasionally a barrel-shaped, convex cylinder is used.[1] But afterwards smaller seals, not more than 2 to 3 centimetres in height, become universal until Kassite times. Then taller seals are used again, to accommodate the prayers which it now becomes customary to engrave upon them, and this shape continues down to early Assyrian times (Pl. II *k*), while Syria and Palestine still retain the older and smaller models of the First Dynasty of Babylon. In Mesopotamia shorter shapes reappear in Assyrian times, often with convex sides (Pl. II *e*).

The foregoing remarks about material and shape give but a crude and simplified picture of the actual facts. Exceptions are numerous at all times. It is, in the last resort, always the *seal design* upon which we must base our dating.

§ 3. THE INSCRIPTIONS

A number of cylinders are inscribed. These are cut reversed so that they can be read on the impression of the seal.[2] The value of these inscriptions is largely chronological, for they sometimes contain peculiarities of grammar, writing or nomenclature which are characteristic of definite periods and which thus allow us to assign a date to the seal upon which they occur. The actual interpretation of the seal design is rarely furthered by the contents of the inscriptions.

Texts first appear on cylinder seals of the Second Early Dynastic period. At that time they are still very uncommon and seem to consist of nothing more than the owner's name.

In the Third Early Dynastic period a title is habitually added to the name of the owner; it appears that not all citizens but only officials had their seals inscribed.

Under Sargon of Akkad this is changed. The name of the owner and that of his father now appear commonly on seals, the mediocre quality of which betrays the fact that these people cannot all have occupied positions of importance. Thus we find one seal inscribed as follows:

Dababa, scribe, son of Ibea, the weighing master.[3]

[1] Cros, *Nouvelles Fouilles de Telloh*, p. 252; As. 32/120.

[2] There are very rare exceptions at all times, but on the Assyrian cylinders the former exception becomes the rule and the signs can be read on the cylinder itself.

[3] A–72. Translation by Dr Thorkild Jacobsen.

Sometimes the signs are engraved between the figures of the scene, having evidently been added at the request of the buyer to an already completed cylinder.[1] More often the inscription is written in a panel consisting of several "cases" or columns, supported by pairs of heroes struggling with beasts (Pl. XVII *a–d*).

This simplest form of inscription, giving the name of the owner and that of his father, and sometimes his rank or title, continues in use through the succeeding ages. But we also find in Akkadian times a new type of inscription which enjoys great popularity until the end of the Third Millennium B.C. The seal inscription is in this case elaborated so as to include an expression of dependence upon some authority, the text occasionally taking the form of an invocation. Thus we read as a straightforward declaration of dependence or loyalty:

To Ibil-Ishtar, brother of the king: Kalki the scribe is thy servant (Pl. XXIV *c*).

This formula is customary for officials, but seems to have been obligatory with the rulers of formerly independent city-states which had become subject to the King of Akkad or, later, to the King of Ur. Text-fig. 31 (p. 99) gives such an inscription in the form of an invocation:

O Shargalisharri, strong hero, King of Akkad:
Lugalushumgal, governor of Lagash, is thy servant.

There is no doubt that these seals were actually used, since impressions of them have been found; it is also certain that the phrase expressed a very real relationship between "master" and "servant", and this significance of the seal inscriptions, which one might call political, should be remembered when we consider subsequent phases of Mesopotamian glyptic. For the same formula remained in use under the Third Dynasty of Ur, but at that time allegiance was not always expressed to the King of Ur—though that was the rule—but sometimes to a god. It has been credibly argued that this dedication must have as concrete a meaning as that which underlies the older "political" use of the same formula, and that we should err by taking it for a mere expression of piety. While officials in the Civil Service styled themselves "servants" of the governor, just as the governor in his turn was "servant" of his overlord, the king, so the temple officials and priests were obliged to express their dependence upon a higher authority with the

[1] Pl. XXI *i* shows the square for the inscription outlined but unused; the cylinder is perfectly finished. Similar, *American Journal of Semitic Languages*, XLIV, 232 ff., No. 17, and Newell 103.

customary formula of "thy servant" or "his servant"; but in their case a god would take the place of the master.[1]

This view, that the seal inscriptions possessed a concrete significance, is well supported by the fact that dependents had to change their seals when their overlord died and a new king came to the throne. Thus we possess another seal of the same Lugalushumgal whose inscription we have reproduced on the preceding page, and there he styles himself servant of Shargalisharri's predecessor Naramsin. It has been observed[2] that this change of seal did not always follow immediately upon the death of the king, a point of some importance where seal inscriptions are used for dating-evidence. At Drehem numerous tablets were found, many of which bore seal impressions. It appeared there that a certain vassal prince continued to use the seal which proclaimed him the servant of King Shulgi during the first five regnal years of Shulgi's successor Bursin; another similarly changed his seal inscription for one expressing loyalty to Gimilsin, Bursin's successor, four years after the latter's death.

Besides cylinders which were actually used as seals, a few survive with a much longer inscription, whose shape is probably the only point of resemblance to true seals. One of them shows next to the design reproduced in Pl. XXV*c* an inscription reading:

To the god Meslamtea, right arm of Lagash, for the Life of Shulgi, the strong hero, king of Ur, Killula-Gazala, son of Urbaga, has made (this seal). Of this seal "May the king in his benevolent purpose live", such is its name.[3]

Here the cylinder seal, once an accessory in legal transactions, has become a simple monument, dedicated to a god, proclaiming the dependence of a vassal upon his overlord, and even called by a name of its own. Such a cylinder, presented to a temple, was treated as a costly jewel. There is textual evidence regarding such presentations,[4] and in the Tell el Amarna letters seals are mentioned among the gifts sent by the kings of Mitanni and Babylon to Amenhotep III of Egypt.[5] At Ishchali was found an amethyst cylinder seal bearing the following dedication:

Mattatum, daughter of Ubarrum, for her health to the goddess (Ishtar) Kititum has presented (this seal),

[1] This is the view of Dr Thorkild Jacobsen. It seems to me that it gives the best explanation of the fact noted by J. Krauss, *Die Götternamen in den Babylonischen Siegelcylinder-legenden*, pp. 14 f., namely, that a man is quite often "servant" of a god different from the one appearing in his personal name.

[2] N. Schneider, in *Orientalia* 45–46 (Rome, 1930), p. 109.

[3] De Clercq, 86.

[4] *Journal of the Royal Asiatic Society*, 1926, p. 446.

[5] Thomsen, in Ebert, *Reallexikon der Vorgeschichte*, II, col. 119.

and this cylinder was actually found in that part of the temple where the ornaments of the cult-statue were preserved.[1]

But seals of this type are not common. Rare also are those used as gifts between men. One, found at Tell Asmar, was presented by a ruler of Eshnunna to his son and heir (Pl. XXV *e*). The inscription rather awkwardly combines the usual dedication formula with the commemoration of the gift. This is no doubt due to the force of the tradition that seals of independent princes might begin with a dedication to a deity, a tradition based on the pre-Sargonid theocratic view of kingship according to which the ruler was governor and steward on behalf of the god, and in accordance with this view we find that Tishpak, the god of Eshnunna, is given quasi-regnal epithets in our seal inscriptions:

O Tishpak, mighty king, king of the land of Warum, Kirikiri, governor of Eshnunna to Bilalama, his son, has presented (this seal).[2]

Even if the ruins in which this cylinder was found had not revealed its age, we should on the evidence of the inscription have assigned it to the Isin-Larsa period. For under the Third Dynasty of Ur only the King of Ur expressed allegiance to the god while local rulers were "servants" of the king. With the collapse of the central government these former vassals assumed royal prerogatives.

Under the First Dynasty of Babylon the old formula of the seal inscriptions of ordinary people slightly altered. Formerly it had consisted of: god's or ruler's name, owner's name, owner's father, owner's title and the addition "thy servant" or "his servant". The inscription began henceforward with the owner's name, and the final phrase became "servant of NN".

Moreover, an entirely new, short type of inscription made its appearance in the Isin-Larsa period. This consisted only of the name of one or of several gods. It would seem natural to assume that these short inscriptions were intended to elucidate the scenes depicted by the naming of some of the figures. But this view, which seems so obvious, is in numerous cases manifestly erroneous and loses sight of the historical perspective. For we have found that throughout the periods preceding the age of Hammurabi the inscriptions were entirely independent of the designs upon the seals. To return once more to the inscriptions of Lugalushumgal (Text-fig. 31, p. 99), we recall that they proclaim him the servant of Naramsin and Shargalisharri of Akkad, but the

[1] *Oriental Institute Communications*, No. 20, pp. 83 ff.

[2] Jacobsen in *Oriental Institute Communications*, No. 13, pp. 42 ff.

scenes in both cases show a worshipper, presumably the owner of the seal, approaching the Sun-god with a kid as sacrificial gift at the moment when the deity rises in the mountains of the east. Another seal inscribed by a "servant of Naramsin" shows the owner worshipping a goddess of vegetation (Text-fig. 32, p. 116). It is illogical to assume that the short inscriptions of the Isin-Larsa period and the First Dynasty of Babylon should be related to the scenes depicted on the seals while such a relation is demonstrably absent from all the more explicit texts. These later short inscriptions are, in fact with a few exceptions, debased and standardised survivals just as the seal designs of the period represent a simplified mass-product in which but a minute proportion of the earlier seal-cutters' repertoire survives.

Already under the Third Dynasty of Ur a single subject, the presentation of a worshipper to a god by an interceding deity, tends to oust all other designs. This phenomenon will be discussed in a later chapter (Section IV, Chapter I, p. 142); it is without doubt the result of mass-production, explicable when we remember that the use of written documents suddenly increased a thousandfold in the second half of the Third Dynasty of Ur, and that the spate of contracts, letters, receipts and agreements does not subside before the end of the First Dynasty of Babylon.

In the Isin-Larsa period the inscriptions on the seals are affected by a standardisation such as had already restricted the variety of their subjects in the preceding centuries. Thus we find the short inscriptions which consist merely of divine names, the standardised remnants of the declarations of loyalty which had been in common use hitherto, the names of gods replacing those of local rulers, which would possess a very restricted validity in the prevalent political confusion.

Some texts, giving name and rank of the owner, retained an individual character, and the old formula "servant of NN" was still used, and probably still referred to a social reality. But the new short inscriptions seem either to reflect the personal attachment of the owner to some deity, or more often to possess in their standardised form magical rather than religious significance with a view to imparting power rather than expressing belief. If occasionally a seal-cutter brought variety into the design, which then became again distinctive, his clients' religious inclinations were apt to influence the purport of the inscription. It is obvious that these two forces need not coincide. Only those seals which were entirely cut to order, or those at the other end of the scale, which were purely conventional, showed congruity between text and scene. In the latter case we find, for example, a god with a turban and without attributes, recalling Shamash on the Stela of Ḥammurabi, who receives a worshipper introduced by a goddess, while the inscription names Shamash and his spouse Ay; Pl. XXXIX*l* illustrates a peripheral, provincial version of this type. But inscription and scene are not really connected. Each represents the final outcome of two parallel but independent processes of standardisation which the much enlarged output of the seal-cutters had brought about.

In this manner we may understand the occurrence of numerous discrepancies,[1] such as the conventional scene of presentation before a personage who may be king or god, while the text describes the owner as "servant" of one of the royal princesses.[2] In other instances the usual dedication to Shamash and Ay is written beside figures which can be recognised as representing other gods.[3] Or we find three renderings of the conventional scene of audience before a bearded figure (Shamash or the king) which are almost identical in all details, but the inscription in one case gives the owner's name and calls him "servant of the god Nergal", while the second seal bears merely the names Ishtar and Tammuz and the third names two goddesses, Ninsianna and Kabtu.[4] Another seal depicts two goddesses but names Adad;[5] another again names two goddesses but portrays a god and goddess, and also shows Adad's symbol and a scimitar;[6] or the text may proclaim the owner to be servant of the god Amurru, but the scene shows a man offering a kid to Ishtar.[7]

Examples of similar discrepancies could be multiplied, but what precedes may suffice to prove that there is, in fact, no connection between text and scene on the vast majority of seals from the time of the Isin-Larsa and First Babylonian Dynasties. It follows that the utilisation of the inscription for iconographical purposes will only be possible in exceptional cases, which can be checked by comparison with non-glyptic material. These would be found among the seals cut to order.

Towards the end of the First Dynasty of Babylon the seals develop in two diametrically opposed directions. On the one hand secondary detail overcrowds the main scene and the inscription disappears (Pl. XXIX*m*); on the

[1] They are too widely spread and too many-sided for Langdon's explanation (*Revue d'Assyriologie*, XVI (1919), 49–68) to appear adequate when he maintains that the worshippers relied on the protection of particular patron-gods (which they named) when approaching the "Great Deities" presumably depicted on the seals.

[2] A–255.

[3] E.g. Ward, 313, and sometimes there are no major deities depicted at all: Hague, Pl. I, 3; A–251, etc. See also following notes.

[4] Bibliothèque Nationale, 110, 111, 113.

[5] A–527*c*. [6] A–334. [7] A–372.

other, the seal designs become more and more jejune, until they contain no more than one or two divine figures with an inscription giving the name of the owner, sometimes with the addition "servant of NN" (Pl. XXX*e*, *g*).

The Kassite seals are a development of the last-named group; but the inscription becomes elaborated to an unprecedented extent. In some cases there is an obvious connection with past usage:

O Nabu,...lord of understanding, compassionate ruler, who reignest with benevolence, Ibni-Marduk is thy servant who worships thee.[1]

Besides these there is an entirely new variety, a regular prayer; thus the text of our Pl. XXX*k* reads:

O Nineanna, thou hast created, thou has given him a name. Have mercy, love, protect, have compassion, and deliver the worshipful servant thy worshipper.[2]

And on our Pl. XXX*m*:

O Marduk, great lord, prince into whose hands has been entrusted the counsel of heaven and earth, may the servant thy worshipper before thee prosper.[3]

In Assyrian times usage reverts to the opposite extreme. Though a few inscriptions are found on seals of the last centuries of the Second Millennium B.C., most Assyrian seals are entirely devoid of texts. Such inscriptions as do occur are mostly cut straight on to the seal and are therefore no longer readable in the impression. We may mention the seal of the Royal Assyrian Mail, which is, however, an eight-sided prism and not a cylinder[4] (Pl. XXXVI*k*). More aptly we conclude this discussion of the seal inscriptions with a translation of the text of Pl. XXXVII*d*. The Persian text reads: "I am Darius the king", the Assyrian: "I am Darius, the Great King".

[1] After Langdon, *Revue d'Assyriologie*, XVI, 70.
[2] *Ibid.* XVI, 73. [3] *Ibid.* 76.
[4] The text reads, after Delaporte, "Seal of the royal communications".

SECTION I

THE SEALS OF THE PREHISTORIC AGE

CHAPTER I. THE ACHIEVEMENT OF THE URUK PERIOD

§ 4. INTRODUCTORY

THE EARLIEST products of the Mesopotamian seal-cutters achieve an astonishing perfection. In the fifth and fourth archaic layers at Warka (biblical Erech) seal impressions were found which, being fragmentary, give but an inadequate idea of their makers' ability (Pls. III *f*; IV *a–f*; Text-figs. 3–6, pp. 20, 23).[1] But they have fortunately solved the enigma of a number of cylinder seals bought from time to time by collectors and museums which had defied classification to such an extent as to be sometimes pronounced forgeries; they possess stylistic as well as purely external characteristics which establish their affinities with the Warka sealings (Pls. III *a–c*; IV *h*; V *a*, *b*; Text-fig. 2, p. 19).[2]

The stylistic qualities will appear in the following paragraphs, where they are treated together with the seal impressions found in excavations. But the external characteristics alone form a strong body of evidence. Several of these cylinders possess a loop for suspension cut in one piece with the cylinder (Pl. I *a*) or a small metal figure of a recumbent ram, horizontally pierced and mounted upon a metal rod fastened into its axis (Pl. I, *b*). These devices survive into the Jemdet Nasr period but are unknown in later times; this also applies to the curious curved object (Pls. III *a*, *e*; V *c*), which has been identified as a gatepost with streamer used in the reed architecture of the earliest inhabitants of the country.[3] Even more important is its recognition as the prototype of the written name-sign of Inanna, the Mother-Goddess.[4]

Thirdly, we find that the dress of the persons depicted in the Uruk period is peculiar and that the same pair of figures often recurs. It consists of a bearded man followed by a long-haired beardless attendant. Sometimes

[1] They have been collected and studied by A. Schott in *Uruk Vörlaufiger Bericht*, v, where he has also mentioned some of the seals adduced by us in the next footnote.

[2] To the Uruk period belong moreover: Louvre, A–116; Newell, 22, 61, 690, 695; Iraq Museum, 16669; V.A. 3902, 8796, 10893; *American Journal of Semitic Languages*, XLIV, 232 ff., No. 6.

[3] Andrae, *Das Gotteshaus und die Urformen des Bauens im alten Orient*, p. 49; see on this type of architecture also Heinrich, *Schilf und Lehm* (Berlin, 1934).

[4] Deimel, *Sumerisches Lexicon*, Bd. I, nr. 103, I.

figures appear with both head and face shaven, and all wear a short skirt with a seam or hem along the lower edge and a vertical opening. This skirt is covered with cross-hatching (Pls. III*a*, *e*; V*c*; Text-fig. 2, p. 19).

Finally, the bought seals often depict a number of objects which recur on a magnificent alabaster vase recently discovered at Warka[1] in a deposit buried in the Jemdet Nasr period, one of several objects which had, as is often the case, continued to be used in the temple, though made in the preceding epoch. For we know the relief style of the Jemdet Nasr period from the Blau monuments,[2] the age of which is unequivocally established by the semi-pictographic signs of their inscriptions. And these reliefs are related to the Warka vase exactly as are the seals of the Jemdet Nasr to those of the Uruk period (compare Pl. V*c* with Pl. V*g*); the subject is the same, but the rendering has lost directness in the later examples and is lifeless and coarsened to a degree. Moreover, there are specific signs of declining technique, both in the seals and in the vases.[3] The alabaster vase and the seals which resemble it in subject and style must therefore be assigned to the Uruk period.

The uncertainty which attaches to these earliest seals must needs influence our treatment. More emphatically than in later chapters we shall have to insist on the various connecting links which unite the scattered material, and especially those which bring the bought seals of unknown date and provenance into relation with the sealings discovered in regular excavations. We shall therefore discuss first the subjects and then the style of the seals.

The seal designs of the Uruk period fall into three groups. Some appear to have none but decorative significance (§ 6, p. 23), others depict action, and a

[1] Heinrich, *Kleinfunde*, Pls. 2, 3.

[2] King, *History of Sumer and Akkad*, Pl. VI.

[3] See also p. 30, n. 1. The alabaster vase referred to in n. 1 above and the limestone trough in the British Museum (Moortgat, *Frühe Bildkunst in Sumer*, Pl. 30) differ from such objects as the green stone vase from Khafaje (*Oriental Institute Communications* xx, Fig. 54) in exactly the same way as the cylinders of the Uruk and the Jemdet Nasr period differ from each other. As soon as sites other than Warka are sufficiently taken into account the situation becomes much clearer. The discoveries at Jemdet Nasr itself, including the few seal impressions found on its tablets, and those at Khafaje, support the method in which we distinguish the two periods. It is particularly significant that only two small seals which we should assign to the Uruk period (Kh. VII/154 and Kh. VII/222) were found in the deepest layers at Khafaje, and at that site we discovered several well stratified layers belonging to the Jemdet Nasr period; these are much more convincing evidence than the position of the deposit at Warka, since these deposits always contain material of older periods alongside objects made shortly before the deposit was buried. Moortgat's book (*Frühe Bildkunst in Sumer*) is marred by his wholesale adoption of the distinctions used in the work at Warka, where the two successive periods cannot very well be separated. Whatever terminology is ultimately adopted, a period of great achievement, which is named the Uruk period, can be distinguished from one of decline in glyptic art, named after the site of Jemdet Nasr.

third group consists of figures which we know in later times to have symbolical value (§ 5). It is a little unsatisfactory to base our interpretation on later evidence, but in the absence of contemporary texts we have no choice but to make use of such indications as we possess.[1] Fortunately there can be no doubt that the Uruk stage of Mesopotamian civilisation shares numerous traits with those of which we have more definite knowledge.[2]

§ 5. RELIGIOUS AND SECULAR SCENES

(*a*) *Religious Representations.*

The two cylinders of Pl. III *a*, *b* introduce us to the religious sphere within which the new glyptic art flourished. Their subject may appear to be purely decorative. But the strange selection of animals which appear side by side on Pl. III *b* has a very definite religious meaning in Early Dynastic times, and their combination is too peculiar for us not to try to account for it by an appeal to the known religious symbolism of a later age with which the Uruk period is in any case connected by a number of similarities. All the figures appearing in Pl. III *b* are afterwards related to a god who personified the generative force of nature.[3] A variety of epithets expressed the many aspects of his being. One of these names, which the Bible preserves as Tammuz, conveyed even in later times the original complexity of his nature. Tammuz was the god of corn, but also the "Lord of sheepfolds". Plants of various kinds, and the wild species of sheep and goats, served as his symbols in Early Dynastic and Akkadian art. A third symbol was the lion-headed eagle, Imdugud. It signified the warlike aspect of the god, his power to vanquish evil and death, and it was habitually (but not always) shown above an antithetically placed pair of animals, sometimes beasts of prey, sometimes his own sheep or goats, just as the eagle hovers above the moufflon rams of Pl. III *b*. The snake emerging from Mother Earth with the sprouting corn

[1] Professor Andrae maintains that these later representations are, in fact, dependent upon those of the earliest inhabitants of Mesopotamia, who in their nearness to nature intuitively found symbolical expression for certain transcendental truths. See above, p. 15, note 3; also *Die Ionische Säule, Bauform oder Symbol?* (Berlin, 1933) and especially "Tier-, Baum-, Haus-Symbole im alten Orient", in *Forschungen und Fortschritte*, XIII, nr. 20 (July, 1937). His profoundly stimulating interpretations are also largely intuitive and therefore, as he admits (*Ionische Säule*, Vorwort), incompatible with the rational method of scientific enquiry.

[2] Frankfort, *Archaeology and the Sumerian Problem* (Chicago, 1932), and Falkenstein, *Archaische Texte aus Uruk*, pp. 37 ff.

[3] See *Iraq*, I, 2 ff.; *Oriental Institute Communications*, No. 17, pp. 47 ff.; *Miscellanea Orientalia Antonio Deimel dedicata* (Roma, 1935), pp. 105 ff.

was another of the god's symbols, sometimes elaborated (with an obvious reference to his generative aspect) into a pair of copulating vipers, the origin of the caduceus. Thus the incomprehensible group of animals and flowers with which Pl. III *b* confronts us appears as a consistent reference to the god of fertility if we admit the relevancy of the later documents; we can hardly refuse to do so, since this single assumption completely solves the problem of our seal.

There are a few other seals of this period, which are less explicit but nevertheless show the god's essential symbols in conjunction. In one case a pair of sheep face each other over a pair of rosette flowers,[1] in another a goat and mountain-sheep are separated by stems of barley placed on either side of the symbol of the Mother-Goddess.[2] This last detail explicitly confirms the religious nature of these representations, but they are yet distinguished from the "ritual scenes" (which we shall now proceed to discuss) by the absence of action, just as the abstract symmetry of the composition differentiates them from the "animal friezes" of §6, and the absence of playful intertwinings creates a contrast with the "heraldic groups" and underlines the earnest intention of the symbolism of these seal designs.

(*b*) *Ritual Scenes.*

The same pair of deities whose emblems provide the sole decoration of the seals which we have just discussed appear as the objects of a cult in other seal designs of the Uruk period. Some of the ritual acts remain inexplicable for us. Those of which the tenor is clear are either sacrifices or concern the flocks or herds sacred to the gods.

The clearest representation of a sacrifice is given in Pl. V *c*. A bearded figure lifts an animal-shaped vase[3] as if to add it to the paired offerings in front of him—two baskets of fruit and vegetables surrounded, perhaps, by portions of meat; two low food tables, two goblets and the fellow of the animal-shaped vase which he holds. The attendant carries a ewer. All the objects depicted here find their counterpart on the alabaster vase from Warka which we mentioned before, and Andrae's description of the latter applies to the scene on our seal: "The problem of what went on in the temple is here quite simply and clearly answered: it was the communion of man with God through oblations drawn from the whole realm of nature, and that not by destruction but by dedication."[4]

[1] Newell, 690. [2] *American Journal of Semitic Languages*, XLIV, 232 ff., No. 6.

[3] Originals of these have been recently discovered at Khafaje, in a temple of the Jemdet Nasr period. See *Illustrated London News*, 20 June 1936.

[4] *Antiquity*, 1936, p. 146.

Closely related is the seal of Text-fig. 2, which connects the scenes of sacrifice with those of a less transparent character. Here the bearded figure seems to be offering a lioness or panther with cut off paws[1] before a shrine dedicated to the god whom we have described on page 17. For the space left between the "back" of the shrine and the two main figures is filled by the significant combination of plants—here barley—and animals.

The string of beads carried by the attendant connects this seal with the tantalising design of Pl. III *d*, which at the moment defies explanation. This unique seal was discovered at Tell Billa, north-east of modern Mosul, far beyond the region from which most monuments of the Uruk period are

Text-fig. 2. Offerings at a shrine.

found. If the two nude figures approaching the shrine from the right with the necklace of our Text-fig. 2 and a strip of woven stuff are really presenting these as offerings, it would seem that here sacrifice is part of a larger ritual, the nature of which we can only guess. The nudity of the two figures may, by analogy with Early Dynastic times, be taken to mark them as priests. The kilted man walking between them seems to approach the shrine in a mood and function differing from theirs. He seems to be weighed down by two heavy objects at the shoulders. Since we notice on the other side of the shrine a boat with plants at either end, we are reminded of the stones which Gilgamesh tied to his feet in order to reach the depths of the primeval waters in his search for the plant of life.[2] It is conceivable that the Epic preserved a trace of ancient ceremonial. In any case it is with ritual, not with myth, that the seal-cutters of the Uruk period seem to be concerned.

[1] Von der Osten, *Newell Collection*, p. 83, speaks of a long-horned animal, but the build of the body is that of a feline, and I can see no trace of horns. Perhaps the rope, by which the animal is carried and which seems to be tied round his muzzle, was mistaken for horns.

[2] Gilgamesh, XI Tablet, 272. See below, p. 63.

Other ritual scenes on seals of this age defy even hypothetical explanation. The boat of Pl. III*d* recurs on a seal from Warka (Pl. III*e*), where it contains, besides the usual pair of figures, an object which is perhaps an altar in the shape of a temple tower supported by the figure of a bull. This, again, appears upon the vase from Warka and upon two seal fragments,[1] and is thus a valuable link in the chain which unites the disparate monuments of Uruk glyptic.

The scenes of Text-figs. 3, 4 and Pl. III*c* must certainly also be classed as ritual compositions. The last-named shows a late stage of this type of cylinder with perhaps the prow of a boat on the extreme right. The excessive use of the drill and the awkward attitude of the squatting figure, which recurs exactly on the Blau monuments, show that this fragment must be placed at the very end of the Uruk period. The same applies to Text-fig. 12 (p. 36), a border case best discussed together with Jemdet Nasr seals.

Text-fig. 3.

Text-fig. 4.

Text-figs. 3, 4. Impressions from Erech: offerings at a shrine.

It is questionable whether Pl. IV*h* should be called a ritual scene. The group on the right is enigmatical, unless one man is filling a tall goblet from a waterskin. On the left a leather-worker's shop seems to be depicted, the master sitting behind a sloping cutting-out block while the attendant brings a skin. A pointed shoe of the so-called Anatolian type and possibly a quiver are finished products lying on the ground. Whether or not the serpent-necked monsters impart to this design a religious character, they certainly establish its age, and their testimony is borne out by the modelling of the figures, the method of rendering the further of two joined arms and by the rams' heads which serve as filling ornaments (cf. Pl. IV*a*).

Text-fig. 5. Impression from Erech: sacred herd and byre.

On several seals the temple herd is represented (Pl. V*d*, *j*; Text-fig. 5). Its sacred character is indicated by the symbol of the Mother-Goddess, which appears sometimes in the field and some-

[1] It occurs in the same manner on the seal fragment, Newell 22, and on I.M. 11501 it is mounted upon a lion, while the usual bearded figure stands upon the structure with hands lifted in prayer between two symbols of the Mother-Goddess.

times above the byre. The animals are either fed by the usual pair of men, or are depicted near their enclosure from which the young cattle emerge. The latter theme also occurs on sculptured vases.

The feeding of the herd represents a ritual act no less well-defined than those discussed in the preceding pages. But the animals and plants which played a part in this ritual also possessed symbolical significance, and the representation of this cult-act can therefore assume a much more stylised form than sacrifices and other ritual performances. The most realistic rendering of the scene occurs perhaps on Pl. V*d*. The herd is represented by a plurality of animals, and no abstract signs are used at all. On other seals actuality is transformed into symbolism by a reduction of the number of animals, whereby room is gained for pictograms (Pl. V*i*). The group on the right recurs to the left of Pl. III*a*, with the addition of two tall goblets known from the Warka alabaster vase and sacrificial scenes like Pl. V*c*. The main group of Pl. III*a* is a much more ambitious stylised version of the feeding of the temple herd, in which the various elements are so arranged as to form a finely balanced antithetical group.[1]

The food tendered to the herd varies in the same manner; in the more realistic versions it is barley, but elsewhere (Pl. V*g*) it is the rosette-shaped flower which appears to symbolise vegetable life in general.[2] It would seem that the plants as symbols are interchangeable, because the ceremony is in fact concerned with the sustenance drawn by the herds and flocks from the vegetable kingdom.[3]

When the sacred herd is represented with its pen or byre, men are absent and the emblem of the goddess stands above the structure; it is this theme that appears on seals (Text-fig. 5) and vases and survives into the Jemdet Nasr period.[4] The method of rendering a herd by making the animals overlap (Pl. V*e*; Text-fig. 5) seems to belong to the Uruk period.

[1] It should be noted that this seal is suspended by means of a pierced copper figure of a ram (Pl. I*b*), while rams are depicted on it. Similarly, the sacred herd of Pl. VI*a* occurs on a seal in the Louvre (A–25) crowned with the pierced figure of a bull.

[2] So, for instance, on Pl. III*b* and on the trough in the British Museum. The fragment A–116 is probably derived from a cylinder showing the offering of barley to the flock.

[3] Mrs van Buren, *Miscellanea Orientalia Antonio Deimel dedicata*, pp. 327 ff., rigorously separates plants and animals symbolising the goddess from those symbolising the god. But only a minority of monuments, such as the British Museum trough, support this view, and in all functions, barley, rosette and branch on the one hand, and goat, sheep, antelope, calf or stag on the other, seem to be interchangeable.

[4] See p. 16, note 3. There is of course no objection to using in the present discussion seals of the later style to elucidate variations of a motive of which but few early examples are available, and we have done so in referring to Pl. V*d*, *g*, *i*.

We have not yet attempted to explain the human figures appearing in the scenes. Since the gods of Mesopotamia were at all times conceived in human shape, it is practically impossible to distinguish them from men unless they wear a distinctive attire. The horned crown which remains a divine attribute in later ages appears first in the Jemdet Nasr period, and that time the Mother-Goddess is rendered in person. She is represented on the seals of the Uruk period by her symbol only. The bearded figure whom we meet there might well be the ruler of the city. During the Early Dynastic times he wears his hair in the same fashion as on the Uruk seals; and the Blau monuments and cylinders of the Jemdet Nasr period would supply the intermediate stages in the survival of that mode of coiffure. We know that the king played an active part in the ritual concerned with the fertility of crops and herds, and there is thus some likelihood that the bearded and skirted figure, who wears his long hair tied in a knot at the back of the head, is a local ruler, while the nude clean-shaven figures appearing on some of the seals are priests. This view is confirmed by some secular scenes, in which the bearded figure appears in a function which well behoves a king.

(*c*) *Secular Scenes.*

Two types of secular scene are depicted in the Uruk period. One shows a herdsman defending a calving cow against a lion, a subject which lies at the root of the greater part of Early Dynastic—and, in fact, of most Mesopotamian—glyptic, since the friezes of combat between men and beasts develop on this basis.[1] An entirely different type is represented by a number of sealings found at Warka. We must call these historical scenes. One, including a war chariot, is too badly damaged to give much information.[2] The other can be reconstructed from a number of impressions (Text-fig. 6). A bearded figure, surely the king, stands, spear in hand, upon the battlefield, where some of his followers are still dealing with the enemy. Most of these

[1] Newell, 695. Von der Osten has pronounced this seal, with several others of the Uruk period, to be a forgery, an excusable mistake since no stratified material of this type was known at the time of his writing. If Newell, 669 and 690 may now be considered above suspicion, there remains a slight possibility of doubt in the case of 695, since it falls well below the standard of most authenticated seals of the period. It is for this reason that we have not illustrated it. Nevertheless, it shows two peculiarities which a forger would hardly invent, much less combine on the same seal, and which yet appeared combined on a seal impression discovered at Warka after the seal reached Mr Newell's collection. The volute of the lion's tail and the use of the antelope's head as filling ornament recur identically in our Pl. IV*a*.

[2] *Uruk Vorläufiger Bericht*, IV, Pl. 14*c*, *h*.

are lying at their mercy with hands tied behind them. It is clear that a definite victory, an actual historical event, is commemorated on this seal.

Text-fig. 6. Impressions from Erech: the king on the battlefield.

(*d*) *Summary.*

This is an astonishing subject for a seal design. It draws attention to the curiously dual character of the art of the period. Its vitality is manifest. It strives so vigorously for expression that difficulties are overcome which the more critical and deliberate artists of later periods would hesitate to face. But the Uruk period did not distinguish between monumental and applied art, representation and decoration. Seals are hardly appropriate to serve as commemorative monuments. Historical and religious scenes which required the ample space of mural designs, or at least the scope offered by a stela, were used to decorate carved vases or cut as miniatures upon seals. The truth that each branch of art has its own limitations and its peculiar possibilities of achievement remained to be discovered. Glyptic art had not yet recognised its own basic laws or constituted itself as an independent means of expression. Yet the creative power of its first manifestations is such that we meet among its astonishingly varied products anticipations of every school of glyptic art which subsequently flourished in Mesopotamia.

§ 6. ANIMAL FILE AND HERALDIC GROUP

The seal designs of Pl. III *a*, *b* are heraldic groups in their formal aspect, but we have excluded them from this class because the former appears, in the light of other representations, to depict an action—though in a stylised manner—while both possess definite religious significance. The designs which we are about to discuss seem to lack such meaning. It is always hazardous to declare a work of ancient Oriental art to be secular; but as far as we are able to judge this description applies to most of the designs on Pl. IV. The animal file of Pl. V *b* may conceivably represent the god of fertility in the manner of Pl. III *b*, the bull taking the place of the ram, and the ear of corn that of the rosette.[1] But this explanation loses probability if we consider the literal meaning which must probably be assigned to the bull in Pl. V*a*. Uncertainty must needs result from the fact that objects playing a predominant part in the life of the Babylonians served at the same time, and for this very reason, as religious symbols.

The other seals which we place in this class do not allow of any allegorical explanation. They show mere additions of animals placed in file, and often display great variety. Sometimes beasts are drawn large, and with calligraphic outline (Pls. IV*a*; V*a*, *b*).[2] Elsewhere we find two rows of smaller figures superimposed (Pl. IV*c*). In one case we meet a rudimentary feeling for landscape, in the sense that the animals' environment is indicated (Pl. IV*b*). A similar interest may have prompted the seal-cutter of Pl. V*f* to set the trefoils of small rock plants between the mountain-sheep and goats.

The animal file is found at all periods of Mesopotamian glyptic, and always with a variant where, instead of ruminants of one kind or another following each other, we find carnivores alternating with herbivores. It seems that the idea of herds, flocks or game brought to mind inevitably the depredations of the beasts of prey. The motive which Pl. V*a* shows in detail appears in four variants in the frieze of Pl. IV*m*, where the victims are game, namely boar, stag, ibex and moufflon. The gesture of attack remains entirely abstract, ideogrammatic; the attitudes of struggling animals are nowhere suggested, but each pair of figures is connected by the forefoot or jaw of the beast of prey.

An entirely different connection between adjoining figures is shown in the designs which we call "heraldic groups". Their composition can be more appropriately studied in § 7, which is devoted to the style of the Uruk period. Here we are merely concerned with the elements of which they are composed. Two animals combined to form a heraldic group are always of the same kind, and their connection is purely ornamental. Tails may be intertwined, paws may be brought into contact, but there is no attempt to depict a situation which might arise in actuality (Pl. IV*d*, *e*, *f*, *j*, *l*). This circumstance explains the presence, in the heraldic groups, of two elements which we do not encounter in the animal file. These are inanimate objects and fabulous monsters.

[1] This seal and Pl. V*a* can be dated to the Uruk period not only by the modelling of the animals, but also by the shape of the ear of corn, especially the way in which the leaves spring from the stalk. Cf. *American Journal of Semitic Languages*, XLIV, 232, No. 6, and Louvre, A–116.

[2] Also *Uruk Vorläufiger Bericht*, V, Pl. 24*b*, and with excessive use of drill, Louvre, S. 311.

The inanimate objects are various types of pottery, amongst which two are of special importance for us, since they are widely used, even in Syria and Persia, but only during the Uruk and Jemdet Nasr periods. One is a tall pointed vase with a neck and two long band-shaped handles, which are made sufficiently strong for use by numerous little struts which connect them with the body of the vase (Pl. IV*e*, *f*, *g*, *i*). This would seem to be a metal vessel. The other vase is also an amphora, but with smaller handles and a conical foot. It may well have a clay prototype (Pl. IV*k*).

These vessels appear also with animal files (Pl. IV*i*, *k*); but there they are alien elements, while in the ornamental frieze they have a comprehensible function as space-filling motives between the main groups, and we find, in fact, both types of vase in an antithetical group on a sealing at Warka, which antedates a little the bulk of the Uruk material.[1] Its intrusion into the animal file is illustrated by examples derived from Elam, a somewhat peripheral region where, as we shall have occasion to see in a subsequent chapter, the Mesopotamian styles are taken over, but seldom preserved in their original purity.

It is also in Elam that the second element which distinguishes the heraldic groups from the animal file is most flourishing. The seal-cutters at Susa enjoyed the representation of monstrous and fantastic creatures. Though these do also occur at the time in Mesopotamia proper (Pl. IV*d*, *f*), at Susa there is a much greater variety; for as the Elamites took such delight in these inventions, they are sometimes comical, sometimes gruesome, but always convincing (Text-figs. 7, 8).[2] Occasionally they depict normal animals in abnormal attitudes, and so achieve a monstrous effect (Pl. IV*l*). Some of these designs may be assigned to the Jemdet Nasr period, for the proto-Elamite tablets on which they occur belong partly to that and partly to the Uruk period, and it is not yet possible to separate these clearly. But the thorough modelling of the animals which characterised the Uruk period, and is lost in the succeeding epoch, definitely connects some of those sealings with the examples now under discussion (Pl. IV*g*; Text-fig. 7).[3] This feature is comparatively rare, however, because the Elamites showed a marked preference for replacing the modelling by decorative lines, mainly relying on

[1] *Uruk Vorläufiger Bericht*, II, Fig. 44. Compare the space-filling function of the vases in Heinrich's *Kleinfunde*, Pl. 15*f*.

[2] The seals and seal impressions from Susa are published in volumes VIII, XVI and XXII of the *Mémoires de la Délégation en Perse*, in drawings which often miss the stylistic essentials of the originals. The best of those now in the Louvre are published photographically in Delaporte, *Catalogue des Cylindres Orientaux*, prefixed by the letter "S".

[3] Louvre, S. 253, S. 301, S. 332.

the expressive force of the silhouette to characterise the creatures depicted (Pls. V*f*; IV*j*). Notwithstanding this stylistic peculiarity, the seal impressions from Susa and Warka show many resemblances of detail. The landscape element of Pl. IV*b* recurs in Text-figs. 10, 11. Religious scenes with

Text-fig. 7. Impression from Susa: griffin.

Text-fig. 9. Impression from Susa: bulls and crosses.

Text-fig. 8. Impression from Susa: monsters in boats.

Text-fig. 10. Impression from Susa: hunting scene.

Text-fig. 11. Impression from Susa: river scene.

shrines,[1] historical scenes,[2] animal file[3] and heraldic group,[4] are all represented at Susa, if often in an impure form, the limitations of the various categories being less clearly realised by the somewhat barbaric highlanders.

[1] *Mémoires de la Délégation en Perse*, XVI, 225, 232. [2] *Ibid.* XVI, 226, 235.

[3] Louvre, S. 301, S. 303, S. 323, S. 324, S. 340; *Mémoires de la Délégation en Perse*, XVI, 96, 104, 105, 125, 146, 149, 151, 153, 183, etc.

[4] Louvre, S. 294, S. 315, S. 320; *Mémoires de la Délégation en Perse*, VIII, Fig. 13; XVI, 182, 313.

In addition to the confusion between the diametrically opposed classes of (realistic) animal file and heraldic group which we have already discussed, we see another in Pl. IV*j*, where the fine heraldic group is robbed of its decorative effect by the obliquely placed animals which serve most inappropriately as filling, but which are obviously derived from such a procession as that of Pl. V*f*, where their attitude admirably enriches the liveliness and unity of the design.

In Mesopotamia fantastic creatures appear on the early impressions mentioned above, and assume most commonly the shape of serpent-necked felines, either with a serpent's head or with that of a lioness or panther (Pl. IV*d*, *f*). The lion-headed eagle is found (Pl. V*h*) along with the serpent-necked panthers on a seal preserved in the Louvre and only datable in the light of the recent discoveries; for the motive is characteristic of the Uruk period at Warka, but the coarse use of the drill indicates the incipient Jemdet Nasr period for this particular specimen. It is of great importance that its age can be established, for its main motive recurs almost identically on a proto-Dynastic slate palette commemorating the conquest of Lower Egypt by Narmer-Menes, the first king of the First Egyptian Dynasty.

§ 7. THE STYLE OF THE URUK PERIOD

The seals of the Uruk period which we have discussed possess all the characteristics of a first achievement. When a new technique has been mastered all the fresh possibilities of expression are simultaneously explored. The creative impulse is not canalised by tradition. Contrasting formulae are evolved and applied side by side. The use of abstract religious symbols (Pl. III*b*) did not at this time exclude the accurate illustration of ritual procedure (Pls. III*d*; V*c*). The composition of highly decorative heraldic groups (Pl. IV*e*) did not discredit the production of mere juxtapositions of separate animal-studies (Pl. IV*a*). It is wellnigh impossible to name stylistic features common to all the seals of the period.

Single figures. Let us first consider the figures of these seal designs in isolation. The animals possess a taut, vivid outline which unwaveringly summarises the essential points of their forms (Pls. III*a*, *b*; IV*a*; V*b*). Within this outline the modelling is vigorous and thorough, and the artist relies on actual relief rather than on linear details. Compare, for instance, the lion and bulls of Pl. V*a*, *b* with those of Pls. VI*a* and VII*a*. When engraved lines are used at all in the Uruk period, they remain subsidiary elaborations of detail, such as the eyes of the bulls or the breast-mane of the moufflon, on the well-modelled bodies of those creatures.

Human beings present a more difficult problem since they cannot be adequately shown in pure profile; the characteristic feature of the trunk, the breadth of the shoulders, appears in a front view. The Uruk period shares with all ideoplastic art the expedient of combining aspects which would be to our vision mutually exclusive. Wherever the influence of fifth-century Greek art has not penetrated the attitude of the bearded figure in Pl. III *a, f* is used. Ultimately the same formula serves as basis for the servant with the pole in Pl. III *e* and all the figures in Pl. III *c*, but the Uruk seal-cutters also introduce profiles and three-quarter views almost unwittingly into their designs. These remain inconsistent and therefore eventually ineffectual, but they are typical of the period. At this time figures with both arms uplifted are habitually presented with the nearer limb overlapping the farther, except for the elbow and a portion of the lower arm (Pls. III *e*; V *c*; Text-fig. 2). Towards the close of the period the increasing use of the borer tends to accentuate the inherent inconsistencies of these "free" attitudes; note the two shoulders in the stooping figure of Pl. III *c* which is rendered in profile.

As to the modelling of the human figures, it rarely achieves the excellence of the animal designs. Sometimes the muscles are shown (Pl. III *a*). More often the human shape is summarised in somewhat full and rounded forms (Pls. III *d, e*; IV *h*; V *e*) which are quite typical for the Uruk style of glyptic, and which sometimes even show through the clothing of the figures (Pls. III *e*; V *c*; Text-fig. 2).

Composition. In considering the composition of the Uruk seals we find two clearly distinguished groups. Some betray no preoccupation with those aesthetic considerations which constitute the *raison d'être* for the second group of designs.

In the first class the composition is that of a continuous narrative, of which the content alone is relevant. Sometimes a certain action is depicted, and then no attempt is made to balance the forces introduced upon the decorated surface. The pronounced gesture of the figure on the left of Pl. V *c* is not absorbed, nor even counterbalanced by the two meagre symbols of Inanna which bound the frieze on the right. The animal file possesses the same one-sided direction (Pl. IV *a*). Sometimes the seal-cutter counteracts the movement in a desultory way by reversing one or more of the animals (Pl. IV *c*).

Another type of Uruk seal is, however, deliberately composed with a view to static balance. The designs are thus basically different from those just discussed. In this second group everything is subordinated to decorative effect. The meaning of Pl. III *a*, for instance, which we have recognised as the feeding of the temple herd, is not by any means patent, and could only be disclosed by comparison with seals of the former, purely narrative, group—like Pl. V *d*. The clearness of representation, which was the main concern of the maker of this latter seal, is sacrificed by the cutter of Pl. III *a* to the production of a finely spaced and balanced decorative design. By the same token the frieze of Pl. IV *m* is composed of four pairs of animals in which those facing each other in one register bridge the gap between an averted pair below or above. A more explicit attempt to avoid hiatus in design is shown in Pl. III *b*, where the eagle and the vipers bracket the mountain-sheep.[1]

The seal of Pl. V *e* is another example of the ability of the early artists, though the device by which balance is achieved is in this case less obvious, but none the less effective. The pronounced directions of the figures in the top and bottom row balance each other, while the rippling movement of the advancing flocks is summarised by the wavy line.

Yet another aesthetic consideration has often influenced the seal-cutters of the Uruk period. They betray a predilection for an even covering of the surface with design. Filling motives such as heads or limbs of animals, birds and vases, are used for this purpose (Pl. IV *a*, *e–l*). More ingenious are those compositions in which the main theme is made to result in an evenly divided disposition of masses (Pls. III *a*, *b*; V *a*, *b*). To achieve this and to produce at the same time a continuous frieze has been the main preoccupation of the seal-cutters of later ages. Thus we find the glyptic of the Uruk period astonishingly rich, not only in subject-matter, but also in the varying tendencies of its style. And in many directions it achieves results which excel most and are equalled by few of the works of later periods.

[1] For the benefit of those readers who are not accustomed to the formal criticism of works of art it may be added that the facts revealed by the analysis of the artist's achievement are not necessarily supposed to have been present in his consciousness at the time of production.

CHAPTER II. THE DECLINE IN THE JEMDET NASR PERIOD

§ 8. THE DISINTEGRATION OF THE OLD REPERTOIRE

No sudden break intervenes between the Uruk period and the succeeding age, which is named, after a small hill where its remains were first discovered, Jemdet Nasr. Some seals may be considered as the latest products of the older, or the first manifestations of the new epoch. In any case it is sound to take the seal impressions actually found at Warka in layers IV and V as a standard of the glyptic of the Uruk period (Pl. III*f*; p. 16, n. 3). Now such technical qualities as are possessed by the seals of Pls. III*c*; V*g–j* and VI*a* are not represented among the stratified impressions and are therefore counted by us as denoting the incipient style of Jemdet Nasr. They are obviously related to the older themes and are in every respect transitional.[1]

The glyptic of the Jemdet Nasr age, considered as a whole (Pls. VI–VIII), presents an entirely different physiognomy from its predecessor. At first sight the contrast seems equivocal. As regards design and execution the Jemdet Nasr period means decline, but the seals show a richer variety of shapes than is found in Mesopotamia at any other time. It is possible, however, to claim a common root for these two apparently conflicting qualities in a change of purpose on the part of the seal-cutter. The impressions of the Uruk period, for all their variety of style, are homogeneous as regards quality and execution. They suggest the work of a fairly restricted group of high-class engravers concentrating upon the design and accepting throughout the oblong cylinder shape, and limestone or marble as their material. But the seal-cutters of the Jemdet Nasr age seem bent upon producing a serviceable article for common use. They experimented with shape and material, size, and mode of suspension (see § 2, p. 4). Writing, invented in the Uruk period, became simplified and more commonly used in the Jemdet Nasr age. Trade found, in consequence, increased opportunities, which is proved by the extraordinary abundance of vessels and ornaments of imported stone characteristic of deposits of this period wherever they are found. The in-

[1] Mere quality cannot serve as criterion, but our distinction between seals of the Uruk and the Jemdet Nasr periods is based upon definite stylistic characteristics such as the omission of facial detail, the decrease in modelling and the excessive use of the drill which serve us as guide. Indifferently executed seals like V.A. 3902 or our Pl. V*c* obviously belong to the Uruk period. Other seals, such as those quoted in our text, or A–26, Moortgat, *Frühe Bildkunst*, Pl. 36, 1, or Heinrich, *Kleinfunde*, Pls. 17*b*, 19*a*, may date either to Uruk or to Jemdet Nasr; the transition being gradual, it is impossible to draw a definite line, but a comparison with the seal impressions from Warka suggests that the seals just indicated belong to the later age. See also p. 16, n. 3, and p. 32, n. 3. The age and affinities of a cylinder and of sealings on gypsum tablets from Warka remain enigmatical: *Uruk Vorläufiger Bericht*, VIII, Pls. 49*a*, 51*c* and pp. 52 f.

creased use of seals would explain the experiments undertaken to produce more practical shapes, as well as the simplification of design and execution. We may, however, suspect that the coarse use of drill and graver (Pl. VII *h*) was an indirect result of the marvellous development of stonework at this time. Subjects given to the seal-cutters of the Uruk period were now considered suitable for sculptured vases and stelae only, and glyptic art must thus have lost much of its talent to another rapidly expanding craft.

However this may be, compared with those of the Uruk period the seal-cutters of the Jemdet Nasr age show less invention, and a much inferior technical skill. The very few subjects which were added to their repertoire will be discussed in the next paragraph. They do not make up for the loss of the majority of those in use up to that time. The subjects continue to be used in very much simplified versions, coarsely engraved (Pls. V *g*, *j*; VII *i*) or cut so deeply with the drill that its traces could not be deleted by the subsequent work of the graver (Pls. V *h*; VI *b*, *c*; VII *d*, *g*, *h*). In the Uruk period the surface of the figures was always vigorously modelled, as we have seen (Pl. III *a*, *d*), but the engraved examples of the Jemdet Nasr period show a flattened surface within the outline (Pl. VIII *k*). These seals, in which drill-work is absent, are large, often measuring two inches or more in height, and they are often devoid of axial perforation. In Elam this class of seal retains a higher standard (Pl. VII *a*), although the tendency to indulge in an exuberance of decorative line-work, which we noted in the previous age, now prevails unchecked. The designs are often carefully composed and adequately engraved, but their character is changed. Instead of designs which represent observed nature (Pls. IV *j*; V *f*) we find, for instance, the bull and lion motive reduced to the gorgeous ornament of Pl. VII *a*. The graduation of relief by which the various parts of the body were originally differentiated has become in Elam a group of separate engraved surface patterns.[1]

In Mesopotamia there are no equivalents to these fine Elamite seals.

[1] Though the seal of Pl. VII *a* was bought in Baghdad for the Iraq Museum, its Elamite origin cannot well be doubted. The division of the animal's body recurs at Susa: *Mémoires de la Délégation en Perse*, XVI, Nos. 90, 93. The first of these also resembles the Baghdad seal in its combination of striding animal, upright animal and plant motive. For the latter see *loc. cit.* Nos. 161, 169 and our Pl. IV *j*, which may be transitional between the Uruk period and the Jemdet Nasr style of Elam. Note that the early occurrence of the tree upon the mountain, a motive more common in Akkadian times, is well certified by *loc. cit.* No. 97, an impression upon a proto-Elamite tablet. Our Pls. IV *j* and V *f* (which also show the division of the animal's body) are, like Pl. VII *a*, devoid of axial perforation. While fine seals like our Pl. VII *a* occur in Elam in the Jemdet Nasr period and have no equivalents in Mesopotamia proper, we find in Elam the same disintegrated designs which are common in the Plain during that period (e.g. S–311).

There we find crude versions of the offering scene of Pl. V *c*, in which—of the various objects of sacrifice—only the two baskets remain. In one respect, however, these coarse seals show important innovations. The goddess, hitherto represented by a symbol, now appears in person (Pl. V *g*). Moreover, she wears upon her head the horns of a cow, forerunners of the horned crown which later formed the distinctive headgear of the gods.[1] The male figure, on the other hand, appears in the same garb as before, another testimony to his human character.[2]

On technical grounds and judging by analogy with the stratified examples, we consider that certain other seals illustrate the survival of older themes into the Jemdet Nasr period. These are the serpent-necked monsters (Pl. V *h*), the sacred herd and its byre (Pl. VI *a*), the animal file of Pl. VI *b*, *c* which shows the mountain-goats with spreading horns so well known in the Uruk period and also the occasional reversal of direction (cf. Pl. IV *c*).[3] The lion-headed eagle, threatening the lion, is not known on seals of ascertained Uruk age.[4] The bulls on this seal show for the first time both horns, placed in front view on the profile of the head. The same feature distinguishes the largest figure of Pl. VI *c*, which is also provided with a trunk. This elephant-bull combination is not uncommon at Mohenjo Daro in the Indus valley, and the different treatment of this composite monster in Pl. VI *c* may well be the result of a gap in time, the Indian seals dating from the end of the Early Dynastic or the Sargonid period.[5]

The few impressions found on the tablets from Jemdet Nasr[6] also seem to

[1] Heinrich, *Kleinfunde*, Pl. 18. In our illustration (which we have used for other reasons) the rendering of the horns is not free from ambiguity, but other examples, such as V.A. 11041, 11042, leave no doubt on this point. A good Jemdet Nasr version of our Pl. V *b* is N.B.C. 5988, illustrated in *Archiv für Orientforschung*, XI, 9, Fig. 10.

[2] See above, pp. 22. Detailed discussions of dress have been avoided throughout since the miniatures on the seals present no more than convenient abbreviations.

[3] From the point of view of technique our Pl. VI *a* stands halfway between Fig. 5 and Louvre, A–25. Our Pl. VI *b*, *c* resembles closely an unpublished seal in Baghdad (I.M. 2806) which has the "loop-bore", a method of suspension used exclusively in the Jemdet Nasr period (Pl. I *c* and p. 6).

[4] It perhaps occurs on two other seals of the Jemdet Nasr period; I.M. 2806 and in *Mémoires de la Délégation en Perse*, XVI, No. 185.

[5] *Oriental Institute Communications*, No. 16, pp. 48 ff. For a survey of the differences and resemblances between the Indus culture and that of Mesopotamia see *Annual Bibliography of Indian Archaeology* for 1932 (Leiden, 1934), pp. 1–12. For the Indian cylinders, see below, p. 304, § 47.

[6] Langdon, *Oxford Editions of Cuneiform Texts*, VII. The seal impressions are most inadequately published. They show two-handled pots (No. 121), large figures of animals (No. 7) and perhaps a shrine (Nos. 45, 64).

be survivals of older themes cut in a rough and ready way without modelling, resembling seals found in the Sin Temple at Khafaje which repeat the old frieze of standing and resting animals.

Another survival of older themes lies at the root of the numerous Jemdet Nasr seal designs resembling Pl. VII *d*, *g*.[1] Their ancestry includes both those of Text-fig. 5 and Pl. V *d*; they combine therefore two themes which appear separately in the Uruk period. Then the temple herd was depicted, either in connection with a domed byre (Pl. VI *a*; Text-fig. 5, p. 20) or receiving food (Pl. V *d*). In an entirely different setting we found sanctuaries depicted (Pl. III *e*; Text-figs. 2, 3). But in Jemdet Nasr times the sacred flock is habitually represented beside the shrine to which it belongs (Pl. VII *d*, *g*, *h*, *i*), and these seals are especially common in the excavated temples of the period. It may well be that they had only their shape in common with the seals and served in reality a dedicatory purpose. I do not know, in any case, of impressions of this type of design.

Not only the theme but also the general appearance of these seals recall the Uruk period. Those depicting the sacred herd are often large cylinders of limestone or marble. The designs show various degrees of completeness. The Inanna symbol is sometimes retained (Pl. VII *d*); at times a tree like that of Pl. VI *c* appears beside the shrine, or a boat (A–31) or a watercourse flows below (Pl. VII *g*). The animals sometimes include cattle as well as goats or sheep. Fish, or more rarely scorpions, are occasionally added. Every one of these motives is in some way or other relevant to that of the fertility gods which prevailed in Mesopotamia in early times. Occasionally spouted vases appear in these designs (Pl. VII *g*), and they sometimes form the sole decoration of smaller cylinders (Pl. VII *f*). The bird (Pl. VII *k*) is exceptional and the curious face of Pl. I *f* is in juxtaposition with a temple of the type shown in Text-fig. 13 (p. 36) surmounted by a band of rosette flowers as known in the Uruk period (Pl. III *a*). In the progressive disintegration of the designs, the temple (or perhaps more specifically the pattern made by the roofing-beams in the façade, cf. Pl. III *d*; Text-figs. 2, 3, 4, 12, 13) seems to turn into the ladder design of Pl. VIII *h*, *i*, *j*.

The animals too are drawn carelessly—the whole group gives the impression of being always hastily executed. Geometric filling motives deserve attention, since they are characteristic of the Jemdet Nasr age and do not occur in the Brocade style of the succeeding period which reintegrated the

[1] Pl. VII *d* has an engraved design added in Early Dynastic times. In addition to the large numbers of this class found at Tell Agrab and Khafaje see also Newell, 24, 26, 27, 28; De Clercq, 2; Heinrich, *Fara*, Pl. 62 *e*; Billiet, *Musée de Cannes*, 15 A.

traditional subject in a new and vigorous manner. In these first products of the Early Dynastic period we shall find neither the ladder design of Pl. VIII *h, i, j,* nor the eye-shaped designs of Pl. VIII *j, k,* nor the curious little star of Pl. VII *f, h* consisting of a drill-hole made at a point where two incised lines intersect, a common occurrence in the Jemdet Nasr age.

§ 9. NEW ELEMENTS OF THE PERIOD

Along with the seals showing a progressive disintegration of the old repertoire we find a class of cylinders which represent an entirely new departure. They are long and thin, and but rarely made of any other stone than steatite which has been glazed (Pl. I *h, i*).[1] Often the seals of this class are made of faience (Pl. I *n*). The glaze was originally bright pea-green, but has turned white in all but a few cases. The designs are geometrical and very varied. Pl. VI *e–i* gives some characteristic examples. It would be tempting to call these cylinders decorated beads, but impressions are known.

The shape, material and the designs are all without precedent. The fact that this class is well represented at Susa does not entitle us to claim for it a foreign origin, because Elam grew increasingly dependent upon Mesopotamian art forms. Moreover, Fara in the Sumerian south,[2] as well as Nineveh in the far north,[3] have both produced examples of this class of seal.

The vitality of this new glyptic can best be gauged by the high quality of an exceptional adaptation of one of the older subjects (Pl. VI *d*). The rendering of animals in their natural setting was known in the Uruk period (Pl. IV *b*). The flatness of modelling in the drinking and ruminating mountain-goats of Pl. VI *d* is characteristic of the Jemdet Nasr period, recurring in certain seals found at Khafaje.[4] The cylinder is of glazed steatite and obviously presents an old subject in the new medium. The makers of this class of seal had, however, a strong predilection for geometrical decoration and this becomes manifest in almost all the specimens which include natural motives. Pl. VI *j* shows how such motives were subjected to piecemeal absorption by their geometrical environment. This subordination of representational to geometrical design differentiates the class of tall slender seals from the

[1] Brett, 30–35, a set of seals evidently belonging together, are made of lapis lazuli, which explains the slight difference in design between them and similar seals from Khafaje. They serve however to date a remarkable cylinder with a snake-coil to the Jemdet Nasr period. *American Journal of Archaeology*, XXX (1926), 405 ff., Fig. 6.

[2] Heinrich, *Fara*, Pls. 69*l, m*; 72*c, d, e*. From Telloh: Louvre, T–1, T–2, T–6.

[3] *Liverpool Annals of Anthropology and Archaeology*, XIX, Pl. LXIII, 11, 14; XX, Pls. LXV, 21–35; LXVI, 3, 4, 7, 18–26.

[4] *Oriental Institute Communications*, No. 20, Fig. 28.

remainder of the Jemdet Nasr glyptic, which developed in the opposite direction. The contemporary existence of such seals as Pl. VII*g–k* and the newly introduced seals with geometrical design eventually resulted in compositions like Pl. VIII*j*, *k*, where the traditional animal file predominates and remnants of the geometric repertoire are used as filling. The "eye" design on these two seals is clearly derived from rosettes or patterns like Pl. VI*f*; in Pl. VIII*k* it appears once with two of the four original leaves. Observe that the disintegration affecting the subjects inherited from the Uruk period ultimately overcame even the new geometric designs. Thus the class of long seals, so obviously an innovation of the Jemdet Nasr period, appears from every point of view to be contrary to the prevailing tendencies of the time. It is impossible to say whether these seals were produced by people freshly arrived in Mesopotamia and unable to hold their own, or whether the innovation is a purely native reaction against the prevailing deterioration of the seal-cutters' craft, and therefore no more than a movement in the field of art which failed to achieve its object. The tall glazed seals appear suddenly and in great numbers in an early stage of the Jemdet Nasr period and survive but sparsely in its concluding phases; but this distribution in time would be explicable on either of the above hypotheses.

Somewhat apart stands a class of stone cylinders with animal designs, scorpions (Pl. VIII*b*) or birds (Text-fig. 14) to which oval incisions are summarily added to make a design. Discoveries at Khafaje have established the age of this group.[1]

During the later part of the period we find an increased number of small stone cylinders of the ordinary shape (Pl. I*k*) which were decorated with simplified geometric patterns derived from the long seals (Pls. VII*b*, *e*; VIII*a*). It is important that this simplification was selective and became standardised. The simple geometric patterns of the three seals to which we have just referred are entirely typical of the Jemdet Nasr period, like the ladder design discussed above (p. 34), and we are able to trace by means of these typical patterns imported seals of the period in Persia and Syria (§ 35, p. 229) and Egypt (§ 45, p. 292).

In addition to the various types of seals so far discussed, the Jemdet Nasr period evolved yet another class, a squat seal, roughly as high as its diameter, often more or less concave and generally made of red, green or grey limestone (Pl. I*j*). These short seals are commonly found wherever town ruins are excavated, at Jemdet Nasr, Telloh, Tell Asmar and Susa, and their impressions occur on proto-Elamite or slightly later tablets. But they are completely

[1] Kh. VI/208; cf. Heinrich, *Fara*, Pl. 67*b*.

absent from the temples of Tell Agrab and Khafaje and rare at Warka. Most of their designs consist of groups of drill-holes (Pl. VIII *c–f*); their most usual subject is a pigtailed female figure, either standing or squatting on a bed or bench. A spider-like design is equally typical though less common (Pl. VIII *f*) and occasionally the drill-holes do not combine into any but a rough geometrical pattern (Pl. I *j*). These seals may be the counterparts of the rough representations of the sacred herds on the large limestone seals. Both classes can be traced back to an ancestry in the Uruk period. This is clear in the cases where a squat seal shows the traditional goat file (Pl. VIII *g, i*); and on Pl. VIII *h* (which is better executed than most) we find in addition not only the ladder design discussed on p. 33, but also the two-handled jar from Pl. IV *e, f, g, i*. Similarly, Text-figs. 12, 13 connect the

Text-fig. 12. Drinking scene and shrine.

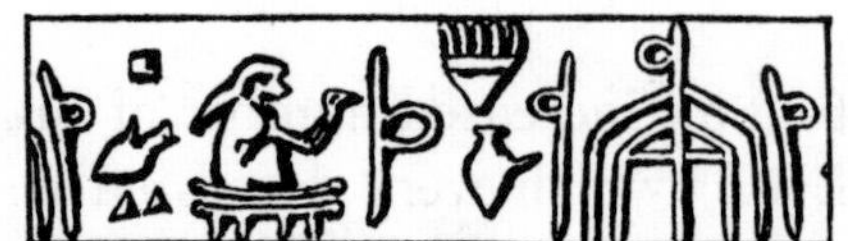

Text-fig. 13. Female figure and shrine.

Text-fig. 14. Birds.

pigtailed figures with the scenes of sacrifice or other ritual which are common in the Uruk period.

These figures often appear in procession, holding some object, or are alternately placed upside down or separated by vertical lines. Some representations are more explicit, and these have been connected with Text-fig. 12 and explained as women spinning, perhaps in the service of a temple.[1] A similar subject occurs on a squat seal (Text-fig. 13). But while it is true that the figure on the left resembles the pigtailed figures of the squat seals, both

[1] Heidenreich, in *Orientalistiche Literaturzeitung*, 1926, pp. 625 ff. The date of Text-fig. 12 is well established by the attitude of the figure on the left which recurs on the Blau monuments. See above, p. 16. Heidenreich has enumerated the seals belonging to this class, to which must be added *Fara*, Pl. 64 *d–g, m*; Newell, 29–31; *Revue d'Assyriologie*, XXV, 176, Nos. 24, 25.

in coiffure and in the fact that she is shown seated on a couch, Text-fig. 12 seems rather to suggest a banqueting or libation scene. Though the couch often becomes a mere ladder design, it is shown with the full detail of its clawed or hoofed feet in Pl. VIII *d*, which is characteristic of the early furniture both in Egypt and Mesopotamia.

The objects with which these women are occupied are too summarily depicted to give us a clue to the meaning of the scene. In some instances we recognise a spouted pot (Pl. VIII *c*, *d* and Text-fig. 13), which also occurs beside goats or birds together with the shrine (Pl. VII *f*, *g*, *k*);[1] and the same applies to the objects represented by various combinations of triangles and drill-holes (Pl. VIII *d*, *e*, *f*).

On a valuable seal from Chatal Huyuk with loop-bore (Pl. XXXVIII *f*) we see the squatting figures engaged with two vases of the types known from the Uruk seals, a motive recurring fairly frequently.[2] We may take it to represent potters at work or people cleaning ritual vessels, since the combination in which the group occurs may trace descent from the ritual or sacrificial scenes of the previous period, and it may be significant that the potters on Pl. XXXVIII *f* appear together with a bull, goat and some pieces of fringed cloth which are also found on proto-Elamite sealings in conjunction with vases or animals.[3] It is thus possible to surmise that the squat seals such as Pl. VIII *c*, *d*, *f* are abbreviations of more elaborate scenes of offerings. A commemoration of a donation to the gods would not be inappropriate as a seal design.

Once (Pl. XXXVIII *k*) the vases are held by scorpions while the presumed "potters" take hold of the scorpions' sting.

In a few instances a mechanism which may be a loom is added to the scene (Pl. VIII *d*, right-hand side).[4] Resuming, we may say that the pig-tailed figures on these seals are depicted in a variety of actions which it is

[1] Newell, 29; As. 32/1189. But Heidenreich's supposition that the spinning woman uses a ewer to keep her fingers moist is rather invalidated by its recurrence in connection with animals and shrines, which suggests that it is a libation vessel for ritual use (Newell, 26, 28; *Hittite Seals*, 36; Louvre, A-29; Kh. VI/174; As. 35/965). Moortgat, *Frühe Bildkunst*, p. 62, suggests that the vessels were used for milking the herds.

[2] *Fara*, Pl. 67 *g*; *Mémoires de la Délégation en Perse*, XVI, 192, 216, 218, 221.

[3] A-115, like the seal from Chatal Huyuk, shows a man and an animal. The fringed material occurs with the vases on *Mémoires de la Délégation en Perse*, XVI, 190, 204, a seal from Tell Basher in Syria, our Pl. XXXVIII *c*; Heinrich, *Kleinfunde*, Pl. 15 *k* and on a seal from Sialk, our Pl. XXXVIII *b*; with vases and animals on *Mémoires de la Délégation en Perse*, XVI, 193. *Ibid.* XVI, 217, two small figures of men, apparently carry a piece of this stuff in either hand. They alternate in the design with a large amphora.

[4] Also Newell, 31.

often impossible to understand but which may well have a religious character.

It will no doubt be useful to summarise finally the facts which we have ascertained as regards the manifold glyptic of the Jemdet Nasr period, without considering the problems of origin or development. We find, then, in the temples a number of large limestone or marble cylinders with representations of the sacred herd, and in addition tall glazed cylinders with geometric designs. The latter occur also in private houses, together with squat, often concave, cylinders of coloured limestone. The designs of all three classes occur again on small seals of the usual cylindrical shape with a height of 1½ to 2 times the diameter. In this latter class limestone of a light grey colour, not found at other times, is often used.

SECTION II

THE EARLY DYNASTIC CYLINDERS

CHAPTER I. THE NEW CONTRIBUTION OF THE FIRST EARLY DYNASTIC PERIOD

§ 10. THE BROCADE STYLE

WITH THE Early Dynastic period[1] we pass into the recognised confines of history. The earliest objects found at Telloh (Lagash) were for many years the only indication of this proto-historic age. Now the famous tombs at Ur are its best-known representatives, falling within the period of which historical tradition preserved some memory. But elsewhere, and only quite recently, the gap has been closed which separated the Jemdet Nasr glyptic from the sealings of Fara and the cylinders from Ur.[2] The new material is of great variety. A peculiar kind of design, which we have called the Brocade style, is characteristic of the period. It is never found in a Jemdet Nasr context, and though, as in other cases, some specimens may appear in later levels of the Early Dynastic period, its first emergence and most common use occur at the very beginning of that age.

The cylinders which belong to the First Early Dynastic period (Pl. IX) do not seem, at first sight, to rise much above the low level to which glyptic art had sunk in the preceding epoch. Their elongated narrow shape (Pl. II *a*) recalls the cylinders with geometric design (Pl. VI *e–j*). Their subjects are little varied and fall almost without exception within the range of the simplest and most conventional scheme of composition, the animal file. It is usually composed of goats, stags or cattle, with the occasional addition of fishes and birds (Pl. IX *b*).

Yet these seals differ fundamentally from those of the preceding period. What is new is neither shape nor subject, but the manner in which the subject is rendered. The actual subject-matter, in fact, was clearly considered only of secondary importance, and all the ingenuity of the seal-cutters went to the creation of a satisfactory pattern to fill the frieze produced by the seal's impression. The disparate motives of Pl. VIII *i, j, k* are reintegrated under a new and strictly applied stylistic principle.

[1] Variously called "Sumerian", "Pre-Sargonid", "Archaic" or "Period of planoconvex bricks". For a clear summary of recent discoveries, see Seton Lloyd, *Mesopotamia* (London, 1936); for a discussion of the relation between the Early Dynastic and the earlier periods, see Frankfort, *Archaeology and the Sumerian Problem* (Chicago, 1932).

[2] *Oriental Institute Communications*, No. 20, presents the evidence now available.

Sometimes the animal designs retain a certain volume (Pl. IX*a*), more often, however, they are reduced to groups of lines which are disposed on the surface so as to produce an evenly divided decoration. The drill is rarely used and then sparingly (Pl. IX*b*). Filling motives such as crosses, lozenges, birds and fishes are constantly used along with the quadrupeds, and not as a result of *horror vacui*. For that much abused term is too negative to account for a decorative scheme applied as deliberately to these seals as a weaver or embroiderer might use it in his own material. The scope of the innovation can best be appraised by comparing the new seals of Pl. IX with the products of the Jemdet Nasr period, and especially with Pl. VIII*j*, *k*.[1] There is no doubt that the older seals provided the material which the new style utilised. Yet we find on the one hand the spiritless fabrications of craftsmanship in decline, and on the other the lively, ever varying experiments of artists in possession of a new formula. For these quasi-simple, quasi-primitive seals of the Brocade style contain the principle which underlies all the great subsequent development. It is characteristic of the best and most original glyptic of the whole Early Dynastic age that it suppresses the narrative—in favour of the decorative value of its designs.

The Brocade style in its most consistent manifestations reduces its subject to a purely linear pattern. The basis of Pl. IX*e* (cf. Pl. II*a*), for instance, is nothing but two goats, one upright and one upside down, with a few strokes judiciously placed to carry the same weight of design across the intermediate spaces. Pl. IX*a* is stylistically "older", the goats having retained a certain substantiality, though here again the use of one filling ornament at top and bottom and three short strokes suffice to effect an even filling of the frieze. There is a great variety of design even without introducing any other subjects than those of Pl. IX*a–e*. We have chosen the goat file as the most common example[2] to illustrate the tendencies which prevail at the beginning of the Early Dynastic age. But these tendencies manifest themselves simultaneously in a number of subjects (Text-fig. 15). At Ur, for instance, a quantity of sealings was found in the rubbish into which the Royal Cemetery was later

Text-fig. 15. Bull, ass and scorpion.

[1] For similar seals see Ward-Morgan, 138; Newell, 62, 63.

[2] In addition to the many seals in collections of which the origin is unknown there is now a considerable number from Khafaje, Tell Asmar and Tell Agrab (*Oriental Institute Communications*, No. 20). Also: *Fara*, Pl. 61*f*; *Kish*, IV, Pl. XV; Ur, 83; *American Journal of Archaeology*, XIV, Pl. LXV, 2; Nineveh, *Liverpool Annals of Archaeology*, XIX, Pl. LXIII, 13.

dug,[1] and these impressions show how the seal-cutters experimented with geometric designs and even with writing signs (Pl. IX*g*) to build up "textile" patterns evenly divided over the whole surface (Text-figs. 16–19). Sometimes old motives, like the cattle byre with symbols projecting from the roof

Text-fig. 16.

Text-fig. 17.

Text-fig. 18.

Text-fig. 19.

Text-figs. 16–19. Impressions from Ur.

(cf. Pl. VI*a*), provide the starting-point (Text-fig. 18). Or other figures known in the Jemdet Nasr period, such as the pigtailed women squatting on a couch, appear in addition to a Brocade style pattern of a geometrical

[1] L. Legrain, *Ur Excavations*, III: *Archaic Seal Impressions*. Not all the impressions from layers S.I.S. 4–5 belong to the First Early Dynastic period, and a glance at Woolley, *Ur Excavations*, II: *The Royal Cemetery*, Pl. 270, where S.I.S. 4–5 are marked, shows that we must reckon with intrusions of earlier and later remains in these parts of the rubbish dumps. Evidently Sir Leonard's remarks as to the higher levels S.I.S. 1–2 (*Ur Excavations*, III, Introductory note) apply to the layers which interest us here with equal force. On Plates 44–47 we see a number of sealings from the Second Early Dynastic period, comparable with our Pl. X*f–h*.

At Warka (see p. 42, note 2) some of the complicated geometric designs were found in strata which show by their combination of planoconvex bricks and pottery of shapes used in the Jemdet Nasr period that they belong to the First Early Dynastic period (see Chronological Table at the end of *Oriental Institute Communications*, No. 20, and Mallowan's conclusions, based on first-hand knowledge of the material from Ur, in *Liverpool Annals of Archaeology*, XX, 141).

The tablets found with these sealings are stated by Burrows (*Ur Excavations Texts*, II: *Archaic Texts*) and by Falkenstein (*Archaische Texte aus Uruk*, pp. 19, 28) to belong to a palaeographic stage between the Jemdet Nasr and the Fara tablets. This agrees with our view as to the date of the contemporary sealings. The discoverers assign the sealings to the Jemdet Nasr period, but the glyptic of that age was insufficiently known, and that of the First Early Dynastic period almost entirely unknown, at the time when they were writing.

character (Text-fig. 19). These patterns are evidently related with those of the seals of glazed steatite which were used in the Jemdet Nasr period, and which formed the starting-point of the Brocade style. The difference between a closely interwoven pattern as we find in Text-fig. 19 and Pl. VI*e–h* is exactly similar to the contrast between Pl. IX*c* and Pl. VIII*j*. But some examples from Ur illustrate in a particularly striking way the fascination which the problem of space filling exercised over the minds of the seal-cutters of the First Early Dynastic period. In Text-fig. 17 we see a design consisting of geometric figures, archaic writing-signs and the combination of two human heads and two bulls' heads into a rich pattern.

Sometimes the short side of the seal is impressed in the clay alongside the rolled impression, whether it is decorated with a rosette of which the axial perforation is the centre, or plain, or even showing the whorl of the shell from which the cylinder was cut.[1]

These seal impressions from Ur have their equivalents at Warka[2] and Fara.[3] All of them are difficult to bring into line with the remainder of the material, because only one actual cylinder of this type is known (Pl. IX*h*); for the rest we are dependent on impressions which, being old and worn and not made with a view to recording the style and composition of the design, are often almost useless for our purpose. They suggest, however, that the Brocade style is richer and more varied than we are at present able to demonstrate. Text-fig. 15, for instance, gives an example with more than one motive, arranged at right angles. There may be local differences too. In the Dyala region, where the seals of the Brocade style are almost exclusively of the type of Pl. IX*a–e*, we find on contemporary painted pots of "scarlet" ware the scenes which decorate the seals in later parts of the Early Dynastic period, and with which the seal-cutters at Ur, and perhaps at Warka, experimented already at an earlier date. Usually the civilisation of Mesopotamia is remarkably homogeneous and local differences can be discounted entirely. But the First Early Dynastic period was a transitional age of short duration, and it may be that the submerging of local styles in a glyptic *koine* coincided with the emergence of the Second Early Dynastic period. The wide variety of the Brocade style can be estimated sufficiently from the examples here illustrated in Pl. IX and Text-figs. 15–19.

[1] Legrain, *loc. cit.* Pl. 43, Nos. 126, 128; Pl. 47, No. 253; Pl. 48, No. 286; Pl. 49, No. 368 etc.

[2] Heinrich, *Kleinfunde*, pp. 10, 32, and Pl. 16*a, b*. The seals, *ibid.* Pl. 19*d*, and *Uruk Vorläufiger Bericht*, II, Fig. 13; V, Pl. 27*d*, seem to be survivals of the heraldic groups of the Uruk period.

[3] Heinrich, *Fara*, Pls. 67*b*; 72*g, k*.

With the Brocade style, glyptic art in Mesopotamia had discovered the means to realise its peculiar potentialities. The function of the seal cylinders was to impress a surface of varying extent with a distinctive design. What could be more appropriate to this purpose than a decoration, which does not require—like a narrative scene—a given minimum of surface to be comprehensible, nor which fills the space beyond this minimum with redundant repetitions, but depends for its effect entirely upon the harmony of its constituents, a harmony which becomes equally manifest in a long frieze as in a short fragment? In fact it was a small fragment which the seal-cutter composed, namely just as much as filled the perimeter of his cylinder.

It is worth while to realise in what manner the seal-cutter brought about the effect which we have analysed above. The seals of this period are long and narrow (Pl. II*a* is the seal from which the impression of Pl. IX*e* was made). The slenderness of the seals admitted only of one rendering of each motive. Thus, in the case of the seal of Pl. IX*b*, the goat was probably cut first and the fish and bird added. The bird's tail ended just in front of the goat's head, but below, between the forelegs of the goat and its tail, there remained about three-eighths of an inch of open space, the figure of the goat being just that much too short to go round the whole of the circumference of the cylinder; there, as a filling, the lozenge was added.

In this way the reader can easily imagine how each design occurs on the actual seals. The impression of these seals presents an endless pattern, because the beginning and the termination of each design are dovetailed upon the cylinder itself. We need not therefore credit the ancient seal-cutter with great power of abstraction. The same qualities on which the aesthetic value of the seal impressions rested were present in the actual design which he was cutting in the stone.

CHAPTER II. THE STYLISTIC DEVELOPMENT OF EARLY DYNASTIC GLYPTIC

§ II. THE IMAGINATIVE AND LINEAR STYLE OF THE SECOND EARLY DYNASTIC PERIOD

THE NARROW basis of the Brocade style underlies all the rich variety of Early Dynastic seals. The principle which had been discovered, after the chaos and decline of the Jemdet Nasr period, to constitute the independence of glyptic art continued to be applied. The value of the seal designs resided as before in the rhythm of recurring motives, forming a frieze of indefinite extent. But the monotonous repertoire of the experimental period (Pl. IX*a–e*) was now discarded. Other motives, even human figures, were introduced and their composition was based on more intricate schemes than the mere file (Pl. X*a*, *b*). The exclusive use of lines was sometimes maintained (Pl. X*b*) but flat surfaces were also incorporated. The interweaving of motives was assisted by their animation. Formerly the friezes had consisted of a mere scattering of unconnected figures. But in Pl. X*a* the lions are not only spaced so as to form an evenly divided pattern, but they are united by their action into a continuous design, the jaws of each animal closing over the leg or tail of its neighbour. The divergence from the older seals seems slight, but is significant; it betrays a revival of the interest in subject-matter.

A transition, represented by our Pl. X*a*, *b*, leads by way of Pl. X*d*, where the same lions appear again, to that infinitely varied group of cylinders of which Pl. X*c*, *e*, *i* show the execution and Pl. XI some designs.[1]

We have qualified this style as linear and imaginative, partly with a view to that of the succeeding age, the Third Early Dynastic period. For this excelled, on the one hand, in a decorative rather than imaginative use of motives, and, on the other, reintroduced the modelling in relief which had been in abeyance since the Uruk period. These innovations will be discussed

[1] The seals found together in the Square Temple at Tell Asmar afford objective evidence that this combination is correct. See *Oriental Institute Communications*, No. 19, Fig. 23, and our forthcoming publication of the cylinders found in the Dyala region. It should again be remembered that the cylinders illustrated in our plates and used in our demonstrations have exemplary value, and are not arbitrarily chosen nor are, on the whole, exceptional. Thus the series which lead from the Brocade style via Pl. X*d* to the fully developed style of the Second Early Dynastic period is paradigmatical, but the same development can be demonstrated in different ways. Further examples will be found in my forthcoming *Cylinder Seals from the Diyala Region* (University of Chicago Press).

in the next paragraph. Here we must insist on the linear character of the older style.

We have already pointed out that the Second Early Dynastic period abandoned the exclusive use of incised lines to which Brocade style in its purest form[1] rigidly adhered. But the flat planes which replaced it, mainly to render the bodies of the figures in the friezes (Pl. X), are in no way vehicles of artistic expression. They are merely surfaces enclosed by outline. They have no plastic value whatever. Such detail as was needed was added by engraving, not by modelling. The contrast of Pl. X with the earlier seals of Pls. III, IV and V, as well as with the later seals of Pl. XII, is striking, and in this sense the style of the Second Early Dynastic period is a linear style, even though it has abandoned the exclusiveness of the Brocade style and reintroduced flat surfaces. It is important to realise the validity of this stylistic discrimination. If such a seal impression as Pl. X *i* suggests that the seal-cutter resorted to modelling especially in the case of the legs of his figures, we need only consider his result more closely to recognise that first impression as erroneous. The enlargement of Pl. X*j* shows beyond a doubt that the suggestion of roundness of the limbs is merely due to the narrowness of that part of the design. The seal-cutter used his graver at an angle. Arms and legs, consisting of two contours cut with a tool sloping in opposite directions, are seen in apparent relief, but as soon as the contours diverge the surface left between them becomes entirely level, without plastic differentiation, and its curved edge is recognisable as the slope of the incised outline. Pl. X*g* represents a provincial version of the same style. Just as its composition reflects in all its detail the more sophisticated designs of the type of Pl. XI *c*, so its execution follows the same principles as the seals which we have just analysed, in a broader, simpler and somewhat coarser manner.

In addition to its linear characteristics, we have attributed to the Second Early Dynastic style imagination, a term which need not be qualified. It is a curious fact that its abundance of fantastic designs seems to be due to some sudden expansion of the repertoire, not to a slow process of evolution. For the seal of Pl. X*a* is still closely related to the Brocade style, and was actually found in the Square Temple at Tell Asmar which immediately succeeded the Archaic Shrine in which Brocade style seals were found. Yet this lion seal cannot be separated from Pl. X*d*, where the same animals recur in the identical attitude, to the right of the main theme. And that theme

[1] Seals such as Pl. IX*a* actually precede the full-blown Brocade style seals with linear designs such as Pl. IX*e*. That was shown by stratified examples from Khafaje.

already belongs to the "Fara" class of Pl. XI. As a matter of fact the lion seal was itself discovered in association with seals of this class.

Leaving out of account ceremonial and other scenes represented in Pl. XI, since they may be considered a secondary development with which we shall deal in the next chapter, it seems that the artistic vitality which had been guided during the previous age into channels of decorative invention was suddenly set free to develop the repertoire once a sound stylistic formula had been evolved in the Brocade style. The result is a seemingly endless variety of friezes in which human, mythological and animal figures are all in action.

They still present to a large extent variations upon a single theme. Their subject is, in essence, the defence of flocks and herds against beasts of prey, especially against lions, but this is rarely presented in a straightforward manner or with any intention of depicting actuality (Pl. X*f*). On the whole, the facts of the situation, which must have been a commonplace of daily life, are taken for granted, and the seal-cutter gives full rein to his inventiveness in the combination of the few given elements into ever-changing groups.

We shall presently study these elements in detail; here we are concerned with the part they play in the composition of the seal design and the value which some of them possess as characteristics of the Second—in contrast with the Third—Early Dynastic period. Suffice it therefore to say that the human herdsman appears but rarely (Pl. XI*d*) and never, as in the later period (Pl. XV*i*), unaided. The brunt of the battle is usually borne by divine or mythological beings, who are often the sole antagonists of the wild beasts.

Thus they are already present in Pl. X*d*; the central figure of the group is the carcase of a goat. The lion—or should we say lions?—standing over it is being attacked by figures wielding that dagger with crescent-shaped handle which we actually possess among the grave furniture from Ur.[1] The person on the right wears a kilt, tucked into the girdle to increase the freedom of his movements. This motive is not uncommon in the Second Early Dynastic period (e.g. Pl. X*i*, small figure), but is not found in the Third. Sometimes a human-shaped figure (Pl. X*d*) has two small projections from the head, perhaps horns, but more probably locks of hair or a cap. The other figure is definitely horned, but only one horn is visible, projecting forward. This is the usual rendering in the case of the Bull-man, a creature combining the horns, tail and hindlegs of a bull with a human torso and face; he is often ithyphallic, especially in Sargonid times. In the Second Early Dynastic period his figure, drawn with striking elegance (Pls. X*e*; XI *b*, *c*, *d*, *k*), occurs

[1] Woolley, *Royal Cemetery*, Pl. 152.

on the majority of seals. Here again it is interesting to refer to the rustic seal of Pl. X*g*, which certainly belongs to the ripe style of the Second Early Dynastic period, as the filling motives, for instance, show (cf. Pl. XI *c*). But while at Shuruppak (Fara) the seal-cutters produced such consummate designs as our Pl. XI *b*, the provinces not only failed to achieve elegance in the individual figures, but also preferred a plain realistic rendering of the main subject to the decorative intricacies of Pl. XI *a*, *b*.

If we leave such exceptional seals out of account we may observe certain methods in the drawing of individual features which are entirely characteristic of the period. Long-haired and bearded human figures, shown in front view, are rendered with an exclusive reliance on incised lines (Pls. X*i*; XI *d*, *m*, *n*). The manes of lions are in this period suggested by lines forming a kind of scale pattern (Pls. X*i*; XI *b*, *c*, *d*, *m*).[1] The hair of goats and the wool of sheep tempted the craftsmen to cover these animals' bodies with lines, and the occurrence of these "zebra-ed animals" forms another cleavage between the Second and Third Early Dynastic periods (Pl. X*c*).[2] Even the necks of bulls are sometimes decorated in this way (Pl. X*i*).

Besides the elegant profile of the Bull-man, the rendering of the tucked-in kilt and the complete hatching of the bodies of animals, we find a fourth distinctive feature of the seal designs of this period in the use of detached animal heads as filling motives (Pls. X*f–h*; XI *d*, *g*, *h*, *k*, *l*, *m*). These bring us back from externals to the stylistic characteristics of the age. The use of filling motives betrays the same predilection for textile pattern already observed in the First Early Dynastic period. We now notice a similar prevalence of dovetailed designs resulting in friezes without hiatus, so that it is, in fact, impossible physically to isolate the impression made by one single revolution of the cylinder. If we try to cut out such an impression we are bound to include fragments of figures at either end. The same applies, of course, to the Brocade style (Pl. IX), but that achieved continuity of design by a mere addition of unconnected figures and filling ornaments. In the more ambitious scheme adopted during the Second Early Dynastic period, the very gestures which express the action weave the evenly divided pattern

[1] It is interesting that this design occurs on one of the few objects from Telloh which antedates Urnanshe, who belongs to the Third Early Dynastic period. This earlier object is the copper spearhead, De Sarzec, *Découvertes en Chaldée*, Pl. 5, ter 1. The mane of the lion shows the same scale-pattern and the nose, upper lip and ear are moreover drawn identically as on our Pl. X*i*. The design of the mane recurs on another object antedating Urnanshe, namely the macehead of Mesilim, *loc. cit.* Pl. 1, ter 2. Other seals belonging in this context are B.M. 89538 (L. W. King, *History of Sumer and Akkad*, Pl. IX) and Ur, 47, 109.

[2] Similarly: Heinrich, *Fara*, Pl. 55*f*.; Newell, 81; Ur, 8, 148, 149.

which had become the recognised requirement of glyptic decoration. The Third Early Dynastic period continued to employ this method, but in the period of its invention it was applied with a clarity of design which is afterwards lost. In the Second Early Dynastic period the action of the figures and their interrelations remain intelligible throughout, whether the original meaning of the theme is explicitly stressed (Pl. X*g*) or whether it is resolved in an ingenious pattern of figures (Pl. X*i*). The filling motives, such as the plant and calf's head in Pl. X*g*, can be accounted for, even though their main function is decorative. The occasional use of hindquarters or forelegs, in place of the usual animal's head, indicates that these motives represent remains of a victim of the beasts of prey.

The figures are widely spaced and often grouped according to a clear symmetrical scheme. A mythological figure between two lions makes a group of three (Pl. XI*m*) which can be extended to a group of five by adding one more antagonist to the lions on either side (Pl. XI*c*). The central figure may sometimes be a victim (Pl. XI*b*), and if space is left on the perimeter of the cylinder after the main group has been engraved, a secondary unit is added, often in a similarly symmetrical scheme (Pl. XI*b*, three figures on left). Even when this is not so, or when room for only one additional figure remains, care is taken to dovetail it into the main group in a way which ensures a continuous frieze (Pl. XI*b–d*).

Our illustrations, which must include various significant representations even though they are exceptional, do not do justice to the fact that the vast majority of seals of the Second Early Dynastic period show friezes such as we have discussed in the foregoing lines. Though no two of them are alike, the subject is the same in all cases. The friezes, as explained above, represent ingenious variations on the conflict between the domestic animals or game and their human and divine protectors, and predatory lions. But it is clear that in the best seals there is no attempt to depict actuality, nor would it seem sensible to enquire whether any ancient narrative can account for the fact that sometimes a Bull-man is shown singlehanded (Pl. XI*g*) and sometimes assisted by two kinsmen in his struggle (Pl. XI*c*). In describing Pl. X*d* we have been in doubt as to the number of lions which were prevented from devouring the goat they killed. There are two bodies, it is true, but only one head.[1] It is quite clear that our question is irrelevant. The seal-cutter was merely concerned with producing a satisfactory composition. Alternative solutions to the one adopted in Pl. X*d* are shown in Pl. XI*b*. In the last instance the two lions are completely separated and form a symmetrical

[1] *Fara*, Pl. 50*e* (V.A. 3956), also shows a lion with two bodies and one head.

group above the goat. This is a very popular design in the Third Early Dynastic period, but at no time has the duplication of the beasts any but a decorative significance; it is the exact counterpart of the increase of their antagonists when a group of three is changed into a group of five. In Pl. XI *b* symmetry is achieved, not by getting one head within the axis of two bodies, but by using the upright body of the goat as axis and duplicating the head, while the variation of the filling on either side, namely star and foreleg, connected as they are with the difference in the position of the lion's claw, make for richness and complication.

These monstrosities, which we are taught by Pls. X *d*; XI *b* to derive from necessities of design, sometimes become independent, and are so used in a considerable number of friezes. In Pl. XI *a* we see a man whose arms consist of the foreparts of lions; much more common is the Bull-man with doubled hindquarters (Pl. X *c*) or the man whose legs end in lion's legs (Pl. XI and Text-fig. 25, p. 55). In Pl. XI *n* the lions are made to bite their neighbours in the manner of Pl. X *a*, *e*, and the animation of the design goes so far that the lions' tails are made to end in snakes which are again held in check by the arms of the human upper part of the figure. The same happens in Text-fig. 25, which belongs to the Third Early Dynastic period. It is quite clear that there is no point in searching mythological literature for the identification of these composite creatures. They have come into existence in the workshop, as it were, and occasionally the hybrids shaped by one seal-cutter in a playful mood caught on and spread to others.[1] The lion-legged man of Pl. XI *n* may well have originated in some such group as appears in Pl. XIII *a*, though that particular seal belongs to a later age.

Besides the groups of combatants we regularly find a peaceful trio of a man holding in either hand a ruminant (Pl. X *i*; cf. Pl. XIV *d*). It is the simplest pictorial expression of the fact that man and the herbivores belong together. It is impossible to say whether the idea of protection or of dominance or domestication prevails in the conception of this group, especially since the throttling of lions gives rise to a similar design (Pl. XI *c*, *m*). Again we have to deal with a device of mainly pictorial significance which allows

[1] Bull-men with doubled hindquarters occur: *Fara*, Pl. 50 *e* (V.A. 3956); Bibliothèque Nationale, 1; Newell, 77; Louvre, A-108; Pennsylvania, 67, 111; *Revue d'Assyriologie*, VII, Pl. 7, No. 4. Lion-legged men occur: Kh. IV/338; Kh. V/1; As. 32/1125; Pennsylvania, 67; *Fara*, Pls. 51 *k* (V.A. 6362), 52 *c* (V.A. 8596), 59 *a*, *d* (V.A. 8632, 8552). In *Fara*, Pl. 48 *c*, the legs are of goats, not lions; *Fara*, Pl. 51 *m* (V.A. 8654), is of special interest, since one of the lion legs resembles our Pl. XI *m*, while the other shows the head in the profile usual with lions at this time.

a greater unity of design to be achieved by an animation of the motives of which it is composed.

In the seals so far discussed in this paragraph the narrative content of the decoration is taken for granted. But when subjects of a less general nature than the war of men and gods against beasts of prey are depicted, the emphasis has to be shifted to the narrative. Even then, as in the case of the wrestlers of Pl. XI *l*, the outcome is sometimes a strictly symmetrical design of great decorative value. More often the seal-cutter had to be satisfied by maintaining an evenly divided closeness of pattern without aiming at any symmetry or balance between his various groups (Pl. XI *f*, *j*). Unusual subjects were often quite frankly represented for their contents only, without any attempt to achieve a satisfactory artistic solution (Pls. XI *m*; XV *j–n*). But with the content of the Early Dynastic seal designs we shall deal in a later chapter.

§ 12. THE DECORATIVE RELIEF STYLE OF THE THIRD EARLY DYNASTIC PERIOD

The change that took place between the Second and Third Early Dynastic periods is seen, in the field of glyptic art, to be not less definite though more subtle than in the case of sculpture or ceramics. The cylinders were still most commonly decorated with friezes of struggling beasts and human or divine beings, composed into closely interwoven continuous patterns. But the character of the individual figures has changed. They became, first of all, more massive (Pl. XII *a*).[1] Each figure now occupied a larger surface than before; but these broad surfaces called for detail, and this was added, sometimes exuberantly, but at first without departing from the habitual two-dimensional methods of the linear style. If we compare the upper part of the figures of Pl. XII *a* with those of Pl. X *i* the change is evident. But a comparison of the lower halves of these friezes is even more instructive. The very size of the later figures leads almost inevitably to modelling, even when purely linear detail has been inserted. Note, for instance, in Pl. XII *a*, how the groin is distinguished by extending the muscle of the thigh into the torso. And the later seals of the Third Early Dynastic period are all deliberately carved with a view to relief (Pls. XII *b*, *c*; XIII *a*). This is clear in Pl. XII *c*, where the hindleg of the goat passes in front of the lion's shoulder. Note also the strong contrast between the modelling of hindquarters and belly on this seal, and the older usage of Pl. X.

[1] Similar seals are found at Khafaje (Kh. III/265, 700) and prove that they come early in the Third Early Dynastic period. Somewhat later are: Ur, 58, 151; Louvre, A–96; Nies-Keiser, Pl. 75 *d*; *Recueil de Travaux*, 1916, p. 166 (plate facing), No. 2.

It is quite clear that this innovation came about gradually and was at no time conceived as the antithesis of the linear style, though the development did, in the end, lead to an almost opposite extreme. Yet many of those seals which have been most thoroughly modelled in relief demonstrate by the extreme delicacy of their linear design in the narrow parts of the figures that they are directly descended from the earlier types. We look, for example, at the animals' legs of Pls. XII *b*, XIII *b*, *f* and perceive the graceful elaboration of the tufted tails and the curly locks below the knees of the Bull-men and human-headed bulls, indicated by formal volutes, as were the bulls' beards in Pl. X *i*. A design such as Pl. XIII *g* hovers on the borderline marking the transition between the Second and the Third Early Dynastic period.

Though the change was gradual, it profoundly altered the character of seal designs. The development led from linear abstraction to three-dimensional realism.

We have already seen that the broadening of the figures did not at first transcend the limits of two-dimensional engraving (Pl. XII *a*). The carved designs remained, to all intents and purposes, reinforced drawings. But after a while depth was no longer treated as an inevitable but indifferent ingredient of the design. It became dynamic and was made to express form. The figures acquired mass (Pl. XII *b*, *c*). Thus the contrast between the seals of the Second and Third Early Dynastic period is the same as that between Egyptian and Greek relief.

Innovations of detail illustrate also the character of the new development. In the Second Early Dynastic period the lions' heads generally appear in profile. If they are shown full-face, or rather seen from above, as in Pl. X *a* and Pl. XI *n* below, their proportions do not exceed those of the side-view. The later craftsmen used the full-face exclusively and with an obvious delight in the massive effects thus obtained from the head and mane (Pl. XII). The faces of the long-haired and bearded figures are also broadened, and especially the arrangement of three tresses on either side of the face emphasises its width; compare Pls. XIII *a*, XIV *d* with Pl. X *i*. A figure which appears in this period for the first time is the human-headed bull. And this creature too is shown full-face (Pls. XII *a*, *b*; XIV *b*).

It is interesting to note that these highly characteristic faces are carved in a manner entirely at variance with Sargonid usage.[1] The Early Dynastic seal-cutter stressed the pupil of the eye and neglected the lid; he accentuated

[1] Compare our seal of Pl. XIII *a* with full-face renderings on typically Akkadian seals such as Pls. XVI *d*; XVII *c*, *g*, *i*.

the nose and cheek at the expense of mouth and chin. Works of sculpture, like the alabaster lamps found in various sites, show the same contrast between Early Dynastic and Sargonid work.[1] The Akkadian artist gave more detail and that with greater verisimilitude, but his predecessors created a far more vivid whole out of the few salient features upon which they had concentrated their attention.

The formal division between the glyptic styles of the Second and Third Early Dynastic period is that between drawing and relief. But there is also a contrast in the spirit of the designs which can be defined as the opposition of imaginative and decorative art. These terms are not, of course, mutually exclusive. Both apply in varying degree to either period. But the earlier seal designs seem, on the whole, to be original compositions, conceived *ad hoc* in many cases, and the later productions mere dexterous applications of customary formulae. We have already pointed out that the earlier designs, for all their close texture of motives, retained sufficient clarity for the interrelations and actions of all the figures to be apparent at a glance. This is by no means the rule in the subsequent period, whose seals replaced, in fact, the symmetrical groups of the earlier style by a repetition of crossed animals, drawn with undoubted virtuosity. Monotony was avoided by the introduction of various new species, such as the stag and the leopard (Pl. XIII *b, f*) and by sudden inversions of figures within the groups (Pls. XII *c*; XIII *d*). The natural attitude which some animals retained in the earlier style (Pl. XI *g*), the not quite erect position so well suited to semi-human creatures (Pl. XI *b, c*) disappeared. Henceforward all animals stood upon their hind-legs, and their bodies crossed each other more often than had been customary till now. Thus the increased massiveness of the individual figures found its correlation in the greater compactness of the groups. Consequently the later style had less need of filling motives; they did sometimes occur, the scorpion (Pl. XIV *b*) or other small animals (Pls. XIII *a, b, g*; XIV *d*) being now used for the purpose instead of detached heads. As a rule the massive main figures, crossing and recrossing, were sufficient to cover the surface without recourse to extraneous matter.

The new method of composition is well illustrated in the conception of the man dominating two animals. The spacious arrangement of Pls. X *i*; XI *c, m* is now replaced by a gesture in which the human being presses the two animals against his sides (Pl. XIV *d, g*), so that the figures stand more upright and more closely together.

[1] An Akkadian and an Early Dynastic lamp in the shape of a human-headed bull are conveniently shown together in Woolley, *Royal Tombs*, Pl. 182.

It is also significant that the seal-cutters of the Third Early Dynastic period rarely employ the symmetrical groups of three and four figures so numerous in the preceding age. With the increased compactness of the friezes, continuous design had become of more importance than balanced composition. Symmetrical groups occur, such as the group of five in the upper register of Pl. XIII *c*; and Pls. XII *a*; XIV *b*. But a symmetrical group is apt to interrupt the rhythm of the frieze by the stability of its own inherent balance, and this is especially the case if the group consists of an odd number, so that its

Text-fig. 20.

Text-fig. 22.

Text-fig. 21.

Text-fig. 23.

Text-fig. 20–23. Impressions from Lagash, 20, 21, 23, seals of Lugalanda.

central axis coincides with a figure which acts as pivot or central support (Pls. XI *c*, *m*; XIII *f*). It is interesting to see how the semi-erect attitude of the Bull-man in Pl. XI *c*, and the disposition of the heads and forelegs of the goat in Pl. XI *b*, counteract the tendency to stagnation about the central figure of the group. But the more closely spaced and vertical figures of the later friezes did not allow of such expedients. If, therefore, in the Third Early Dynastic period symmetrical groups are used at all, those composed of even numbers are preferred. The fact is easily established (Pl. XII *a*, *c*) and its explanation follows from what has been said. The symmetrical group of even numbers does not only lack a static and ponderous central axis. But its centre, being the point where two crossed figures intersect, is essentially a point by means of which movement is carried in the direction of the frieze (Pls. XII *a*; XIV *b*; Text-figs. 21, 22). Occasionally separate units are altogether omitted, the scheme of composition consisting exclusively of pairs of closely grouped combatants (Pl. XIII *b*; Text-fig. 23), so that the distinction between protagonists and subsidiary figures, often possible in the Second Early Dynastic period, can no longer be made. Thus the new style was in several ways a simplification of its predecessor, especially as regards the means of obtaining the required effect. It was, in fact, more severe. It imposed approximation to the vertical upon all figures and placed their heads, or rather their most conspicuous feature—the eyes—as nearly as possible along one horizontal line (isokephaly) (Pls. XII; XIII; XIV *b, d, g*).[1] The rigorous application of these rules of composition sometimes produced an effect of dry efficiency, especially in the lower part of the friezes (Pl. XIII *b, f*; Text-fig. 22, but see the contrast with Pl. XII *c*), which was entirely absent in the preceding period.

Moreover, the interrelations of the figures were almost as strictly regulated as their composition.[2] When a human or semi-human figure attacks an animal he either takes it by the throat and foreleg, or, if the beast has turned away, by the tail. But in such a case the quadruped always looks back towards the aggressor, who grasps his throat with the other hand. As an alternative he may stab the animal with a dagger. It is significant of the wide deviation of the Third Early Dynastic subject-matter from the original conception of these friezes,[3] that in the later period the man but rarely attacks the lion, the traditional destroyer of herds and game. It is true that a human figure occasionally appears, rather emphatically, at the edge of a group (Pls. XII *c*; XIII *f*; XIV *b*), and that when this happens his function is always the slaying of beasts. As often as not the one-time protectors of the ruminants are shown to be in league with the panthers and lions (Pls. XII *a*; XIII *c* (lower half)), or they fall out amongst themselves, the human hero and the Bull-man, for instance, coming to grips in Pl. XIV *h* to suit the seal-cutters' convenience. We have seen that decorative considerations also dominated the glyptic of the preceding age, but these were never allowed so to obscure the original subject of the frieze. In the Third Early Dynastic period, however, compact chains of interlocked figures are to be found which defy rational explanation from any but an aesthetic point of view.

The most refractory elements of these seal designs is the inscription which

[1] Curtius, who was the first to appreciate the very remarkable stylistic qualities of these seals (*Sitzungsberichte der Bayerischen Akademie*, Munchen, 1913, 7e Abh.), aptly speaks of the severity of these rules of spatial arrangement as "Raumzwang".

[2] See Heinrich, *Fara*, 92–137.

[3] See above, p. 46.

appears in the Third Early Dynastic period with increasing frequency. In the rare instances of the use of writing on older seals the signs were strewn between the groups of figures, but kept together (Pl. X *i*). A group of figures on a smaller scale filled but incompletely the gap left underneath. In the succeeding age the spacing of the signs was clarified by the introduction of "cases" for the separate lines of inscription, and a double line formed the lower edge of the inscribed space, but no such delimitation was drawn to the left or right, a proof of the seal-cutters' preoccupation with the continuous frieze (Pls. XII *b*, *c*; XIII *a*, *c*, *d*; XIV *d*). Often designs were cut in advance and a space was left for the insertion of the buyer's name if he so desired (Pl. XII *a*). In those seals it is particularly clear that the use of an inscription is really incompatible with the fundamental principle of Early Dynastic glyptic. The half-hearted solution of Pl. XII was indeed to be refuted by the Akkadian seal-cutters, who adopted the opposite formula, in which the inscribed panel became the central shield of a static heraldic group which replaced the continuous frieze (Pl. XVII *a*, *c*).

Text-fig. 24. Seals from Fara.

Thus until the end of the Early Dynastic age decorative considerations are allowed free play. On some seals[1] there are curious intertwinements of figures like the lion swastika of Text-fig. 24 and Pl. XIV *e*, and the human wheel of Pl. XIV *h*. These are on a par with the composite monsters which occur in the preceding age, and which survive into the Third Early Dynastic period, as is shown by Text-fig. 25, which follows the new fashion of modelling; the composition is also more complicated than in the older examples, since the lions evolved from the legs of each of the two creatures curve upwards to bite their fellows.

Text-fig. 25. Composite creatures.

In this design, as also in the human wheel of Pl. XIV *h*,[2] we find a movement returning on itself, and this, indeed, is very popular in the Third Early Dynastic period. In the human wheel we see four figures each pursuing

[1] See also Heinrich, *Fara*, Pl. 45 *h* (V.A. 6434), and Ur, 54.

[2] Also Legrain, *Archaic seal impressions*, No. 518.

with a dagger the man before him, whose ankle he clasps with the other hand. In Pl. XII *b* and Text-fig. 20 we see the lions which are grasped by the lion-headed eagle, turning to bite back into the wings of the bird which attacks them, and the decorative formula underlying these designs is explicitly given in the arabesque formed by the figures themselves, which consists of a line returning on itself through a complicated movement. The formal arrangement necessary to the cylinder seal, with its beginning and end dovetailed together, is yet another instance of the same movement, and it recurs on numerous spherical monuments of the Third Early Dynastic period such as sculptured maceheads or the silver vase of Entemena. There, for instance, four lion-headed eagles grasp in their claws alternate pairs of lions and ruminants, the latter being held in their turn by the lions' jaws, so that birds, beasts of prey and victims are all links in a chain of interlocked design which encircles the vase without hiatus. Considering this vase and the maceheads which show a similar decoration[1] we realise that a complete change has taken place in the relations between the various branches of art since the Uruk period. We found that at that time their respective limitations had not yet been recognised, so that the seals were used for purposes better served by stelae and mural paintings. By the First Early Dynastic period the seal-cutters had discovered the full requirements necessary to the perfect functioning of their products, and the result was the powerful development which we have surveyed in these paragraphs. So it came about that, by the end of the Early Dynastic period, glyptic had assumed a leading position among the arts, to the extent that its inventions were used by metal-workers, jewellers, sculptors and cabinet-makers. Many of the harps, for instance, and the gaming boards and caskets of which remains were found at Ur, were decorated with inlaid designs directly derived from the seal-cutter's repertoire.

This phase of the Early Dynastic period covers the last few generations preceding the rise of Sargon of Akkad, and includes the earliest seals which can be dated with precision because they bear royal names. Those of Lugalanda of Lagash and his wife Barnamtara have long been known and remain the classical examples of the glyptic of the period (Text-figs. 20–23).[2] At Ur seal impressions were found of Mesannipadda, a king of the First Dynasty, and of his wife Ninturnin.[3] While Lugalanda belonged to the last generation

[1] See *Miscellanea Orientalia Antonio Deimel dedicata*, pp. 105 ff., for a discussion of the maceheads.

[2] For these seals see Allotte de la Fuye, *Documents présargoniques* (Paris, 1908).

[3] The date of the Royal Cemetery has been much discussed. See now *Journal of the Royal Asiatic Society*, 1937, pp. 330–43. Burrows notes that two seals from the Royal Tombs

before Sargon, these rulers of Ur lived a little earlier. Their seals very clearly illustrate the wide range of quality and workmanship prevailing at any one time. Mesannipadda's seal shows the human wheel of Pl. XIV *h* and resembles in style those from the grave of Shubad (Pls. XII *c*; XIII *d*), while that of his wife (Pl. XIII *c*) is much more cursorily engraved. Differences in quality, as distinct from differences in style, can never serve as a basis of chronology.

In the Third—as in the Second—Early Dynastic period we find a number of seal designs primarily intended to tell a story. Even here aesthetic considerations sometimes assert themselves, and the scenes of Pl. XV *g–k* present continuous friezes of a textile pattern in the same manner as the friezes already discussed. But such themes are often treated without any attempt at artful composition. They are therefore omitted from the present paragraph which is concerned with stylistic development.

Before that period drew to a close, such development, hitherto uninterrupted since the emergence of the Brocade style, took a significant turn which foreshadowed impending change. Among the seals which must be placed towards the end of the Third Early Dynastic period there are a small number which again show clearly separated groups of figures (Pl. XII *b*).[1] The subject and the details of the frieze are the usual ones, but its structure has been dissolved. There is no longer a close chain of interlocked figures forming one continuous pattern. The figures have fallen apart into groups and the fundamental principle of Early Dynastic glyptic is thereby denied.

It would seem that the introduction of relief is responsible for the change. Once the depth of the figures has obtained significance it is awkward to have them cross and intersect. The inconsistency and the overcrowding with heavy masses which we see in Pl. XII *c* can, however, be avoided by disentangling the interwoven figures and placing them in groups side by side. This procedure was but rarely adopted and only towards the end of the Third Early Dynastic period, but the instances in which it occurred created the formal basis for the glyptic art of the succeeding, the Sargonid, age.

retain the random arrangement of seals which at Lagash is already rare under Urnina. One of these seals (Ur, 54) is too much damaged to be judged. The other (Ur, 65) is of the type of our Pl. XII *a* and therefore belongs to an earlier stage than the majority of the seals (e.g. Pl. XII *c*), as we have shown in the text.

[1] Compare also De Clercq, 43, 45, which belong to the very last stage of Early Dynastic glyptic, and—in the distortion of the Bull-men—already display Sargonid features. But the panel with the small figure below, the curls at the joints of the animals and Bull-men, and the locks of the bareheaded human figure, distinguish them from true Akkadian seals, such as the otherwise very similar De Clercq, 42 and 44.

CHAPTER III. THE SUBJECTS OF THE EARLY DYNASTIC SEALS

§ 13. THE ANIMAL FRIEZE

The majority of the Early Dynastic seals can hardly be said to have a "subject". It is true that the friezes of struggling animals and human or mythological beings were ultimately derived from a theme which was to be popular at all times and already familiar in the Uruk period,[1] namely the defence of the flocks against beasts of prey, but we have seen how this theme became a mere pretext by which the seal-cutters could display their ingenuity in forming a restricted number of figures into new and often pleasing patterns.

Sometimes the composition is simpler. The victims of the combatant friezes, the goats and cattle, may be depicted in single file. The goat especially appears so often on poorly worked seals that it is seldom easy to date these examples. Even the group of the lion attacking a goat or a bull from behind occurs, once or twice repeated, as the sole decoration of certain small Early Dynastic cylinders. In these designs two lines of development converge. Some of them are merely disintegrated resolutions of the more elaborate friezes. On the other hand, it is quite likely that a number of these simpler seal designs represent an unbroken tradition reaching back to the Uruk period (Pl. IV*c*, *k*, *m*). This is certainly the case with such fine compositions as Pl. XIII*e* (cf. Pl. V*b*) in which ruminants and plants appear in conjunction. While there is no doubt that the Early Dynastic applications are mainly decorative in purpose (the same groups occur on gaming boards, harps, caskets, etc.), it would be wrong to assume that the relationship of this combination of animals and plants to the chief person of the Sumerian pantheon would be ignored by contemporaries of the seal-cutters. The lion-headed eagle (Imdugud) (Pls. XII*b*; XIII*a*; XIV*c*) is another of his symbols; it is uncertain whether the ordinary eagle which appears in the same position up to Sargonid times (Pl. XIII*b*) is interchangeable with the composite bird, especially as the latter form was well known in the Jemdet Nasr period (Pl. VI*c*).

Any of these simple and repetitive designs may be used to decorate one half of a tall cylinder which shows another subject above or below a double or triple line. Animal heads, or the foreparts of animals (Pls. X*h*; XI*e*), may achieve the same purpose. In Second Early Dynastic times they can be employed as filling motives (Pl. XI), a usage already known in the Uruk period (Pl. IV*a*), but discontinued in the Third Early Dynastic period.

[1] See p. 22 above. An unpublished seal in Bagdad (I.M. 13831) represents the motive in the Jemdet Nasr period, when it is common on stone vases.

Of the various beings which assume human shape on the seals, the bald-headed kilted figure of Pl. XV*d, i, m* is certainly human, since inscribed statues of men show the same features.[1] The flat-capped person of Pl. XI*f* is similarly known from historical monuments derived from Kish and Mari. But the various types of naked heroes cannot be said with any certainty to represent human beings. There are three known varieties: front-view with long hair and beard (Pls. X*i*; XI*m, n*; XII*b*; XIII*a, f*; XIV*d, h*); profile with curly hair and beard (Pls. XII*a*; XIII*b*); profile with curly hair but without beard (Pls. XII*c*; XIII*f*; XIV*b, g*). The last type does not occur in the Second Early Dynastic period, which, on the other hand, knows a figure whose head has two little projections (Pls. X*b, d*; XI*d, h, n*), not to be found afterwards. Certain reliefs[2] and copper statues[3] suggest that these two projections represent long tresses left to grow while the rest of the head is shaven. It seems certain that we should not look to these projections for an early rendering of the horns of divinity, since these are clearly worn by the god in the boat on Pl. XI*m*, and have a different appearance.

The beardless figure is not found before the Third Early Dynastic period. There is no parallel for his appearance among the statues, which first show men wearing long hair and beards while only the priests are shaven. With the arrival of the Third Early Dynastic period this priestly fashion was increasingly adopted by laymen, but beardless figures with long hair were exceedingly rare and most likely represent adolescents. One may wonder whether the long-haired but beardless figure of the seals represents Tammuz, the "Lord of the sheepfolds" defending his charges, though it may be an anachronism to project the conception of the ever-youthful son and lover of the Mother-Goddess back into the Third Millennium B.C. Perhaps the curls are meant to indicate the unkempt person of a shepherd-boy while the statues represent, of course, the upper classes.

The long-haired and bearded naked hero occupies a prominent position in Mesopotamian art of all periods. His locks, first indicated by a varying number of drill-holes (Pl. XI*n*) or loops (Pl. X*i*) round his face, are later reduced to three on either side (Pl. XIII*a*). His may well be the figure shown in profile on such seals as Pls. XII*a* and XIII*b*, where his beard appears to begin below the jaw, a detail apt to disappear when a seal is somewhat worn or when a careless impression has been made, in which cases there would be confusion with the supposed shepherd-boy just discussed.

On elaborately carved stone vases of the Jemdet Nasr period, the bearded figure appears in the same action as on the seals, namely restraining lions

[1] This figure seems only to appear in the Third Early Dynastic period.

[2] Heinrich, *Fara*, Pl. 20 f.

[3] *Oriental Institute Communications*, No. 13, Fig. 33.

from their attack on cattle. In one instance[1] he wears a triple girdle and the shoes with upturned toes which are still characteristic of the mountaineers living to the east and north of Mesopotamia.[2]

Once in Early Dynastic times this figure is shown in connection with the gatepost symbol which appears on either side of the shrine of Text-fig. 13 (p. 36),[3] and in later ages he is commonly seen as standard-bearer or attendant to one of the great gods. It is therefore impossible to consider him a leading figure of the pantheon, as has sometimes been suggested.[4] In fact we have for once inscribed evidence as to the identity of this figure. A terracotta plaque shows the nude and bearded hero holding the same emblem as on the seals.[5] Upon his right arm is written: "Come in, Guard of what is good." On the left arm we read: "Go out, Guard of Evil." The preparation of these very figures is actually described in a cuneiform text found at Assur, which directs that such terracottas should be buried in the corners of courtyards to protect them against evil influences. This tallies well with the function of this personage on the many Akkadian seals where he stands as attendant or porter at the shrine of Ea or other gods holding the same object as on the terracotta relief (Pl. XXI*c*; cf. Pl. XVIII*k*). The text names these figures *talim*, meaning twins or companions, and our bearded hero represents, therefore, in this case one of a pair of benevolent demons.

But it would be rash to assert that the bearded and naked hero shown struggling with animals personified the same dæmon. It is equally possible that the Sumerians represented in this way a whole class of heroic or dæmonic figures, and this is, in fact, suggested by the very varied functions later fulfilled by this figure on Akkadian seals (see § 17 and p. 87 below).

The same argument applies to the Bull-man; in fact his usual appearance as the companion of the bearded hero on Sargonid and later seals (Pls. XVI, XVII) would make the two of them into another pair of twins.[6] Yet it is possible that here again several mythological figures are shown in the same guise while we, unlike the seal-cutters' contemporaries, lack the means to distinguish them.

[1] *Illustrated London News*, 12 Sept. 1936, p. 434, Figs. 14, 15, 16.

[2] The triple girdle is usual with the Bull-man, but B.M. 89538 shows it on the nude hero.

[3] B.M. 102546.

[4] Heidenreich, *Beiträge zur Geschichte der Vorderasiatischen Steinschneidekunst*, pp. 1–26. See further the discussion of these figures in § 17 below, but note that the god of animals and vegetation, who is Tammuz, often appears on Akkadian seals but always wearing the horned crown, in contrast with the naked hero.

[5] Published by Ebeling, *Archiv für Orientforschung*, v, 218.

[6] Note that on Pl. XVII*d* the Bull-man's companion is clothed and wears the shoes with upturned toes worn by the naked hero on stone vases of the Jemdet Nasr period.

The appearance of the Bull-man is always the same. A human torso is supported by bull's legs, while the creature possesses horns, bull's ears and a tail, and is often ithyphallic. A long beard is in the early instances shown to grow from the edge of the jaw (Pl. XII *a*) and a pigtail, or perhaps long hair curling at the end, hangs over his shoulders. Assyriologists of an older generation have identified the Bull-man with Enkidu, and though this identification is now generally abandoned we shall see in a following chapter that it has some points in its favour, though insufficient to make it a certainty.

In the Second Early Dynastic period the Bull-man appears exclusively as a slayer of lions, after which time he plays a less discriminate role in the frieze. The horned crown of divinity, which he wears under the Third Dynasty of Ur, does not belong to his attire in Early Dynastic times.

As to the equipment used by the various combatants, a dagger with a crescent-shaped pommel is of common occurrence (Pls. X *d*, *i*; XI *b*, *c*, *d*). Both Bull-man and hero sometimes hold an object which remains unexplained (Pl. XII *a*). Rendered more cursorily it has been mistaken for a bow,[1] and in many a crowded scene of the Third Early Dynastic period it is impossible to know whether this object is depicted or whether the fighter grasps the tail of the lion as is usual at that time (Pls. XIII *f*; XIV *b*, *d*; cf. Pl. XII *c*). The complete absence of arrowheads in Early Dynastic layers, strongly contrasting with the numerous fine chipped flint specimens which appear under the Sargonid Dynasty, forms another argument against the assumption.

Once (Pl. XII *b*) the Bull-man is shown holding a socketed battle-axe of the type so well known at Ur. It hangs head downwards from his right hand or is perhaps slung from his wrist by means of a leather thong drawn through a hole in the shaft.

Among the animals appearing in the friezes, the human-headed bull is the most remarkable. He has been said to represent the bison whose bulging forehead and long beard, vaguely suggesting human features, might be treated as frankly human after the animal became extinct in Mesopotamia.[2] But there are alabaster lamps which portray the creature in the round and leave no doubt as to its composite nature.[3] We find furthermore that bulls' heads of metal fitted to harps from Ur and conforming to the aurochs and not to the bison type are provided with broad human beards, which are actually made as appendages tied round the muzzle.[4] Moreover, the true

[1] Smith, *Early History of Assyria*, p. 372, note 10.
[2] Breuil, in *Revue Archéologique*, 1909, I, 250–54.
[3] Cf. Woolley, *Royal Cemetery*, Pl. 182.
[4] Heinrich, *Fara*, 99; Woolley, *Royal Cemetery*, Pls. 114, 115, 117.

bison does occasionally appear in the seal designs.[1] Finally, composite monsters and semi-human creatures are so characteristic of Early Dynastic work that it seems irrelevant whether the creation of the human-headed bull could have been derived from acquaintance with the bison.

The other animals of the friezes do not require comment, except in so far as they provide us with chronological evidence. We have already pointed out that the lion appears in profile in the Second Early Dynastic period, unless held upside down, and that in the next age he is always represented with his face shown from above. The leopard, characterised by its spots, appears in the Third Early Dynastic period (Pls. XIII*f*; XIV*b*) like the stag, whose coat is often dappled (Pl. XIII*b*). The leopard is always shown in profile. The bull, of the aurochs type, it normally drawn with one horn projecting forward. Sometimes he wears a girth.[2] The various goats, gazelles and antelopes are hard to distinguish from one another.

Filling motives are especially common in the Second Early Dynastic period; daggers, animals' heads, plant motives, crescent and star are used. In the next period they are rarer. The scorpion however now appears and sometimes birds or complete animals are used as filling ornaments (Pls. XIII*b*; XIV*b*).

§ 14. MYTHOLOGICAL SUBJECTS

(*a*) *The Epic of Gilgamesh.*

It has been commonly assumed in the past, and is now generally denied, that the seal designs contain illustrations of figures and scenes from the most impressive work of Babylonian literature, namely the Epic of Gilgamesh.[3] Neither standpoint is susceptible of proof. If, on the face of it, there seems no necessity to postulate that a work esteemed by the literate should have left its mark on works of art intended for general use, we know, on the other hand, that this is precisely what did happen in the case of the Homeric poems. The problem therefore deserves consideration.

The Epic of Gilgamesh describes the adventures of a legendary king of Erech, and of his friend Enkidu. The latter was created by order of the gods to serve as a diversion for Gilgamesh, who was oppressing his people. And indeed the king, having found his equal, left the city to start with his comrade on a series of exploits in which their extraordinary power found full

[1] Heinrich, *Fara*, Pl. 51*a*, left.

[2] Heinrich, *Fara*, Pl. 42*e*; also Kh. II/742.

[3] Now available rendered literally into English hexameters by R. Campbell Thompson, *The Epic of Gilgamesh* (London, 1928). A translation in German blank verse, including some new fragments and the Sumerian versions: Albert Schott, *Das Gilgamesch Epos.*

scope. They killed a monstrous demon in the wooded Elamite highlands and slew the "Bull of Heaven" sent by Ishtar to destroy the citizens of Uruk after Gilgamesh had refused to become her lover. This act of *hybris* was, however, punished by the death of Enkidu, and Gilgamesh, inconsolable, set out to discover the truth about death. He ultimately reached Utanapishtim, the Babylonian Noah, who had not succumbed to the Flood, and, when the gods discovered his survival, was removed from the earth to become immortal. Utanapishtim recounted to Gilgamesh the story of the Flood to prove that death is inescapable and that he himself had only obtained immortality by a specific act of the assembled gods. Moreover, he demonstrated that Gilgamesh, mightiest of men, was even unable to vanquish sleep. At the moment of departure he took pity on the distraught hero and indicated where in the "Ocean deep", the primaeval waters, grew the plant of everlasting life. Gilgamesh dived and found the plant, only to be robbed of it by a serpent. As a last expedient he called up Enkidu's ghost and enquired of the nature of the hereafter. But his friend, not unlike Achilles answering Odysseus, evaded a direct reply but suggested that horror and emptiness were the essential features of his present existence. On this note of utter desolation the Epic ends.

The foregoing synopsis is mainly based on a version found in the library of Assurbanipal at Nineveh. But it is no anachronism to use it in connection with Early Dynastic seals, since the Epic certainly goes back to the Third Millennium B.C. In fact the extant fragments of old-Babylonian and Sumerian versions show that these included further episodes omitted by the Assyrian scribes upon whom we are mainly dependent.

On the other hand, it is well to realise from the outset that the comparisons which we shall make are bound to remain hypothetical. For not a single figure or scene in Mesopotamian art is accompanied by an inscription connecting it with the Epic. Contemporaries had as little difficulty in identifying such figures as we in recognising, for instance, John the Baptist among the figures of a mediaeval painting. In dealing with ancient Babylonian art, the conventions of which are lost for us, we are throughout confined to inferences from circumstantial evidence.

Let us then, first of all, consider the appearance of the two main figures of the Epic. Gilgamesh is described as of superhuman stature, two-thirds god and one-third human. This indication does not lead us far since the gods were conceived in human shape and Gilgamesh would thus appear entirely anthropomorphic.

Enkidu, on the other hand, was of more extraordinary appearance. True, it is nowhere explicitly stated that he was not of human shape, but it would be unwise to attach much value to such negative evidence. His body is said to have been entirely covered with hair, and his head with long tresses "like a woman".[1] His garb is that of Sumukan, a god of cattle. This phrase may, therefore, refer once more to Enkidu's pelt. But when we read next:

> Even with gazelles did he pasture on herbage, along with the cattle
> Drank he his fill,[2]

then surely we must ask ourselves whether we are not interpreting the allusions of the Epic too soberly if we assume them to evoke in the vivid imagination of the ancients nothing more than the absurd picture of a hairy man going down on hands and knees in the grass. And this quasi-careful interpretation is the less justified since we possess in the Bull-man of the seal designs a figure admirably expressing the complex and heterogeneous nature with which the Epic credits Enkidu. The Bull-man of the seals is, in fact, constantly associated with cattle and game; he is often depicted with strikingly long hair, hanging down his back "like a woman", as the Epic describes in more than one place (Pls. XII *a*, *b*; XIII *b*, *f*; XIV *d* and still on XVI *a*, *g*). This looks so incongruous, descending from between the bull's horns, that one naturally seeks an explanation such as a well-known poetic reference would provide.

In the Epic, Enkidu, lured away from the beasts with whom he lived, is taken to a shepherd's shelter. Then he

> ...taking his weapons,
> Hunted the lions which harried the shepherds o' nights; and the jackals
> Caught he. [So] he having mastered the lions, the shepherds slept soundly,
> Enkidu he was their warden.[3]

The Epic here expresses in words the very theme which underlies the many pictorial variations of the friezes. In the Second Early Dynastic period, before the friezes became meaningless decorations, the Bull-man was consistently a slayer of lions, often in evident defence of flocks and game. The latter variant reflects, of course, his long and intimate relationship with the milder animals. Now this theme plays a subordinate part in the Epic. In fact, it is confined to the early passages from which we have quoted, and in the exploits which form the main body of the story no further reference is

[1] Schott, *loc. cit.* p. 17, lines 36–7; p. 25, lines 210 f.; perhaps also p. 26, line 6.

[2] Campbell Thompson, *loc cit.* p. 11, lines 40 f.

[3] Campbell Thompson, *loc. cit.* p. 17, lines 30–35.

made to this original state of Enkidu. All the traits of the Enkidu of the Epic which we have found to recur in the seal designs belong to one, almost self-contained, episode. This adds considerably to their weight.

Elsewhere in the Epic scattered observations occur which might tempt one to relate them to the seals. But they appear to be of very little value. Gilgamesh, in bewailing Enkidu, refers to him as the slayer of the wild ass and leopard.[1] Gilgamesh himself, like Pharaoh, is compared with a wild bull.[2] All these sayings are of a general nature and merely illustrate the valour of the two heroes. But the peculiarities and the mode of life of Enkidu which we find in the early part of the Epic, and which agree so well with the seals, are quite specific. Moreover, they suggest to us a creature who has little in common with the hero who later accompanies the king of Erech on his journeys. Conversely, we find the Bull-man of the Second Early Dynastic cylinder seals (when the friezes still retained some meaning) performing his feats alone,[3] in perfect accordance with the Epic when describing Enkidu's life prior to his meeting with Gilgamesh. The Bull-man of the seals of Pls. XI and XII is not the companion of the king of Erech, but a lonely semi-human creature of the wilds. It may well be that some author working on the Epic utilised the traditions of folk-lore concerning such a being, in creating the Enkidu of the beginning of his narrative. The section from which we have given quotations and which agrees with the seals does, in fact, seem to be woven but loosely into the fabric of the poem.[4] The evidence appears to justify the assumption that the seal designs do depict the wild creature described as Enkidu in the First Tablet of the Epic. And if, at various times, Bull-men appear in Mesopotamian art and fulfil a variety of functions (as attendants for instance of the Sun-god) they may well represent survivals or elaborations of a tradition, which, though it was

[1] Campbell Thompson, *loc. cit.* p. 40, lines 8–9.

[2] Schott, *loc. cit.* p. 16, lines 8, 20.

[3] When more than one Bull-man appears in one seal this is to be considered in the same manner as the two heads of the goat of Pl. XI*b* or the two bodies of the one lion's head of Pl. X*d*.

[4] The connection between the group of Schott, *loc. cit.* p. 23, lines 108–115 (Campbell Thompson, *loc. cit.* p. 17, lines 29–36), and its context is difficult to appraise, since it is followed by a gap. But line 131 would link up well with lines 104–7. Enkidu's renewed intercourse with the hetaera would conclude the process of his "becoming human" just as it had been the opening phase, and the main narrative continues in any case with the arrival of the man from Erech who induces Enkidu to proceed thither. See Mowinckel's suggestion to interpret Enkidu's name as meaning "Lord of the place of abundant recreative force", *Acta Orientalia*, XV, 156 ff., which agrees well with Jacobsen's reply to the question how the creation of Enkidu could have been thought of as a means of relieving the inhabitants of Erech from the oppression of Gilgamesh—*Acta Orientalia*, VIII, 62 ff.

utilised by the authors of the Epic, existed independently in Mesopotamia.

Whether or not then we should call the Bull-man Enkidu depends on this: Was Enkidu originally the friend of Gilgamesh, or was Enkidu the name of a creature described in Mesopotamian folk-tales and assimilated to the friend of Gilgamesh by a poet working on the early part of the Epic? If the latter assumption could ever be proved correct, we should be justified in giving that name to the Bull-man of the friezes. But the question cannot be answered at present, and thus we shall continue to refer to the Bull-man by his descriptive term, since we are, at most, only entitled to dub him Enkidu in the friezes of fighting figures. Conversely, it would be wrong to assume that the Enkidu of the Epic may never appear on the seals in any but the Bull-man's guise.

There is, in fact, one group of figures which occurs fairly frequently and which—if the Epic of Gilgamesh really predominated in the consciousness of the ancients to the extent that we have suggested—must have recalled that dramatic moment when Enkidu, meeting Gilgamesh for the first time, engages him in a bout of wrestling:

snorting (?) like bulls (and) the threshold they shattered, the (very) wall quivered,[1]

to emerge as inseparable friends. A group of wrestlers repeatedly appears on the seals, down to the end of the Third Millennium (Pl. XI *d*, *l*); and an Akkadian instance (Pl. XVII *f*) proves that they are of heroic stature and not ordinary mortals.

Let it be said once more that there is nothing illogical in the assumption that Enkidu might appear in vastly different shapes upon the seals. In the present preliminary stage of the interpretation of seal designs we must keep an open mind on this subject in order not to exclude *a priori* possibilities of understanding. After all, these designs were not produced serially, like the illustrations to a modern tale, in which the persons throughout appear with the same characteristics or attributes. Rather must we assume that the details of the Epic were—like those of Greece or India—a source of vivid imaginings, upon which pictorial artists could always draw. There is therefore no likelihood that in all cases and at all times the personages of the Epic would be depicted in the same manner. On the other hand, it is certain that happy pictorial inventions would be repeated through the length and breadth of the land. This has happened, in fact, with such fantastic designs as the lion-legged man or the double-crouped Bull-man (§ 11, p. 49), of which it is

[1] Campbell Thompson, *loc. cit.* p. 19, lines 15 f.

impossible to say where they originated. If our assumptions are correct we may even find on one and the same seal (Pl. XI *d*) two different traditional renderings of Enkidu. The religious texts—in Mesopotamia as elsewhere—abound in similar inconsistencies which did not trouble those to whom poetry and pictorial richness meant more than logic.

The question now arises as to whether Gilgamesh certainly appears upon the seals. This seems not to be the case; the naked and bearded hero, thus named by earlier Assyriologists, has no specific marks, nor does he come into scenes sufficiently detailed to substantiate the identification.[1] The possibility must be admitted that his constant association with the Bull-man on Akkadian seals was due to a contemporary interpretation as "Gilgamesh and Enkidu", but this is without proof. On the other hand, there is, besides the groups of wrestlers already discussed, one scene which seems to depict an event described in the Epic. Our Pl. XI *m* may well portray Gilgamesh, holding the herb of life, while Utanapishtim, wearing the crown of divinity, sits opposite him in a craft poled by the boatman Urshanabi.[2]

We shall meet a few more scenes on Akkadian seals which may be explained by references to the Gilgamesh Epic. For Early Dynastic times the boat scene on the one sealing from Fara, and the common group of wrestlers, the Bull-man and, finally, some isolated motives like the "Bull of Heaven", may well be derived from the great poem. It is valuable to realise these possibilities, the conditions under which motives might be translated into glyptic art, and the necessary limitations of our insight into these matters. Only if figures were accompanied by inscriptions should we be able to pass beyond the realm of surmise. But since the contemporaries of the seal-cutters did not require written explanations, we are, perhaps, never likely to receive such enlightenment.

(*b*) *The Sun-god.*

The Sun-god appears on Early Dynastic seals in one scene only, which is drawn with a varying degree of completeness (Pl. XV *j*, *n*). The god is seen steering with a paddle a boat which moves of its own accord. This, at least, is the most likely interpretation of a design in which the prow ends in a

[1] The literature on this subject is discussed in full by Mrs E. Douglas van Buren in *The Flowing Vase and the God with Streams*, pp. 12 ff. She endorses, with some modification, Heidenreich's view which we consider untenable. See above, p. 60, note 4.

[2] Medieval iconography teaches us once more that painters would thus bring three persons together even if the texts did not describe such a situation, in order to make their representation intelligible.

human body manipulating a punting pole. This figurehead wears the crown of the gods and long hair; the stern of the boat sometimes ends in the head of a serpent.

The character of the god is plainly indicated in Pl. XV*n*, which shows the two attributes which habitually appear on Akkadian seals; the saw in his hand—with which he "cuts decisions"— and the rays of light emanating from his body.[1] Moreover, the Sun-god's boat is sometimes preceded by a Scorpion-man (Pl. XV*j*),[2] which confirms the solar character of the scene, for we read in the Epic of Gilgamesh:

> ...as he reached the mountains of Mashu,
> Where ev'ryday they keep watch o'er the Sun-god's rising and setting,
> Unto the Zenith of Heaven uprear'd are their summits (and) downwards
> (Deep) unto Hell reach their breasts: (and) there at their portals stand sentry
> Scorpion-men, awful in terror, their (very) glance death: (and) tremendous,
> Shaking the hills, their magnificence; they are the wardens of Shamash,
> Both at his rising and setting.[3]

It may be that the journey of the sun during the night is depicted, since the moon and the stars are sometimes a part of the scene even when there is little room for their inclusion, as in Pl. XV*j*, where they have found a place in the curve of the Scorpion-man's tail. The agricultural associations, of which we shall obtain more explicit proof in the Akkadian versions of this subject, might suggest the nightly journey by which he passes beneath the earth from west to east; it is true that the plough may refer to a constellation and need not, therefore, impart a chthonic significance to the scene. But the seals show an accumulation of associations with agriculture which makes me inclined to accept the chthonic interpretation as correct and this with the more conviction as no traces of Sumerian astronomical or astrological texts have so far been discovered.[4] It seems significant that on Early Dynastic, as on Akkadian seals, three symbols are always depicted together with the Sun-god's boat: a quadruped, a plough and a pot.

The quadruped is, with two exceptions, a lion, or—in detailed renderings —a monster with a human face and a leonine body, ears and tail (cf.

[1] The rays on Pl. XV*n* end in knobs; this feature is entirely exceptional and there is no justification for the assumption of Mrs Van Buren (*Archiv für Orientforschung*, x, 240) that a god of fertility is represented with plants sprouting from his shoulders. The rays in Sargonid times are depicted in the same way as are flames rising from altars (Pl. XIX*e, f* with Pl. XXI*b, f*). Even on Pl. XV*n* the god holds the "saw" of Shamash.

[2] Probably also As. 33/191.

[3] Campbell Thompson, *loc. cit.* p. 42, lines 1–10.

[4] See the most recent and comprehensive discussion by A. Schott in *Zeitschrift der Deutschen Morgenländischen Gesellschaft*, XIII (1934), pp. 302–26.

Pl. XIII *h*). The characteristic volute of the tail is especially easy to recognise, and once a typical attitude of the great cat is faithfully depicted.[1] Sometimes the mane is suggested, as in the animal friezes by a kind of herring-bone pattern.[2] More often a group of vertical lines represents a mane or a beard; this, at least, may be the artist's intention, since in Akkadian times the quadruped usually possesses a bearded human head (cf. Pls. XV *n*; XIX *e*, *f*).

The plough, which is the second component of the group, is of the usual type, with a long shaft fitted into a short transversal yoke, and the coulter fixed between two wooden steering handles, with the sowing funnel between them.

The pot is cut with great detail on Akkadian seals, but is often a mere drill-hole in Early Dynastic cylinders. In both instances which we are illustrating, however, a handle—and perhaps a spout—is indicated.

A decision as to whether this scene has a purely astral or a chthonic significance would be easier if we could be sure of the relevancy of the design of Pl. XI *j*. There two lions draw a plough guided by a Bull-man, while an indeterminate figure drives on the unusual team. Before them we see an eagle and a scorpion which recur in the Akkadian version of Pl. XX *a*. They occasionally accompany the Sun-god in his boat,[3] so that his journey with plough, pot and quadruped may possibly lead him to this field, where he or his associates labour as true husbandmen. On one Early Dynastic seal[4] the boat, probably with its divine occupant (but the seal is too much worn to show his attributes clearly), is depicted in connection with a snake-coil design, and this stands for the god of fertility in his chthonic aspect (§ 14 (*c*) (ii) and § 20 (*e*), pp. 71, 120). In view of all these associations the scene seems to have some definite relationship with the earth's fertility and seems not to depict the sun's diurnal or yearly voyage.

Less important than plough, pot and quadruped which appear to be indispensable elements in the design, are some other figures with which the

[1] Newell, 48. Mrs Van Buren has been singularly unfortunate in dealing with this scene (see p. 68, note 1). She maintains that the quadruped and the pot stand for a bull attacked by Imdugud, a view which is untenable when one considers detailed renderings on Akkadian seals (Pl. XIX *e*, *f*). It is true that the bull attacked by Imdugud appears once together with the Sun-god's boat (Ur, 137), but then a lion is placed nearest to the vessel. The quadruped never has horns nor cloven hoofs, nor the characteristic tufted tail of the bull, and even on the seal quoted by Mrs Van Buren (Mackay, *Kish A*, Pl. VI, 17) we see the round ear and mane which are typical of the Early Dynastic renderings of lions.

[2] A–124; Ur, 137. Also Kh. II/276, but here the head may be that of a dragon as on As. 31/25, which is Akkadian.

[3] Kh. III/922.

[4] I.M. 13916.

Sun-god's boat is sometimes associated, and which may merely be filling motives placed there to complete the pattern of the main figures. Such uncertain themes are the lion and antelope protome of Pl. XV*j* and the eagle grasping an antelope in either claw on the same seal.

The voyaging Sun-god and his companions are in a number of cases so placed as to fill only one half of the cylinder's surfaces; the other half, divided from it by a line, being occupied by a separate design, most commonly the building of the ziggurat.

(*c*) *The Gods of Fertility.*

(i) *Figures of the Gods.* Representations of gods are not common on Early Dynastic seals, and it is not always easy to distinguish them from human beings, especially in the early part of the period when the horned crown seems not always to have been worn by the gods. But the fragment of an old impression illustrated in Pl. XV*e* represents most probably that deity who personified the generative force of nature and was, as we have already seen (§ 5, p. 17), widely worshipped. The figure looking to the left may, indeed, represent the statue of the god in a niche or under a baldachin.[1] This, at least, would be the most natural interpretation of the curved structure shown behind and above. There is no need to assume, of course, that the god must be in front of the shrine; in ideoplastic art it is quite usual to depict a building apart from what is happening inside it.

The main figure does not wear the horned crown, but he is the recipient of libations—a nude figure holding the customary ewer can be seen at the edge of the fragment—and is therefore most likely the god; his identification is possible by means of the gazelle and the plant placed in front of him, just as they serve as identification signs on the base of a cult-statue from Tell Asmar[2] and on Akkadian seals (Pl. XX*b*); we have already discussed this symbolism in dealing with the Uruk period. The eagle with spread wings, with head destroyed, but intended for Imdugud, the lion-headed bird, appears on the base of the cult-statue from Tell Asmar and is on our sealing, drawn above the temple of the god. The sealing belongs to the First or Second Early Dynastic period, most probably to the latter.[3] It is likely,

[1] Cf. Heinrich, *Fara*, Pl. 66 *f*.

[2] *Oriental Institute Communications*, No. 19, Frontispiece and Fig. 64.

[3] The spacing on this sealing recalls Early Dynastic seals like Pl. X*f* and Heinrich, *Fara*, Pl. 59*i*. The shrine with Imdugud above survives in Akkadian times (V.A. 2112). The asymmetrical arrangement of the eagle above his two victims recalls the green stone vase from Khafaje, *Oriental Institute Communications*, No. 19, p. 48, which is Early Dynastic I or II. The resemblance with Ward-Morgan, 35, which has a subsidiary group of pure Early Dynastic II type, helps our dating.

though not certain, that we see the same personification of nature's vital force in Pl. XV *h*. If the figure is male, as the bareness of the upper part of its body suggests, the beard is indicated in an unusual way, above the shoulder. Only a fragment of the cylinder has been preserved, but we see a variety of living things pressing towards the god, who holds an ear of corn. In front we notice a fish, with water indicated above it. This lies under a break in the surface of the seal which obliterates the forelegs of a kneeling ibex with clearly notched horns. Above it is a scorpion, and next to this a stag or mountain-sheep; the wearing down of the cylinder near its edge has obliterated the connection between antler and head. Below them a cow is suckling her calf, beside a tree which is only just visible.

(ii) *Caduceus, Snake-coil and Hydra.* Whether or not we interpret the two scenes discussed above as representations of the god of fertility, we know at least that the symbol of his chthonic aspect, Ningiszida (§ 20 (*e*), p. 119), is frequently used in Early Dynastic times. In its original form, as a pair of intertwined or copulating vipers, we have met it already in the Uruk period (Pl. III *b*). The resemblance to the serpent-necked felines (Pls. IV *d, f*; V *h*) seems to have more than a merely decorative significance, since the entwined snakes have, even in the Second Early Dynastic period, sometimes ears as if they were lion-headed (Pl. XI *h*).[1]

In Early Dynastic times an elaborate snake-coil (Pl. XIV *i*) is more common than the pair of intertwined serpents.[2] The coils often show a head and tail, and sometimes (Pl. XXXIX *c*)[3] two heads project, thus proving that we rightly identify the coil with the caduceus form. The Akkadian seals confirm this view. A tortoise often appears in addition to the coil, generally near the snake's head. Its meaning is still uncertain (Text-fig. 26). A seal impression from Tell Asmar shows the hydra as a seven-headed snake (Text-fig. 27), which we know under another shape in Akkadian times as an adversary of the god of fertility (Pl. XXIII *j*).

We have mentioned above that friezes such as that of Pl. XIII *e* may well refer to this same god.

[1] So also Ward-Morgan, 35, where the god of fertility is seated before his temple, perhaps drinking through a tube. Above are the two lion-headed snakes, entwined; see also next note.

[2] Also Kh. IV/334; I.M. 2185, 6980, 14334 (see *Archiv für Orientforschung*, x, pp. 56 f.); I.M. 18871; Ur, 60; *American Journal of Semitic Languages*, XLIV, 3 ff., No. 4. In *American Journal of Archaeology*, XXX (1926), 410, Fig. 6, we see a snake-coil on a seal of the Jemdet Nasr period, which may have served as prototype for Ward-Morgan, 35.

[3] The result is a design exactly resembling a steatite lamp-cover in the Louvre: *Encyclopédie photographique de l'art*, p. 223 B. More like a caduceus is I.M. 14840 (*Archiv für Orientforschung*, x, 56, Fig. 3).

(*d*) *Various Mythological Scenes.*

Here again the extent to which seal designs can be understood depends on the preservation of relevant texts, and in this accident plays a considerable part. It is, therefore, not surprising that several scenes, depicting mythological subjects in great detail, remain nevertheless enigmatical.

Let us consider as an example the design of Pl. XIII *h*. The upper frieze shows a symmetrical pattern of two human-headed bulls recumbent on either side of a wooded mountain and attacked, the one by the lion-headed eagle Imdugud, the other by a winged lion or dragon. The figures may refer to the "Bull of Heaven", described in the Gilgamesh Epic as possessing a body filled with flame and producing by his onslaught seven years of famine.[1]

Text-fig. 26. Impression from Fara: snake-coil and tortoise.

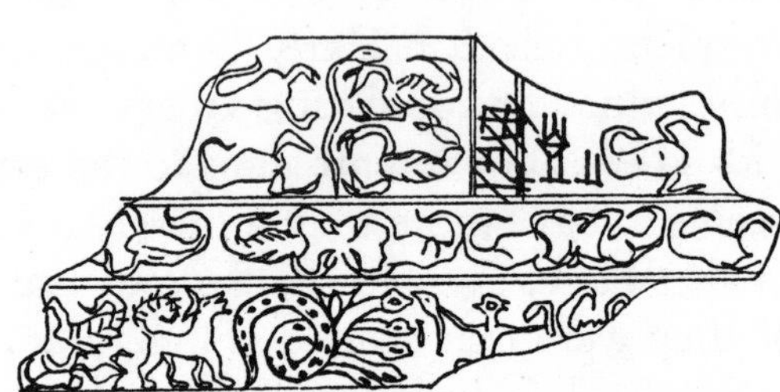

Text-fig. 27. Impression from Tell Asmar: defeat of Hydra.

Since Imdugud is a symbol of the god of fertility, and the winged dragon an adjunct of the Weather-god and Rain-god (§ 21 (*f*), p. 122), our cylinder may represent a conflict between the scorching summer heat of Mesopotamia and the beneficial powers of spring and autumn, especially since the next figure is a combination of plant and ruminant which so often symbolises the god of fertility. If this is the meaning of the upper frieze of our seal, we must admit that it was sometimes lost sight of; the group of attacked couchant bulls beside a mountain recurs on another seal, where a Bull-man on the one side, and the "shepherd" on the other, come to the aid of the bull as if he were one of the figures in the usual frieze.[2] On the other hand, a seal impression from Ur stresses the mythological character of the bulls by letting their elongated bodies end in mountains watched by armed sentinels, and this reminiscence of the place of Sunrise fits in, as we shall see, with what we know of the "Bull of Heaven" (§ 21 (*c*), p. 128); in fact a seal from Susa shows the

[1] R. Campbell Thompson, *loc. cit.* p. 34.

[2] B.M. 22962; Smith, *Early History of Assyria*, Pl. VII *d*.

Sun-god actually rising between two couchant human-headed bulls.[1] In view of these conflicting usages it is impossible say whether or not the upper frieze of Pl. XIII *h* reflects a myth. Perhaps individual symbolism is all that is intended, producing a decorative design which derives additional value from the propitious meaning of its elements.

But the lower frieze can certainly not be explained in that way, though the myth to which its very specific detail refers eludes us. Again we see a wooded mountain; upon its slope, beneath a tree which contains a bird, a monkey plays the flute. In front of him a lion has pounced upon a bull. The next two figures are separated by a small antelope which serves as filling motive, from the bull and its assailant. The insertion of the antelope should possibly warn us not to consider the next two figures as following in the manner enumerated here, but to imagine them on the other side of the mountain. They are both fantastic creatures, one the human-faced lion surmounted by a plough, a combination which usually accompanies the scene of the Sun-god in his boat; the other a Bird-man carrying a trident, which may be a stylised representation of a plant or tree branch. For the punishment of a Bird-man for a theft of this kind is of common occurrence on Akkadian seals (Pl. XXIII *d* and § 21 (*f*), p. 132).[2]

A star and crescent are drawn above antelope and lion, but since the gazelle is undoubtedly a filling motive of the type which occurs, for example, on Pl. XIII *b*, the moon and star may serve a similar purpose and need not signify that the action takes place in heaven.[3] It is true that the plough is the name of a constellation. But the very fact that the Mesopotamians mapped out the sky with symbols derived from the earth makes it impossible for us always to decide where we must locate a scene. Even if we disregard this particular ambiguity, we can only note the possibility that the various mythological motives to which we have just referred are somehow related to the lower frieze of Pl. XIII *h*. There exists no clue to the meaning of the very precise and abundant detail of this scene.

We are in a similar position as regards Pl. XI *m*, which has been tentatively interpreted as a scene of the Gilgamesh Epic. The wrestlers of Pl. XI *d*, *l* may belong to the same context. The curious agricultural scene of Pl. XI *j* remains as inexplicable as the animal musicians of which a few instances

1 *Revue d'Assyriologie*, XXVIII (1931), 44, No. XI.

2 I.M. 2479 also shows the combination of the Bird-man holding a stick or branch and the human-faced lion and plough, but the frieze is for the rest filled up with two ordinary groups of men and goats from the usual friezes.

3 Compare our Pl. XV *j* and its discussion in section (*c*) above.

occur (Text-fig. 28).[1] Conversely, certain scenes which are to be treated in the next sections, because they seem to us devoid of mythology, may quite well have had some mythological meaning which escapes us.

Text-fig. 28. Impression from Ur: lion feasting.

§ 15. RITUAL AND SECULAR SUBJECTS

(*a*) *Adoration and Offerings.*

A number of seals show scenes of adoration before gods whose identity remains undefined. The simplest form (Pl. XV*m*) shows a shaven priest introducing a bearded worshipper to the deity seated at the shrine; it is uncertain whether a god or goddess is depicted. We find, then, already in the Early Dynastic period the so-called "Presentation scene" which is considered typical of the Third Dynasty of Ur and the Dynasty of Hammurabi—one more proof that the subject-matter of seal designs is untrustworthy as dating evidence.

Somewhat more common than the "presentation" is the offering of gifts to the god. In Pl. XV*k* such a scene is rendered with the characteristic Early Dynastic tendency to produce a closely interwoven pattern. The deity, not so much characterised by the head-dress as by the offering-stand placed in front, may be male or female; the latter is rather more probable, especially in connection with the scorpion drawn behind the throne. But this may be, together with the crescent and the star, a mere filling ornament, though the star is rather large and carefully drawn with eight points, as when in later times it refers to Ishtar. A nude priest piles offerings upon the stand, apparently loaves of bread and a trussed duck. He is followed by a worshipper carrying a sacrificial kid. A lance serves to fill the space between worshipper and priest. The divinity holds an ear of corn.

[1] Compare Heinrich, *Fara*, Pl. 65*d–g*.

Since there is little convention in this period, we find numerous variants of the scene. In a case like Pl. XIV*f* it may be that a goddess is depicted drinking through a tube, since she resembles in every detail the main figure of Pl. XV*k*. Once the god is depicted on the one side of his shrine, attended by two persons, while on the other side the worshipper with the kid approaches a collection of jars and a sheep or similar carcase all ready for roasting.[1] At times the preparation of this animal is in itself the subject of the design.[2] Branches of trees and bunches of dates are occasionally placed in the offering-stand.[3] A fine example, probably of the Second Early Dynastic period,[4] shows a bearded god seated on a throne covered by a tasselled plaid of the type worn by the people of the period. His throne is supported by two *couchant* animals, apparently a wild bull and mountain-goat; before him is an offering-stand in the shape of a rearing gazelle, like those found at Ur.[5] It supports some cups. A man with long hair and a long cloak lifts a libation jar and is followed by a female devotee. It is curious that the worshippers descend towards the god.[6] Behind the divine figure the shrine is shown with all the detail of its two recessed towers flanking the doorway. Let it be said again that in all these instances it is immaterial on which side of the shrine the god appears, the idea being merely to convey an act of worship at—and almost certainly inside—the shrine.

(*b*) *Ritual Marriage.*

Two seals[7] represent the ritual marriage which, according to various texts, was consummated by the god and goddess during the New Year's Festival and immediately followed by a feast in which the whole population enjoyed the abundance now ensured by the completion of the rites. The fertility of nature depended upon this act; it is explicitly stated[8] that at Lagash the union of the goddess Bau and the god Ningirsu at the New Year's Festival brought about the welfare of the city. Pl. XV*l* gives the scene. The couch supporting the two figures has animal-shaped legs, either bull's hoofs or lion's claws, cf. Pl. VIII*d*. The scorpion beneath it may symbolise Ishara, the goddess of love,[9] and the figure at the foot of the couch, present on both seals and on a stela,[10] which depicts this scene, may well be the officiating

[1] A-125. [2] Mackay, *Kish A*, Pl. XLI, 6. [3] Ur, 13.
[4] V.A. 3878 (Weber, 430). [5] Woolley, *Royal Cemetery*, Pls. 87, 88.
[6] This is not accidental. It occurs also in Pl. XXII*h*.
[7] Kh. II/41 and As. 32/934. [8] Gudea, Cylinder B, 5, 17–18.
[9] Campbell Thompson, *The Epic of Gilgamesh*, p. 74.
[10] *Oriental Institute Communications*, No. 17, Fig. 40, p. 45.

priest who is said in the description of the ceremony in the time of Idin Dagan to purify the god and the goddess before their connubium.

(c) *The Building of a Temple Tower.*

This subject never occurs outside the Early Dynastic period, when it is fairly common, often occupying the lower frieze of a seal which shows the Sun-god in his boat in the upper register (Pl. XIV*k*). The ceremony is presided over by a seated figure; whether the ruler of the city or the god is represented is not always certain, but several instances[1] suggest that it is the god, since the figure wears the horned crown. A row of men carrying material (generally indicated by mere drill-holes) moves towards the temple tower, while two builders placed on either side are increasing its bulk by the addition of single bricks, or are putting in place one or two whole storeys at a time, for there is, of course, no intention of depicting the activities with verisimilitude, but merely of expressing them ideoplastically.

Here again there are variations. Ladders or scaffolding, or perhaps stairways, seem to be depicted;[2] or the offerings made for the occasion are a part of the representation.[3] Pl. XIV*j* shows a curious detail: a naked priest is showing the seated deity a planoconvex brick, the characteristic building material of the period, evidently for the purpose of having its quality or measurement checked.[4] Here the god is seated on an animal-shaped throne exactly resembling a stone specimen found at Ur.[5] Sometimes he is shown drinking through a tube, a reference, perhaps, to the feast celebrated upon the completion of the construction.

[1] As. 32/437 (our Pl. XIV*j*); Ish. 35/46; Kh. III/949.

[2] A–126; Brett, 13, 14. Doubt may be entertained whether these seals actually depict the building of the ziggurat or rather an agricultural rite such as the heaping of corn before the god. Since the disposition of the figures is the same and also the association with the Sun-god's boat in the upper register, I have taken these seals to show another version of the building scene in which the scaffolding and pyramidal shape visible during construction replace the final stepped appearance; or perhaps the stairways leading up to the higher storeys from plain level are indicated; it is tempting to see in a design with concentric squares which appears above the ziggurat in Brett, 13, and Ish. 35/46 the plan of the Temple Tower.

[3] Bibliothèque Nationale, 49—a sacrificial animal is brought while the god drinks through a tube from a large vessel. The latter scene also in Ward-Morgan, 8, and Ish. 35/46.

[4] In the texts builders like Gudea make a point of the purity and correctness of the materials they use. The explicit rendering of Pl. XIV*j* explains what is shown more vaguely in Pl. XIV*k* and on seals from the Dyala region.

[5] *Antiquaries Journal*, VI, Pl. LIII*b*.

(*d*) *The Banquet.*

The Banquets and Symposia might be considered secular scenes, but for the fact of their habitual appearance on plaques set up in Early Dynastic temples throughout the land, so that they are more likely to commemorate an event connected with the cult. The seals also which bear this scene are commonly found in temples as well as in the so-called "Royal Tombs" at Ur. But then it is not certain that the occupants of these tombs were royalty. There is some evidence[1] that they were victims of a rite which, performed in some calamitous season with possibly exceptional severity to ensure its efficacy, consigned to the keeping of Earth itself those who had embodied the divine powers in the annual festival. The scene discussed in section (*b*) above formed part of the same ritual, which we know was enacted by the king or his substitute and a priestess. It represented the death of the god and his resurrection, followed by reunion with the goddess. It is said in Gudea's description of this festival that after the completion of the marriage a feast took place in which the gods, the ruler and the population of the city partook together (Cylinder B, 5, 11 ff.); a jar with projecting drinking tubes indeed stands near the couch upon which the ritual marriage is consummated (Pl. XV *l*). The most joyful event in the annual cycle of the god was certainly a fitting subject for a seal design.

On the other hand, divinities or divine symbols do not appear in banquets on the seals (Pl. XV *a*, *c*, *f*) and there were, of course, many occasions for festivities, both ritual and secular, which may have been depicted; without the evidence of the reliefs we should not even be able to surmise as much as we do.[2]

The participants in the feast—often a man and a woman—face each other on either side of a large jar from which they imbibe through tubes, and this seems to have been the usual manner of enjoying beer in the Ancient Near East, similar scenes appearing on Syrian seals; and a Syrian mercenary is depicted thus occupied on a stela found at Tell el Amarna in Egypt. Xenophon describes the Armenians as drinking "sweet wine of barley"

[1] *Journal of the Royal Asiatic Society*, 1928, pp. 849 ff.; *Zeitschrift für Assyriologie*, XXXIX, 83 ff.; *Iraq*, I, 12, note 3.

[2] Ravn (*Acta Orientalia*, X, 1 ff.) has studied in detail the scene of two people drinking through tubes and inclines to the view, first propounded by O. Weber, that "the interpretation as a banquet for the deceased seems for the present to be the one best warranted" for Syria, where stelae show funerary banquets. But for Babylonia we have no such evidence. And though it is true that no divine crowns appear in the case of Symposia, gods are occasionally shown drinking through tubes (Ward-Morgan, 35; Ish. 35/46—the god assisting at the building of the ziggurat). The scorpion and eagle may determine the drinking of the single figure on Pl. XIV *a* as a religious act.

with corn swimming on top of the liquid, which had therefore to be sucked up through "straws without joints". And metal strainers, fitted probably into the base of these straws, or tubes made entirely of metal, are found in Egypt and Syria, as well as in Mesopotamia.[1] Sometimes the jar is placed in a square wooden frame (Pl. XIV*f*); occasionally the feasters drink from cups handed to them by attendants; a lower register may show the service in greater detail (Pl. XV*c*) with a sideboard loaded with food, butlers and servants, a man bearing a basin and ewer for washing the hands;[2] or we see men carrying a large store-jar (Pl. XV*f*) suspended from a pole, or kids or calves. Or a band of female musicians appears (Pl. XV*a*), one playing the flute, another the bull-headed harp so well known from the graves at Ur, here carried by two dwarfs or children. Three dancers, clapping their hands, execute passes and no doubt sing to the rhythm of the instruments.

Other women, sometimes bearing flag-shaped fans, are shown in attendance upon the female participant of the feast. The regular presence of women, both on these seals and on the reliefs, differentiates them from the so-called "Standard" found at Ur,[3] where a ruler is shown with his chiefs and councillors celebrating a victory.

The seals so far discussed belong to the Third Early Dynastic period. To the preceding age belongs the rendering of the same subject in Pl. XI*f*; and in the Square Temple at Tell Asmar, which is also dated to the second stage of the Early Dynastic period, we found a clumsy rendering of the main details, two men sitting on either side of the big jar with the drinking tubes, the rest of the cylinder being decorated with an eagle and a star. While these instances antedate the majority, we also have later Akkadian renderings of the same subject.[4]

(*e*) *Shepherds and Flocks.*

Here again there is room for doubt as to whether the scenes have a religious import. The temple herd has, since the Uruk period, played a predominant part in the seal designs, and the shepherds in Pl. XV*g* are

[1] Xenophon, *Anabasis*, IV, 5, 26; first quoted in this context by Ed. Meyer, *Reich und Kultur der Chettiter*, pp. 55 f. Originals of the tubes were found at Tell Asmar, *Oriental Institute Communications*, No. 17, Fig. 35, and at Ur, *Antiquaries Journal*, VIII, 444; and strainers occurred in Egypt, *Journal of Egyptian Archaeology*, XII, 22, and at Tell Chagar Bazar, *Illustrated London News*, 27 March 1937.

[2] Originals found at Ur; Woolley, *Royal Cemetery*, Pls. 171, 172.

[3] Woolley, *Royal Cemetery*, Pls. 91, 92.

[4] As. 32/602 (*Oriental Institute Communications*, No. 16, p. 42) and three others; Brussels, 448; Ur, 142; Speiser, *Tepe Gawra*, I, No. 66.

drawn with an appendage to the head which may be intended for a horned crown as well as locks of hair. On the whole, however, these scenes show nothing which cannot be interpreted as secular. Pl. XV *d* is typical; one man holds a goat while the other milks it, and the master, sitting near a tree, drinks the milk from a cup while the dog jumps up against him and licks the hand which lies on his knee. Another seal[1] shows one man milking and another shaking a large suspended pot to make buttermilk.

(*f*) *Chariot Scenes.*

The chariot appears on the seals exclusively as an engine of war. Occasionally[2] a fallen enemy is pictured beneath the wild asses or onagers, which were tamed by the Sumerians only and used for driving. Their stiff manes and long ears are sometimes clearly shown (Pl. XV *n*).

The chariots are of different types. Some have two wheels, some four, some contain more than one person; others are driven by a single man standing astride a wooden saddle. The front is sometimes shown beside the side-view, as is usual in ideoplastic art. It is strengthened with crossbars, and sometimes shows two loops on them which may have been used as hand rails. A quiver with javelins is fastened against it. The design of the chariot in Pl. XV *n* is less clear than usual. The soldiers who follow carrying battle-axes also occur elsewhere.

The chariot scene has been considered as peculiar to art of the northern mountaineers.[3] We see, however, that it is common in Mesopotamia in Early Dynastic times. It occurs, in fact, on a painted vase of the First Early Dynastic period. On its appearance in Anatolia at the end of the Third Millennium it is depicted in an entirely different style. Again it is the style of the rendering and not the subject-matter which is distinctive.

(*g*) *Boating Scenes.*

Leaving out of account the ships with a human prow which are used by the Sun-god, we find that boats appear on the seals in various functions. Sometimes the object of the journey is clear: the vessel is then used in hunting wild boar through the marshes.[4] At other times there is no means of knowing why the occupants have embarked.

[1] *Oriental Institute Communications*, No. 20, Fig. 32; Kh. V/141.

[2] Ur, 54; Newell, 41; Langdon, *Kish*, IV, Pl. 24, 2.

[3] Moortgat, *Die bildende Kunst des alten Orients und die Bergvölker* (Berlin, 1932).

[4] Heinrich, *Fara*, Pl. 65 *n*, *o*; Louvre, A–125.

SECTION III

THE SEALS OF THE SARGONID AGE

CHAPTER I. DEVELOPMENT AND SCOPE OF THE SARGONID STYLE

§ 16. THE DEVELOPMENT OF THE ANIMAL FRIEZE

THE ACCESSION of Sargon brought into predominance an element of the population which had hitherto had no decisive influence upon Mesopotamian civilisation. The language of the written documents, both official and private, was changed from Sumerian to Semitic Akkadian. In religious matters we distinguish less clearly, but it seems certain that the Sun-god gained prestige at the expense of the old chthonic deities. Nor did the arts remain unaffected, and there too the change matured with great rapidity. On the basis of existing traditions, embodied in the practice of the workshops, a new orientation was found within the first reign of the new dynasty, and subsequently little was added to this initial achievement.

As far as glyptic art is concerned we dispose of a number of dated monuments. Several cylinder seals of high officials name the king under whom they served. They prove beyond doubt that the profound change which separates the designs of Pl. XVII from those of Pl. XII was brought about in Sargon's lifetime. The magnificent seal of Pl. XVII *c* belonged to an officer of Shargalisharri. But a similar seal was in use in the household of Sargon's daughter.[1] The one and a half centuries which separated Sargon's death from that of his last descendant Shudurul show no evolution but merely the deadening effect of convention, though designs were enriched and refined in the south as late as the reign of Gudea, who held Lagash after the Guti had destroyed Sargon's dynasty.

There is a restricted number of cylinders which show the change in its early stages, and which we may therefore assign to an Early Akkadian style, though their actual date can differ but little from the most advanced types.[2] Nevertheless, they explain the transition from the style of Pl. XII and Pl. XIII to that of Pl. XVI and Pl. XVII.

[1] Ur 309.

[2] Published seals of the earliest Sargonid style include in addition to those figured in Pl. XVI: Ur, 167, 170–72; 225, 231; Philadelphia, 74; Louvre, T–83; V.A. 3178; Ward-Morgan, 42; De Clercq, 42, 44, 58 *bis*; *Recueil de Travaux*, XXXVIII (1916), Plate facing p. 166, Nos. 3, 4, 5. Several were found at Tell Asmar and Khafaje.

We may demonstrate this transitional style with Pl. XVI*a*. This seal belonged to Adda, major-domo of Enheduanna, a daughter of Sargon, whom the king had invested with the influential position of High Priestess of the Moon-god at Ur. Three seals are known to belong to members of her household. One of these[1] is of mature Sargonid design; the other two, and that of Adda in particular, show great uncertainty in style. The consistency of such seals as Pls. XII*a*; XIII and Text-figs. 20–23, which represent the best glyptic in use at the time of Sargon's accession, is lost in Pl. XVI*a*, and the new harmony of Pl. XVII still remains to be discovered. The "subject" of Adda's seal, the figures and their composition, do not differ from the late Early Dynastic seals of Pl. XII*b* and Text-figs. 20–23. But a disturbing element makes itself felt most markedly in the modelling of the figures.

The tendency to render the figures in relief was not new. We have, in fact, found it the main factor in the evolution of the style of the Third Early Dynastic period. But we have seen how that tendency was kept within bounds and how the linear character possessed by Early Dynastic glyptic, from the first, was never wholly abandoned. Compared with the older seals of Pl. X, those of Pl. XII seem to be worked in bold relief. Now, however, viewed from the vantage point of Sargon's age and with the seals of Pl. XVI as our standard, those last Early Dynastic seals seem amateurish attempts to express something which only the Akkadians entirely grasped, a conclusion which is not justified, since the aims of the Early Dynastic and Akkadian seal-cutters were in reality profoundly dissimilar.

The point at issue indeed exceeds mere technical procedure. In the displacement of mainly linear by wholly modelled figures we observe a change in attitude of mind. For the first time the artists' world of imaginative and decorative values has lost its autonomy. It is now subjected to the claim of verisimilitude.

This change is evidently fundamental. Considered formally early Sargonid glyptic may seem to continue in a direction already foreshadowed by the end of the preceding age. In reality there is a complete change in the mentality which determines artistic expression, and this explains why the ripest products of the new school do not merely differ from, but embody a negation of the principles which had been valid hitherto.

If we once more return to the question of modelling in relief, we must remember that it arose in the Third Early Dynastic period in the manner we have described in § 12 (p. 50), namely an elaboration of linear decoration. In Sargonid glyptic it abruptly becomes the vehicle of the expression of physical

[1] Ur, 309; the third seal of a servant of Enheduanna is Ur, 308.

reality, of muscular and skeletal structure (Pls. XVI *f*; XVII). But the old forms were not suited to the new purpose. The corporeality of the figures in Pl. XVI *a* reduces the traditional composition in which they appear to an absurdity. The same applies to composite monsters like the human-headed bull. In the curiously vital but dream-like designs of the Early Dynastic age the Scorpion-man (Pl. XV *j*), the lion-legged man, the human-faced lions and bulls move in a sympathetic medium; in the fairyland atmosphere of those friezes they are accepted without question. But to the Sargonid seal-cutter this multitude of monsters which he had inherited in the traditional repertoire was an embarrassment. He usually retained the Bull-man only; attempts to render the human-headed bull produced the unsatisfactory results of Pl. XVI *a*, *d* and Pl. XVII *j*; and the single Sargonid rendering, with all the new emphasis on muscles, of the man with two bulls' hindquarters, which we know from Pl. X *c*, is frankly ludicrous since the whole style of the representation aims at suggesting physical reality.[1]

The Bull-man alone could be adapted to the new world which he had henceforth to inhabit as companion of the naked and bearded hero. The hero, at first somewhat awkwardly brought down to the material plane (Pl. XVI *a*, *d*), soon assumed a new dignity and superhuman stature (Pls. XVI *f*; XVII), and this new heroic figure found an adequate partner in the equally powerful Bull-man whose semi-human character served as foil and added point to the more than human grandeur of his companion. Both remain, as in a previous age, the antagonists of wild beasts, but they are no longer absorbed into a chain of struggling figures. On the contrary, they are isolated, and the decorative continuity of the frieze is sacrificed in order to dramatise the representation of the single combat. This change also is in the direction of realism. The struggle between heroes and beasts is no longer treated as a pretext for the display of decorative ingenuity, but, on the contrary, all attention is concentrated on the conflict, which is a matter of life and death for those involved. The seal-cutters made a point of accentuating the fearful power of the combatants, and the merciless ferocity of the struggle. The traditional forms had to be modified to this end. The attitude of the lion, for instance, with body in profile and face seen from above, was at first taken over from the Early Dynastic repertoire (Pls. XII; XVI *a*). It is not in itself unrealistic, but the change of axis makes for an undulating silhouette which lacks power. The Sargonid seal-cutters replaced it by a simple profile, which in its unity of direction expresses the lion's dreadful bulk or steely force (Pl. XVI *d*, *f*). The vainly extended claws and the gasping jaws of the

[1] Ur, 323.

throttled beast serve to emphasise the heroic strength of his opponent (Pls. XVI *f*; XVII *a*, *g*).

The symmetrical group of one hero or Bull-man between two beasts, popular all through Early Dynastic times, but inacceptable as soon as its implications are taken in a realistic sense, is but rarely used on Akkadian seals of high quality (Pl. XVII *f*). The methods of depicting the single combat are, on the other hand, increasingly various. All kinds of attitudes are invented which stress the completeness of the beast's defeat (Pl. XVII *a*, *b*). We see that not only the design and selection of the single figures but also the rendering of their action are determined by a new point of view, which we have called, for want of a better word, realistic. It is true that neither actions nor actors find prototypes in observed reality. But the subject taken for granted, the Akkadian seal-cutter renders it as concretely as possible. Thus he is at pains to differentiate between the substance of muscles, bones and hairy parts of his creatures. Their encounters, improbable in themselves, are nevertheless rendered as true conflicts in which the forces of the combatants are strained to exhaustion. In fact, the realistic tendency or, if one prefers it, the love of the concrete of the Akkadian seal-cutters is well illustrated by some early seals in which they have overshot their mark by elaborating realistic touches to such an extent that they destroyed the main effect. In Pl. XVI *g*, for instance, we see the Bull-man reaching behind the lion to grasp the tail with his right hand while his left drives a dagger into the beast's chest, an excess of concrete detail which distracts instead of reinforcing the desired impression. It is the simpler version of Pl. XVI *f* which became the basis of Akkadian convention.

The postures are sometimes modified, as we have seen. There are also slight variations in the composition of the groups, where the Bull-man is occasionally replaced by a second anthropomorphic hero, while many designs may be considered as a mere reduplication, for purposes of symmetry, of a simple pair of combatants (Pl. XVII *a*, *b*, *c*, *i*, *j*). Sometimes animals replace —somewhat incongruously—both hero and Bull-man (Pl. XVI *h*).

Together with the changes in the rendering of the figures and the action, came a change in the composition which altered the entire nature of the seal designs. In this case again it might seem that Akkadian glyptic merely continued a trend noticeable towards the end of the Early Dynastic period. We have seen that the friezes of closely interwoven, and often intersecting, figures (Pl. XII *a*, *c*) showed in the latter part of the period a tendency to looseness, so that the figures appeared detached (Pl. XII *b*). We found that the increase in volume and relief of the figures as exemplified in Pl. XII *c* led to overcrowding and lack of clarity when the old formula was retained. The increased corporeality of the Akkadian figures left even the scheme of Pl. XII *b* unsatisfactory, as is evident in Pl. XVI *a, d, g*; in the last instance the seal-cutter has indeed resumed the old method of placing small figures in the open spaces—filling motives—a device which is certainly redundant in the new style. For the mass acquired by the individual figures, now that their details were no longer indicated by line-work but by modelling, required the counterbalance of a wider spacing and a larger area of free and neutral background round the figures. This was sometimes achieved by giving them strongly inclined axes instead of the almost vertical stance of the Third Early Dynastic period (Pl. XVI *b*), a method which further increased the verisimilitude of the action depicted. But as a rule the number of figures was lessened and the spacing widened, till the fine effect of Pl. XVI *f* was obtained. It should be remembered that this design is not complete; above the *couchant* antelope a space was left open to receive the inscription giving the name of the owner. If we imagine the cuneiform signs in their proper place it will be realised that the harmony of the composition is entirely due to the careful and deliberate spacing of even the smallest elements of the design; this is particularly clear in the space between lion and water-buffalo. The new style in this instance still applied the principle of an earlier age which required friezes of evenly divided and continuous pattern. Though rarely successful to this degree, the combination of new and traditional elements is, in fact, characteristic of early Akkadian glyptic.

The mature Sargonid style, however, discarded the continuous frieze as a scheme of composition. It favoured the very opposite, the heraldic group (Pl. XVII). And it is significant that of this new type of composition the central figure is the inscription, placed in its well-defined panel. Hitherto, in the frieze, the inscription had constituted the most refractory element of the design (Pls. X *i*; XII *b, c*; XIII *a, c, d*). Its introduction in Early Dynastic times had resulted, as we have seen, in makeshift solutions which aimed at glossing over its isolation amongst the figures, and at effecting a coherence with the rest of the frieze which could never, in the nature of things, be achieved.

The intense vitality and freshness of approach of the Akkadian seal-cutters show nowhere more clearly than in the unprecedented solution adopted, which was entirely to reverse the method of coping with the inscription in their designs. The issue was no longer shirked, as on Pl. XII, where the signs, enclosed on neither side, are made to look as much as possible like the small figures appearing below them. In Akkadian times, after a few uncertain attempts in the old manner (Pl. XVI *d*), the inscription was deliberately made into the central feature of the composition, framed in a panel and "supported" as if it were a shield by pairs of combatants derived from the frieze (Pl. XVII *a*, *c*). The failure to realise the heraldic character of the Akkadian friezes is responsible for the wrongly cut impressions of so many of the seals reproduced by archaeologists. It is true that the supporting pairs are not always strictly antithetical as in Pl. XVII *a*, *c*. Sometimes they differ in detail without thereby destroying the symmetry of the design; i.e. Pl. XVII *d* (wrongly cut). The commonest groups of supporters are the Bull-man fighting a lion and the nude hero attacking a water-buffalo.

It is clear that the fundamental principle of Early Dynastic composition, the production of a continuous frieze of textile design, has herewith been discarded. Occasionally we find a compromise like Pl. XVII *i*, where the kneeling figure bridges the gap of the two pairs of combatants flanking the (erased) panel on the opposite side of the cylinder. A similar continuity of design is achieved by the disposition of limbs in Pl. XVII *b*. But the purest examples of the new scheme of composition have a clearly defined limit at either side and are severely static (Pl. XVII *a*, *c*). It is, therefore, less well adapted to the use of a cylinder which may need to be impressed upon surfaces of varying length. The Akkadian seals show at their best in only one complete impression, since with less the design remains unfinished, and on a larger surface extraneous portions are appended; and these fragmentary impressions are not, as in the old continuous friezes, so closely interwoven with the rest as to produce one consistent pattern of indefinite length (see above, pp. 40 ff.). But the revolution in design accomplished in Sargon's reign was never undone and the principle of the continuous frieze never afterwards revived.

§ 17. THE FIGURES OF THE ANIMAL FRIEZE

Passing in review the reduced number of single figures which appear in Akkadian friezes, we shall begin by pointing out some features which distinguish the early transitional style of the dynasty from its mature manifestations.

We have already remarked that the lion appears at first with face seen from above but later in pure profile (Pl. XVI *a*, *e*); the Bull-man is at first shown in profile, but later always full-face, balancing his heroic partner

(Pl. XVI *f*). Sometimes on these early seals the Bull-man is depicted with the gatepost emblem (Pl. XVI *b*),[1] which belongs to the naked hero in his function as a protective spirit of buildings (p. 60). Whatever may be the relation between the Bull-man with this emblem and the Bull-man slayer of animals, there is no doubt that both are beneficial to man; the slayer of lions having first appeared, in fact, in the Second Early Dynastic period as a protector of the flocks. But Akkadian seals know also of a Bull-man who is an enemy of the Sun-god and is destroyed by him (Pl. XVIII *j*).[2] As in the case of the naked hero several personages seem to be represented in the same shape.

The human-headed bull is comparatively rare on later Akkadian seals and his mane is then rendered by an awkward convention which makes the neck appear as a set of ribbed conical tubes (Pl. XVII *j*). On the earlier seals he often wears a girth (Pl. XVI *a*, *d*). The water-buffalo makes its appearance in the mature Akkadian style. It then takes the place of the wild bull of the aurochs type as antagonist of the naked hero, while the Bull-man habitually fights a lion. This division into pairs was no doubt dictated by the wish to avoid an accumulation of two pairs of horns on one side of the heraldic group. The true bison is also occasionally depicted (Pl. XVII *h*). Sometimes a Bull-man or hero is incongruously displaced by a lion (Pl. XVI *h*).[3] Antelopes, goats or mountain-sheep, so common in Early Dynastic times, are occasionally to be found in the early Akkadian style when the friezes are not yet superseded (Pl. XVI *b*, *c*, *e*); or they are found as filling motives, especially underneath the inscribed panel (Pl. XVI *f*, *g*). In the same subordinate function we sometimes find divine or mythological figures which are derived from such scenes as those illustrated on Pls. XVIII–XXIII, and which remain unconnected with the rest of the design. Thus we see, in Pl. XVII *i*, the goddess of fertility or vegetation inserted underneath the inscribed panel, and the figure of Etana on the eagle (see p. 137, § 21 *g*) used to fill the space left over between the two pairs of "supporters" on the circumference of the cylinder. Sometimes old motives serve the same purpose; thus we once (A–75) find the space between the supporters filled by a figure of Imdugud attacking a buffalo in the manner shown in Pl. XIII *b*, *h*.

The most enigmatical figure of the Akkadian friezes is the nude hero. He is, with few exceptions, shown in full-face, and wears, when not entirely naked, a triple girdle only. Some more fully dressed figures occur

[1] So also De Clercq, 58 *bis*, and Ur, 232.

[2] Newell, 154; Philadelphia, 150; *Proceedings of the Society of Biblical Archaeology*, XIV (Plate), No. 5; Ur, 314; De Clercq, 181 *bis*; A–131; Ward, 193.

[3] So also Weber, 229, 230.

(Pl. XVII *d*),[1] which may represent the same personage, since they wear the upturned shoes with which the nude hero makes his first appearance in the Jemdet Nasr period. In addition we find an unclothed figure with a flat cap, which is in the more elaborate instances decorated with a zigzag pattern, and he, as we have stated, is always shown in profile (Pls. XVI *a*, *c*, *d*, *e*; XVII *f*, *j*). The relationship of these figures is quite unknown. Nor is it clear how many separate personages confront us in the guise of the naked hero shown in full-face.

We have seen that in Early Dynastic times the naked hero appears on the one hand as a slayer of animals, and on the other as a protective demon or spirit. As such he is portrayed with the gatepost emblem on an inscribed terracotta plaque which makes this interpretation certain.

The naked hero fulfils both functions also on Akkadian seals; holding the gatepost he often accompanies Ea (Pls. XVIII *k*; XXI *c*).[2] It is certainly likely that the attendant of Ea, the god of wisdom and magic, the friend of man, who saved Utanapishtim from the Flood by warning him of the gods' intention and teaching him how to build the ark, is the same as the figure appearing as "talim" on terracotta plaques protecting buildings against evil spirits. But the nude hero is often found without the gatepost emblem, and whether in those cases he represents Ea's servants, or the slayer of animals, or yet another or even several other figures, remains uncertain. In the first place we see him in conflict with his double (Pls. XVII *f*; XXI *h*). This reminds us of the group of wrestlers encountered on Early Dynastic seals (Pl. XI *d*, *l*) but with considerable divergences—nor do all Akkadian renderings conform to a given type. In Pl. XXI *h* Ea is present, but is as likely as not a mere filling like the goddess of fertility in Pl. XVII *i*. This last seal has a parallel,[3] where Ea, with another god reporting to him, is placed between the two antithetical groups of hero and buffalo. Here again the two pairs of fighters serve as "supporters" of the inscribed panel, and the group of Ea and his companion is used to cover the surface of the cylinder left bare by the heraldic group, exactly as Etana and the eagle do in Pl. XVII *i*, where there was even less need for such filling. The fact that not only Ea but other gods or motives are used in such cases invalidates the assumption of a connection between the naked hero as slayer of animals and the god Ea.

1 So also *Antiquaries Journal*, XIV, Pl. XLIII, 2; Newell, 96; *American Journal of Semitic Languages*, XLIV, No. 8; Ur, 249.

2 So also B.M. 89771; De Clercq, 83 *bis*; A–158; A–159; Philadelphia, 159; Brussels, 590.

3 Iraq Museum, 7379.

On other seals the two nude heroes are armed with daggers. Once (Text-fig. 29) they stand over a bird while Ea seems to climb a temple tower or a mountain. We know that Ea is only depicted in this attitude in one circumstance, namely when he assists in the liberation of a god from his mountain-grave (§ 19 (*g*), p. 105). Consequently the two struggling heroes do not here represent any specific persons, but merely symbolise the conflict which took place on that occasion. Besides, we know the protagonists in that struggle (Pls. XIX and XXIII), who never appear without their crowns of divinity. In Pl. XVII*f* two nude heroes struggle in the same position as the wrestlers on the Early Dynastic seals, and here again they use daggers in complete symmetry. This seems to be a combination of the Early Dynastic wrestler motive, without daggers, where the figures do not assume the shape of the nude hero (Pl. XI*d*, *l*) and the design of Text-fig. 29, an assumption which is the more probable since Pl. XVII*f* has no specific meaning but consists entirely of decorative groups derived from the Early Dynastic friezes.

Text-fig. 29. Ea, fighters, fisherman.

But we see in Text-fig. 29 a nude hero in yet another function, namely as a fisherman, and his association with water, especially in the hieratic form as two streams flowing from a round vessel, is quite common on seals of the Dynasty of Hammurabi and their Syrian derivatives. On Akkadian seals this occurs in the form of Pl. XVII*c*, where the hero waters the buffaloes which he is accustomed to destroy. But, again, the slayer of buffaloes may be a different person; on the other hand, a seal from Telloh[1] shows the hero standing between two vessels from which water streams, while he dominates with either hand a buffalo in the manner of Pl. XVI*f*. Here, at least, the water-spirit and the slayer of animals appear as a single being.[2]

[1] T–43.

[2] So also on a fine seal from Ur (*Antiquaries Journal*, XIV, Pl. XLII, 1), where the hero is throwing the bull at the moment when it drinks from a stream. One may well suspect a mythological significance, or at least that these groups of fighters suggest by analogy the destruction of the Bull of Heaven who causes drought (see quotations at the end of § 21 (*b*), p. 127). That would explain, not only the seal just mentioned, but also others as T–43, A–75 (conflict between bull and Imdugud), and in general the antagonism between the nude hero as water-spirit and the bulls, or the restraint put on the bulls in Pl. XVII *e*, *h* when they attack

And elsewhere[1] the wrestlers in the guise of the two nude heroes, without daggers, struggle above a water- and rock-border like that of Pl. XVII *c*. In Pl. XXIV *b*, finally, the nude hero punts a boat containing a bull-eared god with his semi-bovine suite; and there we notice that even the water is personified; the waves take the shape of the nude hero's face and their lapping at prow and stern is symbolised by his outstretched arms. Finally we see on yet another seal[2] the nude hero appear once as a fisherman, and once in an entirely unparalleled situation. He stands with uplifted arms which are grasped on either side by a Bull-man who plunges a dagger into his chest.

The conclusion which follows from this survey of the various situations in which the nude hero appears on Akkadian seals is surely this, that more than one person, or even natural forces, such as the water in Pl. XXIV *b*, may be given his form. It is therefore impossible to postulate that the same mythological figure is represented in all these instances, because the hero appears in functions which are mutually exclusive, either watering or killing buffaloes, victor or victim, or even in conflict with himself (Pls. XVII *f* and XXI *h*). These last instances aptly remind us of the fact that in decorative art the motives and themes may often detach themselves from their original meaning and seem to lead a life of their own, appearing wherever they fulfil an artistic requirement. If, for instance, the water- and rock-border of Pl. XVII *c* appears underneath a pair of wrestlers on a seal,[3] it does not necessarily connect them with the spirit of water who is sometimes represented by the nude hero, but merely demonstrates that the seal-cutter appreciated the beauty of the motive as an edge to his design. The influence of decorative conventions on motives is well illustrated by Pl. XXI *h*, where the figures are no longer presented in the attitude of the Early Dynastic wrestlers, which they assume on Pl. XVII *f*; instead, the upright figure stands in an attitude of Akkadian convention, derived from the heraldic group

vegetation, a design which is not unique. We might assume that the nude hero as servant of Ea gave rise to the invention of the hero with the water-pots, and that this leads, on the one hand, to an interpretation of the slaying of the bulls as a symbol of counteracting drought, and, on the other, to representations of his beneficial activities, as in Pl. XVII *c*. But since we can go no further than suspecting vague associations between, on the one hand, designs which are largely decorative in purpose and dependent on an old pictorial tradition, and on the other texts of which we have late versions and no authenticated illustrations, we have not included an argument on these lines. It would, moreover, largely duplicate that held in connection with Pl. XIII *h* on p. 72 above.

[1] T–34. [2] A–91. [3] T–34.

(Pls. XVI *f*; XVII *a*, *g*, *h–j*), and his antagonist's pose is an adaptation of the human form to the victim's attitude; compare the position of his legs with those of the buffalo in the normal group (Pl. XVI *f*).

The nude hero thus appears on Akkadian seals in the following six functions:

1. As a servant of Ea, holding the gatepost emblem. For this there are Early Dynastic antecedents, though in that period Ea is omitted. We may however assume that the protective spirit, known as a twin on later terracotta reliefs, and figured with the gatepost, is, in fact, the same as Ea's servant.

2. As slayer of lion or bull, buffalo or bison. This too continues an Early Dynastic tradition.

3. As a fisherman, found twice only,[1] and there is no means of connecting this type with any of the others or with the texts.

4. As a spirit of water, generally holding a round vessel from which two streams issue forth. This is rare in Akkadian times and common later, and may well be a comparatively late derivation of type 1. It will be discussed in § 26 (*e*), p. 165.

5. As a figure shown in conflict with his double, perhaps used to symbolise the notion of conflict in general (Text-fig. 29) but more likely without any other than decorative significance.

6. As a personification of natural forces, such as the water of Pl. XXIV *b*, a function which may underlie the designs of all or some of the other five groups without our being able to recognise it.[2]

We do not deny the possibility of more detailed explanations of some of the designs, but these must be so hypothetical that their usefulness becomes questionable. The following, for instance, is an apt comment on Pl. XVII *c*: "I think it is clear that we have before us not an ordinary scene from the life of Gilgamesh, but a mythic one. The vase is not the usual instrument from which animals are given a drink: it is meant for something peculiar, and often the water has been conceived of as the water of life. In that case

[1] Compare Legrain, *Archaic Seal Impressions*, pp. 302, 303, but there the fisherman seems to be human.

[2] Heidenreich, in his work quoted on p. 60, note 4, does not only treat all these functions of the nude hero as relating to one and the same person, but moreover connects with him "the dwarf" from seals of the Hammurabi period and the fighting gods of Louvre, S–471. His identification of the nude hero as Tammuz is untenable.

the bull can scarcely be other than a mythical representation of the earth, which we found at the gate of heaven."[1]

It is possible that this is indeed the significance attached by the ancients to that design. We, on the other hand, have noticed the original appearance of the nude hero and buffalo in older designs to which this explanation does not apply. We know that these figures were commonly used on contemporary seals in a purely decorative function, as "supporters" of an inscribed panel. Are we entitled to ascribe to their unusual appearance in Pl. XVII*c* so specialised a significance as that quoted? Or did artistic imagination and not religious symbolism play a part in this new conception? It is the continuous confrontation with this kind of problem which induces us to "stick to the purely phenomenal side" of the designs.[2]

§ 18. THE SCOPE AND INTERPRETATION OF SARGONID SEALS

Compared with the Early Dynastic period the age of Sargon produced but a small proportion of seals with merely decorative designs. Even those already discussed have as their central feature in most cases one piece of factual information, the name of the owner inscribed in a panel. There is no question of a decrease of aesthetic sensibility; the extraordinarily varied application of so austere a formula as the heraldic group proves the liveliness and force of Sargonid artistry. Nevertheless, the strong inclination towards the concrete which we have found to underlie the stylistic innovations of the period led to an efflorescence of designs depicting actuality as was never equalled either before or afterwards.

Occasionally a mythological subject or a scene from daily life had been engraved on an Early Dynastic seal. But when we compare one of these with an Akkadian treatment of the same subject (Pl. XV*j* with Pl. XIX*e, f*), the contrast is striking: the latter aims with singleness of purpose at precision and clearness of representation, qualities which had often been sacrificed in the earlier period for the sake of decorative effect.

Clarity was at all times a necessity of seal design, but variety of subject, singularity in concrete detail, now took the place of variety of composition. If the name of the owner was not inscribed, he was often depicted adoring a specific deity or bringing him or her sacrificial gifts. Frequent subjects

[1] A. J. Wensinck, "Tree and bird as cosmological symbols in Western Asia", in *Verhandelingen van de koninklijke Akademie van Wetenschappen*, Afd. Letterkunde, Amsterdam, 1921, p. 24.

[2] Wensinck, *loc. cit.* p. 37. See also above, p. 17, note 1.

were those cosmic events with which human life was intimately connected, not only because its sustenance depended upon them but also because the rise of the sun each morning, or the rebirth of vegetation after the deadening summer, possessed a symbolical value in relation to human life which the primitive mind is apt to experience as a real bond, almost as identity. It is natural that these cosmic happenings should have been pictured in their current mythological guise. The Sun-god was shown rising upon the mountains of the east; the god of fertility appeared after rescue from his mountain-grave. In all these cases care was taken to define the various actors with precision. The anonymity of the gods, usual in their rare appearances in Early Dynastic glyptic, is an exception on Sargonid seals. But the means of identification remained purely pictorial; the inscriptions stood in no relation to the design and did not name the gods. The standard-like design on the right of the Sun-god of Pl. XVIII *a* has been interpreted as a combination of the two signs with which the god's name is written.[1] This is highly improbable, since it also occurs in connection with other deities (Pl. XX *k*).[2] It occasionally appears on Early Dynastic seals, e.g. Pl. XIV *e*.[3] It has been thought[4] that it is the sign MUSH and consequently the name of the great serpent, and it happens to appear on our Pl. XXI *b* with the Snake-god. But there is no reason to attach greater importance to this occurrence than to the others, and the meaning of the sign thus remains problematical.

It is through their attributes, positions or actions that we must recognise the personalities involved, and it is only to be expected that we are not always competent to do so. Thus the admirable clarity of the artists no longer ensures a correct interpretation of their design.

It is impossible however to resign ourselves to desist from all attempts, however hazardous, to overcome our disability. For no other class of seals contains a greater variety of rare material than that of Sargon's age. In Early Dynastic times, as we have seen, the seal-cutters rarely told a story. During the Third Dynasty of Ur the scope of representation was narrowed to a single ritual act, and the reintroduction of numerous figures under the First Dynasty of Babylon does little to further our knowledge, since they are often ill-defined and rarely shown in any relation with each other. But the Akkadian seal designs embrace ritual and myth, daily life and religious beliefs. While by the end of the Early Dynastic period the seal-cutters had become confined to a groove, and were in the later age to be hampered by

1 Prinz, *Altorientalische Symbolik*, p. 79.
2 Ur, 270; As. 32/593; Philadelphia, 161; A–150.
3 Brett, 26; Heinrich, *Fara*, Pl. 56*i*.
4 Langdon, *Tammuz and Ishtar*, p. 120.

the limited outlook of a theocratic régime or harassed by an excessive demand for seals, they enjoyed, under Sargon's dynasty, freedom to explore new territory. Some subjects out of their limitless repertoire echo through the literature of later ages without ever again finding pictorial expression. Others reveal the trend of religious thought with a directness rarely to be found in the deliberate writings of the priests. It would be unthinkable for us not to attempt to tap this rich source of information, even though we lack the authority of textual comment.

For if the meaning of the Akkadian seals is no longer self-evident, there are indirect methods by which it may be discerned. It should be possible systematically to collect and compare the extant versions of a given subject, and thus to distinguish the accidental from the essential, and to elucidate obscure details by examining variations which may be complementary. We should, moreover, scan such texts as have come down to us with a view to relevant allusions.

It is, of course, with the first of these two steps that we are here particularly concerned. Hitherto almost all interpretations of seal designs have been based on one or two cylinders discussed in isolation. It is evident that such an approach can only be haphazard. Just as the literary form of certain myths has been preserved in more than one copy of the same text or even in more than one version, so certain myths have found pictorial expression on a number of seals in identical or slightly varying renderings, and again on others which show dissimilar versions. We must therefore first of all establish the pictorial equivalent of a standard text: next we must consider the variants as sources of additional information; and only then are we in a position to search the literary tradition for parallels with the pictured stories.

There are a number of texts referring to subjects dealt with by the seal-cutters of Sargon's age. These texts are later than the seals, but though this difference in age may be a source of error, it would be exceedingly unwise to deny the irrelevancy *a priori*. We already know that numerous religious usages and beliefs have come down from very ancient times, though we happen to know them only from late documents. If we refuse to countenance any combination, however prudent, of texts of the First Millennium B.C. with seals of the Third, we are destroying the only bridge between the literary and pictorial expression of Mesopotamian religion.

The results obtained by these comparisons seem, moreover, to justify the method. It is interesting that ritual texts rather than purely literary works supply parallels to the seal designs, and this circumstance should guide further research. Nor is it hard to explain. The literary form of a myth, even when it is rich in metaphor, retains nevertheless a more general character than the acts of a ritual. These acts possess, in fact, the same degree of definition as an image, and ritual thus uses symbolism in the same manner as pictorial art. It is for these reasons that the description of a ritual, or a commentary on it, supplies us more often with a clue to the Akkadian seal designs than the literary description of gods and events in the great epics of Babylonia.

Text-fig. 30. Impression from Tell Asmar: symposium of lion and ass.

I have only adduced in the following pages such quotations as seemed of indubitable relevance. It should be possible for those who have free access to the original texts to find a greater number of literary parallels for the designs, on the basis of the iconography established here. If the scenes are bound to become more comprehensible as a result of such research, the interpretation of the texts is equally certain to profit by a fuller utilisation of the illustrated encyclopaedia constituted by the Sargonid seals.

CHAPTER II. THE SUBJECTS OF THE SARGONID SEALS

§ 19. THE SUN-GOD

(*a*) *Introductory.*

A Sun-god is often depicted on Sargonid seals in accordance with that reorientation of religious devotion referred to at the beginning of the last chapter. He is characterised by rays issuing from his shoulders, by a saw with which, as supreme judge, he "cuts decisions"[1] and by his attitude with one foot upon a mountain. These three characteristics are used singly or in conjunction.

It is questionable whether we are confronted with the same deity each time a Sun-god appears on the seals. We shall not err if we label as "Shamash" the usual rendering of the rising sun in mythological guise (Pl. XVIII *a*, *b*). It is significant that this theme survives into the period of Shamash's greatest popularity, the First Babylonian Dynasty. The Sun-god as judge may also be called Shamash, according to the texts, and because of the imaginative connection existing between the defender of justice and the personification of a heavenly body in its unalterable course.

But presently we shall discuss a Sun-god involved in mythological proceedings in which Shamash was never a participant. It is therefore likely that these figures refer to other gods. The leaders of the pantheon, Marduk and Assur, are commonly equated with the sun, and such deities as Nergal and Ninurta possessed solar characteristics in later times, though their main spheres of action were death and war; and even this characterisation does not seem to reflect the original position but to be rather the outcome of a specialisation of functions which took place after Early Dynastic times. Both Nergal and Ninurta seem to have been aspects of that many-sided

[1] *Mitteilungen der Vorderasiatischen Gesellschaft*, IX, 234. The "saw" has been often called a key to the Gates of Heaven; the extensive literature on the subject is completely summarised by Dombart in *Journal of the Society of Oriental Research*, XII (Toronto, 1928), 1–24. His interpretations of seal designs are entirely fanciful and unmethodical. His own view is that the saw symbolises the first ray of the sun percolating through the crack between the two leaves of the Gates of Heaven when the sun appears behind them at the moment of sunrise. Divine symbols are, however, based on something more definite than a poetical simile; and we cannot explain the sun's attribute on the basis of one amongst the various scenes in which he appears. The oldest occurrence of the saw is, in fact, in the boat scene of Pl. XV *n*. Nor do the rays projecting from his shoulders resemble the saw. Note also that the ring, so common on monuments of the Hammurabi Dynasty whenever Shamash is depicted, does not occur in Akkadian times.

Sumerian deity who was first a personification of the generative force of nature. Whether this deity has in one or other of his specialised forms a solar aspect is by no means clear; we only observe that the chief figures in the later pantheon have a decidedly ambiguous character. They are warriors with solar qualities; but belong at the same time to the category of the "dying god". This incongruous combination of features is best explained as a result of historical syncretism. I do not refer to the excogitations of theologians, for these are concerned, on the whole, with harmonising lesser traits. A combination of essential but ultimately incompatible features, such as we find in Marduk and Assur, can only be explained as the result of a hardly conscious shifting of stress and change of meaning which religious tenets undergo when a body of foreign immigrants accepts certain beliefs inseparable from the new homeland, but at the same time modifies the significance of those alien concepts. In other words, the curiously heterogeneous character of the state gods of Mesopotamia may well result from an interpretation of Sumerian mythology in the terms of Semitic belief. In dealing with the fertility gods in § 20 (p. 110) we shall approach this problem from the opposite side.

The vision of the sun as an invincible protagonist entirely dominates the "Epic of Creation".[1] It is beyond doubt a peculiarly Semitic idea. It has been pointed out[2] that for the Semites especially, the victorious battle of the Sun-god is a part of "the dramatic conception which takes the place of natural law and sees everywhere strife between the cosmic and chaotic powers".

In the Epic of Creation the gods are threatened with destruction by the powers of chaos. The fearful host is led by Qingu, the active principle of anarchy, in contrast with Tiamat, the female and passive personification of primeval chaos, "mother of all", who is postulated as preceding and containing the matter of creation. Marduk alone amongst the gods dares to take up Tiamat's and Qingu's challenge, and in a heroic combat he vindicates cosmic order by destroying chaos. After this victory he is proclaimed "Lord of all", and creates the existing world by the dismembering of Tiamat's body; significantly enough man is formed of the substance of Qingu. The Epic ends with a description of the gods erecting Marduk's sanctuary in Babylon and reciting his fifty names.

The hero of the Epic of Creation played his part also in the New Year's

[1] Langdon, *The Babylonian Epic of Creation* (Oxford, 1923).

[2] Wensinck, "The Semitic New Year and the origin of Eschatology" (*Acta Orientalia*, I, 155–98, Leiden, 1922).

festival, which lasted twelve days and constituted the main event in the Babylonian religious year. A considerable part of its ritual is known and we even possess some commentaries explaining the meanings of symbolic acts. On a certain day the Epic of Creation was recited from beginning to end and part or all of it was moreover performed as a drama. On other days, however, Marduk's role was hardly compatible with the heroic and invincible warrior of the Epic. We hear that he was kept a captive in or among mountains which are in the nether-world and may be considered his tomb. Riot in the city followed his disappearance, a goddess descended into his grave, others forcibly liberated Marduk, who was brought back to life and the light of day, and finally reunited with the goddess in marriage. The texts which speak of these ceremonies date from the First Millennium B.C. We know of similar celebrations under Gudea and Idin Dagan when, however, the chief personage was not a Sun-god but the god of fertility known under the names of Abu, Tammuz, Ningirsu, Ningiszida and many others. It is quite possible that Assur and Marduk were originally aspects of the same deity; their ritual observances had, in any case, absorbed important parts of those which pertained to the dying and resurrected god of vegetation. These, then, are the facts which justify the surmise that the Semites, entering the country towards the middle of the Third Millennium B.C., and attaining to power under Sargon, not only introduced Shamash (whose name betrays his Semitic origin) but must also have imparted solar characteristics to the chthonic gods of the land of their adoption.

It is unlikely that the process was accompanied by any conscious speculation; nothing would be easier, in fact, than for such a change to pass unnoticed. The myth and beliefs connected with both species of divinity possessed sufficient features in common to enable the Semites to accept the native religion of Mesopotamia, but unconsciously to ascribe to their own solar deities the attributes applied by the Sumerians to their gods of the earth. The yearly death and revival of vegetation find a parallel in the decrease and increase of the sun's power through the cycle of the seasons, and even in his daily rising and setting. And the symbolic connection of the god's vicissitudes with human life and death is revealed in either case with equal clarity. Thus a change of interpretation, however slight, on the part of the Semites, would profoundly affect the mythological conceptions which appeared no doubt to them common to both communities.

I am aware of no other view which would explain the ascertained facts of Babylonian religion in the matter which interests us here. At the same time this hypothesis accounts for a number of otherwise inexplicable and conflicting activities of the Sun-god on Akkadian seals. It is for this reason that we have prefaced our treatment of the latter with a digression on the history of religion in Mesopotamia. But classification of the seals remains, of course, based on the subject-matter independent of our interpretation. We shall therefore in most cases speak of the Sun-god without using any of his distinctive names. Sometimes, however, the conventional figure can be shown to refer to Shamash, in others to Marduk. The accepted view that the latter was an obscure local deity until Babylon became the capital of an empire at the beginning of the Second Millennium B.C. seems untenable, in view of the Akkadian seals whereon a Sun-god appears in situations resembling in detail Marduk's performances in the Epic of Creation.[1]

(*b*) *Shamash Rising and Setting.*

The Sun-god is most commonly pictured on Sargonid seals at the moment of his rising. He is habitually shown with one foot placed on a mountain and grasping his saw or pear-shaped mace, or both, while twin attendants throw open the gates (Pl. XVIII *a*).

The seals thus illustrate an incantation:

> O Shamash on the foundation of heaven thou hast flamed forth,
> Thou hast unbarred the bright heavens,
> Thou hast opened the portals of the sky.[2]

The attendants generally wear the horned crown; sometimes they are bareheaded (Pl. XVIII *b*). The gate is at times crowned with lions (Pl. XVIII *a*),[3] and at others the doors pivot upon a lion. These figures may merely symbolise the sound made by the huge doors revolving on their pivot-stones, but they may also depict a true architectural feature commemorating a lion decoration of the temple doorposts. Gudea describes a new temple of Ningirsu as follows: "The doors of cedarwood, installed in the gateway, were like the god of thunder thundering in heaven; the bolt of the temple of Enninnu was

[1] Ravn has shown in *Acta Orientalia*, VII (Leiden, 1928), that the predominance of Marduk in official inscriptions did not coincide with the rise to power of Babylon under Hammurabi, but that it became noticeable under Ammiditana, about a century later. This alone would weaken the argument that Marduk's position in the pantheon is due to the importance of the city where he happened to be worshipped. This quasi-rational argument has been much abused, both by Egyptologists and Assyriologists, and is definitely disproved, as far as Marduk is concerned, by the Akkadian seals discussed here. It is possible that these derive from a region where the theology of Eridu was prevalent, but we shall supply reasons why Marduk may have appealed particularly to the Semites.

[2] King, *Babylonian Mythology and Religion*, p. 32.

[3] B.M. 89110; A–139.

like a savage dog; the pivots were like a lion (Price: groaned like a lion)...on the... placed above the doors he caused a young lion and a young panther to dwell."[1]

The scene of the sunrise at the gate must have resembled so closely the manner in which the statue of Shamash was displayed in the temple by the opening of the sanctuary doors, that we need not be surprised to find the god occasionally pictured as if enthroned (Pl. XVIII *b*);[2] sometimes the gate is omitted (Pl. XVIII *e*), at others the god is shown standing on the level ground. These are mostly abbreviated renderings of the usual scene. Sometimes the attributes are omitted (Text-fig. 31); the god is always shown ideoplastically in profile, but is supposed to be advancing towards us through the opened gate.

Text-fig. 31. Seal of Lugalushumgal, vassal of Shargalisharri of Akkad.

In a few instances Shamash is depicted with mountains and gate while judging evildoers or receiving adoration or offerings.[3] The accessories of the sunrise then serve merely to characterise the god. Whether the tree which occasionally appears on seals (Pl. XVIII *c*)[4] is a mere filling motive or betrays a connection between the Sun-god and the life of plants or the earth, in the sense discussed in § 14 *b* (p. 67), remains uncertain.

Once the Sun-god is shown rising between two human-headed bulls;[5] he leans with his arms upon them instead of stepping forward. This unusual attitude recurs in a few more instances (Pl. XVIII *g*).[6] In the example illustrated his rays end in stars, which suggests that the unusual attitude indicates that the sun was setting, not rising.

The seal of Pl. XVIII *g* has several exceptional features. The doors are

[1] Thureau-Dangin, *Sum. und Akkad. Königsinschrifte*, pp. 118 f., col. 26, lines 20 ff., first quoted in this connection by Heuzey, *Revue d'Assyriologie*, IX (1912).

[2] A–145 may represent a wickerwork seat as is often carved in Early Dynastic statuary, though among seal designs the nearest parallel are the piles of corn upon which the goddess of vegetation is enthroned (Pl. XX *j*, *k*).

[3] A–146; Philadelphia, 185, 186; Kish, 1930–112.

[4] Guimet, 27; Philadelphia, 188; V.A. 4221.

[5] *Revue d'Assyriologie*, XXVIII (1931), 44, No. 11.

[6] T–83; Bibliothèque Nationale, 71; Ur, 227 (Pl. XX *h*), unless the god of Pl. XIX *a–d* is figured there.

crowned with the foreparts of lions; the Sun-god is shown full-face; and the guardians of the gate seem to hold between them a feathered monster with the feet of a bird of prey whom we shall discuss in connection with the liberation of the god from his mountain-grave.[1] Though the general design of the seal belongs to a class which most certainly represents Shamash, we find in the captive monster a feature from the cycle of the dying god. And in the case of Pl. XX*h* it is impossible to decide whether the god emerging from the mountain is the Sun-god of the seals here discussed, the liberated Sun-god of Pl. XIX*a*, or the resuscitated god of fertility of Pl. XXI*a*. Nor is this uncertainty a serious matter, since all three conceptions reflect an identical religious experience and the Ancients would probably not have understood our wish to distinguish between them.

(*c*) *The Sun-god Militant.*

When the Sun-god is engaged in a conflict, his opponent is either an anthropomorphic god, a Bull-man or a composite monster with a human body and a lion's paws, mouth or head.

The Sun-god's weapons are mace or dagger (Pl. XVIII*h*, *i*, *j*); he is often shown pulling up his adversary's head by the beard so as to bare his throat. The human-shaped victim crowned as a god has never any attributes which would enable us to identify him. He is often seen collapsing upon a mountain, in a manner which reminds one of the scenes depicting the liberation of the god from his mountain-grave (Pl. XIX). Though it is possible that the Sun-god's duel merely reflects that "dramatic conception" which considers the break of each new day as a victory over the powers of darkness, the alternative, that the Sun-god appears in scenes connected with the cycle of the "dying god", cannot *a priori* be excluded.

When the adversary is a Bull-man he usually holds a broken mace (Pl. XVIII*j*).[2] On an Early Dynastic macehead,[3] and later on seals of the First Babylonian Dynasty, a human-headed bull is shown as adjunct of the Sun-god, an iconographical function often assumed by vanquished adversaries, but there is no representation of a conflict between the Sun-god and a human-headed bull, and whether Bull-man and human-headed bull are interchangeable in this context remains to be seen.

[1] A similar monster is held captive by two attendants on B.M. 89746 (Cullimore, *Oriental Cylinders*, Pl. 31, No. 166).

[2] De Clercq, 181 *bis*; Ur, 314; *Proceedings of the Society of Biblical Archaeology*, XIV, Pl. 5; A–142. On Newell, 154 and Qe, 5 the maces are there but not actually held by the Bull-man. On Philadelphia, 150, there seems to be no mace.

[3] Woolley, *Royal Cemetery*, Pl. 183.

The third type of antagonist, the monster with leonine mouth and paws (Pl. XVIII *h*), seems to have a female body.[1] It is moreover never shown with a mane, and thus reminds one of the female demons of illness, such as Lamashtu, in the numerous incantation texts of later times. It is once brought for judgment before Shamash enthroned.[2] There a minor deity who holds it captive has also rays issuing from his shoulders, and it seems therefore that the Sun-god's attendants, such as the one carrying the limp body in Pl. XVIII *d*, could also be distinguished by rays.

To return to the foes of the Sun-god, the introduction of later texts may not justify us in interpreting the leonine monster as a demon of sickness, especially as it would separate it rather markedly from the other persons of these seals, who definitely belong to mythology. If we place the third adversary in the same category, we may then refer to the myth of Labbu (the "raging one", or the lion), who is defeated by Ninurta, the warlike aspect of the pre-Sargonid god of fertility. That god appears, indeed, in Pl. XX *e* (left) with a trophy, which may well be the monster's skin; note particularly the claws. This comparison brings us once more to the problem of a possible merging of the Sun-god of the Semites and the earlier chthonic god of Sumer.

On the other hand, the homogeneity of mythological representations may be disturbed in Pl. XVIII *d* by the group on the right, where a winged god with bird's talons subdues three human beings. This group occurs once more,[3] but not with any variants which might elucidate its nature. Whether it is indeed a mythological theme, perhaps referring to Zu and connected with such scenes as Pl. XVIII *g*, or whether on the other hand the winged figure is a bringer of sickness as is probably the case with a similar figure on later seals (see § 27*g*, p. 174), remains uncertain. The connection with the lion-headed demon is established by the other cylinder, where the group of Pl. XVIII *d* appears with the demon and the dragons of the Weather-god; but we shall discuss the non-mythological aspects of these figures presently, since there are no Akkadian texts to prove the existence of the elaborate demonology of later times.

(*d*) *The Sun-god worshipped by other Gods.*

Some seals show the Sun-god being adored by fellow-divinities (Pl. XVIII *f*).[4] In this and several other instances a small attendant appears behind the throne, the shortness of whose stature being shown to be intentional

[1] Newell, 154. [3] Ward, 300 *a*. [3] Ward, 130 = V.A. 611.

[4] As. 32/594; Bibliothèque Nationale, 72; T–95; Philadelphia, 184.

by the two lines drawn above him in more than one example, a method derived from Early Dynastic seals like those of Pl. XII, but meaningless on mature Sargonid seals; perhaps he embodies a deified human or a minor deity.[1]

It is possible that the Sun-god thus adored is Shamash. He may, however, be Marduk, who was reckoned in later times as Enlil's successor to the kingship of the gods. For, contrary to accepted opinion, it seems certain that Marduk appears on Akkadian seals.

(*e*) *Marduk before Ea.*

We have two cylinder seals which show a Sun-god doing homage to Ea. There is no figure in the Babylonian pantheon which would fit this situation excepting Marduk. Ninurta and Nergal are sons of Enlil, Shamash is the son of Sin. But in Pl. XVIII *k* we see a Sun-god worshipping the god of wisdom and of water "who caused his secret chamber to be founded in the primeval ocean", as the Epic of Creation describes it. In this chamber, around which the "waters of the deep" are flowing, a god is seated amid emblematic streams and fishes (here drawn mouth downward), Ea's customary attributes. In front of Ea's "chamber" we see a Sun-god using the gesture which may convey adoration or merely speech. In any case it is the attitude in which inferiors, such as priests, worshippers or minor gods, appear in front of the gods on a large number of contemporary cylinders, and there can be no doubt that the seal-cutter was here describing a hierarchy in which Ea stood above the Sun-god. The latter is explicitly identified, by the rays and by his attitude. The mountain which he climbs is crowned by the gate of heaven through which he habitually appears. Another Sargonid seal[2] is more conventional and therefore strengthens our argument. It shows Ea in his "chamber" summarily drawn but explicitly identified by streams of water and by a plant, the famous "Kishkanu tree". An attendant opens the door of his chamber to admit two gods, drawn in the convention of the adoration scene; the first of the two, however, has rays issuing from his shoulders. The existence, in Akkadian times, of a Sun-god who recognised the authority of a Water-god is thus well attested. The most natural explanation is that the hero of the Epic of Creation, to whom alone, in the whole of

[1] It is interesting to note that the seal-cutter of Bibliothèque Nationale, 72, made two mistakes which show that he did not understand the scene which he was probably copying. He turned round the little attendant so that he appears, incongruously, to close the row of adoring deities. And he added fishes to the rays which characterise the god who is worshipped, and who thus appears with attributes of Ea as well as of the Sun-god.

[2] De Clercq, 143.

Babylonian mythology, this relationship applies, namely Marduk, the son of Ea, was already worshipped in the time of Sargon of Akkad. In contrast with many other genealogies of gods, the relationship of Ea and Marduk was not an empty formula. Not only in the Epic of Creation, but also in the widely used incantations for curing the sick, Marduk refers to his father for advice. It is true that these texts are, like the others, much later than our seals, but there is no reason to assume that they were invented at the time when our copies were written down. In any case, we cannot ignore the coincidence that one of the few relationships between gods which was made an outstanding feature in several classes of literature was also illustrated by the seal-cutters.

Our identification of the Sun-god with Marduk in Pl. XVIII *k* finds support from the group on the left half of that illustration. It is perhaps a little difficult to account for the crouching deity with the lion, though in all likelihood he is Ninurta, often symbolised by the lion and known to have preceded Marduk's son Nabo as the liberator of his father from the mountain-grave. But the double wings between which the Sun-god is shown to appear can be explained. The obscurity of this motive is excusable, since it represents chaos itself, Tiamat. In one of the hymns Marduk is called:

> . . . the lord who dwells at the New Year's festival in the midst of Tiamat,[1]

and the dramatic performances of the New Year merely re-enacted what had happened on the first New Year's day of all, at the creation of the world.

The emergence of the Sun-god, rather conspicuously bearing his scimitar-shaped saw, is also in accordance with the text, for the Epic states that, after killing Tiamat:

> The Lord rested beholding the cadaver;
> As he divided the monster, devising cunning things,
> He split her into two parts, like an oyster.[2]

As it happens we have conclusive proof that the Ancients could symbolise this cutting-up of Tiamat by the two wings of Pl. XVIII *k*. For a commentary on the New Year ritual explains one act in the following terms:

> The pigeon which is thrown is Tiamat. It is thrown and cut into two halves.[3]

Thus our seals leave no doubt but that in some parts at least of Babylonia, and possibly under the influence of Eridu, the theology reflected in the Epic of Creation had become well established in the Third Millennium B.C.

[1] Ebeling, *Tod und Leben*, p. 25, Rs. I, 4. [2] Langdon, *Epic of Creation*, IV, 135–7.
[3] Ebeling, *Tod und Leben*, p. 33; Zimmern, *Zum Bab. Neujahrsfest*, II, 49.

(*f*) *The Burning of Qingu.*

There is yet another group of cylinders which seems to illustrate an exploit of Marduk. In the Epic of Creation one of the god's most formidable opponents is Qingu, the male complement of Tiamat. In the version preserved to us his throat is cut, but in the ritual there are indications of the burning of Qingu. We read the following commentary:

> The fire which blazes before Belit; the sheep which is put upon the oven, which the flames destroy; that is Qingu as he is burned by fire.[1]

The following comment must evidently be understood in this context:

> Firebrands which one lights from the brazier; they are the merciless arrows from the quiver of Marduk.[2]

A scene which recalls this episode is depicted on Pl. XVIII*j*. The victorious god wields a three-tongued weapon, probably a firebrand or a representation of lightning. The victim collapses upon a mountain, burning, and a kneeling man blows the flames brighter through a tube.[3] The victor in our plate bears no distinguishing marks, but in other instances he is shown with the flames characteristic of the Sun-god. These sometimes issue not only from his shoulders but also from his body or legs;[4] there is therefore a possibility that here is a Fire-god and not the Sun-god. But this particular ambiguity suits Marduk very well, for it reflects characteristics which belong to him according to the written records. The same text which identifies Marduk with Shamash calls him also "Lord of the Firebrand",[5] and a commentary once speaks explicitly in these words:

> The fire which is lighted; that is Marduk,[6]

and the Epic of Creation itself at least once identifies Marduk with Gibil, the

[1] Zimmern, *Zum Bab. Neujahrsfest*, I, 131.

[2] Langdon, *Epic of Creation*, p. 30; Ebeling, *Tod und Leben*, p. 36.

[3] So also De Clercq, 176.

[4] De Clercq, 180 *bis*, and in the same style *Aegyptus*, VIII (Dec. 1927), 274, No. Turin 23, where a god covered with flames destroys a kneeling adversary with a mace, aided by an assistant. A–141; A–143; Bibliothèque Nationale, 69; V.A. 2572 (Weber, 359). In the last seal the attacker uses a mace and not a firebrand; this is also the case in A–141, where moreover a burning figure is pictured which might be considered as a Fire-god assisting the protagonist, but is more likely the victim, Qingu, burning after he has been felled by the god's mace on the mountain, since the burning figure is without a crown, and in most scenes of combat the winning party is grasping the crown of the loser, presumably to pull it off.

[5] *Revue d'Assyriologie*, VII, 32, 40, 46, 48.

[6] Zimmern, *Zum Bab. Neujahrsfest*, I, 130.

god of fire.[1] Here again, as in the case of a Sun-god worshipping Ea, we find on the Akkadian seals and in the literature an unusual combination of features in the person of one god, which makes it highly probable that both sources refer to the same divinity, that is, to Marduk.

On all the seals where the burning of Qingu is depicted other pairs of combatants occur. It is always a moot point whether the groups of figures appearing side by side on a seal are really related unless they take part in one continuous scene or action. But it is at least probable that the seal-cutters, remembering that Qingu had arrayed the powers of chaos against Marduk, placed the subsidiary pairs of antagonists to represent the warring hosts.

(*g*) *The Liberation of the Sun-god from his Mountain-Grave.*

On the seals so far discussed the Sun-god has appeared as invincible hero. In another group he is shown in a more passive role. He is still the main actor in the drama but inimical powers have temporarily obtained the upper hand so that he has become dependent for life and liberty upon others who must bring him back to the light of day. We have references to the annual performance of his passion play at the New Year which go as far back as Gudea, or, in other words, almost back to the Dynasty of Sargon of Akkad. Lagash and Larsa, in the south of the Plain of the Two Rivers, maintained pre-Sargonid beliefs in comparative purity over a long period. The dying god, to whom the texts refer, was at first a chthonic deity, connected with the produce of the earth and the flocks. But on the Sargonid seals to be discussed in this section, the god who is liberated combines certain features of this older type of deity with those of a Sun-god, and we have already shown that this is probably the result of the increasing predominance in the country of the Semitic Akkadians.

Pl. XIX*a* shows us the final scene of the drama with all the actors assembled. In the centre a god emerges from a mountain; he holds the Sun-god's saw, and rays spring from his shoulders; but the tree which sprouts forth from the fateful hill proves clearly that the life of nature is affected by the occurrence. For all the stage properties in this scene convey some definite information.

The conflict which preceded the god's resuscitation is depicted on the seals

[1] Langdon, *Epic of Creation,* VII, line 91. The others quoted in the Index A, under Gibil, are less conclusive, especially the often repeated boast of Qingu to his army of monsters that they will quench the Fire-god, and need refer only to the terrific heat or poison of their breath. But see also *ibid.* p. 92, note 5.

reproduced below. The large cylinder which we are describing at the moment merely shows all those who took part in it, and it is interesting to note that it combines, without confusing them, two groups of gods which appear separately on the other seals. On the right stands Ea with his Janus-headed follower, and a bird whose attitude makes clear its connection with the liberation of the god. The part which these three figures played in the drama is shown in detail on a large group of seals of which Pl. XXIII *a–i* give examples and which we shall presently discuss (§ 21 (*f*), p. 132). Suffice it to say here that they are concerned with reducing to impotence an adversary symbolised in our seal by the bird which Ea controls. In the whole of Babylonian glyptic it is only in this connection that Ea, Marduk's father, sets his foot upon a mountain; Shamash appears normally in such a pose, above the eastern hills where the sun rises daily, but the mountain upon which Ea plants his foot is the grave of his son. Usmu, the god with two faces, is Ea's usual attendant.

The figures on the left side of the mountain are those who take an active part in the god's liberation, their action being expressed in Pl. XIX *b–d*. Similarly, we find in the ritual of the New Year's festival a god and a goddess labouring on behalf of the wounded and imprisoned god. The seal-cutters have been at pains to show that the goddess is no mere spectator; in Pl. XIX *b* she holds the victim's foot, in the seal next to it his hair, in that on the right his crown. In three instances (Pl. XIX *a–c*) she is unequivocally characterised as a goddess of vegetation. If the wings in the large seal are unparalleled, the "rays" projecting from her shoulders appear on closer scrutiny to end in leaves or perhaps fruit, while she carries a cluster of dates like that carved upon a sculptured vase-fragment of Entemena portraying a goddess of fertility.[1] We shall presently discuss Pls. XX *g* and XXI *a*, where this goddess is shown at the same mountain as in Pl. XIX *a*.

The presence of the Mother-Goddess, Tammuz' lover, in these scenes confirms our interpretation of the tree present in Pl. XIX *a* as a symbol of the revival of vegetation which follows the god's emergence from the nether-world, and both most definitely connect the scene on that cylinder with the cycle of the Dying God. In a similar way plants sprout from the mountains upon which Fertility-gods are enthroned (Pl. XX *d, i*).

The male protagonist on behalf of the imprisoned god is shown on the left of the large seal with two attributes, a lion and a bow.[2] The former has become changed, like the dragon of St George, from adversary to adjunct. With a

[1] *Iraq*, I, Pl. V *h*.

[2] The long hair of this god is not so exceptional as has been supposed (*Reallexikon der Vorgeschichte*, VIII, col. 209). See, for instance, our Pl. XX *c*.

lack of logic frequent in religious art the god is shown wearing as a trophy a lion's skin, the tail of which can be seen falling down behind him. In Pl. XX*e* the details are clearer. There too we see a well-designed club, which explains the staff held by the god of Pl. XIX*a*. The latter is thus certainly the same person as the Herculean figure on the smaller seal, shown by the plants projecting from his shoulders to be a form of the Sumerian god of fertility.

In Pl. XIX*c* this god, characterised by the bow, is shown in the act of destroying an enemy upon the mountain from which the captive god is soon to be set free. This adversary is represented in Pl. XIX*a* by the bird of prey, in accordance with the ritual of the New Year's festival in which references to the defeat of the storm-bird Zu abound; we shall discuss these in connection with a group of seals where the enemy is indeed depicted with bird-like features or with a bird of prey as emblem (§ 21 (*f*), p. 132). A striking iconographical connection between that group and those we are discussing here is provided on Pl. XXIII*f*, where the bird of prey is driven off the mountain-grave of the Dying God by the warrior with the bow of Pl. XIX*a*, *c*. In Pl. XIX*b* the champion carries no weapons but is identified by the lion-headed eagle Imdugud who assists him. For Imdugud is the best known symbol of the Fertility-god in his warlike aspect, Ningirsu, or, later, Ninurta. The lion-skin also suits Ninurta, since the myth of Labbu, describing him as the conqueror of a leonine monster, fully accounts for such a trophy. In later times it was Nabu who liberated his father Marduk; but Nabu is sometimes significantly called Abu—"The Lord of Vegetation"—a title of Ninurta,[1] and the king who acted the chief part throughout the New Year's festival at Babylon was styled "Ninurta who avenged his father".[2] Thus there is full agreement between the *dramatis personae* of the ritual drama in later times and the personages of Pl. XIX*a*. It only remains to account for the small bull who crouches below the figure of Ea. This is not among the god's customary attributes. The only other figure in the design with which it may be connected is the god emerging from the mountain. That would suit Marduk, the ideograms of whose name may be interpreted "young bull of the sun".[3] The meaning of the signs with which Marduk's name is written suggest that he was originally perhaps more closely connected with the sun than most other Sumerian deities. This peculiarity would make him exceptionally congenial to the Semites, and the fact that Marduk became the centre of the syncretistic theology which followed their assumption of power in Mesopotamia would

[1] Langdon, *Tammuz and Ishtar*, p. 8, note.
[2] Ebeling, *Tod und Leben*, p. 36, line 20.
[3] Ebeling in *Pauly-Wissowa*, Vol. XIV, II, 1669.

thus find an explanation, which his association with the city of Babylon is in no way sufficient to supply.

(*h*) *The Sun-god in his Boat.*

The Sun-god, as we saw, appeared in Early Dynastic times in one scene only, and that theme is retained by the Akkadian seal-cutters (Pl. XIX*e*, *f*). But it is no doubt because it reflects a pre-Sargonid tradition (Pl. XV*j*, *n*) that the representations of the Sun-god in his boat differ so markedly in character from the scenes just described. In most of these the god was actively involved, either as a victorious warrior or as judge, or at least as a figure whose capture gave rise to fierce combats. But the boating scenes possess an idyllic character, where the divinity is seen steering his animated vessel with an oar across the heavenly or subterranean waters. It might be thought, on the strength of Pl. XIX*e*, that the human-faced quadruped represented an element of strife since it is tied to the prow of the boat. But this need not denote capture. On the contrary we see it in Pl. XIX*f* straining on a leash and guided by a stick like any ox or ass which was taken from farm to field. For it is tempting to connect it with the plough which the Sun-god is holding so carefully in the lowest illustration and which is, as we already know, together with the quadruped and the pot, an indispensable feature of the scene (see § 14 (*b*), p. 67). The vessels may well contain the seeds, if we really believe the Sun-god to be on a journey to some field where ploughing and sowing are to be undertaken (Pls. XX*a*; XI*j*), in accordance with an incantation of which unfortunately all but the title is lost:

> The astral Ploughman has yoked in the Plain of Heaven the seed-sowing plough.[1]

We have seen, however, that purely astral associations seem to be irrelevant at this period (p. 68).

The bird which swoops down in Pl. XX*a* and the scorpion which is held by or forms the hand of the foremost god recur in the Early Dynastic renderings of this scene and also in connection with the Sun-god in his boat as we have noted;[2] and the dragon with the worm-like body, who either draws the plough with the lion in Pl. XX*a* or serves as shaft, recalls such designs as the plough in Pl. XV*n*;[3] and in one instance[4] the quadruped has the dragon's head of Pl. XX*a*, while it carries a bucket round its neck and is guided exactly as in Pl. XIX*f*. The god in the boat is seated upon a bird-shaped

[1] Gadd in *Myth and Ritual*, edited by S. H. Hook, p. 43.
[2] See above, p. 70. [3] So also Kh. II/276. [4] As. 31/25.

throne like the goddess in Pl. XIX*f*. All these cross-references suggest that a relation between the ploughing scene and that of the Sun-god in his boat is very probable.

This connection falls into line with a number of other traits which connect the boating scene with plant life. Plants are, in fact, frequently figured in connection with it, appearing close to the boat or carried behind it,[1] or the boat's stern may end in a branch.[2] This adds significance to the appearance of the goddess of vegetation in Pl. XIX*e*, which can hardly be considered a filling motive as it is in Pl. XVII *i*, since another seal shows two gods carrying branches in a corresponding position. Moreover, a goddess recurs in Pl. XIX*f*; though there she has no distinctive attributes, the throne recalls that of Bau on a statue found at Ur.[3] The snake's head in which the boat's stern often ends also suggests an intimate relationship with the earth and its fertility.

How are we to interpret these chthonic connections? Do they merely hint at the influence which the heavenly body exercises on the growth of vegetation? The plough may stand for a constellation, and on some Early Dynastic seals moon and stars are figured above the boat. Is it, then, the intention only to represent the sun's journey along the sky? That explanation does not account for the explicit and manifold symbols referring to the earth and its fertility. It is possible that the scenes refer to fields and vegetation which were projected in heaven, as the incantation which we have mentioned speaks of an astral ploughman and a heavenly plough. But just because such speculations postulate "a pattern laid up in heaven", we are unable to distinguish to which of the two spheres a given scene may refer. For the interpretation of the boating scene the question is this, whether it merely represents a mythological view as to the sun's daily journey through heaven, or reflects some belief in a direct and intimate connection between the sun's action and the success of man's labour in the field.

Both points of view are combined in a third and, to my mind, most probable explanation of the boating scene, based on beliefs which occur in Egypt as well as among the Hittites,[4] namely that the sun passes through the nether-world during the night. The contact apparently established between

[1] Sidney Smith, *Historical Texts*, Frontispiece, Fig. 4; As. 32/50 (*Iraq*, I, Pl. III *e*), where a god carries in each hand an ear of corn behind the boat; on Kh. III/279 (Early Dynastic) the man-shaped prow holds branches in its hands.

[2] As. 32/50 (see preceding note).

[3] *Antiquaries Journal*, VI, Pl. LI *a*, *b*.

[4] Götze, "Kleinasien" (Iwan Müller's *Handbuch der Klass. Altertumswissenschaft*, III, I, 3, p. 130).

sun and earth each evening in the west, to be broken each morning in the east, would create at the same time a connection with sprouting plant life which the usual equation of night, earth and death would reinforce and which may have found mythological expression in texts which are lost and in seal designs which we are at a loss to explain.[1]

Whatever may be the correct interpretation of the boating scene, the combination which it exemplifies between the Sun-god's voyage and the produce of the earth is thrown into strong relief by the total absence of such association in all the other seal designs where the Sun-god appears. All of these are Akkadian inventions, but the boating scene was composed in Early Dynastic times, complete with all the essential details of the later renderings. This divergence from the truly Akkadian representations of the Sun-god, such as Shamash rising or sitting in judgment or Ninurta defeating antagonists, can hardly be a coincidence. It is more likely that we touch here upon the very point in which the Sumerian conception of the Sun-god differed from that of the Akkadians. It seems that the Sumerian Sun-god was closely allied to the gods which we are about to discuss, those which personify the generative force of nature. It is this intimate relation with the earth and its fertility which seems to have been for the Sumerians a prerequisite of divinity, while with the Semites it occupied a secondary place.

§ 20. THE GODS OF FERTILITY

(*a*) *Introductory*.

If the Sargonid cylinders represented several deities in the single guise of a Sun-god, they seem, on the contrary, to have hidden the essential unity of the gods of fertility under a variety of divergent shapes. Our method requires us to follow the seal-cutters in their distinction of Snake-gods, Dragon-gods, gods of vegetation and so on, but we should little comprehend the religious background of the seal designs if this multiplicity were to be accepted at its face value.

Even when dealing with the Uruk period (§ 5, p. 17) we had recourse to these gods and their symbols. Their recognition was, of necessity, based on later, historical, material, texts in the first place, and in addition to these the results of recent excavations,[2] the analysis of pictorial and partly inscribed monuments such as ornamental maceheads,[3] and so on. Thus several distinct

[1] The plants drawn in or carried in front of or behind the Sun-god's boat would then equal the "golden bough" which Aeneus required to cross the Styx. See below, p. 136.

[2] *Oriental Institute Communications*, No. 17, pp. 47 ff.

[3] *Miscellanea Orientalia Antonio Deimel dedicata* (Roma, 1935), pp. 105 ff.

but converging chains of evidence have suggested that the Sumerians, far from perceiving nature in the diffused manner of animism, reduced it to the manifestation of a few great powers, of whom it is unlikely that all are known to us. It is, however, certain that those whom we call gods of fertility were considered of the first importance. The designation is more convenient than correct, for the Great Mother-Goddess and her male counterpart, often considered as her son and paramour, personified the generative force of nature as the most striking manifestation of life.

There was *a priori* much to be said for the assumption that one single form of religion underlies all early Mesopotamian beliefs and that local differences were of a subsidiary nature. For we know from the distribution of Al 'Ubaid pottery and the remains which go with it, that the Plain of the Two Rivers was first colonised by settlers from the Iranian Highlands who were in possession of a homogeneous civilisation. It is impossible to indicate which of the divine names goes back to the original inhabitants of the country. The earliest texts, of Early Dynastic times, already mention several designations. I have tried to show elsewhere that the usual assumption that these denote separate deities fails to explain certain facts. Even if we are unable to distinguish one original name among the many which were current, we may at least point to the fact that many of these names are epithets. They are either of the type of Tammuz, which means "True Son", or Abu, which means "Lord of Vegetation"; or they style the deity Lord of a shrine or of a quarter of a city where his sanctuary was situated. This is the case with Ningirsu, for instance, Girsu being a part of the town of Lagash. It should be remembered that the Sumerians were originally grouped in temple communities, so that the entire social and economic life of a given population was, even in practical matters, centred round and dependent upon its temple. This theocratic communistic organisation,[1] besides greatly encouraging a certain parochialism, obviously furthered the adoption of such epithets as we have mentioned, and since one or two among these might be preferred in each locality to the exclusion of the others, the impression is easily given that a multiplicity of deities was worshipped in Mesopotamia. But upon analysis it appears impossible to find characteristics which distinguish these would-be gods from one another. Monuments discovered in widely separate parts of the country represent them by identical symbols; the lion-headed eagle Imdugud, the snake, or the entwined pair of snakes, the combination of ruminant and plant, are the best known of these. Con-

[1] This organisation is very well studied and described by Anna Schneider, *Die Sumerische Tempelstadt* (*Plenges Staatswissenschaftliche Beiträge*, Heft IV, Essen, 1920).

versely the excavations of Tell Asmar have brought to light an Early Dynastic and Akkadian town clustered round one single shrine dedicated to the Mother-Goddess and a male god of fertility. The symbols and scenes on local reliefs, cylinders, amulets, and so on, must therefore be taken to refer mainly to those deities. If we exclude the clear references to the Sun-god, we find the remainder to exhibit just that variety of representation and symbolism which, according to our interpretation, pertains to the divine pair, but which the accepted view of Babylonian religion would have us ascribe to at least half a dozen deities.

Thus evidence has accumulated to show that the various divine names encountered in the inscriptions of the Third Millennium B.C. are in many cases designations of one male and one female deity. Yet it is likely enough that in the different centres of worship emphasis was laid on different aspects or spheres of activity of these deities. In one place the god's connection with the earth might be stressed at the expense, perhaps, of his active character as a personification of vital force. Elsewhere his power over water, prerequisite of all life, might be made an almost exclusive feature of belief or cult. Moreover, there is inevitably forged in the mind of a devotee a link between the god and the habitual locality of his worship. These secondary differentiations might to some extent be acknowledged in the official cult, and in any case material accumulated from which an extensive pantheon could be formed once the sense of underlying unity was lost.[1] By the end of the Third Millennium B.C. this pantheon seems already to have been in existence. The predominance of the Semites, which had become a fact by 2500 B.C., furthered apparently a more pronounced personification, a falling apart, of the vaguely connected groups of prevailing beliefs. The original unity of several of the deities distinguished in the later texts is apparent from a certain complexity of their nature, or from contradictions between

[1] Prof. Wolfram von Soden draws my attention to Urukagina's declaration that a sin had been committed against Nisaba of Umma, while the goddess Bau was worshipped as the Mother-Goddess at Lagash. Bertholet points out how Roman Catholics have a similar feeling that Our Lady of Lourdes is somehow different from the Virgin Mary as worshipped in their parish church, and his very illuminating and richly substantiated study, *Götterspaltung und Göttervereinigung* (Tübingen, 1933), seems to bring the view presented by us entirely into line with the phenomena generally observed in the history of religion. See especially p. 9 (separate deities developing out of epithets); pp. 12, 14–15 (the assimilation of foreign gods as sources of power when two cultures come into contact); pp. 17 ff. (the incorporation of tribal or local gods with representations of natural forces, which applies especially to the Sun-gods of the Akkadians); and his final sentence: "Bis in die Gegenwart hinein gilt es zu einem guten Teil dasz die Masse die unmittelbare Nähe der Gottheit nur um den Preis ihrer Spaltung glaubt erleben zu können."

ritual and mythological references, which have puzzled systematic minds both in antiquity and in our own time. The reason seems to be that they represent single hypertrophied aspects of the god or goddess of fertility from which it had proved impossible to banish every trace of the broader character of the originals. Thus Ninurta became a god of war; yet he is called "Lord of Vegetation". Tammuz was now a purely passive figure, Ningiszida a chthonic god, and so on. Theological speculation had, in fact, itself created the complications which it was at pains to undo when, in the First Millennium B.C., it attempted a simplification of the pantheon by reducing its then independent deities to manifestations of the State-god, Marduk or Assur.

Just as the Semites interpreted Sumerian myths of chthonic gods as referring to the solar deities of their own tradition, so also they seem to have considered as fundamentally different the various objects of the local cults of Sumer. They endeavoured to comprehend a body of widely ramified beliefs which they found prevailing in the country under their occupation. Approaching from the outside, as it were, the spiritual inheritance of a strange people, attempting to gain an understanding of hitherto unquestioned observances, the intuitive had to become conceptual, the traditional systematic. Confronted by the fruit of an alien mentality, they unwittingly changed, it seems, what they had merely intended to preserve.

In the seal designs of the First Dynasty of Babylon the process which we have just described appears complete. There we are confronted by a number of divine figures, most of which have a pronounced and limited character, regularly indicated by the same set of restricted attributes. But on the Sargonid seals a much more fluid situation is reflected. To understand the designs we must realise the peculiar conditions of pictorial representation. The artist is more definitely committed to precision than the author. He can but render one scene and, on the whole, but one aspect of his many-sided deity. But by the addition of symbols or attributes he may hint at a wider characterisation than he is able directly to present. He may have to depict a chthonic deity but can suggest its connection with animal life. Or he may be commissioned to show the god as the "Lord of Vegetation" without for that reason being prevented from indicating his warlike character by the inclusion of an appropriate symbol.

We shall find the compositions of the Akkadian seal-cutters to be of this nature. Being obliged to classify our material objectively we shall in the following sections enumerate the cylinders in groups based on the main theme which is represented upon each; but we shall constantly find that these groups overlap because their differences are but differences of approach to one common subject.

(*b*) *The God of Vegetation and of Animals.*

The Mother-Goddess, searching for the lost Tammuz, calls him "one grown great in the submerged grain".[1] The unfinished seal of Pl. XX*c* shows the god producing corn, not only around him but on his robe and from his hands, his head and his shoulders. Here is the "garment of grain-heads", mentioned in a Sippar cult-tablet,[2] with which Marduk was clothed in the ritual of the New Year's festival, and which may have symbolised his coffin, since the god of vegetation dies with the ripening and harvesting of the corn. Often a god wearing this "garment" is shown worshipping the goddess of fertility (Pl. XX*k*). On other occasions care is taken that the plants sprouting from his body should be of different kinds in order to express a more universal dominion over vegetable life (Pl. XX*j*).

In another series of seals the enthroned god holds in his hand an ear of corn or another plant (Pl. XX*b*). Here his personification of vital power embraces the animal world. The god is most commonly associated with the wild relatives of the domesticated animals, sheep or goats. The combination, in the figure of Tammuz, of the embodiment of the male principle in general and fertility of the flocks in particular is well expressed in an incantation which addresses him as:

> Husband of Ishtar the bride, leading goat of the land,
> Clothed in the girdle band, bearing the shepherd's staff,
> Creating the seed of cattle, lord of the stalls.[3]

Pl. XX*b* shows the shepherds, with their leather-tongued whips (cf. Pl. XXIV*g*, *h*), who bring kids as offering to the god. But the large mountain-sheep is shown to be on familiar terms with the deity. It is a pretty thought of the seal-cutter to render the god and his two symbols not in the usual stiff way (Pl. XX*d*) but to combine them into an animated group, the ram reaching upwards, with his forefoot on the god's knee, to nibble from the plant in his hand. We probably see the same deity on the Early Dynastic seals of Pl. XV*e*, *h*.

In Pl. XX*d* the god is pictured with two new attributes in addition to the ibex and the plant on the mountain behind him, such as occur also in

[1] Langdon, *Tammuz and Ishtar*, p. 15.
[2] Langdon, *Epic of Creation*, p. 40, line 32 and note 2; p. 44, line 53.
[3] Langdon, *Tammuz and Ishtar*, p. 35.

Pl. XX*i*.[1] His throne ends in a snake's head which provides a link with a group of seals to be treated hereafter ((*e*) below), and the god holds a plough which is elsewhere borne towards him by a worshipping minor divinity.[2] Here, then, his connection with plant life is especially stressed from the agricultural point of view.

Sometimes the god appears enthroned and facing another deity.[3] On other occasions there is curious duplication. The god of fertility is seated upon his throne, well characterised by the plants which sprout from his body or his mountain. But among the figures which approach him to do homage we find one who also wears the "garment of grain-heads".[4] This figure must represent a minor deity; his reflected glory is related to the rays which, as we have seen, sometimes distinguish attendants of the Sun-god.

On the left of Pl. XX*e* the same god appears again. There are the ears of corn sprouting from his shoulders; and the same ram which we noticed in Pl. XX*b* shows his affinity to the god in a similar attitude. But the god is further equipped with all the attributes of Herakles, namely bow, club and lion's skin. Here, then, we find expressed not only the Tammuz—but also the Ninurta—aspect, and that in a manner which strongly suggests that the demi-god of Greek mythology may have been originally an Oriental god of fertility.[5]

Ninurta is, in fact, described precisely in the manner suggested by the figure on our seal. In the "myth of Labbu" he conquers a lion or leonine monster,[6] and we suspect this combat to be represented on the right half of Pl. XVIII*h*. His weapons remind us that he was reckoned in later times as god of war, and they identify him with the god who liberates the incarcerated deity in Pl. XIX*a–d*, whom we can name, on textual evidence, Ninurta As the destroyer of Zu, another form taken by the adversary of the "Dying God", we meet him in Pl. XXIII*g*. The plants which sprout from his body in the seal under discussion bear witness to the title "Lord of Vegetation" which pertains to Ninurta and also to another mythological fragment which contains the statement: "the plants with one accord named him (Ninurta) as their king".[7] In his earlier form, as Ningirsu, he had a field near Lagash

[1] The ibex appears similarly in Ur, 198; the god is seated on a mountain which sends forth plants, Ur, 76.

[2] Ur, 198.

[3] A–175. Delaporte speaks of a "goddess" in the text but the figure seems to be bearded; the other figure is Ea—Pennsylvania, 185.

[4] Ur, 76, 268; Ward, 374.

[5] See Miss G. R. Levy's comprehensive study in the *Journal of Hellenic Studies*, LIV (1934), 40 ff.

[6] Langdon, *Semitic Mythology*, p. 87; Ungnad, *Religion der Bab. und Ass.* p. 61.

[7] Langdon, *Semitic Mythology*, p. 119.

where all sorts of plants were said to flourish[1] and he was called "the child of the she-goat",[2] so that we find here again the combination of plants and animals exemplified by seals like Pl. XX *b, d, e*. His warrior aspect is especially connected with the lion-headed eagle Imdugud. There is one pictured above a shrine where the god receives adoration (Pl. XXII *h*). The worshipping god seems to offer a branch and possibly a bunch of dates; the human worshippers seem to bring liquids which are poured out. As on an Early Dynastic seal they seem to descend towards the god, unless the platform upon which devotees are depicted in later times[3] finds a forerunner in the seal here described. The lion-headed eagle, set above the temple where the act of worship takes place, serves to identify the deity.

(*c*) *The Goddess of Vegetation.*

We find a goddess depicted in most of the situations taken by the god of fertility, with this exception that she never appears associated with animals. As the unfinished figure of Pl. XX *c*, and in Pl. XX *e*, she appears on a footing of equality with the god. In Pl. XX *j* she is enthroned and worshipped by a god of fertility, a situation which is fairly common[4] while its reversal is rare.[5] Sometimes she holds the plough,[6] or the plough is brought to her.[7] Once (Text-fig. 32), seated before her own statue, she carries a bowl from which water streams. We have already noticed her occasional appearance as a mere filling motive (Pl. XVII *i*) or in the train of the voyaging Sun-god (Pl. XIX *e, f*), also that she assists in the liberation of the god entombed in the mountain (Pl. XIX *a–d*). Her appearances are evidently too varied for it to be safe to choose any particular designation as fitting for all of them; Nidaba, Geshtinanna, Inanna, one of these may be appropriate in certain cases which we are unable to distinguish from others.

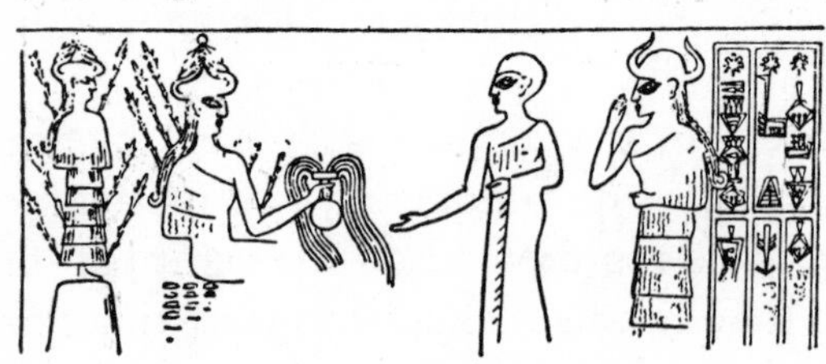

Text-fig. 32. Seal of a servant of Naramsin of Akkad.

In certain cases Inanna, later called Ishtar, "the queen of Eanna who cries 'alas! my husband, alas! my son'", is certainly figured (Pl. XX *g*). Here the goddess is seated not upon a heap of corn as is usual (Pl. XX *j, k*;

[1] Deimel, *Pantheon*, p. 202. [2] Gudea, Cylinder B, 10, 4 ff.

[3] See p. 158, § 26 (*a*).

[4] So also De Clercq, 140; I.M. 12251; Bibliothèque Nationale, 81; Philadelphia, 166.

[5] Ur, 198. [6] Kh. IV/404. [7] Qa, 22.

Text-fig. 32) but on a mountain from which the head, arms and legs of the entombed god project.[1] The question whether the fighting groups accompanying the scene refer to the battle which was waged to liberate the god and which is explicitly represented in Pl. XIX *b–d* remains undecided. A similar allusion might be intended by the subsidiary groups of Pl. XX *h, i, j*.

(*d*) *The Goddess in the Mountain-Grave.*

We have more adequate renderings of the goddess at the mountain-grave of Tammuz, a scene crowning the long search which supplies so many moving details to the Tammuz cult. The extant poem describes the long striving of the desolate goddess to find Tammuz whose disappearance in the nether-world was a cosmic calamity. The curious blend of consciousness that the event has universal significance with the feeling of personal loss is well expressed in some of the laments which were sung at the annual celebrations. The one which follows not only provides apt comment on seal designs like that of Pl. XXI *a* but reveals at the same time the mood in which these representations assume their proper perspective:

For the far-removed there is wailing,
Ah me, my child, the far-removed,
My Damu[2] the far-removed,
My annointer, the far-removed.
For the sacred cedar where the mother bore him
In Eanna,[3] high and low, there is weeping.
Wailing for the house of the lord they raise.
The wailing is for the plants; the first lament is: they grow not.
The wailing is for the barley; the ears grow not.
For the habitations and the flocks it is; they produce not.
For the perishing wedded ones, for the perishing children it is; the dark-headed people[4] create not.
The wailing is for the great river; it brings the flood no more.[5]

Thus the lament continues, enumerating all the forms of life upon which man is dependent and which have ceased to function since the god entered the world of the dead.

Both in the Tammuz cult and at the New Year's festival the goddess seeks and at last finds the god in the "mountain", the land of the dead. In the

[1] In the lower frieze of T. 87 the goddess is seated upon two prostrate persons. The meaning of this scene remains obscure.

[2] Consort or son.

[3] Temple of Ishtar at Erech.

[4] The Babylonians.

[5] Langdon, *Tammuz and Ishtar*, pp. 10 f.

commentary from which we have already quoted on several occasions we find what reads like a literal description of the scene presented in Pl. XXI *a*:

The goddess who kneels with him has descended [to seek] for his welfare.[1]

The god, miraculously revived, emerges from the ground, assisted by the goddess. In the meantime another god pulls up and destroys the vegetation upon the mountain. In one case he is characterised by the rays which mark a Sun-god.[2] He personifies the sun in that redoubtable aspect which the Mesopotamian summer reveals so oppressively, a power inimical to all life, withering the vegetation, threatening man and beast, causing, even in our time, epidemics which spread unchecked. This aspect of the sun the Ancients called Nergal, god of pestilence, ruler of the land of the dead.

Our seal gives a transparently clear rendering of the mythological form in which the annual cycle of climatic change was experienced in Babylonia. When Tammuz had died, after the harvesting of the ripened corn, the sterile summer ruled supreme and the Great Mother suffered on behalf of all the ruin enumerated in the lament. This lasted until Tammuz emerged from the nether-world, whereupon the vegetation revived with the first winter rains. Our seal might have been designed to illustrate the lament which begins:

The scorching heat, verily, verily, the soul of life destroys,

and which continues to describe the goddess' search which ended when:

into the nether resting-place she entered, sat herself before him.[3]

[1] Langdon, *Epic of Creation*, p. 37 with note 5.

[2] Ward-Morgan, 89 (also Weber, 371, and *Iraq*, I, Pl. V *a*); here the god is omitted and Ishtar remains alone within the mountain, a version surviving as late as the Larsa or Hammurabi period (Ish. 34/68). This variant proves that the usual interpretation in which the curved line is taken not as the outline of a mountain but as a bent tree (Ward, 149 f.; Delaporte, *Louvre Catalogue*, p. 10; Meissner, *Beiträge zur altorient. Archaeologie*, p. 27; Opitz, *Archiv für Orientforschung*, VIII, 329 ff.) is not correct. It is based, in fact, on unfortunate photographs of T. 100 where a shadow obscures the fact that the god rises from the ground and does not touch the presumed "tree trunk" at all. Meissner, *loc. cit.*, publishes a cylinder in Moscow which resembles T. 100 closely, and there too the goddess kneels before the god. In the hunting scenes discussed (Text-fig. 36, p. 140) we find a parallel for the two ways in which the mountain is rendered in Pl. XXI *a* and the seals which resemble it on the one hand, and in Pls. XVIII *g*, *j*, *k*; XIX *a–d*; XX *g–j* on the other hand. Both methods occur side by side in Text-fig. 36. It is clear that when detail is to be shown within or in front of the mountain, such as in Pls. XXI *a* and XXIV *a*, the latter is only indicated by an outline upon which plants are shown to grow. On the other hand, when no detail appears in front of it, it is solidly covered by a kind of scale pattern. Only in rare cases, like that of Pl. XVIII *j*, is detail shown against a background of scales.

[3] Langdon, *Tammuz and Ishtar*, p. 20.

It is interesting to recall the subject of Pl. XIX*b–d*. There too a god was depicted in his mountain-grave, but the spirit of that scene is of another kind, the emphasis being laid on the destruction of the hostile powers opposing his resuscitation. The mood of the seals discussed in the present section is elegiacal. The sorrow of the goddess prevails in the consciousness of the seal-cutter to such an extent that in some instances he has even omitted the liberated god (see p. 118, n. 2). Thus a similar, or identical, mythological theme may confront us in entirely different aspects according to the manner of the artist's approach. In the present case available texts suffice to indicate the truth—but how rarely are we thus well informed!

(*e*) *The Snake-god.*

A sculptured and inscribed vase, dedicated by Gudea of Lagash to the god Ningiszida (Text-fig. 33), shows the caduceus and two dragons of the type which was called lion-bird by the Ancients.[1] Ningiszida represents the Fertility-god whom we are discussing in this chapter with special reference to his chthonic character. In addition to the usual functions he was, therefore, invoked for the protection of buildings and their foundations.[2] A house founded in the month Abu, and dedicated to him, was certain to contain children in the future.[3]

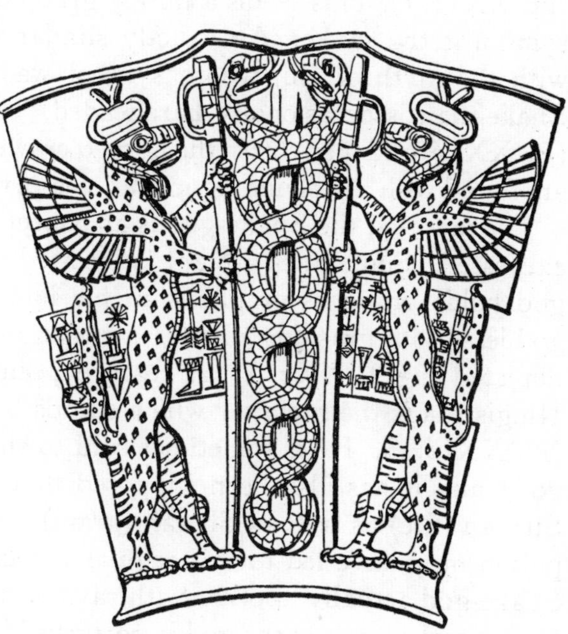

Text-fig. 33. Design on a vase dedicated by Gudea of Lagash to Ningiszida.

His symbol was the snake, or rather, in accordance with his character, a pair of copulating vipers, whose intertwinings were stylised into the caduceus-like design of Text-fig. 33.[4] We have met this symbol, together with other emblems of the fertility god, as early as the Uruk period (Pl. III*b*) as well as in Early Dynastic times (§ 14 (*c*) (ii), p. 71). By

[1] Mrs E. Douglas van Buren, *Iraq*, I, 71.
[2] *Ibid.* p. 68 and note 5.
[3] *Ibid.* p. 66 and note 8.
[4] *Ibid.* p. 12.

Akkadian times it is drawn behind the figure of the enthroned god (Text-fig. 34), or two snakes' heads are shown projecting from his body (Text-fig. 35); or are reduced to one snake with double head;[1] the god was, of course, conceived in human shape, as were all the gods.

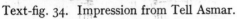

Text-fig. 34. Impression from Tell Asmar.

Text-fig. 35. Impression from Tell Asmar.

The snake-coil, common in Early Dynastic times, is rare in the succeeding period. In Text-fig. 35 it serves as an additional, and in Pl. XXI *d* as the sole, means of identifying the god. Quite often he is pictured as a Snake-man (Pl. XXI *b, f*). This seems a purely graphic device to represent a god whose symbol is the snake. An exactly similar ideogram will be met in dealing with the myth of Zu, whose symbol was a bird (§ 21 (*f*), p. 132). The Snake-man is occasionally bareheaded,[2] but he sometimes wears a flat cap (Pl. XXI *b*) and more often the horned crown (Pl. XXI *f*); but these variations are found with all divine figures at this period.

The fact that the Snake-god is an aspect of the god of fertility is variously expressed. Sometimes a plant is inserted in the design (Pl. XXI *f*),[3] or the god holds branches or plants in his hands.[4] Once he is shown facing a goddess, both grasping plants,[5] a situation corresponding exactly with that depicted in Pl. XX *c, e*. A feature peculiar to the god in his aspect of Ningiszida is the fire-altar which stands before him in most representations (Pl. XXI *b, f*). He is sometimes said to share qualities with Gibil the Fire-god,[6] and it has also been supposed that the name of the serpent may be Shahan (fire) as well as Sherah (grain).[7] Or the "burning" of the snake's poison may have led to this regular association with fire. On one seal the Snake-god actually appears with rays or flames arising from his shoulders.[8] On several occasions the god is portrayed in or near his shrine, with a porter

[1] V.A. 3303 (*Archiv für Orientforschung*, XI, 5, Fig. 2).

[2] Bibliothèque Nationale, 78; A–151.

[3] As. 32/132; Kish, 1931–112.

[4] Musée Guimet, 30; Philadelphia, 164.

[5] As. 31/281.

[6] But this concerns the protection of the foundation of buildings (*Iraq*, I, 63), and since the site of a new building, at least if it was a temple, was purified with fire, the connection may be rather distant.

[7] Langdon, *Semitic Mythology*, p. 90.

[8] Weber, 392 (V.A. 2931).

opening its door,[1] or as if he were entertaining another deity or were entertained by him (Pl. XXI *b*),[2] a scene which still requires explanation.

Occasionally the sign for snake, MUSH, seems to appear in connection with this god (Pl. XXI *b*), but it so closely resembles similar "standards" depicted with Sun-gods and other deities, or even in simple friezes (cf. Pl. XIV *e*), that its relevancy may well be doubted, especially as the seals of the period never carry any writing which could be connected with the design.

(*f*) *The Dragon-god.*

The various dragons of Mesopotamian iconography are mostly adversaries of the gods which have been overcome and made into adjuncts of their conquerors; in the same way, as we have said, the dragon which accompanies St George on medieval monuments is by no means always shown at the moment of defeat. The type shown in Pl. XXI *g*, *i* pertains to Ningiszida. In Text-fig. 33 two of these monsters act as "supporters" for the emblem of the god, in Text-fig. 37 (p. 143) it closes the procession which its master conducts towards Ea. On one seal (see p. 120, n. 1) the god stands on the dragon, and the gatepost emblem probably shows that he is to be considered as within his shrine; next to the emblem a double-headed snake is drawn.

The occurrence of the dragon affords interesting evidence as to the interchangeable character of names or epithets where the god of fertility is concerned. Its connection with Ningiszida is well established. But it has also been found as supporter of Tishpak, a northern, Hurrian, Weather-god who displaced Ninazu ("Lord of the Waters") at Eshnunna before or during the arrival of the Akkadians.[3] In this instance even the fire-altar stands before Tishpak.

In Pl. XXI *g* the dragon identifies the victorious god in the combat, a function similar to that of the snake-coil in Pl. XXI *d*.

The lion-bird wears an elaborate crown on its snake-like head; it has the hindlegs of a bird of prey, and a scorpion-sting as tail. It is sometimes, but not always, winged. Its actual subjection is not shown on any seal, but it is possible that the lion-bird is an iconographical substitute for the hydra of Pl. XXIII *j*. The point cannot be proved, but arguments in its favour are the following:

At Tell Asmar (Eshnunna), where the Hydra seal was found in a temple dedicated to the "Lord of Vegetation", there turned up in the private

[1] Bibliothèque Nationale, 78; Ward-Morgan, 86; A–151.

[2] As. 32/1232; A–151; De Clercq, 141; Weber, 392; Kish, 1931/112.

[3] Thorkild Jacobsen in *Oriental Institute Communications*, No. 13, pp. 51 ff.

houses an alabaster group[1] where a dragon looking like a simplified version of the lion-bird appears as an adjunct of the Snake-god, and this dragon resembles in every detail, except the multiplicity of heads, the Hydra of the seal.

The Hydra is, in any case, subdued by the fertility god discussed in this chapter. That is proved beyond a doubt by the circumstances in which the seal of Pl. XXIII*j* and the sealings of Text-figs. 34, 35 were found. These combine, therefore, with Pl. XX*e* to refer the Greek traditions regarding Herakles to an early Mesopotamian god of fertility. In Pl. XXIII*j* we see four heads hanging limp in death while three are striking at their assailant. Just as Herakles was assisted by Iolaus, so here a second god supports the main combatant. And even as Herakles had finally to resort to fire before he could destroy the monster, so we see flames rising out of the back of the Hydra on the Babylonian seal.

Material has been increasing to show the way, through North Syria and Anatolia, along which these themes reached Greece. Leviathan is shown, by parallels in the texts from Ras Shamra, to have had seven heads; in the Ras Shamra texts he is, moreover, attacked with a lance, as on our seal. There is archaeological and philological evidence of a settlement throughout the Aegean and in Greece of immigrants from Anatolia early in the Third Millennium B.C. Archaeologically they can be traced by the spread of "Urfirnis-ware" and related fabrics, philologically by the "-ss-" and "-nth-" infixes in place-names. The myth of Herakles and the Hydra may be a trace of their presence in the field of religion.[2]

§ 21. OTHER GODS, MYTHS AND OTHER SUBJECTS

(*a*) *The Water-gods.*

Enki, the god of the deep, later called Ea, was intimately connected with man's cultural activity. That his oldest name means "Lord of Land" while his element is water has long puzzled scholars unacquainted with life in the marshes of Southern Mesopotamia, where conditions still prevail which determined the life of the first settlers of the Plain. Even to-day the marsh Arabs cut down reeds and pile them to obtain a comparatively dry spot whereon to build their huts. Life is divided between these flimsy settlements and their boats.[3] We know from the excavations that the earliest settlers,

[1] *Oriental Institute Communications*, No. 17, Figs. 44, 45.

[2] *Journal of Hellenic Studies*, LIV (1934), 40 ff.

[3] See the excellent description of Fulanain, *Haji Riqqan, Marsh Arab* (Chatto and Windus, London, 1927), especially plates facing pp. 26 and 38.

arriving from the Iranian Highlands, lived in precisely similar circumstances. Ea's centre of worship was Eridu, one of the southernmost towns of Sumer, situated at the edge of the lagoon behind the bar of Basrah which separated it from the Persian Gulf. Here the identity between the Lord of Land and the Lord of Water was a matter of course.

Ea was the source of all knowledge, teacher of magic and of handicrafts and protector of humanity against the wrath of the more elemental gods such as Anu of the sky and Enlil of the air. When his son Marduk created the extant cosmos it was Ea, according to the Epic of Creation, who made man out of the remains of Qingu. In an earlier epoch he had succeeded, merely by his great command of magic, in vanquishing one of the powers of chaos, Apsu, the primeval waters. Next we read:

After he had bound his enemies and had slain them
And he, Ea, had established his victory over his foes,
And in his chamber he had become composed as one who is soothed,
He named it Apsu, and they determined the holy places.
Therein he caused to be founded his secret chamber.[1]

It is this conception which we find illustrated by the Akkadian seals. Pl. XVIII *k* indeed depicts a god "who layeth the beams of his chamber in the waters" (Psalm 104, *v.* 3).[2] On other occasions his presence within a building is summarily indicated by a porter or attendant holding the gatepost emblem (Pl. XXI *c*),[3] a feature which completes the picture even in Pl. XVIII *k*. We have in an earlier chapter refuted the assumption that the nude hero, who acts as Ea's attendant, must in all scenes in which he appears be understood as a member of Ea's suite (§ 17, pp. 85 ff.).

We know of another attendant of Ea, a *sukallu* or minister, or master of ceremonies, who had two faces, and was named Usmu.[4] This personage frequently occurs on the seals, either in the act of introducing worshippers to the god (Pl. XXI *c*) or reporting upon events which have taken place. Generally this is the capture of the enemy Zu (Pl. XXIII *d, f*) or an event symbolising that victory (Pl. XXIII *i*); once it is the victory of the Sun-god, presumably Marduk, Ea's son (Pl. XVIII *i*).

In later times, after the Third Dynasty of Ur, the most usual symbol of Ea is the goat-fish. But this monster is never depicted on Akkadian seals.

[1] Langdon, *Epic of Creation*, pp. 78 f.
[2] So also B.M. 89771; Brussels, 590; De Clercq, 143.
[3] B.M. 89771; Brussels, 590; A–158; A–159; T–96; De Clercq, 83 *bis*; Philadelphia, 159; V.A. 3329.
[4] Furlani in *Miscellanea Orientalia Antonio Deimel dedicata* (Roma, 1935), pp. 136 ff.

It is usual there, however, especially when the Apsu is not figured, to identify Ea by two streams of water issuing from his body and often enlivened by fishes which are shown swimming along those streams (Pls. XVIII *i, k*; XXI *e, h*; XXIII *d, e, f, g, i*).

In what precedes there is no reason to connect Ea with the fertility gods which we have discussed in the preceding chapter. But his iconography in Sargonid times includes certain features which do not recur later, but show that he too was somehow related to the life-giving forces of nature, a characteristic which seems to have distinguished all the gods of Sumer.

One may doubt whether the tree which occasionally appears in the god's "secret chamber" is to be interpreted in this way.[1] It most probably represents the "Kishkanu tree", which was supposed to grow there and to produce powerful medicine. But in Pl. XXI *e* we find amongst the minor deities who approach Ea one who carries the plough exactly as we have noticed before in scenes where a god of fertility was worshipped. In Pl. XX *f* not only fishes but also sprouting plants rise from the streams at the god's shoulder. This detail is the more telling since the seal gives us a fresh rendering of Ea; the mythological abode is omitted and instead of the "secret chamber" we see Ea in a boat which is poled through the marshes near his city Eridu, where reeds grow high and conceal wild boar; and in Text-fig. 37 (and perhaps Pl. XXV *d*) a plant is growing from the flowing vase. Again, Ea is sometimes depicted in company with a god or goddess of fertility.[2] Conversely, we find on Akkadian seals that it is sometimes a goddess who commands the flowing waters (Pl. XX *e* and Text-fig. 32, p. 116), just as a male and a female deity are interchangeable in several of the scenes in which gods of fertility are portrayed. One may even wonder whether Ea is conceived as the figure on the Early Dynastic seal fragment of Pl. XV *h*.[3]

The role which Ea plays in the liberation of the god from his mountain-grave has been discussed above; and we shall have occasion to revert to that again in dealing with the myth of Zu.[4]

(*b*) *Weather-gods*.

Sargonid seals do not enable us to identify the god and goddess who ride a fire-spitting dragon or harness it to a chariot (Pl. XXII *a, d*). But a cylinder of the First Babylonian Dynasty (Pl. XXVII *i*) shows this dragon to be an adjunct of Adad, who, seated upon it, wields his triple lightning—

[1] De Clercq, 143. [2] A–175. [3] Also As. 32/1276.

[4] All the monuments from Western Asia which may be connected with the gods discussed in this section have been collected and studied by Mrs E. Douglas van Buren, *The Flowing Vase and the God with Streams* (Berlin, 1933).

neither this forked lightning nor the thunderbolt occur on Akkadian cylinders.[1] But no image could, indeed, be more adequate than that of Pl. XXII *a*, where the god cracks his whip in the thundering chariot drawn by a winged monster spitting fire.

The goddess who habitually accompanies the god appears on later seals as "Ishtar of War",[2] but this symbol may stand for a variety of deities. Adad's spouse Shala is not known in early texts,[3] otherwise one would naturally expect her to appear in this scene. The objects which she holds are in no case distinct; once they look like the swaddling-bands which typify the Mother-Goddess Ninharsag.[4] It is more likely that she bears the rain which accompanies the storm and is unmistakably shown in Pl. XXII *e*, of which the designs of Pl. XXII *a*, *d* are abbreviated renderings.[5] Adad often appears in the texts as god of rain and floods;[6] and at a later period he is depicted with the typical attribute of a beneficial agricultural deity, the plough (§ 26 (*c*), p. 164). We may use Adad, the name employed in all subsequent periods, for the Weather-god on Akkadian seals.

The dragon may have been originally vanquished by Adad, as is so often the case with animals appearing closely connected with the gods. The beast occasionally occurs as filling beneath an inscribed panel, and is once or twice thus represented on Early Dynastic monuments.[7] Its characteristics distinguish it sharply from the other dragons of Sargonid glyptic. It has the head and forelegs of a lion, but the hindlegs, wings and tail are those of a bird of prey. In Pl. XXII *a* the hindquarters are clearly shown to be covered with feathers.

The chariot, which may be of the two-wheeled type,[8] is sometimes omitted, in which case the gods appear standing upon the dragon (Pl. XXII *d*, *e*);[9] once the goddess drives the chariot.[10]

[1] See p. 127, note 1 below.

[2] B.M. 89058 and Newell, 220.

[3] Deimel, *Pantheon*, p. 248; but see Schlobies, *Der Akkadische Wettergott in Mesopotamien*, p. 9.

[4] See *Antiquaries Journal*, XIV, Pl. XLII, and *Archiv für Orientforschung*, IX, 165 ff.

[5] This interpretation is the most likely, though the rough way in which the neck of the figure in the rain is engraved in Pl. XXII *e* might suggest a beard; but the vertical lines are absent and, moreover, there is a clear difference in the coiffure of this small figure and that of the two gods; the breasts also seem to be indicated. She may have possessed a crown which has been worn down, placed as it was at the very edge of the seal. But she appears also without crown in Pl. XXII *d*.

[6] See Schlobies, *Der Akkadische Wettergott in Mesopotamien*, pp. 22 f.

[7] A–40; Newell, 73. Also on engraved shell inlay from Lagash.

[8] *Antiquaries Journal*, XIV, Pl. XLII.

[9] B.M. 89367; A–153; A–154.

[10] V.A. 242.

The beneficent powers of the gods are stressed in Pl. XXII *a*, where a man, pouring a libation over an altar, faces the terrifying group; the type of altar is known from the excavations at Assur and Khafaje; it is made of baked clay in the shape of a house, and supports loaves of bread and other offerings. On another seal, however,[1] emphasis is laid entirely on the dangerous character of these deities. Both appear mounted on their dragons, while between them rages the lion-headed monster of Pl. XVIII *h* and a winged god with the talons of a bird of prey crushes three men as he does in Pl. XVIII *d* (cf. § 27 (*g*), p. 174). In the midst of these dreadful figures a forlorn human being lifts his hands in prayer. We are here reminded of a recent identification of the dragon with the constellation Ukatukha, which was assigned to Nergal, the god of pestilence.[2] This scene remains exceptional; the beneficial aspect of the thunderstorms naturally prevailed in a country like Mesopotamia, and this aspect finds clear mythological expression in Pl. XXII *e*, a scene which in abbreviated form recurs elsewhere.[3] Drought is symbolised by a bull; here we must quote the Gilgamesh Epic, which obviously refers to the Bull of Heaven as a symbol of the aridity of the Mesopotamian climate. It is thus described when Ishtar asks her father Anu to give her the bull that she may destroy Gilgamesh who has scorned her:

> Father, Oh make me a Heavenly Bull which shall Gilgamesh vanquish
> Filling his body with flame.[4]

But Anu warns her of the dangerous character of the creature:

> If I the Heavenly Bull shall create for which thou dost ask me
> (Then) seven years of (lean) husks must needs follow after his onslaught.[5]

And a Sumerian fragment makes it even clearer that Ishtar plans to punish Gilgamesh by striking his city with famine:

> It was reported to the Lord Gilgamesh:
> Inanna has brought forth the Bull of Heaven!

[1] V.A. 611.

[2] Schott in *Zeitschrift der Deutschen Morgenländischen Gesellschaft*, 1934, pp. 319 f. But in the relief on which this conclusion is based the dragon is pursued by a god wielding lightning, so that the relation with Adad still seems valid. Thureau-Dangin also connects the dragon with Nergal, *Revue d'Assyriologie*, XVI, 140; but see on this whole question § 27 (*g*) below.

[3] Ward, 129*a*, shows the bull killed in the same manner before the god and goddess mounted on their dragons; the rest of the design consists of four more of these dragons.

[4] R. Campbell Thompson, *The Epic of Gilgamesh*, p. 34, lines 94 ff.

[5] *Ibid.* lines 103 ff.

She made him pasture in Erech
And drink at the waxing river:
A double-hour the waxing river flowed, then only his thirst was slaked;
Where he pastured the earth is bare.[1]

The heroic king of Erech succeeds in killing the bull:

Gilgamesh, like an able slaughterer, strikes with his sword the Bull of Heaven forcefully and precisely between shoulders and neck.[2]

It is this action which we see illustrated in Pl. XXII *e*. The kneeling god there is hardly the Gilgamesh of the Epic, for the scene appears on our seal, not as part of the personal conflict between Ishtar and the King of Erech, but in the more general cosmic form which may have supplied the epic poets with the theme. But it is clear that the killing of the bull on the seal signifies the breaking of the drought. The Thunder-god with mace and leather-tongued whip is seen approaching from the left on his dragon of lightning, and abundant rain descends, called up by the goddess who appears with outstretched arms in the sky.[3]

[1] Schott, *Das Gilgamesch Epos*, p. 90, lines 15–20.

[2] *Ibid.* p. 44, lines 150–52.

[3] The fact that the earliest Mesopotamian representation of the Weather-god's lightning is not the thunderbolt or lightning fork but the whip has a direct bearing on a problem of classical antiquity, namely the whip wielded by the god worshipped at Baalbek. Macrobius has already explained Jupiter Heliopolitanus as a combination of a solar deity with a Weather-god, and recognised Hadad, the Syrian form of Adad, as the origin of the latter. He assigned the whip to the solar aspect of the deity, referring to Helios Auriga. Furlani has recently shown that this view, doubted by some modern scholars and supported by others, is untenable ("La Frusta di Adad", Reale Accademia Nazionale dei Lincei, *Rendiconti della Classe di Scienze morali historiche, filologiche*, Ser. VI, Vol. VIII, pp. 20 ff.), but the matter is confused by attempts to connect the whip with the lightning-fork or thunderbolt which has three tongues. We now see that this latter symbol, which remains prevalent in Syria at all times and entered Mesopotamia about the time of Hammurabi (Pl. XXVII *i* gives the earliest instance), has an origin entirely independent of the whip; the latter is shown by our seals, moreover, not to be a scourge but a whip such as goatherds use, with one long leather tongue. Furlani demonstrates that in late Assyrian times, under Adad-Nirari III, the metaphor of the lightning as the god's whip was still in use, and the distance of time separating the Mesopotamian instances from Jupiter Heliopolitanus is thus reduced. A. B. Cook (*Zeus*, II, i, 824–6) has shown that in Greece the whip occurs as a symbol of lightning, and *Iliad*, II, 782, proves that whip and thunderbolt are separate attributes in the gods' hands; Jacobsthal, in his monograph *Der Blitz in der orientalischen und griechischen Kunst* (Berlin, 1906), takes the forked lightning symbol as the more original form and explains it as a stylisation of fire. Its Syrian origin is likely because of its persistence there, and also because it first appears with the Amorite First Dynasty of Babylon in Mesopotamia, where hitherto the whip had exclusively been used as a symbol of lightning. See also p. 162, § 26 (*c*) below.

(*c*) *The Goddess at the Gate, and the Bull of Heaven.*

The motive which we have encountered in connection with the Weather-gods, namely the Bull of Heaven as a symbol of the drought which can be catastrophical to the community, seems to recur in another group of seals under another aspect. We have seen that in the Epic of Gilgamesh the bull is at the disposal of Ishtar. But if the wrath of the goddess was an epic theme, the ordinary man was more apt to dwell on her beneficent influence, especially when choosing a subject for the decoration of such objects as cylinder seals, since the image always partakes of the quality of what it depicts. In Pl. XXII*g*, *i* we seem to have representations of Ishtar holding the Bull of Heaven in check.

The Sumerian fragment of the Epic, from which we have already quoted on the preceding pages, describes in some detail Anu's concern when his daughter Ishtar asks for the Bull of Heaven; we have mentioned how he warns her that seven lean years will follow the bull's onslaught. He is moreover preoccupied about another matter which is more difficult for us to understand. He refuses to let the Bull of Heaven go with Ishtar before she has promised that she will prevent it from reaching the "Place of Sunrise"; to make certain, Anu takes as forfeit a bowl of lapis lazuli belonging to his daughter. But Ishtar reassures him as follows:

> I am the one who commands, and heaven and earth obey;
> But if fear does not subdue him, the rein will restrain him.[1]

A number of seals show us the goddess seated in front of a gate which may well be the gate of sunrise (cf. Pl. XVIII); for the projections on either side, which are generally described as wings, might conceivably render the light of the sun behind the gate. It is not unlikely that here we see Ishtar, or, to give her ancient name, Inanna, the Lady of Heaven, as a beneficent power who protects the land against drought and famine. Sometimes she actually holds the bull by a rein passing through his nose (Pl. XXII *i*),[2] or grasps his horns (Pl. XXII*g*).[3] Often, however, she holds in the other hand a rope which is fastened to the gate, while opposite her, on the other side of the gate, a deity holds a similar rope or touches the gate itself as if to keep it closed. This second figure generally helps at the same time in the subjection of the bull. It would seem that the "Bull reaching the Place of Sunrise" would stand metaphorically for the heat of the sun reaching that scorching intensity

[1] Schott, *Das Gilgamesch Epos*, p. 89, lines 22 f.
[2] As. 33/146; Philadelphia, 161, 162; Ur, 267.
[3] Banks, *Bismaya*, p. 303; A–150.

which makes the summer in Mesopotamia nearly unbearable. The seals suggest that the danger which Anu feared was the bull's irruption through the closed gate to release the heat of the sun whose rays can be seen extending from behind it.

This interpretation of the very common scene is of course largely hypothetical, but there is no alternative and it does account for the particular features which we have enumerated. There are a number of variants which are partly abbreviations, and sometimes, as it would seem, the result of confused ideas, as when the goddess is shown with rays, perhaps intended for plants.[1] Sometimes the group is conventionalised to the extent that two almost identical figures appear on either side of the gate;[2] or the gate is omitted though the ropes leading to it are indicated.[3] Sometimes the group forms part of a more elaborate design which unfortunately contributes nothing to our understanding.[4]

(*d*) *Other Goddesses.*

In Pl. XVIII *j* a Sun- or Fire-goddess seems to be pictured, on Pl. XIX and Pl. XX *c*, *e–h* a goddess of fertility, in Pl. XXII *a*, *e* a goddess of rain. Some or all of these may be aspects of the Great Mother-Goddess, whom we recognise in Pl. XXI *a*, and who seems to be represented in Pl. XXII *g*, *i*. She must also be the subject of a number of cylinders which depict a goddess holding a child on her lap, while worshippers bring offerings (Pl. XXII *c*). The secondary scene of our seal, which recurs with the Mother-Goddess, is interesting; we see a servant occupied with the device which is still used in Mesopotamia to obtain regular supplies of fresh and clean drinking water. A large porous pot on a stand contains the water as it is drawn from river or canal. It percolates through the sides of the pot and while some of the moisture evaporates, keeping the pot and its contents cool, the remainder collects at the pointed base and drips down into a bowl placed beneath. On one seal[5] a man, perhaps intended for the owner of the cylinder, carries a goblet with water from the filter to the child. On another a flask, bowl and bunch of dates are brought.[6] Once the goddess holds a flower[7] and we should take her for a vegetation goddess but that the servant with the filter connects her with the seals just discussed, another proof that the figures which we

[1] A–149; the goddess actually holds plants on As. 32/1231.

[2] A–150; Bibliothèque Nationale, 76; As. 31/279.

[3] As. 32/1231; A–148.

[4] Ward, 361; Ward-Morgan, 85; Oriental Institute, A 7227; *Revue d'Assyriologie*, XXVIII, 44, No. X.

[5] A–176. [6] Ur, 291; but this may be a human domestic scene. [7] D–21.

distinguish iconographically as Mother-Goddess, goddess of fertility and so on, appearing as they do with distinct names or epithets in the texts, are not essentially different.

In one instance a worshipper stands between the Mother-Goddess and her infant, and Shamash rises.[1] The latter motive may have no connection with the rest, since such groups are used as filling motives, as we have repeatedly demonstrated. But it is worth while pointing out that Shamash and Tammuz appear similarly combined in a text,[2] and in both cases this unexpected association may well be due to the thought that each of these two gods alone, each in his own way, is able to pass through the nether-world, through death, in fact, and to emerge alive.

Another goddess appears on the right-hand side of the inscription of Pl. XX*e*. This is Ishtar of War, with scimitars and maceheads projecting from her shoulders, and in a characteristic attitude, one leg standing free from the draped shawl which hangs smoothly round the limbs of those goddesses who are not committed to violent action. Though the texts reveal that Sargon and his dynasty showed her special deference, she occurs but rarely on the seals.[3] One worn cylinder[4] leaves us in doubt whether the warlike or the fertility aspect of the goddess is depicted, since the projections from her shoulders may be either plants or weapons. Two women musicians play the harp and sistrum before her, and since the goddess is seated on a lion throne it is probably Ishtar of War. Once she is depicted in full panoply, seated on a lion throne and in full-face, as is her usual attitude from the Isin-Larsa period onward; and again the essential unity of all the aspects of the deity is demonstrated, since behind the worshipper bringing her a sacrificial kid appears a minor goddess bearing a flowering branch.[5] Often a goddess appears without attributes or with only a goose or scorpion or both of these; or else with a star behind her (Pl. XXII*j*; cf. Pl. XV*k*). It would be wrong to use in these cases the names Bau or Ishara or Ishtar with the implication that all other designations are excluded, for the narrowly circumscribed spheres of action allotted to separate gods in later times are not

[1] Ward-Morgan, 88.

[2] R. Campbell Thompson, *Devils and Evil Spirits of Babylonia*, I, 200 ff.:

"...the Kishkanu tree...
In an undefiled dwelling, like a forest grove
Its shade spreadeth abroad and none may enter in.
In its depth (are) Shamash and Tammuz."

[3] Ward-Morgan, 90.

[4] A-172.

[5] Ward, 407 (Weber, 439). Since this seal is known only from drawings its style cannot be judged and it may belong to the Third Dynasty of Ur.

distinguished in the middle of the Third Millennium B.C., when the great gods were known and worshipped with a full understanding of the complexity of their characters.

(*e*) *Battles of the Gods.*

We have on several occasions discussed conflicts of gods where either attributes or situations made possible a specific identification of the warfare. We have seen a Sun-god destroying a Bull-man, a leonine monster or a human-shaped god. We have found a god armed with bow and arrow and assisted by a goddess, subjecting a god upon the mountain in which another god is incarcerated. We have recognised the burning of a human-shaped adversary in a series of scenes which place the battleground again on a mountain side. But in several cases subsidiary pairs of combatants appeared beside the protagonists. These anonymous fighters, of whom nothing but their divine character is indicated, sometimes form by themselves the decoration of a seal cylinder (Pl. XXII *b*). They are shown in all the various attitudes already observed in the more detailed scenes, and even the mountain upon which the victim collapses occurs in these designs. We cannot decide whether such seals refer to any of the conflicts discussed, or merely render in a general way the victory of benign over malignant powers. In some cases even very detailed renderings leave us uncertain because we are unable to recognise the situation. Thus we have in Pl. XXII *k* a very full rendering of the building by various gods of a temple composed of the usual material, mud brick. One god hacks up the soil with a hoe and mixes it with water to make mortar, another carries this substance in a basket on his head up a ladder. One of the masons at the top is ready to receive the load, another catches bricks which are thrown up one by one from a builder standing on the ground. At the top of the seal a seated god is probably making bricks by filling wooden moulds and levelling the tops with his trowel. Next to this building scene a large figure of a god dispatches his kneeling victim with a mace, while another seems to express astonishment. It has been suggested[1] with great probability that we have here an illustration of the final episode of the Epic of Creation, when the gods worship Marduk after he has defeated the powers of chaos:

> Unto Marduk their Lord they said:
> O Nannar my lord, thou who hast brought about our deliverance,
> What shall be our sign of gratitude before thee?
> Come, let us make a shrine.[2]

[1] Opitz in *Archiv für Orientforschung*, VI.

[2] Langdon, *Epic of Creation*, pp. 171 f., lines 35–8.

If this quotation is relevant, as is likely, the kneeling victim would, of course, be Qingu.

Another scene containing ample detail which we are unable to interpret is shown in Pl. XXII*f*. Needless to say the inscription does not bear on the representation at all, containing merely a proper name; and I at least do not know of any literary source which will enlighten us.

The killing of a creature who is depicted in human shape and accompanied by a boar in Pl. XXIII*h*, and whose death seems to be represented by the slaughtering of the boar in Pl. XXIII *i*, is more easily explicable. The festival of the New Year again gives the enlightenment which we need. On that occasion a criminal was said to be with the imprisoned Marduk, and represented in the ritual under the form of a pig which was slaughtered at a later stage of the celebrations.[1]

We have good reason to connect our seals with this ritual. In Pl. XXIII *i*, we see the two-faced Usmu reporting to his master Ea upon the scene depicted on the remainder of the cylinder's surface, that is, the slaughtering of a boar below a bird of prey. What is the connection? We can answer that question by the study of the next group of seals, the result of which we must here, for the sake of clarity, anticipate. Both boar and bird stand for the hostile powers which have to be overcome before the god upon whom the life of nature depends can be liberated from his mountain-grave. We have seen that in the ritual of the New Year's festival a boar was killed; we also know that in mythology this hostile power is referred to as the storm-bird Zu, and we shall see that the seals which represent the subjecting of the enemy in the shape of a bird habitually add the group of Ea and Usmu to the scene. Pl. XXIII*h* is based on the ritual; Pl. XXIII*i* depicts the ritual but drives home the meaning of the scene by adding the mythological references.

It now remains to study the seals where the scene is rendered solely in its mythological guise.

(*f*) *The Myth of Zu.*

In describing the seals with the Snake-god we have found that three methods of representing that deity were in use in Sargonid times. The god was always conceived in human shape, but in order to distinguish him an animal—connected with him either as vanquished adversary or as emblem—could be depicted by his side (Text-figs. 34, 35, p. 120); or secondly the animal symbol could stand by itself (Text-fig. 33, p. 119, where the god's

[1] Langdon, *Epic of Creation*, p. 39, lines 24–5, for the identification of the criminal and the pig, and p. 43, lines 44–6, for the slaughtering.

adjunct, the dragon, acts as heraldic "supporter"); or, lastly, this god was represented by an ideogram which consisted of the upper part of a man placed upon a serpent's body (Pl. XXI *b*, *f*).

In exactly the same three ways an evil being whose symbol is a bird of prey occurs upon the seals.

In Pl. XXIII *a* the victim is identified by the bird on the right, just as one of his two executioners is characterised by the mountain-sheep which we have met with already in this attitude to indicate the god of fertility (Pl. XX *e*). The latter appears in both these cases in his warlike aspect as Ninurta. In the seal impression of Pl. XXIII *b* we have a confirmation of this view, since there the collapsing victim is grasped by one of the claws of the lion-headed eagle Imdugud, an emblem of the god in his Ninurta (Ningirsu) aspect; the victorious upright god is connected with his symbol by a gesture: he holds the tail and one wing of the bird. Another version of this scene[1] is even more complete. Beside the attacking god and his lion-headed eagle is another small bird pictured to identify the kneeling figure exactly as it does in Pl. XXIII *a*. And here too we meet Ea standing with his foot upon a mountain, an attitude so exceptional for this god that we must seek a special reason for it,[2] for the consistent use of definite groupings, attitudes and attributes is the very language of all religious art, which would be incomprehensible without it. We shall presently analyse the attitude of Ea. For the moment it serves merely as a link between the seal impression just mentioned, which goes together with our Pl. XXIII *a*, *b* and, on the other hand, Pl. XXIII *e*, which also shows Ea with his foot upon a mountain and in front of a bound captive in the shape of a Bird-man. This detail connects all the seals so far discussed with a numerous group of which Pl. XXIII *d*, *f* are examples. The Bird-man is, evidently, an ideogram of the same nature as the Snake-man whom we met previously, and it may stand for a figure elsewhere represented by a man-shaped being accompanied by a bird (Pl. XXIII *a*) or by a bird alone (Pl. XXIII *c*, *i*). The animal-headed gods of Egyptian art and the animal-headed evangelists of certain romanesque capitals[3] originated in a similar manner as graphic symbols.

The judgment of the Bird-man is a very common subject on Akkadian seals. Usually the two-faced herald Usmu introduces the captors or restrains

[1] *Iraq*, I, Pl. V*g* (Ward, 454*c*).

[2] So also Ward, 291, where in the drawing the mountain under Ea's foot is omitted. I have to thank Mr J. M. Upton of the Metropolitan Museum, New York, for letting me have a photograph of this seal.

[3] Emile Mâle, *L'Art réligieux du XIIIe siècle en France*, p. 3, n. 2, and fig. 5; Bernheimer, *Romanische Tierplastik*, pp. 138 f.

the captive before Ea enthroned, and the owner of the seal has had himself depicted as approaching the god at this auspicious moment (Pl. XXIII*f*). We should once more remember the variants like Pl. XXIII*e*, where Ea stands with his foot planted on the mountain. In Pl. XXIII*d* we see another type of composition in which the Bird-man is carried like a game-bird, his feet tied to a mace which one of the gods has slung over his shoulder. On this seal we notice that the god preceding the Bird-man's captor carries some uprooted plants tied to a stick.[1] It seems as if they were intended to explain why the Bird-man was caught; it is apparently suggested that he has done damage to these plants or that they were illegally in his possession. Here we have a link with yet another illustration of this story. A group of seals depicts a bird of prey being caught or destroyed by two upright figures, and in one case at least in the act of seizing a plant (Pl. XXIII*c*).[2] The identity of the bird of this seal with the kneeling figure accompanied by the bird in Pl. XXIII*a* is supported by the peculiar character of the group. As a rule, on Akkadian seals, combatants appear in pairs, and not in groups of three.

Now that the various versions of the theme have been collected we may attempt its interpretation. For this purpose the attitude which Ea twice assumes is decisive. Normally the god is portrayed in his "secret chamber", as we have seen, or merely enthroned without indication of locality. His character does not suggest any relation with mountains. In one case, however, the combination is relevant, namely when he attends at the liberation of his son Marduk from his mountain-grave, as represented in Pl. XIX*a*. If the seal-cutters have occasionally added Ea in this posture to the seals where the capture or judgment of the Bird-man was depicted, it was no doubt to convey the idea that this victory was but the prelude to an even more momentous event, the emergence of the resurrected god from the netherworld. Conversely the bird was shown in the hands of Ea in Pl. XIX*a* to indicate that the capture and conviction of the enemy had preceded the god's liberation. And we may well doubt whether the group on the left half of Pl. XXIII*a* is merely the conventional picture of the sunrise added as space filling, or whether it refers to the liberated god mounting upwards, as pictured in Pl. XIX*a*, after the enemy symbolised by the bird had been destroyed. I incline to the latter interpretation, since we see near the Sun-god a stand with sprouting plants, unexpected in connection with Shamash but highly appropriate if this Sun-god is the "dying god" after his resurrection.

[1] So also B.M. 103317; for a possible Early Dynastic rendering of this motive see Pl. XIII*h* and p. 72.

[2] Also As. 32/46; As. 32/84; Ward, 126.

And again there are iconographical indications supporting our interpretation, since in the hands of dealers I have seen a cylinder with a scene like Pl. XXIII*c* where one of the gods destroying the bird is identified by his bow with the victorious god of Pl. XIX*a–d*, just as in Pl. XXIII*g* the god whom we recognise as Ninurta drives the bird off the mountain.[1] Another seal shows the Sun-god adored, while a man carries over his shoulder the uprooted plants of Pl. XXIII*d*, in reference to their recovery from the enemy before the god's resurrection.[2]

I am inclined to see in these plants another symbol for what is called in the texts of later times the "tablets of destiny". In the myth of Zu it is told how that personage stole the "tablets of destiny" while the king of the gods was bathing "and had put off his crown (and his ornaments) and put them on a chair". The nature of these tablets is unknown; remembering the magical qualities of the herb of life which Gilgamesh obtained we may imagine that in the early period from which our seals date, some such plant as seems to have been stolen by the bird in Pl. XXIII*c*, *d* may have played the part of the later "tablets of destiny". One of the most common beliefs regarding sacred trees is their aptness for providing oracles[3] and the transition to the "tablets of destiny" is therefore by no means far-fetched. Or, if destiny is taken in the pregnant sense which it often holds in the Near East, namely the destiny of death "allotted to man", then we may quote in this connection not only the plant of life from the Epic, but also the curious objects which Gilgamesh had to bring from a nearby grove before Urshanabi would ferry him over the waters of death.[4]

It is important to remember the concrete character of all that the primitive mind conceives. Even such notions as "life" and "death" partake of the nature of objects:

> "... the gods, in their first creation of mortals,
> Death allotted to man, but life they retained in their keeping."[5]

It is also clear from this quotation, that "life", in its opposition to "death",

[1] The rest of the design consists of a mere enumeration of gods without any attempt to depict a scene. Two of these we recognise as interested in the outcome of Ninurta's struggle, the Sun-god, who here no doubt represents the god to be liberated, and his father Ea. Similarly the Sun-god is shown as a spectator at the killing of the bird on As. 32/46.

[2] Philadelphia, 185; Sidney Smith, *Historical Texts relating to the fall of Babylon*, Frontis piece No. 4, shows two Bird-men carrying plants behind the Sun-god's boat, a scene which I am at a loss to explain unless these Bird-men are implied to be subjected, just as the Bull-man is shown sometimes in conflict and sometimes in attendance upon the Sun-god.

[3] So Mowinckel in *Acta Orientalia*, xv, 154.

[4] See below, p. 136, n. 2.

[5] R. Campbell Thompson, *The Epic of Gilgamesh*, 46.

means everlasting life. And thus the theft described in the Myth of Zu would signify the loss of the immortality which the gods had "retained in their keeping" and consequently a true "Götterdämmerung". The iconographical relations between the seals with bird or Bird-man on the one hand, and those of the liberated god on the other, add probability to the assumption that in the first-named group a plant may stand for "life", since these seals are evidently connected with the cycle of the god of fertility. If the plant were the "external soul" of a god of fertility,[1] it is clear that his resuscitation could only follow the defeat of the enemy who had robbed or damaged that plant. In this manner the various seal designs become understandable as consistent illustrations of a well-defined group of beliefs. Let us once more summarise the evidence. We find scenes of the subjection of a bird or Bird-man under circumstances which suggest that he had stolen or damaged a plant. We see that a captive bird or Bird-man figures in a scene where the liberation of the god from the mountain is either explicitly represented or implied by the attitude of his father Ea. Sometimes plants are figured as sprouting from the mountain-grave. They may indicate the revival of vegetation which is to follow the god's resuscitation; on the other hand they may also stand for the "life" of the god, restored to him after the defeat of the evil bird which endangered it. A similar ambiguity attaches to the plants appearing in or with the boat in which the Sun-god travels (§ 19*h*, p. 108). They may either signify in a general manner the connection between the god and the life of vegetation, or they may represent the "golden bough" which Aeneas had to break before he was taken across the Styx, just as Gilgamesh had to fetch something from a nearby grove before his boat journey.[2] But ultimately both interpretations are aspects of the same sombolism in which the plant represents abiding life.

It remains a matter for surmise, but we shall see presently that there is good evidence for connecting Zu with the hostile power on the seals under discussion, apart from the nature of his actual crime. Returning to the myth, we learn that

[1] According to the scheme of thought studied by Sir James Frazer in *Balder the Beautiful*.

[2] This connection is established by W. F. Jackson Knight, *Cumaean Gates*, especially pp. 24 f., 41. Miss G. Rachel Levy, in discussing the "Oriental Origin of Herakles" (*Journal of Hellenic Studies*, LIV, 44), mentions an orphic hymn, in which Herakles is said to be "whirling a branch, no dead club, to scatter the evil plagues". The reference is especially interesting in connection with our seals depicting the Sun-gods journey since Herakles on that occasion travelled in the sun's cup to the West...Sir James Frazer has pointed out (*The Golden Bough*, XI, 294 ff.) that Orpheus and Adonis too are sometimes depicted holding a branch to indicate that they "might yet be brought back from the Gates of Death to life and love".

the loss of the tablets makes Enlil powerless; on the other hand they bestow on Marduk the highest power, when he receives them in the Epic of Creation. In the myth of Zu, Lugalbanda, a son of Enlil and another form of the pre-Sargonid god of fertility, conquers Zu and recovers the "tablets of destiny" for his father. Here then is a parallel with the myths which underlie the New Year's celebrations. There too a god made powerless by enemies is liberated by his son. We have seen that in Pl. XIX*a*, and all the seals discussed in this connection, a hostile power symbolised by a bird is overcome before the god is liberated. And the probability that the "myth of Zu", in the late form in which it has come down to us, is but one variant of the same story is strengthened by the repeated references to Zu in the celebrations of the New Year. Once Ninurta's victory over the warder of the captured god is closely associated with a defeat of Zu.[1] Another commentary speaks of "the race which in the month of Nisan before Bel (i.e. Marduk) and all the sacred places they run in a frenzy", and this race is said to represent, in the yearly ritual, the defeat of Zu by Ninurta.[2] This is an equivalent in the texts to the regular appearance of Usmu reporting to Ea in connection with the capture of the Bird-man. If, in the following quotation, we read *Ea* for *Assur*, and *Usmu* in lines 58 and 59 where the name of a god is lost, we have an exact account of what the seals seem to depict:

58 That means, when Assur sent Ninurta to conquer the god Zu, the god so-and-so.
59 Before Assur spoke, saying: "Zu is conquered"; and Assur spoke, to the god so-and-so,
60 Saying: "Hasten unto all the gods, announce the tidings".[3]

It is important to remember that the evidence which led us to identify with Ninurta the liberator of the incarcerated god of Pl. XIX*a–d*, and on the other hand the material pointing to Ninurta as the conqueror of the bird in Pl. XXIII are mutually independent, being separate chains of iconographical connections leading us to certain texts. The agreement which appears to exist between texts and seal designs is thus accentuated, and once more shows the value which they possess as a potential source of information regarding the religion of the Ancients.

(*g*) *The Myth of Etana and Scenes of Daily Life.*

It is difficult to decide whether seal designs which appear merely to reflect scenes from the daily life of the people do not also possess some religious

[1] Ebeling, *Tod und Leben*, p. 33, lines 24–39.
[2] Langdon, *Epic of Creation*, pp. 44–7, lines 57, 58.
[3] *Ibid*. p. 45, lines 57–60.

significance. Agricultural subjects are not rare; we are shown an orchard watered by "shadufs"—water-buckets on long poles from which the runnels are filled to surround each tree trunk;[1] or we see the gathering of the date-harvest in a well-stocked garden of various plants (Pl. XXIV*d*);[2] or we witness ploughing and sowing (Pl. XXIV*e*).[3] But then we remember an Early Dynastic seal where the dates seem to be no sooner harvested than they are offered to a goddess.[4] And though it is true that birds are normally to be seen behind the plough and the sower, nevertheless their regular occurrence in these ploughing scenes reminds us of the "astral ploughman" of Pl. XX*a*. Similarly one wonders whether the flocks appearing in such seals as Pl. XXIV*g* are perhaps connected with the temple, since the temple herds played so large a part in the glyptic of earlier periods.[5] Moreover, this particular motive occurs quite frequently together with one which is frankly mythological. On the right-hand edge of Pl. XXIV*h* we see a man mounting to heaven on the back of a large bird. Interpreters agree to recognise in him Etana,[6] a man who assisted an eagle which had got into difficulties after betraying its friend the serpent with whom it had entered into a covenant. Etana rescued the bird and as his reward asked to be carried up to heaven to obtain the plant of birth, since he had so far remained childless notwithstanding his ceaseless offerings to Shamash.[7] Since the flight apparently ended in disaster (but the text is badly damaged there) it is not quite clear why this myth should appear on seals. Perhaps in early times there was an alternative good ending, or perhaps another story is illustrated. There seems no doubt that the man lifted from the earth is a shepherd. His dogs are regularly depicted looking up at their master, generally on either side of a bag or vessel which he left behind. Sometimes companions look up with the dogs or express their amazement by the lifting of an arm in the attitude

[1] A–156.

[2] So also Ur, 341; Kh. VI/153; and perhaps *Revue d'Assyriologie*, XXVIII (1931), p. 45, No. XII.

[3] So also As. 32/290; Bibliothèque Nationale, 7; Brussels, 572.

[4] Ur, 13. In Ward, 388, a god and goddess are seated on either side of the palm from which they take the bunches themselves. This is an Akkadian seal.

[5] In dealers' hands I have seen two seals which connect this scene with the gods, but none of the published specimens is unequivocal.

[6] Jolles (*Orientalistische Literaturzeitung*, XIV, 387–90) objects that the eagle lifting Etana in the poem is supposed to do so with his claws, since he invites the man "Place thy breast against my breast"; but the fact that the man on the seals is heavily bearded surely disposes of Jolles' alternative explanation, namely that we see here the eagle saving the baby Gilgamesh thrown from the window of a tower by the servants of his grandfather who feared for his throne, a story moreover only preserved in a late source (Aelian, *De nat. anim.* XII, 21).

[7] Langdon, *Semitic Mythology*, pp. 166 ff.

shown in Pl. XXIV*h*.[1] Otherwise the gesture in our plate would suggest that the shepherd is driving off the two lions, for two Akkadian seals are known to depict the age-old theme of the defence of the flocks, which we remember from the Uruk period onward.[2] But the comparison with other variants of the Etana theme suggests that the shepherd in Pl. XXIV*h* lifts his hand while looking at or calling out to Etana, shown rising on the other side of the tree. The lions would then not be preying on the flocks but would be part of the Etana story. In the text the eagle betrays the friendship of the serpent by devouring its young. It seems that on our older seal the place of the serpent is taken by the lion; one of the pair, at least, seems to be threatening the eagle in the tree, while the bird grasps a small animal which might be a cub.[3]

Once Etana is pictured with his dog and a shepherd who stands beside him carrying a leather-tongued whip, but the rest of the cylinder is filled with a hunting scene in the mountains,[4] a fact of some importance for the dating of such compositions.

Whether or not the scenes so far discussed have a religious meaning, they are certainly rendered with a delightful freedom and without trace of hieratic conventions. Thus we see in Pl. XXIV*g* the herdsman, who has driven the flock out of the reed enclosure where they passed the night, halting at the door to turn and speak to a companion who remains behind for dairy work. He is cleaning a large vessel while others stand around, among which we recognise a churn for the preparation of buttermilk. Outside the enclosure some cheeses are shown put out on a mat to dry. The suggestive atmosphere of the early morning of a rural day is completed by the bird perched on the top of the enclosure.[5]

The dairy work is regularly depicted at one side of the flock, and Pl. XXIV*g* may be a fresh elaboration of certain motives which play a subsidiary part in the complete scenes of which Pl. XXIV*h* is an example. Thus the first named scene may appear to us secular only because it happens to omit the main motive which was mythological.[6]

[1] See T–87; Ward, 391, 392, 394; Pinches, *Babylonian and Assyrian cylinder seals in the possession of Sir Henry Peek*, No. 18 (Ward, 393).

[2] As. 32/174; Unger, *Sumerische und Akkadische Kunst*, p. 87, Fig. 31 (seal of Dannili, Vienna).

[3] So Langdon, *Semitic Mythology*, p. 172, but he wrongly states that all these seals are "Early Sumerian"; the scene occurs exclusively on Akkadian seals.

[4] Kish, 1932/114.

[5] I have shown rather more than is necessary of this impression because it is one of the few successful survivals into Akkadian times of a frieze as a composition scheme.

[6] Similarly the herd alone is pictured in Ward, 396.

Of the secular nature of the seal design of Ibil-Ishtar there can be no doubt (Pl. XXIV*c*). The figure in cloak and cap is probably some official guided by tribesmen of the mountains and followed by a shaven scribe or priest, while in the background, or rather beneath the inscribed panel, two servants are carrying their master's requisites for the wild districts which he is visiting, namely a bed and some provisions.

Purely secular also are certain hunting scenes. Pl. XXIV*a* gives a fine seal which is unfortunately much worn. Text-fig. 36 renders another seal more remarkable for its composition than for the fineness of its modelling.[1]

Text-fig. 36. Hunting in the mountains.

The date of these seals has been much in doubt, but the plant appearing on the left in Text-fig. 36 leaves no doubt as to its Akkadian affinities (see for instance Pl. XVII*d*). Moreover, there is only one group of monuments with which these can be compared. It is true that their spirit recalls the Assyrian reliefs, but their closest affinity, especially in the manner in which the landscape element enters into the design, is with the stele of Naramsin.

The realism and love for the concrete of the Akkadian seal-cutters show indeed to no greater advantage than in the modelling of the animals on these seals. The composition, of course, is unrealistic in the sense that it is overcrowded by lions, game, hunters and dogs. A similar hunting scene, not in

[1] Other seals belonging to this class are: Orleans, C. 185 (*Assyr. und Arch. Studien Hilprecht gewidmet*, Plate facing p. 84, No. 4); Newell, 680. Compare the hair of the hunter on that seal with our Pl. XXIV*e*. Or perhaps a helmet is meant; in any case a similar rendering of hair or head-dress occurs on a fragment of a large stela found at Khafaje and belonging to the very end of the Early Dynastic period. See my *Early Dynastic sculpture from Tell Asmar and Khafaje* (*Oriental Institute Publications*, XLIV, Chicago, 1938), Pl. 110A. The genuineness and the date of these cylinders is shown, moreover, by the appearance of a similar scene, abbreviated, on a seal from Kish. See p. 139, note 4. It is interesting to notice in Text-fig. 36 that a mountain is rendered with a scale-like pattern when there is no need to draw detail in front of it, while otherwise it is merely outlined.

a mountainous setting but in the north-west Mesopotamian plain,[1] shows a lion driven off a wounded gazelle, while antelopes, a fox, an ostrich and a stag fill the rest of the field.

These hunting scenes are not particularly well adapted to the purposes of a cylinder seal. They crowd on to the small surface scenes which require whole walls to be adequately displayed. But their exceptional value lies in this very quality, that they reflect the greatness of an art of which nothing has been preserved for us but a few damaged stelae.

[1] Newell, 680, see previous note.

SECTION IV

MESOPOTAMIAN GLYPTIC FROM THE END OF THE AKKADIAN TO THE KASSITE DYNASTY

CHAPTER I. THE STYLISTIC DEVELOPMENT

§ 22. THE SEALS OF THE GUTI PERIOD AND OF THE THIRD DYNASTY OF UR

THE LAST KINGS of Sargon's Dynasty had to contend with barbaric hordes who invaded the country from the north-east. Eventually the mountaineers prevailed and the Akkadian empire collapsed amidst confusion. Part of the country experienced a serious setback of culture. This was demonstrably the case in Central Mesopotamia, and the poor glyptic found in strata of the Guti period at Tell Asmar contains but coarsened versions of a few of the older themes, especially presentations of worshippers to the gods. The style is linear and angular, lively, lacking charm but not vigour (Pl. XXV*a*).[1] Its craftsmanship might be explained as a purely local disintegration of Akkadian glyptic, were it not that evidence to be discussed in a later part of this book suggests that we have in the Guti technique a first instance of the intrusion into the Plain of one of the derivative styles which had sprung up in the surrounding regions which were culturally dependent upon Mesopotamia. These peripheral schools existed in all periods; another of their manifestations in Akkadian times is represented by Pl. XXV*b*, one of several cylinders found at Tell Asmar, but also closely resembling in material and design certain specimens from Susa, Assur and Telloh. This type of cylinder seems to be at home at Susa and to be ultimately derived from the Early Dynastic animal frieze.[2]

The cylinders so far discussed are truly characteristic of the Guti. But along with them we find the Sargonid style surviving in its purest form, and that especially in the south, where the results of the invasion were less disastrous. The city-states, though perhaps limited in the scope of their activities, maintained a considerable degree of prosperity, as the monuments of Gudea of Lagash show, and culture remained unimpaired. But later

1 Other seals of this period are: Newell, 114, 158, 160; A–179, 181, 185; and several from Tell Asmar.

2 Andrae, *Archaischen Ischtartempel*, p. 83; S–388–399; Kish, 30–114, Kish, 31–115; Ur, 97; As. 31/202, 227, 1101; As. 32/420; As. 33/46.

commentaries demonstrate that the domination of the barbarians was felt as deeply humiliating; compensation was found apparently in dwelling upon the intimate relationship with the gods which was the prerogative of the lawful inhabitants of the country. This spirit, which finds clear expression in Gudea's inscriptions, had a deplorable effect in the field of glyptic art. The rich variety of Akkadian themes vanished. Neither mythology nor the life of the people henceforth supplied subjects to the seal-cutters. Their repertoire became confined to ritual scenes, which illustrated the close relationship of men and gods. In Text-fig. 37 the god Ningiszida is shown introducing Gudea to the god Ea. In Text-fig. 38 the owner of the seal Urdun pours out a libation before the god Ningirsu while an anonymous deity intercedes on behalf of her protégé. Often the main deity who is thus approached remains similarly anonymous, at least to our knowledge.

Text-fig. 37. Seal of Gudea of Lagash.

Text-fig. 38. Seal of Urdun.

The divergence from the Akkadian treatment of this theme is not striking but nevertheless significant. In Pl. XX*b* or XXI*f* the setting is not specified, but, whatever the intention of the seal-cutter may have been, the impression prevails of an open-air scene. In Text-figs. 37 and 38, on the other hand, there can be no doubt that the presentation and the libation took place in a temple. The seal-cutter betrays a truly pious delight in ritualistic detail. The offering-stand with its palm branches and bunches of dates, the side-panels of the throne, are most carefully rendered. Various details appear for the first time at this period, for instance the panther-headed scimitar, the multiple mace and the double-headed eagle of Text-fig. 38, while the interceding deity, following the worshipper with uplifted hands, is also a contemporary design. Previously the introducing god had led his protégé by the hand as in Pl. XXV*a*. It is, of course, possible that in both cases the design was intended to convey that the interceding goddess stands beside the worshipper in front of the main deity, but for us it suffices to note that the rendering differs.

The peculiar spirit which became manifest in the Guti period under the

Gudea Dynasty at Lagash remained characteristic of the glyptic art of the country after the Guti had been expelled, 125 years later, and unified rule was established and maintained for over a century by the kings of the Third Dynasty of Ur. The seals reached a high standard of technical perfection (Pl. XXV*d–j*) and in many specimens a true piety has found adequate expression. But they repeat one or two subjects over and over again.

It is refreshing to find a few decorative designs which survived from the Akkadian repertoire (Pl. XXV*f*, *g*; Text-fig. 39). The narrative subjects occasionally found in Early Dynastic times, and so strikingly developed under Sargon's Dynasty, did not survive the latter's disappearance. Decorative designs did, however, survive to a larger extent than is generally acknowledged.[1] On the whole there is an instructive difference in their presentation. On Akkadian seals we find scenes of combat conceived in a heroic spirit, with well-matched antagonists, equals in strength whether they be human, animal or demoniacal (Pl. XVII). In the rendering of the Third Dynasty of Ur (Pl. XXV*f*) the nude hero relies on a weapon to supplement his physical power. Moreover, he does not touch the lion which he has engaged, and the futile gesture of his left arm weakens the action of the group. But it is a goddess who restrains the lion by grasping its tail. Though the motives are derived from the Akkadian repertoire we have travelled far from the original conception of this kind of scene. They are indeed ill-suited to express a belief in the gods as the ultimate source of all power, and this may explain their comparative rarity during the Third Dynasty of Ur. On the other hand, a number of seal impressions are known which show the well-established Akkadian arrangement of two pairs of combatants serving as heraldic supporters of an inscribed panel (Text-fig. 39). It is an innovation that the Dragon of the Weather-god (see §§ 21 (*b*), p. 124, and 27 (*f*), p. 174) now appears as the antagonist of the Bull-man; in the succeeding age he is to become even more thoroughly dissociated from Adad. But the usual pairs of "hero versus bull" and "Bull-man versus lion" do occur (Pl. XXV*g*) and a seal impression from Ilishuilia, prince of Eshnunna (Tell Asmar) and vassal

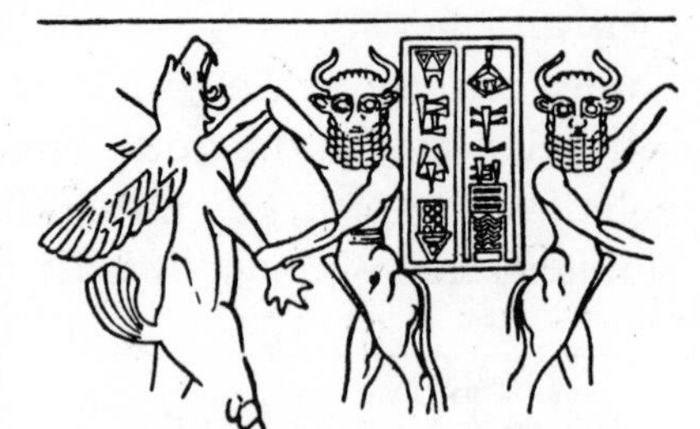

Text-fig. 39. Seal of Namu, servant of Shulgi.

[1] It so happens that very few actual cylinders of this type are preserved, or perhaps they are assigned to Akkadian times, in the collections. But there are a number of dated impressions: T–48, 50, 51, 67, 71–4. C. E. Keiser, *Selected Documents of the Ur Dynasty* (*Yale Oriental Series, Babylonian Texts*, XIV, No. 196).

of Ibisin of Ur, shows a design obviously inspired by such monuments as the stela of victory of Naramsin.[1]

The almost universal application of writing to seals now weakened any tendency on the part of the craftsmen to vary the seal designs, for it was no longer on the design that the individuality of the seals depended. Even Pl. XXV *d* was meant to receive a text, and the two crossing lions and the crescent are awkwardly superimposed on a square reserved for an inscription which the buyer of the seal apparently did not require. Our Pl. XXV gives, in fact, a greater impression of variety than can be considered as representative of the glyptic of the period. For each small variation which we show one must postulate several score of seals of the type of Pl. XXV *e* and *j*.

The ritual scenes differ from those of the Sargonid period in externals as well as in style. The shaggy worshippers of an earlier age (Pls. XX *b, d*; XXI *c, f*; XXII *c, j*) are replaced by clean-shaven priests or by men wearing a turban or skull-cap, and sometimes a long well-kept beard (Pl. XXV *d, e, j*). Though it is sometimes impossible to identify the gods even on good seals (Pl. XXV *j*),[2] they have, as a rule, a characteristic attribute. In Pl. XXV *d* it is Ea with the flowing vase and the goat-fish as a footstool. In Pl. XXV *c* Meslamtea holds a scimitar and a stalk with three flowers or poppy heads.[3] This seal is dated to the reign of Shulgi, that of Pl. XXV *e* to Ibisin's reign. The god Tishpak, worshipped at Eshnunna where this seal was found,[4] is shown with two dragon heads projecting from his shoulders, a characteristic which in the south pertained to Ningiszida.[5] Elsewhere a god of fertility is shown holding a rope which is ringed through the nose of a goat upon which he is seated, thus distinguished, as an emblem, from the thrones decorated with animal figures.[6] Imdugud appears on this seal, and apparently often, though not always, with the same god. This also applies to the lion,[7] who stands before or behind an enthroned god, sometimes holding a standard with five globes not unlike the symbol occurring in the Jemdet Nasr period

[1] See Frankfort, Lloyd and Jacobsen, *The Gimilsin Temple and the Palace of the Rulers at Tell Asmar* (*Oriental Institute Publications*, No. XLIII).

[2] The god may be Nusku, since the seal is dedicated to that god "for the life of Shulgi"; see the translation of the similar inscription of Pl. XXV *c* on p. 10 above.

[3] The translation is given on p. 10 above.

[4] *Oriental Institute Communications*, No. 13, Fig. 14 and pp. 42 ff.

[5] T–111; reign of Shulgi.

[6] *Revue Archéologique*, 1909, Pl. 13, Fig. 1, pp. 250–53.

[7] C. E. Keiser, *loc. cit.* Nos. 155, 195; Louvre, A–301; Newell, 173; Bibliothèque Nationale, 116. The last three are probably later in date.

upon the byre or pen of the sacred herd (Pl. VI *a*).[1] At times the lion, Imdugud, a goose or a monkey appear as ensigns mounted on poles (Pl. XXVI *e*).[2] Other animals such as a bull or goat may occur as a footstool or standing free behind the throne, or beneath the panel with the inscription as in the Akkadian epoch.[3] Occasionally small shapes of gods or worshippers are inserted between the larger figures (Pl. XXV *e*). The nude hero with a flowing vase may appear in this function.[4] A pot-stand may identify the female divinity with the Mother-Goddess discussed in § 21 (*d*), p. 129.[5]

Once Abu or Ninurta is shown (Pl. XXV *h*) carrying in one hand a plough and in the other a lion-headed club; his attitude might be an allusion to the liberating of the incarcerated god from the mountain (§ 19 (*g*), p. 105). But mythological motives are very rare at this time.

In one respect the seals of the Third Dynasty of Ur show a completely new departure. Among the gods worshipped there now appear the deified kings. Repeatedly a subject, especially a high official, pays homage on his seal to his enthroned lord, and is introduced to the august presence by an interceding goddess exactly as in religious scenes of presentation. The only difference is the headgear of the occupant of the throne, who does not wear the horned crown when the earthly ruler is intended (Pl. XXV *i*).[6]

The stylistic difference between the seals of the Third Dynasty of Ur and the Dynasty of Sargon of Akkad is considerable. The bold cutting of the older period is replaced by a much more minutely elaborate manner. The instruments used were apparently finer, the incisions are narrower and far more numerous. The flounces of the garments of the gods, the fringes of the shawls worn by men, are rendered with precision; the folds of the shawl where it passes across the chest or hangs down from the arm are given graceful curves. The style, as a whole, is somewhat anaemic, and of limited scope, but its delight in *minutiae* balances to some extent the loss of vitality.

[1] T-111, 213; Keiser, *loc. cit.* No. 155. The symbol also occurs on the seal quoted on p. 145, note 6, and on Newell, 129 (a poor seal of the Ur III dynasty); also on a stela-fragment of Gudea, Fondation Piot, *Monuments et Mémoires*, xvi, Pl. II, 3.

[2] Keiser, *loc. cit.* No. 201, and perhaps 58. Pinches, *Behrens Collection*, p. 27 and frontispiece. The Hague, Pl. III, 11 (our Pl. XXVI *e*), and Pl. VI, 29; Newell, 158. Note that the alabaster monkey found in the Shamash temple at Ishchali and dated to a slightly later period was perforated below as if for mounting on a stick (*Illustrated London News*, 5 September 1936, p. 389, Fig. 12).

[3] De Clercq, 106, 108.

[4] T-156, and impression on a tablet dated to the reign of Bursin.

[5] *American Journal of Semitic Languages*, xxvi, 170; De Clercq, 113.

[6] Also A-225; B.M. 89129, the seal of a servant of Urnammu.

§ 23. THE SEALS OF THE ISIN-LARSA PERIOD

The disruption of the realm of Ur by the joint action of Amorites from the Syrian desert and Elamites from the eastern mountains led to conditions reminiscent of pre-Sargonid times. A number of city-states competed for a hegemony without on the whole succeeding in establishing their authority beyond a more or less restricted neighbourhood. Internal strife prevailed from the fall of Ur, about 2186 B.C., until the fall of Isin, conquered by Hammurabi of Babylon in the 30th year of his reign about 1924 B.C. The two intervening centuries are named after the two cities which stand out as more powerful than the others.

In these cities Babylonian culture probably maintained a high standard; we know very little of this, but we do know that the city of Babylon, under the earlier kings of Hammurabi's Dynasty, was an insignificant place, and that works of art dated to the reign of Hammurabi, such as his stelae and the bronzes recently obtained by the Louvre, are part of an artistic tradition which must reach back uninterrupted, at least to the Third Dynasty of Ur.

The extraordinary number of tablets dated to the Isin-Larsa period proves the liveliness of commercial intercourse. We have remarked already that this may well have been detrimental to glyptic art, since the great demand for seals led to standardisation and a decline in workmanship. Stratified material is unfortunately rare. At Tell Asmar we excavated a town which flourished during the decline of the central power, and the cylinders found there are merely coarsened renderings of the presentation scenes of the Third Dynasty of Ur (Pl. XXVI *a–c*). It is for this reason that the new glyptic style, established by the end of the Third Millennium B.C., is called after the First Dynasty of Babylon. But the innovations can be traced as early as Sinmuballit's—and to some extent into Sumalailum's—reign, and we can hardly assign a leading position to the city of Babylon at that time. Artistic and political development need not proceed at the same rate. But in the absence of precise data it will at least be convenient to call after the Isin-Larsa period the style in use during its earlier half, and to call after the First Dynasty of Babylon the new style which had become established throughout Mesopotamia by about 2000 B.C.

§ 24. THE STYLE OF THE FIRST DYNASTY OF BABYLON

The low level to which glyptic art had sunk in the Isin-Larsa period created considerable practical difficulties. Unless the owner's name was clearly impressed it was generally impossible to distinguish one sealing from another.

Towards the end of the Isin-Larsa period the makeshift was adopted of drilling a couple of holes into the cylinders; and these, being arbitrarily placed between the conventional figures, made it possible to recognise the impressions of individual seals (Pl. XXVI *d, f, h*). A similar attempt to make the seals easily distinguishable may have led to the reversal of certain figures in the design (Pl. XXVI *f*). These simple devices were occasionally used at a later date when a more varied style had already been developed;[1] they were poor substitutes nevertheless which proclaimed the inability of the seal-cutters to respond to the requirements of their clients. And during the First Babylonian Dynasty a new style was developed which aimed at restoring the distinctive individuality of each seal design by the variety of components. The earliest dated impressions of this style belong, as we have said, to the reign of Sinmuballit, Hammurabi's predecessor.

The ritual scene remained, at first, the main theme of decoration, but variety was obtained by filling the cylinder surface with several secondary motives, unconnected with the main theme. These motives consisted either of divine figures, or of sacred symbols or ritual objects such as maces and vases, or of purely decorative designs. The last-named group was largely derived from the Sargonid repertoire, which had survived, at least in its more common decorative designs, during the Third Dynasty of Ur. The nude hero, with or without flowing vase, the Bull-man, crossed lions or animals attacked by hero or Bull-man, again make their appearance (Pls. XXVI *h*; XXVIII *k*; XXIX *a, e*). Even the grotesque figure of the human-headed bull is dragged from oblivion to appear in connection with the club with two lions' heads (Pl. XXVI *g*). The way in which these archaisms are used proves the motives to have been derived from ancient seals which might turn up accidentally (as they do to-day) or which were still in use. The crossed lions (Pls. XXV *g*; XXVI *h*) are shown with their heads seen from above, as was normal in Early Dynastic but not in Sargonid glyptic.[2] The regularity with which such features as the association of human-headed bull and club occur in the glyptic of the First Babylonian Dynasty demonstrates their derivative character. Motives invented by the Babylonian seal-cutters, such as the god with the multiple mace, are handled freely; but the motives which were, perhaps in one workshop only, derived from ancient seals were somewhat anxiously repeated under the single form in which they were first adopted. Thus the lions never cross with another animal as they

[1] De Clercq, 74, 96, 107, 125, 126, 170; Louvre, A–276, 281, 205, 341, 372, 350, 406; Bibliothèque Nationale, 134; Weber, 450; Weber, 101.

[2] Hague, 3; V.A. 3419; Newell, 166.

do in Early Dynastic times, but always appear as a rigidly symmetrical pair, although symmetry is not habitually used by the seal-cutters of the period.

It is curious that with the revival of Sargonid motives something of their spirit seems occasionally to be recaptured. Often the modelling of the figures is vigorous and life-like as in Pls. XXVIII*k* and XXIX*a*; the latter seal shows a bold acceptance of spatial depth as an element of the relief; note the hero's leg passing in front of the lion; once we even find an enthroned god depicted in full front view (see below, p. 245, note 5). These experiments with perspective remain isolated instances within a glyptic school which is nothing if not conventional.

The small animals, monkeys, goat-fish, lions, antelopes and the ritual objects such as vases, maces and so on, and even small human or mythological figures which are freely interspersed between the main figures on the seals (Pls. XXVI–XXIX), recall the filling motives of Early Dynastic times. But their function is not the same. The development of Mesopotamian glyptic had been decisively influenced by the innovations of Sargon's age. Even though the most outstanding qualities of Sargonid art, its love for the concrete and talent for narrative, were misunderstood by a later age, its mode of decoration by means of a single clearly limited design remained the only one recognised during the First Dynasty of Babylon. The textile patterns and continuous friezes of Early Dynastic times were not revived as principle of composition before late Assyrian times. And the small designs strewn between the larger figures on Babylonian seals serve no decorative purpose but are an additional means of distinguishing individual sealings.

It is a curious fact that no unifying principle can be discovered in these seal designs. Neither decorative harmony nor the rendering of a story or myth serves as a basis of representation. We are faced with juxtapositions of entirely unrelated figures, sometimes added to a presentation or offering scene, but often forming by themselves the decoration of the cylinder. When neither decorative nor narrative coherence is required as a basis of design, an unstable equilibrium ensues; and we notice, in fact, a double development which, starting from the usual designs, leads to two neatly opposed extremes; and each of these has a decisive influence on the further development of Mesopotamian glyptic.

The usual design of the First Babylonian Dynasty represented, after all, a compromise. The traditional subject of man's approach to the divine powers was maintained, but additional matter served to make the seals distinctive. It is obvious that the accent could be shifted either to the traditional or the subordinate elements of the design, and this is what we actually find.

On the one hand the ritual scene was maintained, but since it was not distinctive as a design, interest centred on the inscriptions. Only two or three figures were preserved and those widely spaced and clearly cut. Commonly we see only a male deity, with whom one or two goddesses intercede on behalf of the worshipper named in the inscription, which thus becomes the main feature of the seal (Pls. XXVII *m*; XXVIII *f*); occasionally the worshipper himself is depicted (Pls. XXVIII *e*; XXX *g*). Among the seals of less quality (which occur of course at all stages of development) we find therefore a further simplification in the omissions of the main deity, so that only the interceding goddesses appear. Pls. XXIX *j*; XXX *a* are examples of this class; the paradox which always results from mechanical deterioration led in the present case to the production of seals with only these figures and no inscription. On the other hand we see in Pl. XXIX *j* two interceding goddesses facing a panel, in addition to certain other motives. But as a rule[1] the inscription, accompanied by one or two purely conventional figures, is all that the seals of this type display. This extreme simplification of the style of the First Dynasty of Babylon underlies the glyptic of the Kassite period.

The opposite pole is represented by such seals as we illustrate in Pls. XXVIII *k*, *l*; XXIX *c*, *e*, *g*, *m*. There the accent is shifted from the scene of worship to the additional motives; in fact the latter often hold the field alone. In Pl. XXIX *m* they run riot while of the original scene nothing but the male god, the interceding goddess and symbol of Marduk remain.[2] Pl. XXIX *a* is an interesting instance of the reversal of the original situation; the interceding goddess and the worshipper (a nude woman) are reduced to small scale figures filling open spaces between decorative groups. It is this development, in which the secondary motives have crowded out the scene

[1] E.g. Qb, 23; Newell, 234, 235, 260, 273; A–460–469, etc.

[2] This seal is very interesting since it presents all the more common groups of the contemporary repertoire; the two registers are separated by a row of nude women; above we see a male worshipper, the dragon, the mace with the double panther-head, and a lion devouring a gazelle; below there is a dragon devouring a man, two wrestlers and a bow-legged dwarf beside a nude figure. Similar seals are A–388, 459, 517 (top); 869, 877; De Clercq, 288; Ward-Morgan, 210, 211; Qd, 18; Newell, 261; Ward, 845, 849. For some reason which I fail to understand these cylinders are generally clssed as foreign ("Syro-Hittite"). They do not however answer to the requirements of foreign seals (see p. 224, § 34) and the foregoing analysis of the seal of Pl. XXIX *m* shows once more its exclusive dependence upon the Babylonian repertoire.

of worship and the inscription, which underlies the "Mitannian" style of the Kirkuk seals.

The two contrasting styles which developed out of the compromise during the First Dynasty of Babylon have one element in common; the destruction of the ritual scene which had been the predominant pictorial element under the Third Dynasty of Ur. Its lack of individuality was now apparently considered a decisive argument against its use. In the line of development which made the inscription the central feature of the design, the scene of worship was simply neglected as superfluous. The contrasting school, in agreement with all strong schools of glyptic art, concentrated on achieving distinctions by means of the design alone, and thus had no use for the conventional scene of worship.

The two developments which we have outlined took place simultaneously; this, in fact, is what we should expect, since each of them realised one of the two extremes inherent in the compromise effected under the style of the First Babylonian Dynasty. Their evolution was also rapid, and this reduces the usefulness of the seals of the period as dating evidence; they cannot serve for distinguishing remains of successive reigns. But we have to accept this fact; we actually find side by side the complex seals of the First Babylonian Dynasty and the two extreme forms which are potentially present in that complexity. Towards the end of the Dynasty the extreme types become more numerous. At the same time we notice certain technical changes which may thus serve as chronological evidence. These conclusions follow from a consideration of impressions on dated tablets, and of a few dated cylinders.

At the beginning of the First Dynasty the style of the Isin-Larsa period is still predominant, as proved by a seal impression of Sumuabum.[1] In Sumulailum's reign we find the presentation scenes still used, but the god is no longer seated.[2] Another impression[3] shows the more elaborate variety of the new style, in the manner of our Pl. XXVIII *k*. But only with the next reign does dated material of the new style become common. Along with the usual designs which maintain the presentation scenes but add numerous secondary motives, we already find in Sinmuballit's reign representations of the two extreme forms: one impression[4] shows the design reduced to three figures; another[5] the crowding of a number of small figures into two registers in the manner of our Pl. XXIX *m*.

A valuable envelope dated to the reign of Hammurabi's successor Sam-

[1] *Museum Journal*, 1922, Fig. 25.
[2] Bibliothèque Nationale, 138.
[3] A–477.
[4] A–518.
[5] A–517, top.

suiluna contains twenty-five impressions of seven different seals. It is reproduced in our Pl. II*m* and, partially, in Pl. XXX*a*.

The new style is, as always, observable throughout the whole of Mesopotamia and stands in no relation to the particular region where the central power became ultimately established. Tablets dated in the reign of Hammurabi's rival Rimsin, and therefore sealed by cylinders made, presumably, within his realm, show the same style.[1] Hammurabi's political genius gained hegemony for Babylon, but there is no proof that the Babylonian artists had previously played a leading part in the country. Since the new features are reflected in the Cappadocian tablets which are contemporary with the early reigns of the First Dynasty of Babylon, it is clear that the new glyptic art must have developed in Isin and Larsa, which were, indeed, older centres of culture than Babylon.

The style of yet a century later, about 1800 B.C., is exemplified by the impressions on tablets dated to the reigns of Ammiditana and Ammizaduga[2] which correspond in style with our Pl. XXX*c–f*.

The subjects are identical with those of preceding reigns; the *guilloche* of Pl. XXX*e* has been wrongly considered a Syrian motive; it is at home in Mesopotamian art from the Early Dynastic period onwards and occurs on seals of the contemporary native style (Pl. XXIX*l*) and a seal on the tablet of Pls. II*m* and XXX*a*.[3] On the other hand, a reflex of the exceedingly strong influence which Mesopotamia was exercising in Syria at the time may be seen in the presence of two winged sphinxes in a Babylonian sealing on a tablet dated to the 5th year of Ammizaduga's reign[4] and perhaps also in the fact that Adad in Text-fig. 40 stands on two mountains as is usual with the Syrian and Hittite Weather-gods.

But if the subjects of Pl. XXX*c–f* are Babylonian, their execution shows a great difference from those so far discussed (Pls. XXV–XXVIII).

In the later seals the drill has been used excessively. It shows in the shoulder, hands and hair of Pl. XXX*c*, *e*. In fact, the whole design was apparently first roughly outlined, and then, instead of being carefully incised with the burin, the main points were fixed with a drill. Thus, for instance, for the divine figures of Pl. XXX*c*, three points—the crown, the shoulders and the feet—were first drilled. The coarse cylindrical shapes of this seal are also due to an excessive use of the drill. We have reproduced a fragmentary

[1] E.g. A–485, 486, 498; *Amtliche Berichte der Preuss. Kunstslg.* XXX (1909), pp. 129 f.

[2] A–569, 572.

[3] A–877 is also purely Babylonian.

[4] A–570.

impression of an unfinished seal of this period from Ishchali (Pl. XXX*b*) which shows that a first removal of stone by the drill makes it impossible to produce the finer details by a subsequent use of the graver. And we note in yet a third method the influence of a slackened technique upon the design. Here as many motives as possible are reduced to strings of drill holes, as in Pl. XXX*f*, with the curls of the nude hero's beard, the streams of water flowing from his vase, the fringed edges of the shawls of the subsidiary figures. Marduk's traditional flounced or hairy garment had to be done by straight lines, and the same applies to the head of his dragon and the minute figure of the libation priest behind him, where drilling would have merely created chaos. But the sun symbol was reduced to a rosette of drill holes and the prevalence of the drill technique may have accounted for the renewed popularity of the staff with the seven globes which was a motive in use during the Third Dynasty of Ur, then disappeared almost completely and now apparently took the place of the saw of Shamash.

That the god of Pl. XXX*c*, *d*, who steps upon a mountain and carries this symbol is indeed Shamash, is proved by one seal, where his foot is placed on a human-headed bull;[1] elsewhere he holds the saw in his other hand[2] and the emblem itself is once held, as a standard, by two Bull-men (Pl. XXX*h*). The use of the drill, and especially the tubular drill, reduces the *guilloche* to a series of concentric circles, just as happens in the Mitannian style.[3]

The decline of technique is also emphasised by cylinders with the simplified design accompanying an inscription (Pl. XXX*e*, *g*). There is indeed no reason why the subject should affect the execution, and sometimes the sun reduced to a rosette and other traces of the excessive art of the drill occur in this class also.[4]

It will be clear that the last part of the First Babylonian Dynasty presents a complicated aspect in matters of glyptic. We have already successively described three lines of development: firstly, the simplification of design which destroys the main theme, does away with the inscription and results in a more or less careful composition of isolated motives (Pls. XXVII *l*; XXVIII *k*, *l*; XXIX *j*, *k*, *m*);[5] secondly, a simplification of the subject in which the secondary motives are suppressed and the inscription made into the main feature (Pls. XXVII *m*; XXVIII *i*; XXIX *j*; XXX *g*);[6] thirdly, a

[1] A–863.
[2] Bibliothèque Nationale, 154.
[3] Bibliothèque Nationale, 230; a purely Babylonian seal of the late style.
[4] A–470.
[5] See p. 150, note 2.
[6] Similar seals are exceedingly common, e.g. Qb, 23; Newell, 234, 235, 260, 273.

coarsening of the technique by an excessive use of the drill (Pl. XXX*c–f*).[1] But all three tendencies worked simultaneously; thus, for instance, we have from Ammizaduga's reign not only seal impressions showing the increasing use of the drill, but also simplified yet carefully executed seals of the type of Pl. XXX*g*.[2] In fact, the best glyptic of the First Babylonian Dynasty continued to exercise influence for some considerable time after its manufacture had ceased. It seems unlikely that seals in the fine linear style, without preponderant use of the drill, were made after the Dynasty had been swept away, under Ammizaduga's successor, by the invading Kassites. But the curious seal of Pl. XXXI *a* shows how the products of a higher craftsmanship were valued by those who could not equal them. It shows a cylinder of the Hammurabi Dynasty of a late simplified design, one god and two interceding goddesses, purely conventional but beautifully executed. Between the figures designs in the Kirkuk style have been subsequently carved to bring it up to date. And this is not an isolated instance.[3] Elsewhere fine seals of the First Dynasty of Babylon are found together with those of the Kassite period;[4] in Palestine one of these late Babylonian seals appeared in an Eighteenth Dynasty context.[5] Indeed the impressions on tablets from Hana[6] show that during the first reigns of the Kassite Dynasty seals like Pl. XXX*c* were still in use.

However, by the end of the sixteenth century two new indigenous styles had come into being, the Kassite style in the south, based on the simplified Babylonian designs with few figures and the text as their main features, and a northern Babylonian style or rather one which deserves another designation, since it is by no means confined to the region of Kirkuk but is found as far east as Tepe Ghiyan in Persia, and as far south-west as Tell ed Duweir in Southern Palestine; this is in reality a Mitannian style.

We shall find that during the last centuries of the Second Millennium B.C. these two opposing styles were blended by the young genius of Assyria into

[1] Similar seals, often considered Syrian, but in fact purely Babylonian, are: De Clercq, 156, 235; Newell, 204 (water), 252 (sun and crescent symbol); *American Journal of Archaeology*, II, Pl. V, No. 7; *American Journal of Semitic Languages*, XLIV, 232 ff., No. 38; Musée Guimet, 122, 123; Bibliothèque Nationale, 148, 232, 430, 437, 438 (439 is peripheral); *Hilprecht Festschrift* (1909), Plate facing p. 90, Nos. 20, 21. With Bibliothèque Nationale, 437, cf. Pl. XXIX*a* and *Revue d'Assyriologie*, XXIII, 18, No. 7; De Clercq, 162.

[2] Ranke, *Babylonian Legal and Business Documents from Sippar* (Philadelphia, 1906), Pl. X, No. 15.

[3] De Clercq, 66; Louvre, D–48.

[4] *Uruk Vorläufiger Berecht*, VI.

[5] *Museum Journal*, 1928, p. 161. The layer is dated to Amenhotep III, about 1400 B.C.

[6] A–596.

something novel and valuable. But their paternity of this distant offspring is not the main claim to distinction of the seals of the First Babylonian Dynasty. They had, in fact, an immediate and contemporaneous influence of unusual scope and great historical significance. This by no means brilliant stage of Mesopotamian glyptic art was mainly instrumental in disseminating Babylonian motives and designs throughout the Near East.

The expansive force (which was largely commercial) of the Hammurabi Dynasty had greater influence than artistic merit. The Babylonian seals which reached Egypt and Crete during this time could not influence the development of the highly individual art-forms of those countries; but the Asiatic fringe of the Mediterranean did not harbour people of equal originality and artistic power; and the whole of Syrian glyptic during the Second Millennium B.C., and a considerable part of its applied art, is dependent upon the seals of the First Dynasty of Babylon for its motives.

CHAPTER II. THE SUBJECTS OF THE SEAL DESIGNS OF THE FIRST BABYLONIAN DYNASTY

§ 25. THE ASTROLOGICAL HYPOTHESIS

Since the seal designs of the First Dynasty of Babylon are as a rule mere conglomerations of figures, we can only deal with its subject-matter by discussing these figures one by one.

There is, however, one point of view which would enable us to consider at least the best products of the period as something more than a haphazard collection of motives, assembled merely to be distinctive in its variety. It is possible to see in many of the best seal designs an astrological significance. The mediocre and poor seals would, as always, be mere imitations of the better examples and lack a meaning of their own. But in the case of such designs as those of Pl. XXVI *k* or Pl. XXVII *d* or Pl. XXVIII *k, n,* for instance, it is quite possible to claim that the great gods represent the planets, while the other figures symbolise signs of the Zodiac, either those which according to astrological belief are of special importance because they stood in the Ascendant or in Midheaven at the time of birth, or because they served as "House" to the ruling of other planets. Of the Zodiacal signs in their Babylonian form only two, Cancer and Sagittarius, do not occur on the seals of the First Dynasty of Babylon; Aries, called the labourer, may be represented by the small human figures. Taurus would appear in its usual form; Gemini would be two *talim*, "twins", such as the two nude heroes wrestling (for the denomination of which we have textual evidence; see p. 60) or even hero and Bull-man; Leo appears frequently; Virgo could be represented by any goddess, since her symbol was a woman with an ear of corn[1] and most goddesses were fertility deities. Virgo bore a similar epithet *Banât riḫutum* "who creates seed"—and was identified with Shala. Libra and Scorpio both occur in their modern form, but Sagittarius appears in the immediately succeeding, Kassite, period, as a Scorpion-man or centaur shooting with bow and arrow. Capricorn, on the other hand, is embodied in Ea's goat-fish, which shape it retains even with us, while Aquarius might well be represented by the nude hero with the flowing vase, which alternates with a female figure similarly equipped; for this constellation, though sometimes treated as masculine, is called Gula, a form of the Mother-Goddess. Pisces, finally, would appear in Babylonia as mermaid and bird ("The Tails").

[1] *Revue d'Assyriologie,* XVI, p. 135.

As to the identification of the planets, the equations Sun=Shamash, Moon=Sin, Mercury=Nabu, Venus=Ishtar, Mars=Nergal, Jupiter=Marduk and Saturn=Ninurta are well established. In addition to this double series of equations it would be possible to expect the representation of other groups of stars which played a part in Mesopotamian astrology. Thus the best seals, which were made to order, should present us with a kind of horoscope either conventional or real, of the owner, or of his king or town, even if we do not possess a key enabling us to read them.

But two considerations prevent us from following up this hypothesis in detail. In the first place astrological prognoses are only known in matters relating to the king or the state. It may be a mere accident that we do not possess astrological works concerning individuals; but under the present circumstances we have no right to assume that astrology was thought to be relevant to the affairs of private citizens.[1] In the second place it seems that astronomy as a comparatively exact science dates only from late Assyrian times. In fact its most remarkable developments can be dated to about 700 B.C. and ascribed to the northern town of Calah (Nimrud).[2]

On the other hand, the period with which we are dealing includes the reign of Ammizaduga, the fourth successor of Hammurabi, and in his reign very precise and valuable observations of Venus were made. These remain inexplicable on the assumption that astronomy only dated from the eighth and seventh centuries B.C. Our period differs at least to this extent from those which precede it.

In dealing with early Dynastic or Akkadian seals, written sources supply no justification for the invoking of astrology as an aid to the explanation of seal designs, but as regards the First Dynasty of Babylon this may possibly be allowed. The astronomical observations at Calah may prolong a tradition going back to the beginning of the Second Millennium B.C. It is almost certain, for instance, that signs of the Zodiac and other constellations are figured on the Kassite boundary stones and their names occur in the Isin-Larsa period.[3] There are at least two seals of the second Syrian group which seem to depict the Pleiads,[4] and the seven drill-holes in our Text-fig. 81 (p. 251)

[1] Schott in *Zeitschrift der Deutschen Morgenländischen Gesellschaft*, XIII (1934), p. 313. This quotation which explicitly states that "this sign does not apply to a householder but to the whole realm", suggests perhaps that other signs could be observed which did concern individuals.

[2] Schott, *loc. cit.*

[3] For the early occurrence of names of constellations, see Schott, *loc. cit.* p. 309. The astral significance of the symbols on the boundary stones was at first much over-rated. A reasonable statement is given by Hinke, *A new Boundary Stone of Nebuchadnezzar I*, pp. 71–115.

[4] Ward, 879; A–924.

may have the same significance. For, finally, there is the indubitable evidence already noted of the Venus observations in the reign of Ammizaduga. Whatever the uncertainties due to the present state of our knowledge, the astrological hypothesis deserves consideration, since it is the only one which can confer a degree of unity upon the seal designs of the period.

Tentative research in this direction would naturally take us far out of our course, and we shall, therefore, merely treat the various themes in isolation. Our task, in other words, is purely iconographical.

We have already established the fact that the inscriptions on the seals refer only in exceptional cases to the seal designs. We shall therefore, if possible, deal with each motive by starting from a representation which by its detail establishes the identity of the figure under discussion, and from these follow up the several versions which can be safely called variants of the same theme.

§ 26. GODS AND MEN

(*a*) *Introductory.*

The distinction between deities and mortals has become somewhat vague in the seal designs of this period. The horned crown, it is true, still appears in most of the carefully executed seals as part of the god's attire, but certain divinities like the Sun-god or the god of the west are occasionally depicted with a turban similar to those worn by an earthly ruler. On the other hand, the deification of the kings of Ur had tended to diminish the difference between gods and mortals in the designs, so that subjects and officials were depicted approaching the king of Ur exactly as they would enter the presence of a deity. As we have seen, even the interceding goddess with uplifted hands accompanies her devotee into the presence of his overlord. In some cases it must remain doubtful whether a god or a ruler is represented.

In one or perhaps two types, the distinction between human being and god is always clear. There can be no doubt as to the mortal nature of the priest who is shown on many seals with a bucket of holy water and a sprinkling brush; he often wears a circlet with some object, which remains one of the uraeus of Pharaoh, and is no doubt a part of his ritual attire. Now this priest often stands upon a square box or podium or stool, and wherever he occurs he is the only figure in such a position (Pl. XXVIII *a*, *d*).[1] The stand appears to have the same function in some of the Phoenician ivories found at Nimrud, and its wide use in Syrian and Palestinian religion has suggested that King Josiah stood on such a stool and not near a pillar "to make his

[1] Also Bibliothèque Nationale, 229, 233, 234; A–362, and elsewhere.

covenant before the Lord" (ii Kings 23, *v.* 3).[1] If we accept the modern author's statement that the stool was used to put the worshipper "on a level" with the god, we must interpret his words with the magico-religious connotation appropriate to the times with which we are dealing. It is likely that the mounting of the stool was the final act of a "rite de passage" by which the worshipper left the impurity of his earthly environment, and thereby became able to approach the deities. We have seen already that some Early Dynastic and Akkadian designs may show a similar approach to the deity (§ 20 (*b*), end, p. 116).

Occasionally, however, we see another male figure mounted on the stool. This is comparatively rare.[2] In Pl. XXVI *i* the sprinkling priest is drawn on a small scale but without the stool, and he faces towards Ishtar, who is also the recipient of the sacrificial kid and the prayer of intercession by worshipper and goddess. But the remainder of the scene is occupied by a bearded figure on a stand, whom we might interpret as god, king or man. The inscription runs "Ninshubur, true vizier of Inanna", and refers therefore to the interceding goddess. A similar case is presented by some other seals,[3] where a worshipper approaches Shamash, behind whom a priest with sprinkling brush and bucket stands upon a stool. The remaining space is occupied by a figure who may or may not be divine and who is also placed upon the "stool". Sometimes it is a similar bearded figure as that of Pl. XXVI *i*, standing on a stool between Ishtar and an interceding goddess.

As far as the designs show details there seems to be a difference between the base used in these cases and the stool of the sprinkling priest. The latter, whether in one or two storeys, resembles the design used for rendering either the dais or the mats upon which gods and kings are enthroned (Pls. XXV *d, e*; XXVI *e*; XXVII *a*) and this, as we shall see presently, gives an additional clue as to its meaning. On the other hand, we see on the base of the figure on the left of Pl. XXVI *i* rows of triangles which are most likely a simplification of the scale pattern used for rendering mountains. We know that bases of statues, at least in later times, were thus decorated.[4] On Babylonian seals the gods appear in person; but the figures on the base never show divine attributes, and it seems most likely that they depict statues of the king, such as were placed in the temples, and may conceivably have been included in the scene of worship or sacrifice.

[1] Barnett in *Iraq*, II, pp. 209 ff. See also *ibid.* Pl. XXVI.
[2] Bibliothèque Nationale, 167 (a peripheral seal), 228; Newell, 205.
[3] Bibliothèque Nationale, 167; Newell, 205.
[4] Weissbach, *Babylonische Miscellen*, Frontispiece.

As common as the priest is a nude female figure which is placed upon the stool in the seal designs. She has long been known as the "naked goddess", but there is no reason to consider this figure as a deity. She never wears the horned crown, and is used on the best examples and in the mature style of the First Babylonian Dynasty exclusively in subordinate positions, like the animals and other divine emblems which are interspersed between the larger figures (Pl. XXVI *k*). She is always shown full-face, and is often placed on a small scale between a god and the interceding goddess (Text-figs. 40, 43, pp. 163, 174), but becomes more conspicuous in the latter half of the Dynasty with the simplification of the design, which we have discussed in the preceding chapter (Pls. XXVII *f*; XXVIII *b*; XXIX *k*). Even then the naked woman is often figured standing on the stool, like the priest. On the other hand, no goddess, who is demonstrably such, is ever depicted naked (except Shala on Akkadian seals). The conclusion seems indicated that the naked woman is of the rank of the priest and represents either a priestess or merely a female worshipper who had honoured the deity by once serving as a hierodule in the temple.

In exceptional cases other figures are placed on the "stool"; once it is the kneeling victim of the griffin (cf. Pl. XXVII *g*),[1] and the base of the dragon in Pl. XXVIII *c* may have the same significance. Another time we see the Sun-god and behind him his shaven priest, holding the emblematical saw, standing upon the stool.[2] All these instances agree with the interpretation of the stool which we have adopted; we might specify its meaning perhaps a little more clearly by saying that, both in ritual and in design, it symbolised ritually pure ground, which in most cases would mean the temple. This, again, agrees with the use of a similar design beneath thrones (Pls. XXV *d*, *e*; XXVI *e*; XXVII *a*).

(*b*) *The Sun-god, Shamash.*

The many settings in which Shamash appears on Sargonid seals did not survive the age of their inception. They are of a mythological character and mythology was not, as a rule, considered a suitable basis for seal designs in post-Sargonid days. It is true that the Sun-god is often figured with his foot on a mountain, but this attitude is but an attribute serving to identify the god, though, as we shall see, not quite unequivocably. Shamash is also depicted enthroned, a rather complete version appearing in Pl. XXVII *a*. That the throne is drawn in the convention used for mountains is no doubt

[1] A–406.

[2] Brett, 54. This is probably also the meaning of the coarsely cut seal, B.M. 89681.

an allusion to the more usual attitude which renders the sunrise on the eastern mountains. The enthroned god holds a saw; behind him appears a lion, and a human-headed bull serves as a footstool. This last feature is not altogether uncommon.[1] In Pl. XXVI *k* the god stands upon two of these creatures. This finds its correlative in designs where Bull-men act as standard-bearers to Shamash.[2] The Bull-man has become an adjunct, but was first, as we have seen on Akkadian seals, the sun's adversary. It seems probable that the distinction between Bull-man standard-bearer and the human-headed bull which serves as footstool is not essential but merely a matter of convenience, the quadruped being more suitable "couchant", and the Bull-man upright. These associations suggest that two other figures in the Babylonian repertoire may possibly be identified as Shamash. The one is a god with multiple mace destroying an enemy (Pl. XXVIII *a*, *c*, *g*). He once appears accompanied by Bull-men with the sun's standard (Pl. XXVIII *g*);[3] we shall study it presently. The other figure is a deity bearing the emblem with seven globes (Pl. XXX *c*, *d*), and here the identification with Shamash is well attested. This emblem appears only in cylinders cut in the style of the latter part of the Dynasty. Since this god is once depicted with his foot on the human-headed bull,[4] and the standard is held by two Bull-men in Pl. XXX *h*, his identity is indubitable.[5] This conclusion seems to receive corroboration from the cylinders of the Third Dynasty of Ur discussed on p. 145, where a lion carries this same emblem. The lion is certainly a symbol of Shamash, though not as exclusively as the Bull-man or human-headed bull. Both occur together on an Early Dynastic macehead from Ur.[6]

Whether the god on Pl. XXVI *j* holding the club with two feline-heads is Shamash remains doubtful, since only his attitude is distinctive, and we shall

[1] E.g. A–350, 363; Bibliothèque Nationale, 155, 166, 229. If Delaporte is right in seeing in A–362 a goat underneath Shamash, that would be a result of confusion with Amurru; but it may well be a human-headed bull.

[2] Bibliothèque Nationale, 143, 172.

[3] This seal also names Shamash in the inscription, but we have seen in § 3, pp. 11 ff., that we may not rely on such evidence for the identification; and in fact it would be nothing unusual if the god with the multiple mace represented Nergal and the name *Shamash* were to be referred to the group of standard and Bull-men next to which it is written.

[4] A–863.

[5] Nevertheless, the emblem seems originally to have belonged to a god of fertility. It appears combined with cattle-pens on vases and seals of the Jemdet Nasr period (Pl. VI *a*) and once on a tablet dated in year 9 of Gimilsin (*Revue Archéologique*, 1909, Pl. 13, Fig. 1, and pp. 250 ff.) together with a god seated upon a goat.

[6] Woolley, *Royal Cemetery*, Pl. 183.

see that that is not by itself a certain proof of identity; on the other hand, it is likely that the standing figure in Text-fig. 41 (p. 172) is Shamash,[1] and then he carries the scimitar with two feline heads.

A number of other divine figures on Babylonian seals may well be Shamash, but we are unable to identify them with certainty in the absence of assured emblems. The rays issuing from his shoulders, which were a regular feature on Sargonid seals, are not depicted in the period under discussion; Text-fig. 41 is an exception. We have seen that the inscription "Shamash and Ay" is meaningless at this time. Of actual attributes the saw and Bull-man are conclusive, but when the god merely holds ring and staff or a cup (Pl. XXVII *a*, *g*), when the sun's disk and crescent appear in the field or a lion is placed behind them,[2] his identity is insufficiently established. There is not only a risk of confusing the Sun-god with another deity but even with the king, if it is true that horned crowns are not always worn by the gods on Babylonian seals.

In designs like Pl. XXVII *b* the enthroned figure may conceivably be the king of Babylon. On the other hand, we have in Pl. XXVII *e* a doubtful case when the evidence is slightly in favour of an interpretation as Shamash. The sun and crescent emblem on this seal carries little weight. The inscription is a little more important, naming the Sun-god alone, than it would be if it were in the conventional panel enclosing the names of Shamash and Ay which were added at this time to almost any type of design. The uncrowned armed attendant behind the throne (the impression is cut in a misleading way) might suggest an earthly court official, but we have another seal where he appears again, without crown but standing behind Shamash in full panoply with his foot on a human-headed bull.[3] And we have seen that Shamash was depicted on Akkadian seals with a small attendant, perhaps a deified mortal, behind his throne (Pl. XVIII *f*). This comparison of Pls. XXVII *a* and XXVII *e* illustrates the type of uncertainty with which we have to contend in the glyptic of the First Babylonian Dynasty.

(*c*) *The Weather-god, Adad.*

The Weather-god Adad has lost several of his attributes. He is now but rarely associated with the winged dragon which appeared regularly as his

[1] Compare *Proceedings of the Society of Biblical Archaeology*, XXXIII (1911), Pl. 15, 3; and below, p. 172, note 2.

[2] Newell, 173, 174; Bibliothèque Nationale, 116; Musée Guimet, 37; A–231, 301; Brussels, 604; De Clercq, 117, 128, 129, 130; *Proceedings of the Society of Biblical Archaeology*, XXIV, 89. Some of these may be of the Third Dynasty of Ur.

[3] A–350. Cf. Newell, 179, where the crescent takes the place of the sun- and crescent-emblem, no doubt mere carelessness on the part of the seal-cutter.

adjunct on Sargonid seals; and the wagon and whip have disappeared entirely, though the literary association, which they represent pictorially, survived into late Assyrian times (p. 127, note 3). In one instance (Pl. XXVII *i*) the monster serves as his throne.[1] The dragon is quite common on the seals of this period, but he has separated himself from the Weather-god and exists independently and with a new significance. Even in Pl. XXVII *i* the god holds an emblem which is unknown in the earlier period. The whip of the Akkadian representations has been replaced by a three-tongued fork of lightning, an emblem no doubt derived from Syria. In Anatolia too, it seems to have been used from the beginning, and we know that, at latest during Sargon of Akkad's Dynasty, the Hurrian Weather-god Teshub was introduced into some parts of Babylonia; the Amorite infiltration which took place during the Third Dynasty of Ur, and ultimately destroyed it, would strengthen these Syrian influences and increase the importance of the Weather-god. This explains the complete supersession of the old symbol of lightning and thunder, the whip, by the double- or treble-tongued fork, and also the "Hittite" representation of Adad standing upon two mountains (Text-fig. 40) or mounted upright upon a bull (Pl. XXVII *j*); Adad is actually called "God of the West" on one seal.[2]

Text-fig. 40. Marduk, Adad and other gods.

Occasionally he holds a rein fastened to the nose-ring of his mount. The bull, surmounted by the lightning fork, or the two emblems separate, often appear among the small motives strewn in the field of the cylinders of this period (Pls. XXVI *k*; XXVII *d*; XXIX *f*). It is, of course, in most cases impossible to connect these with any of the larger figures.

On Pl. XXVI *k* the bull and the lightning fork appear in front of a god whose footstool suggests that he is Marduk. In Pl. XXVII *f* the same emblems, combined as usual, appear in front of a god who may be Adad, but with whom we may equally well connect the sun-standard. Adad is known to usurp the place of Shamash to some extent during this period, at least outside Mesopotamia proper,[3] and the curious cylinder of Pl. XXVII *h*,

[1] He is mounted upon it in Newell 220, and the beast follows an anonymous god in our Text-fig. 43 (p. 174) in the old manner.

[2] A–389.

[3] S. A. Cook, *The Religion of Ancient Palestine in the Light of Archaeology*, pp. 130 f.

though it cannot be interpreted with absolute certainty, seems to render Adad in the boat used in an earlier period by the Sun-god (Pl. XIX*e, f*), while the place of the quadruped is taken by the bull with the lightning fork, and the winged dragon is shown as adversary and not as adjunct. A worse source of confusion (for the seal just discussed is after all exceptional) is found in Adad's attitude. Perhaps again under Syrian or Anatolian influences the god is once figured bestriding two mountain tops (Text-fig. 40). More usual is his attitude with one foot on a mountain, and then it is almost impossible to distinguish him from Shamash unless he holds the lightning symbol. Pl. XXVII*c* gives an example of this rendering. We must disregard here the metaphor used in the Ras Shamra texts[1] that Adad fells the cedars of Lebanon with the *saw* of his lightning, for if we assumed the possibility of an illustration of this conception in Mesopotamia, Adad and Shamash would be entirely indistinguishable. But on the beautiful cylinder of Pl. XXVII*d* we see a god with a foot on a mountain and holding a saw, who should probably be identified as Adad by the presence of his two emblems, the bull and the winged dragon.

We have seen that the Weather-god, who dispensed the rain, was to some extent considered a fertility god (p. 126). We may assume that Adad appears once with a vase from which water flows,[2] since Ea is never shown, to our knowledge, mounted on a bull. Moreover, we find Adad associated with a plough. He seems, in fact, the only god using this emblem in the period under discussion (Pl. XXVII*m*).[3]

(*d*) *The God of the West, Amurru.*

The iconography of Amurru is best based on Pl. XXVIII*e*, where he is named in the text "Amurru, son of Anu", and is depicted standing with his foot on a gazelle, holding a crescent standard which is elsewhere shown in the hands of several gods; the curved staff which normally counts as his emblem appears in the field, and is held again by a seated goddess, no doubt his consort. The nature of this symbol remains obscure; it may be a shepherd's crook. Its connection with the God of the West is repeatedly testified[4] alone

[1] Dussaud, *Revue de l'Histoire des Religions* (1932), p. 256. [2] A–283.

[3] Our figure does not prove that the male god is Adad; we chose it because it was most suitable for reproduction. In two other instances his identity is well established. In Bibliothèque Nationale, 253, he holds the lightning fork, and in A–371 he carries a scimitar but places one foot upon a mountain. Our Pl. XXVII*m* belonged to a "servant of Adad" and the plough as well as the inscription were evidently engraved by order to a design kept indeterminate, as is so often the case at this time; see p. 147, § 24.

[4] A–368, 381, 383, 384, 397, etc.

or upon the goat, and it often appears duplicated (Pls. XXVII *l*; XXVIII *b*). The god appears also in an attitude resembling that of Adad or Shamash, his foot placed upon the goat or gazelle while he bears his emblem in one hand and sometimes swings a mace.[1] Occasionally the animal is reduced to a mere square, and then the assimilation to the attitude of Shamash is complete.[2] Amurru is possibly represented in the Third Dynasty of Ur.[3] Once the god appears with his emblems beside a three-storeyed temple tower.[4] Another curious seal shows a procession of four deities mounted on goats.[5] It is likely that the impression should be cut in such a way that Amurru is in the van instead of bringing up the rear, for the other figures are the interceding goddess and a male and female worshipper, all mounted upon the animal sacred to the god.

Pl. XXVIII *h* shows a conventional seal with a god and goddess and a panel naming Shamash and Ay, but the emblem of Amurru has been engraved, no doubt by order of the purchaser, in one column.

(*e*) *The Water-god, Ea.*

Ea is rarely represented on the seals of the First Dynasty of Babylon. Neither his two-faced herald Usmu nor his "secret chamber" survives the Akkadian period. But the two symbols by which he was known in later times, the goat-fish and the sceptre with the ram's head, now make their appearance. The goat-fish is seen on a seal of the Third Dynasty of Ur (Pl. XXV *d*); the ram-headed staff—which indicates the god on the boundary stones of the Kassite period—is held by him on Pl. XXVII *i*. It is curious that even in the elaborate representations of the Guti period at Lagash, these symbols are not employed. In examples such as the seal or Urlama, one of the successors of Gudea in the time of the Third Dynasty of Ur,[6] it may well be that the god shown there is not intended for Ea, but is merely the local form of the fertility god, Ningirsu, in his aspect of sender of water.

In Pl. XXVIII *k* Ea stands upon a goat-fish and a kneeling "nude hero" with the flowing vase. Elsewhere he stands on a mermaid and a goat-fish, but is at the same time attended by a nude hero with the flowing vase.[7]

[1] E.g. V.A. 523; Bibliothèque Nationale, 448.

[2] A–368; Newell, 207.

[3] Louvre, T–214. The inscription reads: "Geshtinanna and Amurru", and since a gazelle is engraved beneath the panels, I do not see any reason for calling the enthroned figure the king as Delaporte does. It is likely that this seal was conceived as a whole and that the two names apply to the two deities actually depicted.

[4] Philadelphia, 346.

[5] A–876.

[6] T–116 and *Revue d'Assyriologie*, v, 139.

[7] *Revue d'Assyriologie*, v, 131, Fig. C.

Goat-fish, mermaid and hero with vase occur frequently among the small motives strewn between the larger figures of these cylinders. As we have seen, the nude hero rarely carries the flowing vase on Akkadian seals (§ 17, p. 85), but is common in Babylonian times, while intermediate instances are known.[1] The device is certainly symbolical and may for that reason not have appealed to the Akkadians; when it does occur, in connection with the watering of buffaloes (Pl. XVII *c*), it is susceptible of a realistic interpretation. But there can be no doubt that the vase merely expresses pictorially the "source" of the water, and probably of all water. Nor would it be safe to assign to the flowing vases whenever they appear a cosmological meaning. In some cases (our Text-fig. 65, p. 213) that interpretation is feasible, in others it is less certain. Albright has studied the importance of water in Babylonian ritual.[2] He defines the pot of our seal designs as the source of the two rivers and of all ritually pure water. In the seals it is better not to insist on these qualifications and to consider the pot purely as a pictorial device intended to indicate the source of water in general, or of such water as the representation requires, though for the Ancients the water of the primeval ocean, of all sources, and of the rain, was ultimately identical.[3]

(*f*) *The Conqueror-god.*

For want of a name we must describe this figure by its characteristic attitude. He appears on a number of seals armed with a multiple mace and sometimes with a less extraordinary weapon, but almost always trampling under foot a crouching human victim.

The multiple mace does not reveal the identity of the god. It is true that Urdun's sealing (Text-fig. 38, p. 143) shows it in the hand of Ningirsu and that Gudea mentions a seven-headed mace, named Shar-Ur or Abubu, as a possession of Ningirsu.[4] But this deity is but the local form under which the Sumerian god of fertility is worshipped at Lagash, where his warlike aspect is especially emphasised. There is no reason to identify as Ningirsu the god with the multiple mace found all over Mesopotamia.

It should also be noticed that his curious weapon is not always depicted with seven heads but sometimes with only six and at others with as many as

[1] T–156, year 3 of Bursin.

[2] "The mouth of the rivers"; *American Journal of Semitic Languages*, XXXV (1918–19), 161 ff.

[3] See A. J. Wensinck, "The Ocean in the Literature of the Western Semites", in *Verhandelingen van de koninklijke Akademie van Wetenschappen*, Afd. Letterkunde XIX, Amsterdam, 1918.

[4] Gudea, Statue B, 5, 37; Cylinder B, 7, 12–23.

nine. The attitude is identical in all these cases and there can be no doubt that the same god is represented throughout. Once a pair of corpses appear in the field beside the victim agonising under the god's foot,[1] on another occasion the victim is omitted.[2] It has been thought that the god represents Shamash, on the strength of one instance where this name is written in the design (Pl. XXVIII *g*). This argument is entirely inconclusive, seeing how generally that name was added to the seal designs of the period, and in the present instance it may refer to two Bull-men holding the sun's standard between them. On the other hand, the conception of Shamash punishing evildoers was very prevalent at the time and may have found expression in the design under discussion. Two arguments, equally inconclusive, could be put forward in support of the identification with Shamash. In Pl. XXVIII *a* the god seems to wield besides the multiple mace a weapon which resembles more closely Shamash's saw than the scimitar as we see it in Ishtar's hands. And again, several variants are known in which the god uses an ordinary weapon and appears in the turban which was more frequently worn by Shamash and Amurru than by any other gods (Pl. XXVIII *d*).[3]

There is, however, an alternative interpretation of this figure. The curious seal of Pl. XXVIII *c* depicts a novel situation. It might appear as if the god with the multiple mace were driving away two demons from a man who has sought refuge at an altar. In view of the standard version of the victorious god stepping upon a human victim, this interpretation is untenable. The demons must be counted in league with this deity, and since, as we shall see, they are most likely demons of disease, this seal would suggest that the god with the multiple mace represents their master, the god of pestilence, Nergal.

Now an unpublished seal from Larsa[4] shows a deity with a scimitar and a mace with two feline heads, trampling a man upon a mountain; the dedication to Nergal and the exceptional nature of the design are probably interrelated. The mace is not a distinctive weapon, but the god of pestilence afflicting a human being might well be represented as described, and the victorious god with the multiple mace may thus stand for Nergal rather than for Shamash.[5]

[1] Bibliothèque Nationale, 441.

[2] A–351.

[3] So also Bibliothèque Nationale, 236, 242; Musée Guimet, 66; Chicago, A–7215.

[4] *Revue d'Assyriologie*, XXX, 179.

[5] Other seals showing this deity are: Bibliothèque Nationale, 130, 241, 242, 243; Qb, 28; A–544; Ward, 445, 448, 449, 451.

(*g*) *The Bull-eared god.*

Twice a male god is figured with bulls' ears, such as we know already from our Akkadian seal, Pl. XXIV*b*. Once he is clothed like other deities and carries a scimitar,[1] elsewhere[2] he appears as if enclosed in one of the slipper-shaped sarcophagi which are known at a later date in Babylonia. He seems to be present on an unpublished seal found at Telloh in which its discoverer identifies the god as Nergal.[3] He is known from terracottas found at Ishchali,[4] where he appears amply supplied with daggers, maces and scimitars, while the surroundings recall a bower of palm leaves or feathered wings, the latter as well as the weapons being especially appropriate for a god of war, death and pestilence ruling the nether-world. The feet are sometimes human, sometimes shaped like claws, and this again suggests an inhabitant of the land of the dead.[5]

(*h*) *The God with the Mace.*

A bearded figure, clothed in plaid and turban, and holding a mace, occurs on a number of cylinders. He may be a god, since he is occasionally represented as the recipient of sacrifices (Pl. XXIX*b*). He also appears in conjunction with the interceding goddess (Pls. XXVII*f*, *i*, *m*; XXVIII*b*, *h*, *i*; XXIX*f*, *h*, *m*). It is, of course, impossible to be sure of the identity of this personage, and the usual designation of Amurru is unfounded. It is, in fact, quite likely that he stands for a variety of deities. In Pl. XXVIII*h*, *i* the crook identifies him with Amurru, in Pl. XXVIII*d* he takes the place of the Conqueror-god. He may also represent the king, or even the king's statue (Pl. XXVI*i*, left). His most distinctive feature is the carefully curled and splaying edge of the beard, but even that occurs in other cases, especially with worshippers (Pl. XXVI*k*). This supports the view that the king may thus be represented.

(*i*) *Marduk.*

Marduk, the god of Babylon who to later generations was to epitomise Mesopotamian religion, is depicted, as we have seen in § 19 (*e*), (*g*), pp. 102, 105, on Sargonid seals. The personal names and other literary sources of the period disprove the assumption that the rise to power of Hammurabi brought with it a dominating position of his City-god in the pantheon,[6] and the evidence

[1] A-362.
[2] Newell, 213.
[3] Parrot in *Syria*, XV (1934), 382.
[4] *Oriental Institute Communications*, No. 20, pp. 92 ff., Figs. 70–71.
[5] Frankfort, "The Burney Relief", in *Archiv für Orientforschung*, 1938.
[6] Ravn in *Acta Orientalia*, VII (1928).

of the seal designs corroborates the gradual nature of Marduk's ascendancy. There are but few seals in the mature style of the period which show the god; on the other hand, his triangular symbol often appears on the overcrowded cylinders which are characteristic of the later reigns of the First Dynasty of Babylon, and both the inscriptions and the seals of the Kassite period prove that it is only in that epoch that Marduk assumes most of the dignities of the other gods.

In Pl. XXVI *k* we may identify the seated god with Marduk, since his footstool is one of the two types associated with his personality. The ring and staff which he holds are not distinctive of any god (Shamash and Ishtar use it) and the bull and the lightning fork drawn in the field of this overcrowded design can be as little connected with any of the figures as the writing seems to be.

Another cylinder (Text-fig. 40, p. 163) shows the two dragons in detail. One has two straight horns (cf. Pls. XXVI *k* and XXVIII *m*), the other resembles in every detail the "lion-bird" of Ningiszida (Pls. XXVIII *n*; XXI *g*).[1]

The same god appears again in Pl. XXVIII *m*, and since this seal is carefully executed and well composed we may probably accept the relevancy of all the symbols. In that case the goat-fish would be a further definition of Marduk, son of Ea.[2] In Pl. XXVIII *n* he appears standing upon his dragon, in a manner much favoured in Assyrian times, while a cylinder from Ishchali[3] shows the god in the attitude of Shamash and Adad, a scimitar dangling from one hand and his foot placed on the back of the crouching dragon; he is also shown seated upon it.[4]

His emblem, widely used in the seals of the late part of the period, is once held by two monkeys (Pl. XXVIII *b*).

(*j*) *The Divine Couple.*

On a small number of cylinders a god and goddess are shown embracing (Pl. XXIX *b*).[5] It is impossible to be certain about their identity; one thinks

[1] Heuzey in *Revue d'Assyriologie*, VI, 95 ff., has described and distinguished these two monsters with precision; he considers the first type a misunderstood rendering of the lion-bird. It is true that the latter is superseded by the former on the Kassite boundary stones, but our Text-fig. 40 shows that they existed side by side in earlier times.

[2] Compare Newell, 190, where a god holds staff and ring while in the field appear Marduk's symbol and Ea's goat-fish.

[3] Ish. 34/119.

[4] Ward, 324.

[5] So also Ish. 35/26 and our Pl. XLI *c*, which is Syrian. Our Text-fig. 82 (p. 254) and Ward-Morgan, 205, may also represent the divine couple.

of the myth of Nergal who forced an entrance into the nether-world and took Ereshkigal for a spouse. The cylinder belonged to a servant of Shulpae, which may support this view, since Nergal is designated by that name also. But mythological subjects are unusual at this time, and it is possible that the union of the gods which ensured the prosperity of the new year is suggested by this design.

(*k*) *The Goddess of War.*

The goddess in war panoply is occasionally represented in Sargonid times (Pl. XX *e*), and also during the succeeding centuries, until she becomes really popular with the seal-cutters of Hammurabi's Dynasty. In her characteristic attitude she appears full-face with one leg placed forward, parting her shawl so as to leave her freedom of movement. Normally she places one foot on a crouching lion but sometimes stands on two of these beasts (Pls. XXVI *i*; XXIX *l*, right). She carries a weapon, usually the ordinary scimitar or the mace with two feline heads, in either hand, while other weapons project behind her shoulders. The seal-cutters sometimes create the impression of having drawn her with a beard in horizontal ridges or curls (Pls. XXIX *a*; XXXIX *i*). In reality this device represents her numerous necklaces.[1] Occasionally the goddess appears with head in profile[2] and in the earlier periods she was often shown enthroned; this becomes rare during the First Dynasty of Babylon.[3]

(*l*) *The Goddess of Water.*

A goddess holding the flowing vase is depicted standing on two goat-fish[4] or supported by a nude hero with the emblematic vase (Pl. XXIX *l*). In these positions Ea too is shown, and the goddess probably represents Damgalnunna, Ea's spouse. She usually appears without supporters.[5] On Urlama's seal a small figure of a goddess stands above the flowing vase which the god holds.[6]

(*m*) *The Weather-goddess.*

The curious seal of Pl. XXVIII *j* shows a goddess full-face, who holds the scimitar with two panther-heads. Since she is mounted on two winged

[1] Compare for a version in sculpture in the round a fragment found at Mari, reproduced in *Syria*, 1935, Pl. 26, No. 1.

[2] Bibliothèque Nationale, 169, 238, 240; A–284; Newell, 220; Kh. VI/73.

[3] Bibliothèque Nationale, 236.

[4] Louvre, A–522 F.

[5] De Clercq, 153; A–543 A.

[6] T–116.

dragons, one must identify her as the goddess regularly associated with the Weather-god on Akkadian seals, in all probability his spouse, Shala.

(*n*) *The "Nude Goddess"*.

This figure seems not to be a goddess at all, but rather a female devotee (see § 26 (*a*), p. 158).

§ 27. MYTHOLOGICAL FIGURES, ANIMALS AND EMBLEMS

(*a*) *Bull-man and Nude Hero*.

These two figures, derived from the Sargonid repertoire, appear on the seals of the First Dynasty of Babylon in combat with animals or with each other. Sometimes the winged dragon is their antagonist;[1] the perspective rendering of the lion's head between the legs of his adversary seen in Pl. XXIX*a* is an innovation of this period.[2]

The nude hero, as we have seen in § 26 (*e*), p. 165, is often equipped with the flowing vase. He may then be standing or kneeling, drawn on a large or very small scale.

The Bull-man is often portrayed, alone or with an identical companion, as the standard-bearer, usually of Shamash,[3] sometimes of Sin;[4] once also of Marduk[5] and once of Adad,[6] the gods being generally not depicted alongside their standards. It will be recalled that in Sargonid times the Bull-man occasionally held the doorpost emblem. Once only he was shown as a bringer of offerings (Pl. XXIV*b*), and this is more common now; he is then carrying a sacrificial kid;[7] thus far have we travelled since Early Dynastic times, when the Bull-man made his appearance in the animal frieze as a semi-savage protector of flocks and herds. Another development is, perhaps, largely graphic, but its occurrence signifies either that the folk-lore of the Bull-man has suffered change or that he no longer plays a part in any but pictorial tradition. Since the Third Dynasty of Ur the horns of the Bull-man have received the graceful curve of those fitted to the crown of divinities and he is, in fact, often quite clearly equipped with that head-dress (Pl. XXX*h*). This is one of the outward signs by which these seals may be distinguished

[1] Numerous examples, e.g. De Clercq, 76; Bibliothèque Nationale, 102, 143, 172, 242.
[2] So also Ward-Morgan, 48; Ward, 212; Brett, 44.
[3] De Clercq, 236; Newell, 149.
[4] De Clercq, 112; A–274. These may be badly drawn sun-standards.
[5] B.M. 89157.
[6] Qb, 28.
[7] Newell, 225; A–359, 553, 557, 558, 540; Ward, 418*a*.

from those of an earlier period.[1] Both Bull-man and nude hero are sometimes depicted along the circumference of the cylinder (Text-fig. 41).[2]

The nude hero had been pictured in this fashion already in Early Dynastic times, grasping snakes[3] or the gatepost emblem[4] or lions (Pl. XV *b*), and there are some examples belonging to the First Babylonian Dynasty, in which he holds the flowing vase.[5] But he assumes this position in one of the very few designs of the period which reflect mythological themes in some detail (Pl. XXIX *d*).[6] Even so the detail does not go very far, and there is no clear connection between the prostrate body and the figures above it. We can be sure that an Akkadian seal-cutter would have made different use of the opportunity for narration. Nevertheless, this much is clear—that the nude hero symbolises in the present design an unfavourable power, another proof, if such were needed, that a variety of mythological personages are rendered in this guise. It may be that the bird drawn between his arms identifies the enemy as "Zu" or in any case as the same figure which is vanquished in the Akkadian seals of Pl. XXIII *a–i*; however that may be, the nude figure furnishes in subjection the foundation for a sanctuary. We see that a religious scene is enacted over his body, and the surface upon which this takes place is used elsewhere (Pl. XXVI *e* and § 26 (*a*), p. 158) to indicate a temple. We notice on the left (Pl. XXIX *d*) a nude hero holding a flowing vase, then a crescent standard, in front of which a deity pours water over a biconical stand; next comes another deity holding a crescent standard; then

Text-fig. 41.
Sun-god, Bull-men and antelope.

[1] The stylistic differences are numerous but cumbersome to describe in words. It may be worth while to enumerate here a number of cylinders which belong to the First Dynasty of Babylon, although their subject is Akkadian: La Haye, No. 3 (cf. A–517, year 14 of Sin-muballit); De Clercq, 52 *bis*, 73–6.

[2] So also with sun-standard, in *Proceedings of the Society of Biblical Archaeology*, XXXIII (1911), Pl. 15, No. 3; V.A. 4249 and V.A. 6298, both in Heinrich, *Fara*, Pl. 78. The first-named seal showing the two Bull-men holding the standard of Shamash, between them a worshipper in front of Shamash and then again a somewhat obscure figure holding a mace and standing with his foot on a lion. The inscription reads here, too, Shamash and Ay, and the fact that the whole representation consists entirely of symbols connected with the Sun-god suggests that the dubious figure in Text-fig. 41, which is clearly related to the other seal, gives an unusual representation of the Sun-god.

[3] As. 34/91.

[4] As. 33/600; Ward, 205.

[5] Philadelphia, 100; Newell, 336; Ward, 204; Ward, 206 without vase.

[6] The nude hero occurs here twice, once as the large figure and another time in the row of figures above, on the left-hand edge; and he obviously impersonates a different power in either case.

another such standard mounted upon a support of two crossed lions, and finally a worshipper on the extreme right.

(*b*) *Wrestlers or Dancers.*

The pair of wrestlers or dancers may also have derived from Early Dynastic times. This cannot be proved, since we do not know its meaning. In Pl. XXVIII*m* it is clear that wrestlers are intended. Pl. XXIX*c* and Text-fig. 40 (p. 163) suggest dancers, and this seems also to account for the cases in which one of the figures appears alone (Pl. XXVIII*l*).[1] Whether the two divine figures in Text-fig. 43 are a variation on this theme (cf. Pl. XXIX*c*) is uncertain.

(*c*) *The Bow-legged Dwarf.*

This little figure is not easy to connect with any of the large personages; he addresses his impudent gesture with equal frequency to gods and goddesses. If the nude goddess were really a deity, then the group at the left-hand bottom corner of our Pl. XXIX*m* suggests that the dwarf was the guardian of the gates of the netherworld robbing Ishtar of her clothes and apparel. But the evidence is not conclusive. He is even depicted holding Marduk's emblem.[2]

Text-fig. 42. Deities and hand symbol.

(*d*) *The Kneeling Man.*

This figure appears sometimes as a worshipper (Pl. XXVII*j*),[3] kneeling in front of a deity, but more often as the victim of either the Conqueror-god,[4] a lion,[5] a lion-headed demon[6] or a winged dragon (Pl. XXVII*g*);[7] like all the other motives he also appears alone.[8]

We have already mentioned the curious scene of Pl. XXVIII*c*; another instance[9] shows the kneeling figure on a platform in the power of a winged dragon. This figure has been thrown together with the bow-legged dwarf and also the hero with the flowing vase[10] without, of course, any justification.

1 See also Musée Guimet, 6; Louvre, A–341, 455; De Clercq, 236.

2 A–891.

3 Qb, 28; A–292, 345, 366, 459.

4 See above, p. 166, § 26 (*f*).

5 Newell, 146; A–312, 885, 892.

6 Bibliothèque Nationale, 445.

7 Qd, 18; De Clercq, 73, 78; A–877, 890.

8 Qd, 43; De Clercq, 74.

9 A–406.

10 Heidenreich, *Beiträge zur Geschichte der vorderasiatischen Steinschneiderkunst*, p. 11.

(*e*) *The Human Victim.*

On a few seals a man is held upside down either by a lion or by a lion-headed demon (Pl. XXIX *i*).[1] We shall presently enquire into the meaning of these scenes.

(*f*) *The Winged Dragon.*

The composite creature to which we refer with this abbreviation possesses a number of features recurring as regularly as the wings, and no less peculiar to a quadruped. The hindlegs are those of a bird of prey and so is the feathered tail, the mouth may either be leonine or a bird's beak. It follows from this description that the dragon is the same beast as that which appears as associate of the Weather-god on Akkadian seals (Pl. XXII *a*), though it had (but very rarely) appeared alone in Early Dynastic times. On the other hand, it is quite common on Assyrian seals. During the First Dynasty of Babylon it is dissociated from the Weather-god, or for that matter from any other deity. There are a few exceptions; in Pl. XXVII *i* it serves as the throne of its traditional master, Adad. In Pl. XXVII *h* a male figure with a scimitar faces the dragon and is thereby shown to be a god, and therefore perhaps the Weather-god. It is uncertain whether the dragon identifies the god in Pl. XXVII *d*, though its combination with the bull makes it likely; but in such a case as Text-fig. 43 the figure in front need not represent the Weather-god; the design is quite non-committal.

Text-fig. 43. Adad and other gods.

Occasionally the dragon holds a standard, although, not, to my knowledge, in the suite of any god. But as a rule this monster, so frequent on seals of the First Babylonian Dynasty, shows itself merely destructive. It attacks either the crouching figure of a helpless man (Pls. XXVII *g* and XXIX *m*) or a gazelle or goat (Pl. XXIX *e*). Exactly in these same functions we meet the lion (Pl. XXIX *e*) and lion-headed demon, and we may therefore consider the meaning of these figures after having passed them all in review.

(*g*) *The Lion-headed Demon.*

A demon in human shape but with lion's head (or at least jowl), and sometimes with claws, is figured on a number of seals. Sometimes he holds a man upside down by the feet (Pl. XXIX *g*, *i*), or stands with one hand raising a

[1] Newell, 146, 157; Bibliothèque Nationale, 445.

dagger (Pl. XXVII *l*).[1] In Pl. XXVIII *c* we see two members of this species. Once[2] the demon kneels beneath the foot of a god who dominates him—and thus, subjected by the gods, have we met him in Akkadian times; usually as the Sun-god's victim (Pl. XVIII *h*). On one occasion he stands in the typical attitude with uplifted dagger, before the Sun-god enthroned as judge.[3] We also found him on an Akkadian seal raging amongst the winged dragons of the Weather-god.[4]

The later literature of Babylonia enumerates a variety of demons with terrifying characteristics like those of our figure.[5] The demons cause sickness and must be exorcised. There is a choice of names and no reason, as far as I can perceive, to prefer one above another; but the dagger regularly seen in the hand of the lion-headed monster supports in a general way the interpretation of a demon of sickness, since the simile "dagger of pestilence" actually occurs in cuneiform texts.[6]

The "lion-man" and the "bird-footed man" are mentioned in an Assyrian text which includes an incantation to protect a household against illness. At Ur the actual images were found buried under the floor of an Assyrian building.[7] In dealing with Assyrian seal designs we shall have occasion to observe the limited usefulness of these texts for our purpose. They attempt to give comprehensive protection by including every known kind of demon and evil spirit in their precautionary measures. We meet there the Bull-man and the nude hero with the gatepost, known from seals two thousand years older than these texts; and we have already seen that the protective functions of these creatures were originally subsidiary to a much more specialised mythological significance. But in the case of the leonine monster and of the bird-footed demon of Pl. XVIII *d* we have, at present, no indications that they had any other function besides that of carrying disease; this may be, therefore, their specific task. The following quotation shows how the later ritual tries to drive out the devil with Beelzebub: "Instructions to make clay figures of the Lion-man; on their sides write: 'Bolt out the supporter of the evil head.' Bury (them) in the gate of the washing water."[8]

[1] Bibliothèque Nationale, 278; A–454; Ward, 475; Qb, 16.

[2] A–523 (year 2 of Hammurabi).

[3] Ward, 300 *a*. On Pl. XXII *f* it also shows with a dagger, but not in situation which can be interpreted.

[4] Ward, 130 (=V.A. 611).

[5] See below, pp. 199, 203.

[6] R. Campbell Thompson, *The Devil and Evil Spirits of Babylon*, p. xlvii.

[7] *Journal of the Royal Asiatic Society*, 1926, 689 ff. on pp. 695–706. Mr Sidney Smith has collected the relevant texts.

[8] *Ibid.* 1926, p. 700, lines 15, 16.

Nor were these precautions relied upon by the poor man only. Near the entrances of the Assyrian royal palaces were found reliefs with the lion-headed monster having bird's feet and uplifted dagger as in our Pl. XXVIII *c*.[1] The persistence of the traditions throughout the ethnic and political upheavals of the Second Millennium B.C. is highly remarkable; it is, of course, irrelevant whether the Assyrian reliefs represent masked men or demons actually believed to exist in this shape.

The standing demon of Pl. XXVIII *c* seems to have the feet of a bird of prey as on certain Akkadian seals and Assyrian reliefs, and this once more supports our connection of the leonine monster with the figure of Pl. XVIII *d*. And their interpretation as demons of illness is strengthened by the fact that the inhabitants of the nether-world are said to be covered with feathers. Enkidu, in the Gilgamesh Epic, sees in the ominous dream which precedes his death a dark-faced figure, with a face like that of a great bird and with claws like those of an eagle, who changes Enkidu's appearance and guides him to the nether-world. This description fits the standing demon of Pl. XXVIII *c* and may explain the half-birdlike figure of Pl. XVIII *d*.

It is strange that demons of disease should be depicted on cylinders, but they never stand alone, and the accompanying figures and emblems of deities may have been considered sufficiently apotropaic. Perhaps there is even a connection; it may be that the owners of these seals (as of Pl. XVIII *d*), having recovered from a disease which had threatened to take a fatal turn, expressed their gratitude to the deity whom they held responsible for the recovery, by depicting them on their seals at the side of their own person when victim to the demon. Perhaps it was hoped that this reminder of his defeat would discourage the visitant from renewing his attacks.

This interpretation implies that we should not consider the winged dragon and the leonine monster as attributes of any particular god, in the manner that, for instance, the Bull-man belongs to the Sun-god. We have seen that both monsters lead a somewhat independent existence, the dragon already appearing alone on Early Dynastic seals and the leonine demon in various scenes throughout Akkadian times. They probably represent a class of evil beings and no single individual, just as the nude hero is used to represent several mythological personages. There is therefore nothing strange in finding the dragon regularly associated with Adad on Akkadian seals and in Pl. XXVII *i*, while, as we have seen, in later times it seems to be related to Nergal. Since it led an independent existence, it was available to enrich

[1] Gadd, *Stones of Assyria*, Pls. 17, 32, and also in his British Museum publication, *The Assyrian Sculptures* (1934), pp. 49 ff.

the mythology of the one god as well as of the other. That the significance of the dragon on Akkadian seals was not exhausted by its symbolic function as fire-spitting mount, or motive power of the Weather-god's chariot, is proved by the seals in which not only are there numerous dragons of this kind in the field, but they are even associated with the leonine monster (see above, p. 165, § 21 (*b*)).

(*h*) *Animals.*

In addition to the lion and the winged dragon which appear independently or as symbols of Shamash and of Adad, we have met already with a number of other animals serving a similar purpose; the human-headed bull attends Shamash, the goat-fish Ea, the goat or gazelle Amurru. But quite often a gazelle or goat is figured by itself, sometimes free (Pls. XXVIII *d*; XXIX *i*), more often the victim of a lion or winged dragon (Pl. XXIX *e*). Its appearance on Pl. XXV *g* is an archaism, that of Pl. XXVI *d* exceptional. In Text-fig. 40 (p. 163) it appears upside down between two lions. It always looks backward and is sometimes seated on a square seat.[1] Its meaning is obscure as is that of an animal resembling a dog or, sometimes, a lion.[2] It is generally depicted crowned by a pole with curved top (Pls. XXVII *j*; XXIX *f*). The dog of Text-fig. 43 may refer to Gula. Once a seated goddess holds the rein of a cow surmounted by a crescent standard; a cow suckling its calf (Pl. XXVI *i*, *l*) may refer to another goddess, perhaps more especially to her form of Ninharsag. The lion-headed or double-headed eagle (Text-fig. 38, p. 143) seems to be connected with several gods.

The monkey, mounted originally on a pole (Pl. XXVI *e*), appears quite commonly between the larger figures, and seems not more intimately related with one figure than with another. The same applies to the fly (Pl. XXIX *f*), the scorpion (Pls. XXVIII *b*, *l*; XXIX *j*), birds (Pl. XXVIII *k*, *l*), frogs or tortoises (Pl. XXIX *f*) or the hedgehog (Pls. XXVII *i*; XXIX *a*). Parts of animals are rarely used in the designs of this period.[3] But curious combinations do occur; beside the goat-fish (Pls. XXVI *l*; XXVIII *k*; XXIX *g*) we meet a lion-fish.[4]

(*i*) *Inanimate Emblems.*

It may be useful to enumerate the emblems which we met in the preceding pages before adding others not used in connection with deities. The double

[1] Bibliothèque Nationale, 170.

[2] A–358.

[3] Bibliothèque Nationale, 142, 170.

[4] A–527, 553, 590.

scimitar or mace with two feline heads seems also to be used by various gods.[1] It appears most commonly in the hands of Ishtar, but is really appropriate to all warlike gods; we find it with Shala (Pl. XXVIII *j*), Ninurta (perhaps Pl. XXVI *j*) or Nergal,[2] while the common association with two human-headed bulls may point to a connection with the Sun-god (Pl. XXVI *g*, *h*). It also occurs by itself (Pls. XXVII *j*; XXIX *f*) or mounted in a support shaped as a pair of gazelles.[3] The scimitar with one panther-head is also in general use and the same applies to the crescent standard. The latter appears on the back of a cow which is suckling a calf,[4] on the back of a goose,[5] held by two dancers (Pl. XXIX *c*), held by two gods (Text-fig. 43, p. 174), held by a Bull-man or mounted on two crossed lions (Pl. XXIX *d*) or held by Amurru (Pl. XXVIII *e*). Once it appears in the hand of a seated god carved on the seal of a servant of Sin and Urash[6] and here it may, therefore, serve as an emblem of the Moon-god, but we can hardly suppose it to do so in most cases where it occurs.

The scimitar with one panther-head seems to be associated with Adad (Pl. XXVII *d*), Marduk (Pl. XXVIII *n*), Shamash,[7] mounted on an animal lying on an altar,[8] or by itself (Pl. XXIX *j*, *k*), and cannot be connected with any one deity. In an older period it was held by Ningirsu (Text-fig. 38, p. 143) but also by Ishtar (Pl. XXV *f*).

Marduk's triangular symbol, not a spear but an agricultural tool, still in use nowadays in Mesopotamia and called *mar*, is, of course, an unequivocal emblem, and so are the saw of Shamash, the lightning fork of Adad and the shepherd's crook of Amurru. The plough may not be emblematic of any particular deity, but seems, as we have seen, to be used in connection with Adad alone.

[1] Scheil, *Revue d'Assyriologie*, XXIII, 39, takes the central part of the weapon as a vase and calls it the "sainte ampoule"; more usual is the description of caduceus (Von der Osten, *Newell Collection*, p. 87; Frothingham in *American Journal of Archaeology*, XX (1916), 175 ff.). This seems to be based on Ward's distinction of the simplified seal design of Pl. XXVI *g*, *h*, *j*, *l*), where the cutting edge below the feline head is well marked, from the maces on the boundary stones drawn in all detail on monuments of a much larger scale (Ward, *Seal Cylinders of Western Asia*, pp. 402, 408). The distinction, therefore, is not justified; the best proof that this object is a weapon lies in a comparison with the single-headed scimitar (Pls. XXVIII *n*; XXIX *j*), which is identical as regards the animal head and cutting edge. Pl. XXV *c* shows a variation without ornamental head. The double-headed weapon, besides being decorative, combines the weight of the mace with the cutting edge of the scimitar. Whether the head is that of a panther, lion or dragon is uncertain. In any case there is no resemblance to the serpent's head which would be necessary for a caduceus.

[2] Parrot in *Revue d'Assyriologie*, XXX, 179, No. 51; Thureau-Dangin also ascribes the weapon to Nergal, on the evidence of the Kassite boundary stones, *Revue d'Assyriologie*, XVI, 140, and Steinmetzer in *Sachau Festschrift* (Berlin, 1915), pp. 62 ff.

[3] De Clercq, 112.

[4] Musée Guimet, 33.

[5] A–339.

[6] Newell, 264.

[7] Bibliothèque Nationale, 121; A–307.

[8] A–374.

The object depicted between worshipper and interceding goddess in Pl. XXVI *d, e* is exceedingly common (see also Pl. XXVII *b, c, e, j*). It may be the arm of a balance and symbolise the justice of the god's judgment, but that is mere surmise. It quite often occurs together with a small jar. It should not be confused either with the ancient "doorpost" emblem or the "ring and staff". The latter, often held by Shamash (as on the stela of Hammurabi) but also by Adad or Marduk (Pl. XXVI *k*), seems however to represent also measuring instruments. On the stela of Ur-Nammu from Ur[1] it is rendered with unusual detail and appears to be a measuring rod and line. The unwonted precision of the rendering is explained by the occasion commemorated by the stela, namely the founding of a temple. In our Pl. XIV *j* a god is shown approving the size of the planoconvex bricks used for his Ziggurat; so Ur-Nammu is shown receiving essential equipment from his deity. Since measuring instruments may metaphorically become symbols of justice, it is understandable that they became a general emblem of divinity, generally simplified as "ring and staff".

(*j*) *Men.*

The human figure, drawn on a small scale, occurs on the seals of the Hammurabi period either singly or in pairs, in which case one figure is drawn upside down below the other (Text-fig. 42, p. 173).[2] Often the manikins then assume the shape of the bow-legged dwarf.

The sprinkling priest has already been discussed in § 26 (*a*), p. 158.

There is a revival of the Early Dynastic and Akkadian fashion of placing a small human being underneath an inscribed panel.[3] Whether an archer who appears occasionally[4] is human or divine remains uncertain. The human countenance, isolated, is clean-shaven in profile (Pl. XXIX *a, h*) but heavily bearded with long locks when shown in full-face (Pl. XXIX *h*).

A man's hand apparently serves as a standard or emblem. In Text-fig. 42 it appears projecting from or mounted upon a hill. In Pl. XXX *a* it is flanked by two interceding goddesses. It occurs amongst other emblems on Pl. XXVIII *k*. Usually this symbol is considered typical of Syrian glyptic, but this is certainly an erroneous view, as Pl. XXIX *k, l* show. We can admit no more than that the peripheral styles of the West frequently show the hand in their designs, along with other motives derived from Mesopotamia.

[1] *Antiquaries Journal*, v, Pl. XLVIII.

[2] Bibliothèque Nationale, 100, 206; Newell, 214; De Clercq, 166.

[3] Bibliothèque Nationale, 233 (see Bibliothèque Nationale, 45); As. 31/591; *Recueil de Travaux*, XXXVIII (1916), Plate facing p. 166, No. 5.

[4] Bibliothèque Nationale, 233. It may be Ninurta.

SECTION V

THE SEALS FROM THE KASSITE TO THE PERSIAN PERIOD

CHAPTER I. BABYLONIAN SEALS OF THE SECOND MILLENNIUM

§ 28. THE SEALS OF THE KASSITE PERIOD

THE KASSITE invasion caused a disruption of the cultural unity of Mesopotamia such as had not occurred since the earliest settlement of the Plain. Then the southern marshes had been occupied by Iranian mountaineers (Al 'Ubaid culture) while the northern foothills and plains had been inhabited by people of North Syrian affinities (Tell Halaf culture). By the middle of the Second Millennium the south, under Kassite rule, was fostering existing traditions, while the north was becoming thoroughly permeated with western influences as a result of its domination by the kings of Mitanni.

The Kassite cylinders stress the traditional character of southern art in a novel manner. They contain elaborate prayers to the gods of the land (Pl. XXX*j–m*), causing the inscription to predominate over the pictorial design of the seal. We have already seen that in this respect the Kassite cylinders merely continue one of the two lines of development discernible during the First Dynasty of Babylon. The very common type of Babylonian seal represented by Pls. XXIX*j* and XXX*g* is evidently the ancestor of the Kassite designs. We know, in fact, that such seals were used in early Kassite times,[1] and Pl. XXX*h, j* illustrate the transition from the older to the later style. Both show motives commonly employed on the cylinders of the First Dynasty of Babylon, and on these seals we notice that excessive use of the drill which transformed the sun-disk and crescent emblem into a rosette (cf. Pl. XXX*c, f*) and made the staff with globes take the place of the older emblems of Shamash (Pl. XXX*c, d, h*). The figures on the two transitional seals are also in the old Babylonian tradition, but the text on the one, and the small designs on the other, are without precedent. In Pl. XXX*h* the text contains a prayer to the god Nabu such as is never found on older seals but became the rule in Kassite times.[2] A similar state of transition is revealed

[1] A–596, dated to the reign of Kashtiliash I.

[2] Similar seals, with Babylonian designs and texts of the Kassite type: Bibliothèque Nationale, 292, 293.

by the earliest dated seal of the new Dynasty, that of Izgur-Marduk, son of Karaindash.[1] Groups of two or three figures which are common on seals of the Hammurabi Dynasty are repeated six times and grouped in two registers, while writing-signs, making up a prayer, are strewn between the figures as in Pl. XXX *h*. The other transitional type, namely that of Pl. XXX *j*, includes with motives of the old repertoire, such as the balance and the sun in rosette-form, a rhombus and a squatting dog, not to be found in earlier times, but common on the Kassite seals (cf. Pl. XXX *l*).[2]

The muddled appearance of the transitional subjects is a measure of the achievement underlying the new style (Pl. XXX *k–m*). There the inscriptions and designs are clearly separated. The scene is simple, and usually consists of one divine figure to whom a few small motives are added. On the whole these lack relevance; they appear to serve the same purpose as in the previous ages, namely to make it easier to distinguish one seal impression from another. The equilateral cross (the so-called Kassite cross) is as common as the rhombus, and of the animals the goat and dog are the most popular. Swallows,[3] grasshoppers,[4] frogs,[5] flies (Pl. XXX *l*) also occur. Once the ears of corn and the calf, emblematical in their combination of the god of fertility, and used as early as the Uruk period (Pl. III *a*), are added to a design which accompanies a text naming the Ṣumerian god Lugalbanda.[6] Elsewhere we see Marduk equipped with the emblems of Shamash; for he is seated on a throne borne by two human-headed bulls.[7] This design illustrates the increasing predominance of Marduk in Babylonian religion, a change which is one of the main innovations of the Kassite period.

Occasionally ritual objects, such as Marduk's symbol, appear mounted on a stand (Pl. XXX *k*). Again some motives are derived from the Mitannian glyptic prevalent in Northern Mesopotamia at this time. The rosettes of Pl. XXXI *b* are a common possession of both styles, the god, worshipper and "naked goddess" are drawn as on other Kassite seals, but the winged dragon at the top and the two antelope heads are clearly derived from the region round Kirkuk and Assur. The antithetical group of bulls and plants in Pl. XXX *l* has the same origin.

[1] Philadelphia, 530.

[2] Other clear survivals of the earlier repertoire are the merman and hero with flowing vase as in Ward, 654; the monkey (D–56); the nude woman (A–604); and La Haye, Pl. VI, No. 27. The rosette also in Newell, 270, and B.M. 89128, 89258; A–598. In De Clercq, 263, not only the sun-rosette but also the "Kassite cross" are rendered by drill-holes.

[3] De Clercq, 256, 257.

[4] A–599, 606.

[5] Ward, 528.

[6] Ward, 517.

[7] Ward, 537 *a*.

The figures are generally without distinctive attributes, though a servant of Kurigalzu had two musicians depicted, of whom one was possibly himself.[1]

A seal found at Babylon depicts a chariot scene (Pl. XXX *i*); whether this too was derived from Syria or was an innovation of the Kassites it is impossible to say. The triangles serving as border to that cylinder have the curious origin described on page 7. The better seals of the period were often mounted in gold caps which were clamped round the ends of the stone cylinder and sometimes covered with gold granulations. These triangles naturally showed in the impression and this effect was imitated in a number of contemporary seals, while during the next period hatching was added to increase the resemblance (Pl. XXXII *a*, *c*).[2]

The new style is not discernible before the fifteenth century B.C. We have seen that a seal impression on a tablet dated to the reign of Kashtiliash I is still in the manner of Pl. XXX *c*, and that the seal of a son of Karaindash is transitional. The disappearance of the Kassite style is difficult to trace, since it was displaced by an Assyrian glyptic containing elements of both Kassite and Mitannian repertoires.

§ 29. THE SEALS OF THE MITANNIAN STYLE OF KIRKUK

The glyptic style which prevailed in the northern part of Mesopotamia during the middle of the Second Millennium B.C. cannot be understood in a purely Mesopotamian context. It came into being in North Syria, and spread within the boundaries of the ephemeral Mitannian kingdom; and its offshoots are found even farther afield. The fitting place for its discussion is therefore a later section of this book (§ 42 (*b*), p. 278). But since the Assyrian seals are decisively influenced by Mitannian glyptic, we shall consider here the elements of the Kirkuk style which connect it with the preceding school, and after that the features linking the Kirkuk style with that of Assur.

We therefore take at the moment the western (Phoenician) features of the Kirkuk style for granted. The panel added to the right half of Pl. XXXI *a* consists of such elements only. On the left half we recognise two interceding goddesses and a male god drawn in the finest style of the First Dynasty of Babylon, but widely spaced, as often on unfinished seals where an inscription, or additional symbols, might be added to suit the purchaser. The cylinder surface thus left over was utilised several centuries later, when the Mitannian style was in vogue. The figures looking to the right, and stylisti-

1 D–56.

2 Other seals of the period of a more popular type like Pl. XXX *i* are V.A. 6937; *Uruk Vorläufiger Bericht*, VI, Pl. 18*f*; Bibliothèque Nationale, 305.

cally related to those of Pl. XXX*c–f*, have been added, together with the animals and sphinxes occupying the space originally reserved for an inscription. The designs of Pl. XXXI *c* and Text-figs. 46, 48, 50, 51, 52, 54 are of the same type as the additions of Pl. XXXI *a*. These northern Mesopotamian seals show, on the whole, a clear division of their surface into two separate groups of designs of different origin. On one side we find various small animals, stylised trees, a *guilloche* or a series of concentric circles which is derived from the *guilloche* or the spiral. In this form none of these motives occurs on the older Mesopotamian seals. The other half of the northern cylinders is occupied by figures derived from such seals as

Text-fig. 44. Text-fig. 45. Text-fig. 46.

Text-fig. 47. Text-fig. 48. Text-fig. 49.

Text-figs. 44–49. Mitannian seals from Nuzi.

Pl. XXX*c–f*; Shamash with one foot upon a mountain faces a worshipper or another god, sometimes accompanied by an interceding goddess (Pl. XXXI *c*). The other groups are similarly derived from those of the First Babylonian Dynasty.

It is true that the figures are curiously deformed, but the composition is based nevertheless on such cylinders as Pl. XXIX*f*, *h*, *m*, where a few large figures remain of what was once the main subject of the seal design, while a number of secondary motives are added in two rows. If the main figures do not look Babylonian, they merely represent the development illustrated in Pl. XXX*c–f* carried a stage further.[1] And if Syrian motives are frequently

[1] This is very well shown by such scenes as Guimet, 120, which closely resembles our Pl. XXX*c*, *d*, but the figures as a whole, and details such as the crowns, have assumed the shape of our Text-figs. 44, 45.

used in the secondary small designs, there are, on the other hand, numerous survivals of the Babylonian repertoire. The two Bull-men with the sun's standard and the large bearded face (Text-fig. 44), the arm of the balance (Text-fig. 51), the hero with the water-pot (Text-fig. 54), all these occur on seal impressions of tablets from Kirkuk. There cannot be, indeed, the slightest doubt that the glyptic of the First Babylonian Dynasty in its

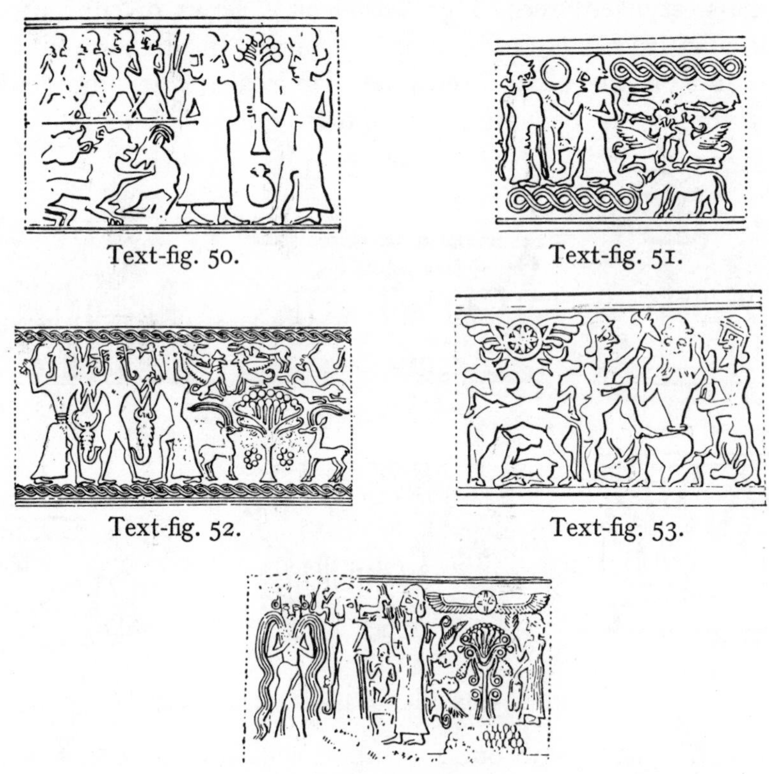

Text-fig. 50. Text-fig. 51.

Text-fig. 52. Text-fig. 53.

Text-fig. 54.

Text-figs. 50–54. Mitannian seals from Kirkuk (50–53) and Assur (54).

latest phase underlies this Mitannian style in so far as the latter does not contain western elements.

Pl. XXXI *e* shows a curious seal which is evidently on a par with such late Babylonian cylinders as Pl. XXX *c*. The figure facing the monster with uplifted arm (which recalls Pl. XXVII *l*) is identical with those in Pl. XXXI *c* and Text-figs. 44–54, and the little antelope "couchant" with head turned backwards is a truly Mitannian motive. The border of the design, formed by two *guilloches*, is not usual in Babylonia, although the *guilloche* is known there; but it occurs in Text-fig. 52. The seal of Pl. XXXI *e* is transitional between the First Dynasty of Babylon and the Mitannian glyptic of the north, just as Pl. XXX *h, j* show us the transition from the older Babylonian to the Kassite style. Our series of connections is completed by Pl. XXXI *b*, which shows a Kassite cylinder which has undergone the influence of contemporary Mitannian glyptic and derives from these, perhaps, the purely decorative use of the rosette, and in any case the winged dragon and the antelope heads.[1] Its main figures, though cut in Kassite style, are derived from certain earlier seals,[2] which show the group of Pl. XXXI *b* in the manner of Pls. XXX *c–f*; XXXI *e*.

But the seals from Northern Mesopotamia do not show their dependence upon the west by the use of Phoenician motives only. They also apply a principle of composition which found little favour in Mesopotamia during the First Dynasty of Babylon.

The Mitannian seals, as we shall see, display a preference for strictly symmetrical groups of designs. And in contrast with what we observe in the south we find that similar antithetical groups are popular at Kirkuk. We notice that antelopes or winged monsters, placed on either side of a palmette or stylised tree, occur quite regularly (Pl. XXXI *c, d*, and Text-figs. 44, 49, 51, 52). The source of these antithetical groups, as of their often hybrid components, is to be found in the eclectic art of Syria. We shall have to return to this point later on. For the moment we must merely point out that the importance of this popular Mitannian style must not be judged by its artistic merits. For it was through the mediocre glyptic of Mitanni that these fantastic creatures and elaborate vegetal designs became known in Mesopotamia, and provided the seal-cutters of Assur with a most promising and entirely unprecedented raw material.

[1] So also Myres, *Handbook of the Cesnola Collection*, p. 431, No. 4301, a Kassite seal with two human-headed sphinxes of Syrian extraction.

[2] E.g. A–470.

CHAPTER II. THE SEALS OF ASSYRIA

§ 30. THE ORIGIN AND STYLE OF ASSYRIAN GLYPTIC

The decline of Babylonian power under the foreign rule of the Kassites led to a precarious independence of the northern districts. It goes without saying that these were completely dominated by Mitanni as long as that curiously artificial power was strong. But when about 1350 B.C. it fell to the aggression of the Anatolian Hittites, Assyria emerged as a more or less coherent and independent realm, too far to the east to be a matter of concern to the kingdom of Hatti, and too far north to be subjected by the Kassite kings of Babylon. A number of seal impressions of this age, which may be conveniently called the Middle Assyrian period[1] (Text-figs. 55, 56, 57, 58, 59), show a refreshing vigour. The motives are traditional and derived largely from the Mitannian repertoire (§29, p. 182; §42, p. 273; Pls. XLII *a*, *b*; XLIII; Text-figs. 44–54). There we find the griffin, the sacred tree of Text-fig. 59, and the sky rendered as a pair of outstretched wings supported by a pillar or by figures as on Text-figs. 57, 59. And the prevalence of symmetrical groups is derived from the same source. Even the two-headed monster of Text-fig. 59 has its forerunner in a sealing from Kirkuk,[2] and the winged disk on the stool of Pl. XLII *b* recurs on an Assyrian cylinder.[3] The historical succession of Assyria to the heritage of Mitanni is thus well expressed in glyptic art.

Text-fig. 55. Middle Assyrian sealing from Assur.

But if the early seal-cutters of the Middle Assyrian period used existing motives, the general character of these seals differs noticeably from the popular Mitannian style upon which it is based. The Assyrian seals (Text-

[1] Sidney Smith, *Early History of Assyria*. The old Assyrian period would fall about 2000, the new Assyrian period after 1000 B.C.

[2] Sidney Smith, *ibid.* p. 326, Fig. 18. There is no need to identify the monster with either Nabu or Marduk, though these two names are engraved on the cylinder, if we realise the dependence of the Kirkuk seals on those of the First Babylonian Dynasty, where such inscriptions only refer in a very few cases to the figures depicted (see p. 13). The monster on the Kirkuk sealing seems not to have a bird's head (though it has a bird's beak), but Pl. XXXI *d* shows that the griffin type occurs in popular Mitannian glyptic.

[3] Ward, No. 1100. The stool is drawn incorrectly.

figs. 56, 57, 58, 59) are much less chaotic and uncertain; if they use the same motives and principles of design, they compose them with a purposeful precision all their own.[1]

There is nothing in the past to suggest the existence of an individual glyptic tradition in Assyria. In fact the Old Assyrian seals, of the centuries just after 2000 B.C., are quite ordinary representatives of the peripheral style of the First Dynasty of Babylon.[2]

Text-fig. 56. Seal of Eriba-Adad.

Text-fig. 57. Middle Assyrian impression from Assur.

Text-fig. 58. Seal of Assur-uballit I.

Text-fig. 59. Middle Assyrian impression from Assur.

Of the seals of Text-figs. 56–9 two belong to Assyrian kings, Text-fig. 58 to Assur-uballit I (1380–1341), and Text-fig. 56 naming Eriba-Adad (1392–1381), rulers who were contemporaries of the kings of Mitanni, but prepared Assyrian independence; Assur-uballit writing personal letters to Pharaoh, much to the annoyance of his traditional overlord, the powerless Kassite in Babylon, whose complaints to Akhenaten are included in the diplomatic correspondence known as the Tell el Amarna tablets.

[1] Perhaps Bibliothèque Nationale, 380, 385 belong to this group.

[2] They are collected by Unger, *Assyrische und Babylonische Kunst*, Figs. 15–19, and are A–284; A–359; Bibliothèque Nationale, 216; and two from Péronne and Graz. They belonged to servants of Shamsi-Adad I, who was a contemporary of Hammurabi. Moortgat, who knows the originals from Assur, compares them all with late examples of Babylonian glyptic (*Kunst der Bergvölker*, p. 34 with note 6).

The political awakening of Assyria found its correlative in the new glyptic style, based on existing elements of Northern Mesopotamian art.[1] So much is clear from Text-figs. 56–9. But Southern Babylonian influences soon enriched this new school. In Text-fig. 59 the "Kassite cross" appears. A cylinder like Pl. XXXI *g* contains a prayer to Marduk. This, and the dog, grasshopper and rhombus, connect it with Kassite glyptic. The lifelike palm trees, the forceful lion, and the scheme of composition in general, present an entirely new departure.

An even finer example of the same school (Bibliothèque Nationale, 301) is difficult to reproduce. It has, according to Kassite custom, a prayer to Marduk written in vertical columns with figures composed in a space beside it. In the field the Kassite cross and the rhombus appear. But the design consists of a naked hero holding in either hand the horns of a rampant ibex. The three figures are magnificently drawn; their curved outlines suggest steely resilience while their surface shows the muscles in strong relief. Above them appears a vulture vaguely reminiscent of the figure of Mut on Egyptian monuments which had been copied by the Phoenicians. It recurs on Pl. XXXI *l*.

While the cylinder just described maintains the traditional composition of the Kassite period, and Pl. XXXI *g* presents an arrangement of old features combined with new designs, Pl. XXXI *f* has done away with southern usage altogether by abandoning the inscription and filling the field with a remarkably free design, probably derived, directly or indirectly, from the west (cf. Pls. LXII *l*; LXIV *b*), but rendered with all the force and interest in physical reality displayed by the other two seals also.

This interest is found throughout Assyrian art, but the particular kind of freedom in the composition attempted in Pl. XXXI *f*, and magnificently exemplified by Pl. XXXI *h*, *j*, is not characteristic of the subsequent glyptic of Assyria. The antithetical group of the third seal, with its strict symmetry but comparatively realistic detail, is much more typical of the later Assyrian style; and of this Pl. XXXI *i*, *l* are fine Middle Assyrian examples. Whether we call the seals of Pl. XXXI *f*, *g* and Bibliothèque Nationale, 301, Babylonian (i.e. late Kassite) seals under Assyrian influence, or Assyrian seals conceived on Kassite lines but with a character of their own, does not really matter much, since they are truly transitional. That the new orientation is Assyrian cannot be doubted, not only because one of its finest mature mani-

[1] Outside Assyria the pre-Assyrian Mitannian designs, especially of the popular type discussed on p. 278, § 42 (*b*) below, continued here and there to be used even after the fourteenth century.

festations (Pl. XXXI *j*), is proved to be so by the name of the owner, but also because of an obvious affinity between these seals of the end of the Second Millennium B.C. and the Sargonid seals of Pl. XXXV. In both cases we find, as a rule, the order imposed by a rigidly symmetrical arrangement, while the elements of which these decorative designs are composed are modelled with vigour and with strong concern for the physical nature of each element. We are reminded, on the one hand, of Akkadian art, and, on the other, of the reliefs of Assurbanipal. The degree of verisimilitude reached in the modelling of such examples as Pl. XXXI *h, j* is truly astonishing. Yet these cannot be separated from Pl. XXXI *i, l*, and the trees and birds of the latter seal go with Bibliothèque Nationale, 301, which we have described and which must be dated to the late Kassite period. Our Pl. XXXI *l* shows, moreover, the Kassite cross at its upper edge. Pl. XXXI *j* is connected with Pl. XXXI *i* by the unusual inscriptions in horizontal lines, and this again with Pl. XXXI *h, k* and some similar seals[1] by the tree-on-mountain design. The whole of this group of fine seals therefore hangs together, and its age is well established.[2]

Nor is there any *a priori* reason to discredit the existence of a high standard of glyptic art during the last centuries of the Second Millennium B.C. It is true that few monuments of the period survive. But it is natural to expect that the renaissance of the country under the first great rulers of a new line, Tukulti-Enurta I (1256–1220) and Tighlathpilesar I (1100–1070), found concomitant expression in the field of art.

The artistic vitality of the country at the time is well illustrated by the fact that an entirely different style existed simultaneously with the one which we have just described. This second Middle Assyrian school is exemplified in Pl. XXXII *a, c*, which utilises the Mitannian tradition more than the Kassite as regards motive, but adheres to the Kassite usage in the size of the seals and in the border of cross-hatched triangles; Pl. XXXII *b* is obviously related to the dated examples of Text-figs. 55–9.

In Pl. XXXII *a–c* purely decorative values are paramount. Moreover, drawing prevails over modelling. And it is this linear and decorative style that ousts the contemporary relief style of Pl. XXXI *h–l*. A comparison of

[1] Louvre, A-712; B.M. 103313=*Early History of Assyria*, Pl. 21 *b*.

[2] Other seals of this class are in the Library of J. Pierpont Morgan (photographs by courtesy of the Metropolitan Museum of Art) and rendered in drawings as Ward, Nos. 1066; 1069, possibly an archaistic neo-Babylonian imitation; 1071, which is closely related to Bibliothèque Nationale 301, but coarser; and 1130, which shows the arrow-like plants on the hill with the tree of our Pl. XXXI *k*, and also the moon and star.

Pl. XXXI *k* with Pl. XXXII *h* shows how the relief style was absorbed by the linear style, Pl. XXXII *c*, *g*, *h*, *i*.

Modelling became important again under Sargon II. It is true that the linear style, predominant, apparently, down to the middle of the ninth century (Pl. XXXIII *a*, dated to about 850 B.C.), was displaced by the more substantial engravings of Pl. XXXIII *b*, *c* (about 790 B.C.) and *f* (about 800 B.C.); but here the relief is very summary indeed, a mere emphasis on the volume of the figures but not a means of differentiation of constituent parts as in Pl. XXXV. On the other hand, the linear style is proved to have survived in Sargon's time (Pl. XXXV *g*, *h*) by finds at Khorsabad, and it remained in use as an alternative for coarse drilling in the manufacture of the simpler seals.

Already by the end of the Second Millennium B.C. the use of the linear style was no longer confined to purely decorative designs. Pl. XXXII *i* shows a worshipper explicitly marked as human, facing a god so designated.[1]

As we have said, the linear style shows obvious links with Mitannian glyptic, the antithetical group, the elaborate palmette and scroll designs being all derived from that source. But they are infused with new life. For instance, there is no doubt that the extraordinary population of monsters which crowd the Assyrian cylinders (Pls. XXXII–XXXVI) were partly derived from the Mitannian repertoire, which in its turn had borrowed from Syrian or Phoenician glyptic, where they were at home from the beginning of the Second Millennium B.C. But their original appearance in Syria can often be attributed to slackness and eclecticism on the part of Phoenician craftsmen, who bungled Egyptian and other designs while they copied them, and by combining heterogeneous elements produced monsters not known in any other region.

The Assyrians found here material which was highly congenial because it gave shape to the prevalent beliefs in demons and evil spirits. But their imagination, once stimulated, was so vivid, and their power of expression so great, that the original designs on the Syrian seals seem bleak abstractions beside the terrifying creations of the Assyrians.

The artistic fecundity of Assyria at this time becomes manifest in yet another way, namely in the variety of principles applied by the seal-cutters. In the matter of composition alone, all that had gone before in Mesopotamian glyptic recurred abbreviated as in a musical recapitulation during those last

[1] This seal is transitional in the same manner as Pl. XXXI *f*; the proportions of the cylinder, the border, the head-dress of the god and the symbol of Marduk point to the Kassites, the subject itself to such Assyrian seals as Pl. XXXIV *e*, *h*.

centuries of Mesopotamian greatness. The continuous textile frieze, which was the prevalent scheme of composition during Early Dynastic times, finds a splendid application in Pl. XXXII *a–d*. Evidently the copying of ancient models is out of the question; for there are no detailed similarities.[1] The Assyrian artists must have rediscovered the appropriateness of this scheme for the decoration of a cylinder seal. We find similarly adept renderings of self-contained scenes of the Akkadian type (Pls. XXXIV *c, i*; XXXV *a, b, c*) or of a series of the unconnected figures favoured by the First Babylonian Dynasty (Pl. XXXIII *b, f*) or of antithetical groups (Pl. XXXV *c, j, k*). The scarcity of inscriptions is, moreover, significant of the self-reliance and creative ability of the seal-cutters. It was, as always in the best periods of glyptic art, in the design itself that the distinction of the individual seal resided.

The variety of Assyrian seals is, indeed, extraordinary; Pls. XXXII–XXXVI *a, d* give an impression of the range of designs, sizes and technique of cutting. But the development of this rich variety remains obscure. The rarity of inscriptions reduces the internal dating evidence to a minimum. The inscribed seals were moreover owned by important officials, while the seals of the ordinary man, like Pl. XXXIV *g* or Pl. XXXV *f, h*, will remain practically undatable so long as there is no material from excavations with which to compare them. At the moment this category contains no more than a score of cylinders from Khorsabad. Nevertheless, we must try how far dated seals will take us.

In Text-figs. 55–9 we have reproduced sealings of the fourteenth century already discussed. Text-fig. 60 shows a hunting scene, found in impressions on tablets from Assur of about 1140 B.C. (Enurta-Tukulti-Assur). It stands quite apart and shows how much remains to be known, but it at least confirms our assumption that there was a naturalistic school of glyptic art in the thirteenth–eleventh centuries of which Pl. XXXI *h–l* are products. Our further assumption that Pl. XXXII *a–c* were contemporary with the relief style is supported by the impression of Rimeni, wife of Enurta-Tukulti-Assur, and another impression on these tablets (Text-figs. 61–2). There we find the griffin-demons which were known in the fourteenth century, but still appear on dated tablets of the ninth century. A dated example of this later period appears in Pl. XXXIII *a*; and Pl. XXXII *e*, a griffin-demon sprinkling a sacrificial sheep on the altar with holy water, is probably roughly contemporary with this seal. At least it is related to the earliest dated seal

[1] Compare the contrasting phenomena of neo-Babylonian times, where we find derivation and the use of archaisms.

of one of the great officials after whom the years were named.[1] Cylinders of about 880 B.C. show a similar creature touching a palmette of a highly stylised "sacred tree". Since these stylised elements as well as this type of demon were also used in the fourteenth century (Text-figs. 56–9) there is

Text-fig. 60. Seal of Enurta-Tukulti-Assur.

Text-fig. 61. Seal of Rimeni, wife of Enurta-Tukulti-Assur.

Text-fig. 62. Middle Assyrian impression from Assur.

little to guide us in assigning the seals of Pl. XXXII *d*, *h* to any century within this period. Pl. XXXIII *a* is less than fifty years older than Pl. XXXIII *f*, but the later seal shows an entirely different technique. At the terminals of its sacred tree, the bows and a number of other details, we notice the use of the drill, which also underlies the deeply cut cylindrical figures, while Pl. XXXIII *a* has the flat texture and finely divided linear

[1] Ward-Morgan, 160.

pattern of a textile. The use of the drill is not in the case of Pl. XXXIII *f*—as it was in earlier times—an indication of decline, nor has it yet become a means of aesthetical enrichment of the design. It is, as we have already stated, a method by which the design can be rendered more substantial and emphatic. Yet the glittering surface produced in Pl. XXXIII *b–k* aptly suggests the astral nature of the deities represented; it achieves this even in Pl. XXXIII *i*, although that seal is somewhat more summarily executed, just as Pl. XXXIV *e*, *g* show a somewhat coarser version of the linear method of Pl. XXXIII *a*. The point is, however, that we may speak of two styles, since in Pl. XXXIII *a*, *f* the two techniques are appropriate to two types of subject and concomitant with two types of composition; and these different styles exist contemporaneously during the ninth and early part of the eighth century. In such circumstances it is wellnigh impossible to attempt a closer dating of individual Assyrian seals. Pl. XXXIII *d* resembles in its subject a cylinder dated to about 808 B.C., and is consequently roughly contemporaneous with Pl. XXXIII *f*, while it shows the same double rhombus as Pl. XXXIII *c*, which is dated to about 797 B.C. The last of this little series of eight dated seals, closely resembling Pl. XXXIII *f*, takes us down to 778 B.C. We have grouped in Pls. XXXIII and XXXIV some other seals which seem to us to belong to the ninth and the early part of the eighth century (with the exception of Pl. XXXIV *c* which should be later), but it will now be clear how little certainty can be obtained in these matters.

With the Sargonid Dynasty, however, a change of style is noticeable. The few seals found at Khorsabad[1] show, it is true, a survival of the older types of design such as Pl. XXXV *e*, *l*, but the other cylinders of Pl. XXXV possess different characters, and one of them (Pl. XXXV *d*) was actually found at Khorsabad. They are distinguished from the seals of the preceding period by a much more detailed modelling without increase in depth, and a more carefully regulated proportion between figures and background. If we add to our little list a seal of King Urzana of Muzam,[2] we have dealt with all the chronological evidence which we possess. This material is clearly much too scanty to serve as a basis for generalisations or to distinguish successive styles or subjects within the range of Assyrian glyptic. It is a pity that we must deal thus summarily with a period so rich in glyptic art of high quality; perhaps this very richness adds to our difficulty. Unless extensive excavations are undertaken in Assyria (which is very unlikely) we shall not be able to distinguish more than three phases: (i) the glyptic of the last third of the

[1] Louvre, *Catalogue*, I, Pl. 57, K. 1–9; and Gordon Loud, *Khorsabad*, II.

[2] La Haye, Pl. VII, No. 32.

Second Millennium B.C., comprising at least two entirely different styles (Text-figs. 60–64 and Pls. XXXI *h–l*; XXXII *a, b, c, i* and perhaps XXXIV *b*); (ii) glyptic from the tenth century to the middle of the eighth century (Pls. XXXII *d–h*; XXXIII); (iii) glyptic of the Sargonid Dynasty (Pls. XXXV, XXXVI *a*). And even then the distinctions are not always clear and the age of a large number of seals remains entirely uncertain.

§ 31. THE SUBJECTS OF THE ASSYRIAN SEALS

It is when turning to the subject-matter of the Assyrian seals that we realise the distance travelled since the beginning of the Second Millennium B.C.; viewed from the advanced point of Assyrian glyptic all older Mesopotamian styles, from their earliest appearance at the end of the Fourth down to the First Third of the Second Millennium B.C., seem to form a coherent group, with which the Assyrian seals have but little in common. That we noticed in Assyria a revival of the different stylistic principles which had found application at one time or another in preceding ages does not attenuate the impression which the Assyrian seals evoke of dissimilarity from the old traditions. For these artistic modes were, if not dependent on, at least strikingly appropriate to the medium, and any school of artists setting out to make cylindrical seals of stones could adopt them.

The newness and strangeness lie indeed in the subject-matter, but the fact that we seem to observe a sudden change during the last centuries of the Second Millennium B.C. is due to the relatively inferior quality of Kassite and Mitannian glyptic. Both of these styles utilised disintegration products of the preceding period, while their new features, the predominance of Marduk and Nabu in Kassite glyptic, the elaborate vegetal motives and antithetical groups of the Mitannian seals from Mesopotamia, are not vigorous enough to prevail over the impression of the lingering decay of traditional possessions which they evoke.

The Assyrian seals are so forcible a manifestation of a new epoch that we realise how little remains of the spirit and material of the preceding glyptic school of comparable achievement—that of the First Babylonian Dynasty.

(*a*) *Ritual Scenes.*

"A race like the Assyrians, living in a land without great natural advantages, condemned by their geographical position to constant struggle with animals and men, as well as with adverse incidents due to natural causes, is likely to hold gloomy views of the supernatural powers, and at the same time to be fanatically devoted to the practice of religion."[1]

In Assyrian times the age-old motive of a worshipper approaching the gods is still in use, but it has entirely changed its character. It has become the rendering of a ritual act rather than the illustration of a religious experience. On Assyrian seals we do not notice the humble figure of former times, protected by an interceding deity, in the actual presence of a god who appears, for all his attributes, to be as accessible as an earthly ruler. Those scenes, dull and formalistic at their worst, were at their most expressive a picture of direct contact intensely realised. But the Assyrian seals show a powerful robust figure, unsupported, making the correct gestures with conviction (Pls. XXXIII–XXXV), while the gods seem to be represented only by symbols or by cult-statues, mounted on flat or animal-shaped bases.[2] The inscription "god" and "man" in Pl. XXXII *i* accentuates the entirely impersonal and general character of the Assyrian seals, where the presentation and offering scene has lost what directness it may once have possessed.

It is possible that we should interpret some of the divine figures not as cult-statues but as personifications of the planets and constellations associated with the gods. On many seals (Pl. XXXIII) they appear studded with stars, and it is clear that Ishtar, at least, is regularly depicted with the planet Venus above her. It is therefore possible that in Pl. XXXIV *f* the temple tower is identified as dedicated to the great goddess by the planet appearing in the field. Another scene depicts a priest near a temple tower and below a fox catching a fish, possibly again an astral symbol.[3]

The Pleiades are never personified as far as we know, but occur very frequently as additions to the seal design, rendered by seven drill-holes, placed either to resemble the actual constellation (Pl. XXXIII *c*, *k*) or adapted to requirements of space (Pl. XXXIII *d*, *f*, *i*). We have seen that they have probably already appeared in this shape at the beginning of the Second Millennium B.C., for instance on Cappadocian seals (Text-fig. 81, p. 251), at a time when the Venus observations during Ammizaduga's reign

[1] Sidney Smith, *Cambridge Ancient History*, III, 69.

[2] The frontispiece of Weissbach, *Babylonische Miscellen*, is proved by its inscription to depict a statue of Ishtar and this resembles many of the seal designs.

[3] The seal, V.A. 7736, is figured by Unger, *Babylonische und Assyrische Kunst*, Fig. 26. For its astral interpretation, see Dombart in *Journal of the Society of Oriental Research*, XIV, 1–10; the fox on Kassite boundary stones is tentatively identified with the fox star of the Great Bear, symbol of Ira, by Thureau Dangin, *Revue d'Assyriologie*, XVI, 37.

suggest an increased interest in astronomy; and we know that astronomy made great strides in Assyrian times.[1]

An object of worship, entirely different from those discussed hitherto, appears in Pl. XXXV *d*. The worshipper seems to address his gesture neither to the sacred tree nor to the symbol of the god Assur who hovers above, but to a stela with the figure of the king. Reliefs depict similar scenes. "The obligation to do appropriate honour to these monuments became a matter of politics when they were set up, as the inscriptions frequently relate, inside and at the entrance of a newly-conquered city, where any defacement of the image or the cessation of the prescribed observances in its honour was an overt act of rebellion.

"It cannot, however, be inferred from this that the Assyrian kings exacted worship of themselves as gods, either from their own citizens or from conquered foreigners. On the stelae it is noteworthy that the king himself is always depicted in an act of worship. He holds out his right arm, making a peculiar gesture with his fingers, towards a number of divine symbols; this is the gesture which the Greeks, as mentioned before, thought to be a snapping of the fingers. The king would certainly not be so represented if the stela itself was to be the object of worship. The fact seems rather to be that such monuments were at once a visible symbol of sovereignty and, when placed in temples (as they sometimes were, both at home and abroad), were intended to associate the king in every act of worship there performed, both as the earthly representative of the gods, and as participant in every favour they might vouchsafe to grant."[2] Exactly the same situation is depicted in Pl. XXXV *d*.

But it is remarkable that even the living king is thus represented in effigy on the cylinder seals and not in person. Note how in Pl. XXXIII *a* the decorative reduplication of the king's figure destroys any suggestion of portraiture or direct representation. Here again, as in the case of the gods, the higher power has become inaccessible, and direct contact apparently ceased. It is in this atmosphere of tension between the ruling powers and helpless humanity that astrology, utilising the newly acquired understanding of the stars and their motions, developed from an amorphous tradition of observed *omina* into a systematic attempt to understand the cosmos and thus to avoid collision with what was ordained.

[1] Schott, in *Zeitschrift der Deutschen Morgenländischen Gesellschaft*, XIII (1934), pp. 302–337.

[2] C. J. Gadd, *The Assyrian Sculptures* (British Museum, 1934), p. 16.

(*b*) *Secular Scenes.*

Here too directness has been lost. The Assyrian seal designs do not introduce us to the life of the individual as in the earlier subjects. Throughout we are faced with official ritual, state functions, or the king's power.

Of the rustic scenes of ancient times, reflecting the care of flocks and herds, nothing survives. We might consider as their successor the design of Pl. XXXV*g*, a horse covering a mare, were it not that horses played little part in Assyrian private life but were essentially a requisite of the army.[1] And thus we find on Assyrian seals battle scenes (Pl. XXXV*l*)[2] and fortresses (Pl. XXXIV*j*), and if a man is shown hunting, he is in military uniform (Pl. XXXIV*i*) as if foraging.

There are a few exceptions to the rule that only official matters form a subject for seal design in Assyrian times; the most interesting are those which represent the curing of a sick man by magico-medical means.[3]

The feasts depicted on Early Dynastic seals somehow conveyed the sensation of enjoyment even if the accompanying music and dance were not depicted as in Pl. XV*a*. Its Assyrian equivalent (Pl. XXXIV*e*) shows an officer on duty uncomfortably snatching a meal, standing at a table, bow in hand, while a servant fans the flies from the food. And this scene is not exceptional but often recurs.[4] Even the king is thus represented.[5] When a figure is seated at table it seems to be a god (Pl. XXXIV*h*); at least it sometimes appears then mounted on an emblematic animal.[6]

(*c*) *Fights and Contests.*

Fights and contests form the favourite theme of the Assyrian seal-cutters. Once again we are reminded of the Akkadian period, but the differences are considerable. In Akkadian times the pairs of combatants were derived from the existing, Early Dynastic repertoire; they served as a rule as heraldic supporters of a panel with inscriptions, and on uninscribed seals were composed as if the panel had merely been omitted. And the scenes of combat were the most conventional of subjects, while the imagination of the seal-

[1] Louvre, K–4; Newell, 408, 409. If it were not for the man holding the female animal's head, one would think of unicorns rather than domesticated animals.

[2] Also De Clercq, 310.

[3] A–831; an Assyrian cylinder from Tell Halaf; and possibly also a cylinder of the second Syrian group in Moscow. These are published by Meissner, who studies this subject in *Beiträge zur Altorientalischen Archaeologie*, pp. 14 ff.; the seal from the Vatican (*ibid.* Fig. 14) does not belong to this group but shows the subject of our Pls. XXXIII*h*; XXXIV*b*.

[4] Bibliothèque Nationale, 342–346; Newell, 397–399, 402, 405.

[5] Ward, 728.

[6] A–727.

cutter was active in the grouping of mythological figures or the rendering of scenes from daily life.

In Assyrian times mythological scenes are almost entirely absent, for the battle between gods and dragons may just as well be considered a specific instance of the group with which we are now dealing, namely the fighting subjects, especially since the gods are never otherwise represented as taking part in any action, but merely as the recipients of worship or offerings. Even those compositions which we might consider to describe daily life are nothing but specific instances of conflicts, generally hunting scenes and scenes of war. It is quite clear that this subject attracted the Assyrians more than any other; it certainly inspired their engravers to an unrivalled display of invention and skill. Occasionally they revived ancient themes such as the hero swinging a lion above his head;[1] the male figure was then no longer naked but wore a kilt. Pl. XXXII *f* shows a revival of the animal frieze, with evident traces of Syrian intermediaries. And we may be tempted to associate the attack of a bowman upon a bird[2] with the ancient myth of Zu, or, in the case of Pl. XXXIV *c*, to think of Herakles and the Stymphalian birds, since other labours of Herakles have been shown to go back to Mesopotamian mythology (§ 20*f*, p. 121).

But all these subjects are of exceptional occurrence on Assyrian seals. As a rule the scenes of battle lack the detail and the tell-tale variations which proved, in the case of Akkadian times, the genuine mythological origin of the designs, and the resemblances to such ancient compositions are rare and may be fortuitous. Thus the conflict of bowman and bird cannot in fact be connected with Zu because it is merely a variant of a long series, in which every conceivable beast and monster serves as the archer's quarry (e.g. Pls. XXXII *h*; XXXIV *g*).

On the whole we do not find even such apparent echoes of earlier legends. For the Assyrians obviously revelled in creating for themselves the weird antagonists of their imagined contests.

Genii with two or four wings, with human or animal heads, dragons, winged bulls, winged horses, griffins, sphinxes, centaurs, unicorns, lion-centaurs (Pl. XXXIV *d*), Scorpion-men mingle and fight. Their spacing is often most sophisticated (Pl. XXXVI *a*); the detail combines decorative effectiveness with a precise understanding of physical substance and function (Pl. XXXV *b*, *c*, *k*). Again, as in Early Dynastic times, the seal-cutters succeed in creating a world of their own, unconnected with the realities of daily life and yet entirely convincing. But it is not the fairyland of the Sumerians into which

[1] Weber, 31. [2] Bibliothèque Nationale, 309.

they introduce us but a sombre world of elemental forces impinging upon each other in battles which are beyond human understanding, both in their origin and their outcome.

Thus the Assyrian seal designs reflect a mentality which is characteristic of ancient Mesopotamia. The texts at all periods prove that for its inhabitants living meant exposure to countless perils. Though these were personified as demons or evil spirits, they did not become better known nor easier to overcome for having received name or shape. Omens were sought and collected in the hope of stealing a march on fate, and, by foreseeing what was likely to happen, of avoiding disaster. Astrological omens were taken from the end of the Third Millennium B.C., and it has already been shown that during the empire of the Assyrians a remarkable advance in astronomical knowledge was made. To what extent is it possible to correlate the seal designs with these other manifestations of Assyrian thought? Can we identify the planets and constellations, evil spirits and helpful genii on the seals where conflicts are depicted?

It seems to me that we cannot go farther than noting a general similarity between the literary and pictorial embodiments of the Assyrian outlook. It is more than likely that the draughtsmen borrowed from the poets, just as the poets may have been stimulated (and not only in Assyrian times) by products of the artist's fancy.

The Epic of Creation enumerates as the Brood of Tiamat, the children of Chaos, a number of fantastic and composite creatures.[1] The seal-cutters may sometimes have derived inspiration from this source. But since we can follow in certain cases the history of a motive with a definite cosmological function such as the Scorpion-man, or can trace it to a foreign source, as with the griffin, we should be careful not to consider literature as the sole origin of these creatures. On the other hand, later writers, faced with the prolific output of the Assyrian artists, looked upon all and sundry as the Brood of Tiamat; thus we find in Berossos an enumeration of those who lived when all was darkness and water, which far exceeds the lists of the Epic of Creation[2] and includes all the figures familiar from the seals.

It would certainly be wrong to "read" each seal design as if it represented a particular conflict between well-defined antagonists. We do not find on Assyrian seals (as we did on those of Akkad) circumstantial renderings of mythological events. We find the mere fact of conflict denoted in great variety but never with any definition of cause, occasion or locality. We have

[1] Langdon, *Epic of Creation*, pp. 87, 88.

[2] Schnabel, *Berossos und die Babylonisch-Hellenistische Literatur*, p. 254.

to deal with a set of designs answering precisely to the requirement of seals in that they are distinctive. It would be unwise to read into them a meaning which they were never intended to convey. We shall presently see that with great impartiality—or we should, perhaps, say indifference—the same figure is shown as victor and as victim. The seal designs are at one with the omens and the medico-magical, astrological and cosmological texts, in expressing the belief that conflict is of the essence of existence. But the seal-cutter, unlike the soothsayer or the exorcist, was not under any obligation to set out the causes and parties of each conflict with precision. He had found, moreover, from the first, that the best way to solve his own particular problem was to produce variations on a general theme. A single specific subject did not allow of sufficient scope to supply all his clients with distinctive seals. At some periods the use of inscriptions supplied a solution. The absence of a leading theme during the First Dynasty of Babylon led to the varying selections of available symbols to be presented on the seals. In Early Dynastic as in Assyrian times the general theme of the seal-cutters was conflict and strife. The spirit in which this theme was treated differed profoundly, but in Early Dynastic as well as in Assyrian times the rule holds good that the peculiarities of the seals are due to requirements of design, and cannot be referred to a particular meaning either of the motives or of their arrangement. If we lose sight of this fact we shall be constructing a mythology based on no other foundation than the fancy and ingenuity of the seal-cutters.

This danger is the less imaginary since certain creatures appearing in the repertoire of the seal-cutters occur also in another context. Thus the lion-centaur and the Bull-man, the four-winged genii and the genii with birds' heads occur in the reliefs and portal-figures of the royal palaces of Assyria. These representations have recently been studied afresh. Mr Gadd describes the "winged bull" from the Assyrian palace gate: "a bull as to his general structure, a man in hand and face except for the taurine ears which wear ear-rings, an eagle as to his wings and breast-feathers and a lion by the curly hair which grows on his breast, flanks and hindquarters." "Winged lions" and "lion-centaurs" are also known, and Mr Gadd concludes: "in all of these figures there is an obvious intention of combining the forces of all the predominant creatures so that they might be the more powerful to resist those adversaries whom it was their function to dispel from the places which they guarded."[1] It seems to me that though this was indeed their function when used architecturally it may represent only a secondary use, a skilful

[1] Gadd, *The Assyrian Sculptures*, p. 14.

exploitation by the architects of the creations of the seal-cutters (and perhaps the poets) who worked in a freedom which the sculptor could never hope to attain. For long before those palace sculptures were made, the composite creatures were engraved on seals, and by no means always as the friendly and protective beings which the sculptors represent.

Thus we find the griffin—related no doubt to the griffin-headed demons who are shown (as we shall see presently) to impart power to the king in such designs as Pl. XXXIII *a*, or to consecrate offerings (Pl. XXXII *e*) and perhaps even to protect gods (Pl. XXXII *g*)—sometimes a prey to demons[1] or even prevented from committing a crime[2] which would be the very opposite of the action just described, namely damaging the "sacred tree", which, as we shall see, is the source of the power which he imparts. Elsewhere the griffin is prevented by a griffin-headed demon from devouring a bull.[3] In Pl. XXXII *h* and elsewhere[4] the griffin is the quarry of a bowman, or is captured by an heroic figure (Pl. XXXII *b*). One might be tempted to apply here a formula which has dissolved similar perplexities in dealing with earlier periods, and maintain that the griffin only became a beneficial power after subjection by a deity. But how can we then explain that the best known guardian of the palace gates, the human-headed bull, appears as a similar prey to bowmen, and that even more frequently[5] than the winged horse[6] or the winged bull?[7]

Or let us take the Scorpion-man, known from the Gilgamesh Epic as a guardian of the place of sunrise, and shown on Early Dynastic seals (Pl. XV *j*) in connection with the sun. We may understand his appearance on Assyrian seals as supporter of the winged disk (Pl. XXXIII *b*, *e*). For this symbol represents, as we shall see, the sky, and the Scorpion-man, stationed at the end of the earth, where the sun rises and sets, is the obvious supporter of heaven. The Bull-man, a traditional adjunct of the Sun-god, appears, though rarely, in the same function.[8] The Scorpion-man becomes a beneficent genius with sprinkling cone and pail,[9] or even attacks dragons or lions[10] with bow and arrow. In this case, as in that of the other creatures which we have discussed, the inconsistencies are only explicable on the assumption that the seal-cutters were not in the least concerned with the meaning of these

[1] Ward, 634.
[2] Musée Guimet, 114; Bibliothèque Nationale, 337.
[3] Ward, 634.
[4] A–650, 651.
[5] Bibliothèque Nationale, 311; Musée Guimet, 96; Louvre, K–2, K–3; De Clercq, 305.
[6] Ward, 580; A–647; Weber, 343; *American Journal of Archaeology*, II, Pl. IV, 16.
[7] A–648, 649.
[8] A–678.
[9] Bibliothèque Nationale, 356, 358.
[10] Bibliothèque Nationale, 313; A–714.

symbols but used whatever material was at hand for the hundreds of designs of combat which they had to produce.

The only composite creature who does not appear in these scenes of conflict is the Fish-man (Pl. XXXIV*b*), no doubt because he is unsuited to any warlike exploit. He belongs to a group of beings of which the texts reveal only the most general and perhaps least characteristic qualities.

The Fish-man and the human-shaped demon with the bird's head and wings are mentioned in Assyrian texts, which consist of instructions for the preparation of apotropaic figures, to be buried in houses as a protection against illness; and at Ur clay figurines including these among other types were actually found buried under the floor of a building and thus supply a welcome illustration to the texts.[1]

These texts, however, have a limited value from our point of view. They are not concerned with mythology, and in their care not to omit any precaution and to exorcise every possible bringer of evil, they tend to include indiscriminately every known demon or monster. We have quoted one section in connection with the lion-headed monster of the Babylonian seals (§ 27 (*g*), p. 174). This creature may, as we have seen, have never had any significance beyond that of a carrier of disease. But we find in these same texts mention made of other creatures, also represented amongst the figures actually found at Ur. They include the Bull-man, whose various functions we have been able to trace on early cylinders, and the Scorpion-man whose cosmological significance appears in the Gilgamesh Epic as well as on Assyrian seals; or the dragon who was the opponent of Marduk or Adad. By explaining the Griffin-man and Fish-man of Assyrian glyptic as protectors against evil we merely describe a quality which they shared with almost all supernatural beings. Their mythological, individual characteristics escape us. Their identification with seven antediluvian sages[2] is fairly certain, since it is just these two types of figures which are buried in groups of seven; moreover, these are described as holding a lustral instrument and a bucket, as they do on the reliefs and in Pls. XXXII*d*, *g*; XXXIV*b*. It has been suggested[3] that they are representations of good weather and favourable winds. It is a fact that the annual outbreaks of cholera, smallpox and other diseases in Iraq are brought to a conclusion by the autumn rains. But in any case we cannot understand the significance of these "sages" from such sources as

[1] Woolley, "Babylonian prophylactic figures", *Journal of the Royal Asiatic Society*, 1926, pp. 689 ff., where Sidney Smith (pp. 695–706) gives translations of the relevant texts.

[2] Zimmern, *Zeitschrift für Assyriologie* (N.F.), I, Band 35, 1924, pp. 151 ff.

[3] Meissner, *Babylonien und Assyrien*, II, 49 f.

the ritual texts, where they are merely included among dogs, Lion-men, children of Chaos[1] and so on, to protect the Assyrians from disease.

Their pictorial rendering is an innovation of Assyrian times, on the model of the leonine demon, the bird-footed demon and other monsters long known to Mesopotamian art. For the Fish-man there are no antecedents; the bird-headed monster was obviously composed with elements introduced by the griffin of Mitannian glyptic into Assyria.

Among the animals which appear in the scenes of combat, we find lions, bulls, horses, with or without wings, all kinds of dragons and the innocent ostrich (Pl. XXXV *i*), which appears in Pl. XXXVI *b* in a hunting scene. This bird, then, stands on an equal footing with the beasts and monsters just enumerated; and Deutero-Isaiah, who was well acquainted with Mesopotamian views, speaks indeed of "the beasts of the field, the dragons and the ostriches",[2] reminding us that the ancients actually believed the wilderness to be populated by strange monsters. In the same manner we find that monsters are mentioned in the official account of Sennacherib's perilous crossing of the Sinai desert.[3] This circumstance makes it yet more improbable that each of the creatures on these seal designs embodies some definite and particular conception.

Finally there are some curious scenes of combat in which the central figure of Pl. XXXII *f* takes part. Though in our illustration he is holding two antelopes, which may perhaps be the quarry which the dragons are seeking, the kneeling man is generally the victim of attack from two adversaries, in fact inseparable from Kirkuk seals (Text-fig. 52), especially because of the curious stylisation of the locks of hair or, perhaps, ornaments dangling from the head-dress of the victim; another Kirkuk version appears in Text-fig. 53 (p. 184). The fact that in Pl. XXXII *f* he holds two antelopes is also a link with Syrian glyptic of the Second Millennium B.C. On the other hand, indubitable Assyrian versions of the First Millennium B.C. are known.[4]

[1] Sidney Smith, *Journal of the Royal Asiatic Society*, 1926, pp. 695 ff., points out the numerous parallels between the protective demons involved and Tiamat's brood in the Epic of Creation; a similar impression is gained from Berossos—all of which shows the limitations of this class of ritual when original significance is looked for. See above, p. 199.

[2] Isaiah 43, *v.* 20. The Authorised Version has "owls", but "ostriches" seems to be the translation accepted by Semitic scholars.

[3] Luckenbill, *Ancient Records of Assyria*, II, 558. Similarly we find at Khorsabad on reliefs depicting the transport of heavy timber by water, among the fish, crabs and tortoises, also a merman with the horned crown of the gods, while a winged bull seems loath to leave the trunks felled, perhaps, in the mountains where he was supposed to dwell. See Pottier, *Catalogue des Antiquités Assyriennes*, Pl. XX, Nos. 43, 44.

[4] Ward, 642, 644, 645.

The symmetrical compositions of the last two seals we have discussed lead us to a fourth group of subjects which are common on Assyrian seals.

(*d*) *Antithetical Groups and the "Sacred Tree".*

In the antithetical groups the decorative principle predominates entirely, and is in reality the *raison d'être* of the design. Certain contests (Pls. XXXII *b*; XXXV *k*) belong to this scheme, but we shall treat here especially those designs in which an ornamental vegetal motive is the central feature.

The scene with the Fish-man (Pl. XXXIV *b*) is included here because its focus is the winged disk which is often observed with anthropomorphic genii flanking that elaborate combination of vegetal motives called "the sacred tree". The winged disk is, in fact, constantly depicted above that "tree".

Mr Gadd points out that there are many objections against the usual explanation of the action of the attendants as the artificial fertilisation of the date palm.[1] Everything, on the contrary, goes to show that the "tree" is rather the source than the recipient of a magical virtue. In Pl. XXXII *d* we see griffin-demons facing this "tree", as they face in Pl. XXXII *g* the figure of a god. Elsewhere (Pl. XXXIII *a*) they stand behind the king, and it is indeed likely that the powerful influence radiating from the sacred branches "is conveyed by the touch of the cones dipped in a lustral fluid contained in the small pails".[2] In this fashion a griffin-demon seems to consecrate the sacrificial sheep in Pl. XXXII *e*. The same gesture is made by another class of genius, human in shape but provided with two or four wings,[3] who may fulfil other functions, such as fighting beasts (Pl. XXXV *i*, *k*) or carrying animals and fruit (Pl. XXXV *j*), in performing which service they also appear in sculpture, and Mr Gadd writes that they seem to be winged messengers of strength and health with the implied accompaniment of prosperity for the harvests of Assyria.

What then is the meaning of the elaborate combination of stylised vegetal motives, the highly artificial "sacred tree" which usually appears as the source of power round which the figures are symmetrically grouped? A tree

[1] See Miss C. Garlick in *Proceedings of the Society of Biblical Archaeology*, XL (1918), pp. iii *f.*

[2] Gadd, *The Assyrian Sculptures*, p. 52.

[3] It is questionable whether these wings are an essential feature; if we take, for example, a striking and surprising adversary in the contests—the ostrich—we sometimes find it (Guimet, 105, and Newell, 424) held, together with an ibex, by a figure which seems merely human, but elsewhere (Bibliothèque Nationale, 330) by a winged creature. Similarly sphinxes are held by creatures with and without wings (Bibliothèque Nationale, 332, 333).

or plant occurs as the centre of an antithetical group from the earliest times. But to refer to that as a "sacred tree" confuses the issue. Throughout Palestine, Syria, Mesopotamia and Persia, and at all times, a simple antithetical group of animals flanking a plant is known (Pls. IV*j*; XIII*h*; XVII*h*). Whether or not it possessed a symbolical significance in addition to its decorative value is at the moment irrelevant. In the arrangement of this group up to the middle of the Second Millennium, we recognise a stylised rendering of one of the commonest sights of the East, and to speak in this connection of a "sacred tree" is gratuitous. But in Pls. XXXII*d* and XXXIII*a*, a highly artificial "tree" is the central feature of a definite ceremonial. It is true that it is also used elsewhere in a purely decorative manner (Pl. XXXII*b*, *c*), but nevertheless we have in Pls. XXXII*d* and XXXIII*a* definite proof of the religious significance of this peculiar motive. It occupies—alone in Pl. XXXII*d*, and together with the king in Pl. XXXIII*a*—the place taken by a god in Pl. XXXII*g*. These seals correspond exactly with the reliefs in which the "sacred tree" appears as a source of magical virtue. But we may define its nature somewhat more specifically. It seems likely that the "sacred tree" on Assyrian seals represents the national god, Assur.

(*e*) *The Gods*.

(i) *Assur*, *"Sacred Tree" and Winged Disk*. It is exceedingly difficult to distinguish the primarily Assyrian features in the official religious texts of the empire. The prestige of Babylon was such that its usages and doctrines were as far as possible adopted by the ruling Assyrians.[1] But it has been discovered that in one respect the Assyrian cult differed from that in the south. "It would appear that at the New Year festival in Assyria use was made of a bare tree-trunk, round which metal bands, called 'yokes', were fastened, and fillets were attached. This is clearly magic of the type called 'sympathetic'; the ritual act is intended to promote that revival of Nature in the New Year which is the most intense desire of primitive man.... There is evidence that apart from the important part this bedecked Maypole played in the New Year festival of the Assyrians, the bare pole itself was the object of ritual practices at other times just as was the case in Syria and Palestine."[2]

[1] The difficulties and the complete uncertainty resulting from this state of affairs become clear, for instance, in a perusal of the article "Assur" in *Reallexikon der Assyriologie*, I, 196 ff., or in Tallquist's Study, *Der Assyrische Gott* (Helsingfors, 1932), in which, however, both the original character of Assur as a god of fertility and his identification with any extant image are denied, in the writer's opinion on insufficient grounds.

[2] Sidney Smith, *Early History of Assyria*, p. 123.

The tree is, in all probability, a cedar tree:[1] and in front of the temples at Khorsabad cedar trees bound with copper bands, decorated with religious scenes, stood on either side of the entrance.[2] The use of the cedar supplies a further parallel with Egyptian usage, especially the erection of the Ded-pillar in the cult of Osiris, which is connected with Byblos by clear mythological traits, revealed by modern research as being possibly echoes of an historical relationship with Syria.[3] It is likely that this cult spread throughout Egypt from the Eastern Delta where it was established in pre-Dynastic times, the natural foothold of those Asiatic elements whose presence is attested by certain features in the Egyptian language and which may, on the other hand, have formed a component of the population of Assyria. The earliest remains found in the northern part of Mesopotamia are more closely related to those of North Syria than to the southern region of the Plain; and the association between tree and fertility god is likely to go back to an early stage of indigenous culture.

The Syrian cylinder of Pl. XLIV*h* gives a dramatic rendering of this association. Three figures do homage to a tree or palm which is topped by a head wearing the horned and spiked crown of the gods. From Ishchali, near Baghdad, but east of the Tigris and thus situated in an area closely connected with the north, comes a terracotta plaque similarly showing a palm tree crowned with the emblem of divinity.[4]

An ancient relief from the Assur temple in the city of Assur[5] shows the god, perhaps as a Tree-god, but in any case as the exact equivalent of the figures on Pl. XX*b–e*, of the type worshipped throughout Mesopotamia. But now we know that at the New Year festival a "bedecked maypole" played—in contrast with the south—an important part at Assur, we understand the religious significance evidently attached to the very artificial structure on such seal designs as those of Pls. XXXII *b*, *c*, *d*, XXXIII *a* and

[1] *Journal of Egyptian Archaeology*, VIII, 44.

[2] See Gordon Loud, *Khorsabad*, I, 97, 104 ff., Figs. 99, 111, 112, and *Oriental Institute Communications*, No. 19, Figs. 95, 96.

[3] Sethe, *Urgeschichte und älteste Religion der Aegypter*.

[4] *Illustrated London News*, 5 September 1936, p. 388, and *Archiv für Orientforschung*, XI, 265, Fig. 9.

[5] Andrae, *Kultrelief. aus dem Brunnen des Assur tempels zu Assur*, W.V.D.O.G. 53 (1931). The place where the relief was recovered provides very strong circumstantial evidence for the identification, which Tallquist opposes. The scolloped design on the god's dress recalls the epithet: "Lord of the Abek mountains, the mountains which he loves" (Tallquist, *loc. cit.* pp. 15 and 112), which may well refer to an important cult centre or to a region where plants or trees, which were in particular considered to be the god's manifestations, are found.

XXXV *d*, *j*, which are unintelligible as the rendering of natural trees but not so if they represent the ritual object consisting of a pole ornamented with copper bands, cloth and ribbons, the *asherah* of pre-Israelite Canaan (ii Kings 23, *vv*. 6, 14—where the Authorised Version has "groves"). In this respect too they resemble their equivalent, the Ded-pillar in Egypt.

The Assyrian seal designs are thus the earliest in which we can be sure that a "sacred tree" is rendered by the seal-cutters. Iconographically this Assyrian design is an inheritance from an earlier period. For it is on the Mitannian seals, both of the official and of the popular style, that we shall witness the transformation of the simple rendering of a natural tree (flanked by two animals) (Pl. XLI *f* and Text-fig. 44) into the "sacred tree" of scrolls and palmettes (Pl. XLII *b*, *i*, *o*, Text-figs. 49, 52, 54). This is well in keeping with our view, since the Mitannian style arose and prevailed within the territory which was subsequently to form the heart of the Assyrian empire. Since the beliefs reflected in the cult of Osiris and Assur are of immemorable antiquity, we should expect them to become recognisable once the peculiarities of these regions could find some spontaneous expression. Up to the great migrations which weakened both Babylon and Egypt in the eighteenth century B.C., the glyptic of the northern regions had been a mere reflection of that of Mesopotamia (Section VI, p. 224). The newly arrived Mitannians succeeded for a few centuries in maintaining an independent North Syrian state; then we find for the first time in the seals of Mitanni a suggestion of ideas which subsequently were more explicitly expressed by the seal-cutters—and scribes—of Assyria.

It is not only the "sacred tree" which refers to the god of the Assyrian empire on the seals. A god himself is often shown hovering above this symbol (Pls. XXXIII *a*, *e*, *f*; XXXV *d*). There is no inscription to prove his identity, but he is probably Assur. The texts prove that Assur is directly concerned with the king's accession and with all the deeds of his reign. The Assyrian kings give to certain accounts of their wars the literary form of a report sent by them, as commanders, to their overlord, the god.[1]

The god in the winged disk appears in all those warlike and peaceful situations on the monuments (Pl. XXXIII *a*; Text-figs. 63, 64), where his association with the king corresponds to the function which the texts assign to Assur.[2] Since, at the same time, the god in the disk appears associated with the "sacred tree" (Pl. XXXIII *a*, *e*, *f*) which independent texts relating to the

[1] Ungnad, *Orientalistische Literaturzeitung*, 1918, pp. 72 ff.

[2] Tallquist, *loc. cit.* pp. 86–92.

New Year festival assign to Assur, there is nothing missing but an inscription actually naming the god in the disk to make the identification with Assur a certainty.

The origin of the winged disk seems at first sight to refute this, but before we enter into the complicated tale of derivation and reinterpretation which forms the history of that symbol, let us realise that in refusing to interpret the winged disk with the god as a symbol of Assur, we should have to assume that the national god of the empire remained unrepresented in Assyrian art.

It is true, of course, that the winged disk as a symbol is older than the emergence of Assur as an imperial god; but that does not necessarily impair the identification. For it seems likely that here again the Assyrians utilised motives derived from older and existing schools of art. In this case, as is evident, they changed the meaning of the borrowed iconographical device.

We can only roughly outline here the history of the winged disk from its emergence in Egypt early in the Third Millennium B.C. down to Persian times and beyond. Its adoption by various Western Asiatic cultures falls in the time of Egypt's greatest expansion, under the early kings of the Eighteenth Dynasty.

The winged disk itself was then copied from Egypt, perhaps not so much because it supplied a religious symbol to the Syrians and Anatolians, as because of a certain display-value which it had received from the immense prestige of the Empire of the Thutmosids. A similar design had already been introduced into Syria under the last kings of the Middle Kingdom. In the tombs of the rulers of Byblos the *cloisonné* pectoral and gold-foil necklaces imitating Egyptian designs are decorated with the Horus falcon with outspread wings.[1] The Mut-vulture spreading its protecting wings over Pharaoh was also well known and frequently appears as a filling motive on Syrian seals of the early Second Millennium B.C. (Pl. XLI *i*).[2] But the winged sun-disk in particular seems to have been considered as a symbol of power and royalty. It was adopted by the Hittites as the upper part of the groups of hieroglyphs with which kings' names were written. It appears on the one royal seal of Mitanni which we possess (Pl. XLII *a*). And it is small wonder that it should be adopted by the Assyrian kings anxious to establish their independence in the midst of the rival claims to suzerainty of Kassites and Mitanni, for its use probably signified that the king counted himself under the "Great Powers". And this was no mere matter of vanity; the notion had a clear political connotation. The Hittite kings, for instance, allowed to the "Great

[1] Montet, *Byblos et l'Égypte*, Pls. XCIV–CVII.

[2] In a Kassite or Early Assyrian seal: Bibliothèque Nationale, 301.

Powers" alone the alternative of alliance to the otherwise binding choice between vassalage or hostility.[1]

We do not know when the Hittite kings assumed the winged disk. We do know that they used the title "my sun" as an equivalent to "my majesty" in the New Hittite Kingdom, from 1400 B.C. onwards, and that this title was not employed in the Old Hittite Kingdom, which came to an end about 1650, during the Hyksos domination of Egypt. There can therefore be little doubt that it was assumed by the Hittites in imitation of Pharaoh, the prototype of an imperial monarch. But we should be on our guard against considering the Asiatic symbols too exclusively from the Egyptian standpoint. The star, which regularly appears with the disk on Hittite and Mitannian monuments, is without precedent in Egypt. It is most likely that the Babylonian usage, as exemplified by our Pls. XXV*e*, XXVII*a*, etc., served as example here, for we must remember that the Indo-European immigrants who organised the states of Mitanni and of Hatti arrived with a well-developed language and religion, but not, to our knowledge, with an art of their own. They used, therefore, art-forms prevalent in the regions in which they settled and where Egyptian influence was insignificant in comparison with that of Mesopotamia. But the meaning attached to the symbols thus acquired need not always have conformed to their original significance. We know, for instance, that the winged disk was in Egypt, at least in the New Kingdom, a solar symbol. We have seen that it was taken over by Hatti, Mitanni, and Assyria because it enjoyed an enormous prestige as symbol of imperial power; but it was adapted to the beliefs of these peoples which differed totally from those of the Egyptians. The Asiatics at first depicted the winged disk exclusively with a support, and considering the outstretched wings the main element of the design, evidently interpreted it as a representation of the sky. The earliest indubitable rendering of the winged disk on an Asiatic monument, the sealing of King Shaushattar of Mitanni (Pl. XLII*a*, cf. Pl. XLII*b*, *e*, *o*), shows it firmly supported by a pillar, and on Hittite monuments two pillars are usual (Text-fig. 89, p. 275). Primitive cosmology often explains the relation of heaven and earth by means of this device, and the Rigveda and Atharva Veda actually mention the cosmic pillar which separates heaven and earth and supports the first,[2] a motive which appears for the first time with the settlement of Indo-Europeans in the Near East. We are therefore justified in using this conception to

[1] Götze, *Kulturgeschichte Anatoliens*, pp. 89 f.

[2] Holmberg, "Baum des Lebens", *Annales Acad. Scientiarum Fennica*, Ser. B, tom. 16, pp. 5, 19.

explain the fact that on Mitannian and Hittite monuments the disk does not form part of the outstretched wings, but rests upon them, and furthermore that even when the pillar is omitted, one or two figures, like Atlas, support the wing-shaped sky.

This idea remained popular in Assyria, though the alien conception of a "pillar of heaven" disappeared from glyptic art before Middle Assyrian times, being in some designs replaced by the "sacred tree". In others a single kneeling figure supports the sky (Pl. XXXIV *b* and Text-figs. 66, 67, p. 219). Note that it is not the sun-disk but the outstretched wings which rest upon their hands. There is an early (Syrian) precedent for the single supporter,[1] but the pair of supporters of Text-figs. 57, 59 is more common. The naked heroes and griffins of Middle Assyrian times are replaced by Scorpion-men (Pl. XXXIII *b*, *e*). Their presence is easily justified, as we have seen, on cosmological grounds. In the Gilgamesh Epic Scorpion-men guard the mountains of sunrise and sunset. But we should not jump to the conclusion that for this reason their association with the winged disk counterbalances the evidence adduced hitherto and proves the winged disk on Assyrian seals to represent the sun. For the essential characteristic of the Scorpion-men, according to the Epic, is that they dwell at the end of the earth; thus they happen to be placed where the sun rises and sets and can guard his passage; but for the same reason they are admirably suited to support the edge of the cupola of the sky.

The star drawn within the disk above the wings on Middle Assyrian monuments may be explained as a rendering of the planet Venus, but since the Hittites use the same convention and since in their case the sun is probably intended, it is perhaps more likely that the old Mesopotamian sun-emblem explains this deviation from Egyptian usage.

And yet we cannot interpret as Shamash the god so commonly occurring in the winged disk on Assyrian seals. For the motive underwent a peculiar development in Assyria which can be followed in great detail. On the seals only a few stages of this development are preserved. We see a god appearing within the winged disk (Pl. XXXIII *a*, *c*, *f*) or a winged disk with a tail (Pls. XXXIII *h*; XXXIV *i*) which is sometimes but faintly indicated (Pl. XXXIV *b*). But other types of monument supply the transitional forms which explain the relationship between these various conceptions.

On the "broken obelisk" in the British Museum (Text-fig. 63) made in the eleventh century B.C., we notice a symbol closely resembling that of Pl. XXXIV *b*. It can hardly be described as a winged disk because the disk

[1] Contenau, *La Glyptique Syro-Hittite*, Fig. 142.

is inconspicuous. The main feature is a pair of wings, compactly drawn and closely feathered, and from these two hands project, one apparently blessing the king beneath, the other holding a bow.

This is an experimental design, soon to be replaced by the less enigmatical figure of Pl. XXXIII *a*. But it is valuable in proving that we must not take the association between god, disk and wings too literally. The original conception as expressed on the "broken obelisk" is clearly this, that the god appears in the sky and extends his protection to the king. If we wish to explain the feathery mass concretely we might regard it as a rendering of clouds. For this there are good parallels in a contemporaneous religion of which we have more detailed knowledge:

Text-fig. 63. The winged disk on the "broken obelisk".

"Now the idea of God, or the Spirit of God, dwelling in a cloud, is a representation that belongs to the fundamental thought of the Old Testament. Jahwe as the guide of the Israelites in the Red Sea and the desert, shows himself or covers himself in a cloud; when Jahwe descends on Sinai the mountain is covered by a cloud; when Jahwe comes to meet Moses in the tabernacle, the tent is seen under a cloud: the cloud is the representative of the godhead. Jahwe in heaven sits on his throne, but in the old poetry of the Old Testament, like Psalm 18, Jahwe in heaven is also conceived as riding on the clouds. So—as pointed out by Gunkel—Jahwe's throne in heaven goes back to the idea of the clouds considered as the dwelling place of the deity."[1]

The setting of clouds is particularly appropriate to a god who, like Assur, embodies, *inter alia*, the generative force of nature, which depends upon rain; and in Text-fig. 65 we see indeed water descending from the outstretched wings.

But before studying that monument we must describe the related but more explicit design of Text-fig. 64, which appears on a glazed tile of Tukulti-Enurta II, who reigned at the beginning of the ninth century B.C. There the god of Pl. XXXIII *a* is seen again, but with all the detail which the rendering on a larger scale allows. He draws a bow, and appears in a disk, but the feathered wings are not attached to this, but to the god. Here the ancient symbol has really been superseded by a new design. In fact the sky which the outstretched wings originally symbolised in Assyria (Text-figs. 57, 59, p. 187)

[1] A. J. Wensinck, "The ocean in the literature of the Western Semites", *Verhandelingen van de Koninklijke Akademie van Wetenschappen*, Afd. Letterkunde, XIX, No. 2 (Amsterdam, 1918).

is depicted in an entirely different manner upon this tile. To the left and right of the god appear clouds, whose rain is to be released. The sky being thus explicitly rendered, the wings have really become redundant. But the artist appreciated the value of the motive, where he was required to depict the god hovering above his protégé. The deity was thus equipped with wings and with a feathered tail, and these wings, which had first symbolised the region where the god dwelt, now became an attribute, almost an organ of the deity. The *disk*, on the other hand, became a "glory", such as the seal-cutters often stud with stars (Pl. XXXIII *b*). This "glory", exalting the god's appearance and terrifying his enemies, is neither on the seals nor in the texts a prerogative of Assur. But it is remarkable that the texts, when describing the part taken by Assur in battle, use a phrase for him alone which applies exactly to the god on the tile of Tukulti-Enurta II, hovering

Text-fig. 64. The god in the disk on a glazed tile of Tukulti-Enurta II.

with drawn bow in his glory above the king's chariot. It is explicitly stated that he intervenes by shooting out of the sky fire and missiles.[1] And he alone owns an epithet which exactly describes the god in the disk which we know from the seals: "he who inhabits the resplendent firmament."[2]

We can go one step farther and prove that the winged disk retained its meaning as a symbol of the sky notwithstanding the new form given to Assur. The connection is again established by the monument on which the diverging symbol of Assur first appears, namely the glazed tile of Tukulti-Enurta II. The rain-clouds about the god are not a mere stage-property, or a sudden touch of landscape-painting. They are an essential attribute of the god, and remind us of the climatic difference between the north and south of Mesopotamia. In Babylonia rain serves at most to supply the nomadic shepherds with pasture, while agriculture is dependent upon irrigation. In Assyria however the country is mostly too hilly for irrigation by canals, and agriculture is dependent upon rain, which is much more plentiful there.

[1] Tallquist, *loc. cit.* p. 98.

[2] Tallquist, *loc. cit.* p. 46.

The seal cylinder of Text-fig. 65 is more explicit than Tukulti-Enurta's tile as to the relations between god, "sacred tree" and rain, and fully symbolises the dependence of vegetal life upon the circulation of moisture through earth and atmosphere. The "sacred tree" is here not merely placed upon a mountain; it emerges from a water-vessel. The winged disk above it has outstretched hands from which the water descends to just such vessels as that from which the tree springs.

The idea is similar to that of the "broken obelisk" (Text-fig. 63). There the god hidden in the clouds (rendered by feathery wings) extended a bow and a hand to the king. Here another aspect of the god's nature is emphasised, and again hands appear from the outstretched wings which symbolise the sky or the clouds, and from them the precious water descends.

The early date of the seal of Text-fig. 65 is well established; its borders recur in Pl. XXXII *a*; it may well therefore belong to the end of the Second Millennium B.C., and cannot in any case be much later than the year 1000 B.C. On later seals the same idea is expressed with less precision (Text-fig. 66, p. 219), or the old beliefs regarding the primeval ocean, the Apsu, are brought into connection with the other design (Text-fig. 67, p. 219) to denote the source of the water, or that this ocean surrounds both the sky from which rain descends and the earth which receives it.

Text-fig. 65. Symbolic rendering of Assur giving rain to maintain vegetal life.

After all that precedes, there can be little doubt that the god represented on the seals which we have illustrated is Assur. If there are cases where this interpretation does not seem to apply, they are very few, and may be explained in relation to theological movements within Assyrian religion in the course of which epithets and qualities originally belonging to one god became assigned to another.[1] Let us once more summarise the evolution of

[1] Pering (*Archiv für Orientforschung*, VIII, 289, 292) quotes a number of references to Ninurta which seem relevant in this connection, but then we know of a movement at Calah which aimed at assigning to Ninurta a place in the pantheon occupied hitherto by Assur in the north and Marduk in the south (Schott, *Zeitschrift der Deutschen Morgenländischen*

the design; Assur is represented as hovering protectively and as active supporter over the king in battle or over the "sacred tree", his manifestation on earth as god of vital force. This conception takes three different forms: the least concrete occurs in Text-fig. 65 and on the "broken obelisk", where from the sky, rendered in the traditional (originally Mitannian) manner as two feathered wings with a disk between them, two large hands either dispense rain or make a gesture towards the king; most concrete is the design on the glazed tile of Tukulti-Enurta II, where the god appears in his glory amongst rain-clouds; and by an intermediate method this idea is represented in a large majority of cases, such as Pls. XXXIII *a, f, j*. This form led, furthermore, to an abbreviated rendering, where the god's figure is omitted, but a ring, the abbreviation of his "glory", appears in the midst and a bird's tail projects below the disk (Pls. XXXIV *i*; XXXV *h*; XXXVI *d*). This form of disk with wings and tail occurs a few times during the ninth century, but only becomes common in the eighth. The disk, which first appeared supported by the wings (Text-figs. 57, 59, p. 187), is shown on the reliefs of Assurbanipal, rather as the "glory" of the winged figure (Pl. XXXIII *a, c, f*). In Pl. XXXIII *e* the disk is reduced to a mere point of the body of the feather-clad god, above whose wings (as in Pl. XXXV *d*) appear two more heads, probably a symbol of the great Triad Anu-Enlil-Ea, with Assur in the place of Enlil, just as Marduk took Enlil's place in Babylon.

On several seals two bands depend from the winged disk (Pls. XXXIII *a*; XXXV *d, h*). It is possible that these are the "Band of Heaven and Earth",[1] or they may be an abbreviated rendering of the rain of Text-figs. 65–8, though sometimes they end in claws or flowers (Pl. XXXV *d*). At first it is only the king who is depicted as holding this connecting link with supernatural powers (Pl. XXXIII *a*). Whatever the exact significance of such a detail, it symbolises in a more abstract but decorative way what the pro-

Gesellschaft, 1934, pp. 302–37). The history of the symbol which we have traced here does not necessitate the assumption that it represents a god whose symbol was a bird, *casu quo* Ninurta, nor is Weber's and Götze's view (*Zeitschrift für Assyriologie* (N.F.), VII, 251) that the symbol originated in Imdugud likely to be correct. On one relief—Budge, Pl. XVII, 1—the "glory" of this god contains the Maltese cross and rays, which were really the Assyrian form of the sun-symbol of Pl. XXVII *a, b*; and on the Bavian stela of Sennacherib, Shamash is mentioned in the inscription, and the winged disk with bird's tail is the only symbol which can be assigned to him. (Frank, *Bilder und Symbolen Babylonisch-Assyrischer Götter*, p. 16; his sharp distinction between symbols alleged to refer exclusively to Shamash or Assur is untenable.) But whether we have here confusion with Shamash or merely a consequence of the tendency to give to the national god and head of the pantheon the attributes of the Sun-god it is impossible to decide.

[1] Pering, *Archiv für Orientforschung*, VIII, 291 f.

jecting hands on the "broken obelisk" denote more realistically, namely that Assur guides and assists his land and people in the person of their king.

(ii) Ishtar is depicted on these seals very much as she, "the lady of ladies, goddess of war, lady of battle", appeared in a dream to one of Assurbanipal's seers: "on her right and left she had quivers, she held a bow in her hand, a sharp sword she held unsheathed for battle",[1] only the last detail being omitted. The planet Venus appears above her or is fixed to her crown, and the ring seems peculiar to her also (Pl. XXXIII *b*, *c* (left); *f*, *i*, *k* (left); also Pl. XXXV *a*).

(iii) In the case of an enthroned goddess, like that of Pl. XXXIII *g*, one may doubt whether the constellation Gula (Aquarius) or the goddess Belit is represented. The stela of Essarhaddon found at Senchirli would suggest the latter. Gula is sometimes represented by her dog[2] and once[3] the dog is shown mounted on a dais and placed under a baldachin or tent and worshipped.

(iv) Amongst the male gods Adad is conspicuous. He normally holds his distinctive weapon the axe, but also the forked lightning (Pl. XXXIII *i*), and is sometimes mounted on a bull (Pl. XXXIII *c*, *f*), and sometimes on a fire-spitting dragon with a scorpion-tail (Pl. XXXIII *k*). A god, armed with a bow, is shown attacking a dragon on several seals (Pls. XXXIV *a*; XXXV *b*), and this god is generally mounted on the same animals as Adad, that is, bull or dragon.[4] Since Adad on such seals as Pl. XXXIII *f*, *k* is identified by his axe, and carries at the same time bow and quiver, there is reason to give the same name to the divine bowman, and this the more likely since his quarry is identical with the animal who was continuously the associate of the Weather-god on the seals for about 2000 years (Pl. XXII *a*, *d*, *e* and also Pl. XXVII *i*). And just as a god and goddess are shown bestriding this dragon, the goddess, in Babylonian times, being armed with a double panther-headed mace (Pl. XXVIII *j*), so again we find Ishtar in war panoply upon this dragon.[5] Again the famous relief from Nimrud, usually

[1] Luckenbill, *Ancient Records*, II, 859 ff. On the stela of Shamash-Resh-Ushur (Weissbach, *Babylonische Miscellen*), where her statue is pictured and named as such, the goddess holds a bow upon which the planet is set.

[2] A-771, 728.

[3] Bibliothèque Nationale, 365.

[4] Weber, 295, 311; Ward, 365-570; Unger, *Babylonische und Assyrische Kunst*, Fig. 74; Musée Guimet, 100; *American Journal of Archaeology*, II, Pl. V. In Bibliothèque Nationale, 313 Sagittarius (a Scorpion-man with a bow) attacks this dragon.

[5] A-681.

called—but without justification—the Battle of Marduk with Tiamat, shows this same monster assailed by a god with a thunderbolt. And even an inscribed lapis lazuli seal of Adad, in neo-Babylonian times, depicts the god with this dragon and another animal on a lead.[1]

These arguments are strongly in favour of identifying the god, who attacks the dragon with the bow, as Adad. On the other hand, his dragon appears on Kassite boundary stones, where Adad is habitually recognised by his lightning or thunderbolt; and it has been identified with the constellation Ukatukha (*cygnus* and *lacerta*), which was connected with Nergal, who, as a plague god, was armed with bow and arrow. The species with the scorpion-tail is never quarry but always support; and somehow Nergal and Adad may both be concerned in the conflicts, since on one occasion both antagonists face the monster, the god with the bows, and behind him the divinity with the thunderbolt,[2] but the exact nature of the connection remains obscure.

(v) Marduk appears occasionally on his dragon,[3] just as his father Ea appears on the goat-fish (Pl. XXXIII *j*);[4] the triangular symbol of Marduk is exceedingly common on seals of this period, often in combination with that of Nabu, and even mounted on one and the same dragon (Pls. XXXIII *b*, *c*, *d*, *k*; XXXIV *i*). In Pl. XXXIII *d* they appear together in a shrine. These would be considered seals made in the southern part of the country but for the fact that the texts too show that Marduk was much worshipped by the subjects of the kings of Assyria.[5]

[1] Weissbach, *Babylonische Miscellen*, p. 17.
[2] Bibliothèque Nationale, 314.
[3] A–686.
[4] Bibliothèque Nationale, 361.
[5] Wolfram von Soden, *Der Aufstieg des Assyrerreichs*, p. 36, with note 2.

CHAPTER III. THE NEO-BABYLONIAN AND PERSIAN CYLINDERS

§ 32. THE NEO-BABYLONIAN SEALS

The city of Babylon retained its influence in spiritual matters throughout the period of Assyrian domination. If during this time its peculiar culture found independent expression we, at any rate, are no longer able to discern it. There are certain purely external features which seem significant, such as the frequent occurrence of the symbols of Marduk and Nabu on Assyrian seals (Pls. XXXIII *b*, *c*, *d*, *k*; XXXIV *i*). But since their subject, style and technique are indistinguishable from the contemporary seals such as Pl. XXXIII *f*, there is no way of distinguishing Babylonian from Assyrian workmanship. The cylinders made during the neo-Babylonian empire, when, after the fall of Nineveh in 611 B.C., Babylon again became the political capital of Mesopotamia (Pl. XXXVI *c*, *e–l*), retain the traditions of the preceding age. The coarsely made examples (Pl. XXXVI *d*), or even those which are merely conventional, are really indistinguishable from an Assyrian seal like that of Pl. XXXVI *e*. We assign this seal to the earlier age because of the occurrence of the rhombus and the *sibitti* (Pleiades), while, in Pl. XXXVI *g*, the excessive elegance of the lion and the wide spacing of the design in general suggest a neo-Babylonian date. But it may well appear, when more dated material is available, that these distinctions are untrustworthy criteria of age, and fall within the range of variations of the Assyrian style. The best neo-Babylonian seals, however, have a character of their own (Pl. XXXVI *f*, *j*, *l*). They possess extraordinary elegance and little force. The contours are neither taut nor powerful, but possess a calligraphic quality. The group of the hero grasping two beasts, so popular in Assyrian times, embodied even in its most sophisticated form (Pl. XXXV *k*) the tension of conflicting forces. On neo-Babylonian seals it becomes a graceful monogram (Pl. XXXVI *l*).

The monsters of the earlier repertoire somehow lose their terrifying aspect. In Pl. XXXVI *f* we see a combination of the griffin of Pl. XXXII with the dragon of Pl. XXXV *b*; though it possesses lion's paws, it seems to be a creature as ornamental and harmless as a pheasant. Another composite beast which occurs with comparative frequency in neo-Babylonian seals is the human-headed ibex (Pl. XXXVI *c*),[1] but there can be no doubt that he too

[1] E.g. A–717, A–658.

is an Assyrian product born in the imagination of the seal-cutters of the Assyrian empire. It is imagination that the neo-Babylonians seem to lack. If they have to picture real animals, like the stag of Pl. XXXVI *h*, or the lions of Pl. XXXVI *i*, *l*, and, perhaps, Pl. XXXVI *b*, their designs, while not equalling those of the Assyrians in impressiveness or force, are nevertheless adequate and have a merit of their own. But everything imaginative is reduced to a minimum. This is especially clear in the case of the most original product of neo-Babylonian glyptic (Pl. XXXVI *j*)—a priest worshipping the gods who are neither depicted nor represented in effigy, but are expressed merely by symbols. Ménant has already proved, with the help of impressions on dated tablets, that similar designs are found from the reign of Nebuchadnezzar II onwards, remaining in use throughout Persian—and down to Seleucid—times. They employ a symbolism which was common on the boundary stones of the previous independent Babylonian Dynasty, that of the Kassites, where similarly divine symbols mounted on square bases represented the gods. A seal like Pl. XXXVI *i*, showing, in addition to Marduk's symbols, Ishtar, with lion, bow and lightning and her star, the Planet Venus, is exceptional. Just as on the Kassite boundary stones, we find on neo-Babylonian seals the arms or symbols of the gods, mounted on their "seats",[1] and these square blocks may well represent the stands on which the sacred emblems were kept in the temple. The fact that the "seats" often seem miniature renderings of temples does not invalidate that supposition, since altars found in private houses often imitate the shrines in a similar way, or are at least decorated with the recesses and niches characteristic of temple architecture.

Another curious feature of neo-Babylonian seals is the revival of certain ancient motives which had fallen into disuse. The antiquarian interest of King Nabonidus is well known; we have proof that he collected ancient monuments or copied ancient texts. And we find at least two older motives revived on neo-Babylonian seals. One is the naked hero, of immemorial tradition. On the rare occasions in which this figure had appeared in Assyrian times either swinging a lion[2] or triumphing over animals in other ways (Pl. XXXII *b*, *f*) he was always dressed in a kilt. In Pl. XXXVI *h* he stands nude with the wild locks of the early seals. The attitude, that of a hunter holding a wild bull by the ear while striking, is known on Assyrian seals, but there the victor is of the fully-robed type usual at that time.[3] The naked hero on Akkadian seals never carries small game as he does in Pl. XXXVI *h*,

[1] Hinke, *A new boundary stone of Nebuchadnezzar I*, pp. 173 ff.

[2] Weber, 31, 270.

[3] Bibliothèque Nationale, 328, 329.

but several figures on Mitannian seals are depicted in that action (Pl. XXXI *d*), and Pl. XXXIII *e* shows a late survival of the type. The stag of Pl. XXXVI *h* finds parallels on another neo-Babylonian cylinder,[1] but the most convincing evidence regarding the date of Pl. XXXVI *h* is an impression on a tablet dated to the reign of Nabonidus, where a similar naked hero appears together with seals showing divine symbols on their "seats".[2]

Text-fig. 66. The winged disk and rain on a neo-Babylonian seal.

There can be little doubt that the reappearance of the hunter is a conscious archaism, but it is impossible to say whether Akkadian, Babylonian or even Mitannian seals were the source of inspiration. Even the prayers of the Kassite seals reappear,[3] alongside with the Kassite symbols which we have noted. A similar revival of motives from a long past school of glyptic art are the various water designs reproduced in Text-figs. 66–8, the flowing vase, Ea's "secret chamber" and the merman, which appear on seals of the First Babylonian Dynasty. Another ancient motive, a hero standing with his foot on the neck of a bull, is also revived.[4] The hero has become a robed genius with four wings, and since a lion attacks him, one may even suspect the inspiration of a chance discovery of some Early Dynastic seal showing the defence of the herds.

Text-fig. 67. Winged disk, rain and world-surrounding ocean.

Text-fig. 68. Mermen on a neo-Babylonian seal.

[1] A–717.

[2] A–776 (Pl. 120). These neo-Babylonian seals resemble somewhat the Middle Assyrian seals of Pl. XXXI *h–l*, especially since the stag is in evidence in either group. But neither the tree upon a hill nor the bird occurs on the neo-Babylonian seals, and the human figures on the latter are naked, while they are clothed—often in a tasselled robe—on the Middle Assyrian seals. A–795 (Pl. 121), unfortunately damaged, occurs on a tablet dated to the reign of Darius, but is either a reused middle Assyrian seal or an archaistic neo-Babylonian work, on a par with those named in the text.

[3] A–717.

[4] Guimet, 106.

However, such speculations have little point. Seals of all but the earliest periods are certain to turn up in Mesopotamia either in building or in work on the land, or merely by the erosion of ancient mounds, and it is instructive to note that these discoveries influenced the neo-Babylonian (in contrast with the Assyrian) seal-cutters, even if the origin of the various archaisms remains obscure. And the derivations are presented in a purely neo-Babylonian style, which had behind it the unrivalled knowledge of the Assyrian artists, both as regards composition (Pl. XXXVI *l*) and modelling (Pl. XXXVI *h*), but which was less full-blooded than its predecessors.

How long this neo-Babylonian style persisted it is difficult to say. A good many seal impressions on tablets dated to the Achaemenid period are indistinguishable from those of the neo-Babylonian age. On the other hand, a seal like Pl. XXXVI *b*, though part and parcel of Babylonian glyptic, can hardly have been made before knowledge of Greek art had reached Mesopotamia: compare the modelling of the male figure with that of Pl. XXXVI *h*, which is in the Mesopotamian tradition. But we count it with the neo-Babylonian seals because it shows none of the features which distinguish Achaemenid work from that of earlier schools.

The seal of Pl. XXXVI *k* is remarkable. Strictly speaking it is not a cylinder but an eight-sided prism. But it is evidently a mere variation of the cylindrical shape and has nothing to do with the only other class of Mesopotamian seals, the stamp-seals. The symbols of Marduk and Nabu stand beside an antithetical group of entwined goats. The seal was used by the royal Babylonian mail service. The inscription reads: "Seal of the royal communications."

§ 33. THE PERSIAN SEALS

The seal of Pl. XXXVII *a* illustrates the ambiguous character of Achaemenid art. The group of hero and dragon on the left is purely neo-Babylonian. The group of king and lion on the right is Persian, and this not only because the costume and crown of the king are the same as those of Achaemenid reliefs, but because in this pair of figures observed reality for the first time prevails over decorative values. The unbalanced group of man and beast exactly reflects their relative sizes. But no Mesopotamian artist would have cared to weaken his design by incorporating unmodified proportions and situations which happened to be those of reality.

We shall first consider which elements of Babylonian glyptic recur on Persian seals. The heroes fighting with animals are among these (Pl.

XXXVII *a*, *b*, *h*) and the antithetical groups (Pl. XXXVII *b*, *c*, *l*). A centaur, armed with a bow, attacks an antelope near a "sacred tree" under a winged disk.[1] The only novelty is that he wears the Persian crown, the cidaris. Instead of the former symbols such as the "sacred tree" we sometimes find a fire-altar as the central feature on certain cylinders,[2] but there is nothing new or remarkable in the composition of these designs. They are in the direct line of Mesopotamian succession.

The hunting and war scenes of Assyrian times are revived; we know that the Persian kings kept in the parks of their various palaces wild animals which they killed for sport. Pl. XXXVII *d* shows an impression of the seal of Darius I in the British Museum;[3] here the king in his chariot attacks a second lion while driving over a victim in agony. The winged disk now symbolises neither Shamash nor Assur, but Ahụramazda, as does also, in all probability, the figure in the medallion of Pl. XXXVII *l*. The border of the latter seal suggests a western, non-Iranian land of origin. And within the boundaries of the Persian empire a number of local styles must have existed which we can neither trace to their source, nor even as yet recognise. Thus we see on Pl. XXXVII *h* a dwarfish figure carrying one of the king's victims, who represents the Egyptian Bes, acclimatised by this time all through the Levant. On the seals so far discussed traditional and observed elements are mingled. On the exceedingly fine seal of Pl. XXXVII *n* we see again the royal hunter in his chariot, but his quarry is the old Mesopotamian dragon of Pls. XXII *a*, *d* and XXXV *b*, who, perhaps via a form like Pl. XXXVII *a*, has now obtained the horns of the common game of Persia, the ibex.

A number of Persian seals are free from fantastic or traditional elements. They are of two types. Some describe in a matter-of-fact way an actual scene. A bird is offered to a noble lady (Pl. XXXVII *e*) or the king destroys captured enemies.[4] Three hunters spear a wild boar in the marshes (Pl. XXXVII *k*), or the king is shown not, now, in a hand to hand fight with a lion but spearing it from the back of a camel (Pl. XXXVII *m*). The attitude

[1] Qc, 28.

[2] *American Journal of Semitic Languages*, XLIV, pp. 323 ff., No. 59; Bibliothèque Nationale, 401.

[3] So also Strelkov, in *Bulletin of the American Institute of Iranian Art and Archaeology*, V (1937), 18. His attempt to distinguish an early from a late style of Persian glyptic leaves me unconvinced so that I am unable to state to which king belonged the Moscow cylinder of "Artaxerxes" published by Strelkov.

[4] Newell, 453, and a seal in the Oxus treasure, and two in Moscow and Leningrad, discussed by Strelkov, *loc. cit.*

of the lion, which recurs on Pl. XXXVII *h*, is not found before Persian times. Agricultural scenes are also found (Pl. XXXVII *g*).

The second class of these narrative Persian seals depicts especially hunting scenes (Pl. XXXVII *f*, *i*), but besides the hunters and their game the design contains another element which had never before been included. This element is three-dimensional space. In the modelling of the figures as well as in their placing we notice a feature which we are accustomed to associate with relief work but which, in fact, did not exist before the successors of Phidias invented it in the fifth century B.C. Up to then a work of plastic art had remained a closed volume, separated from the space in which we move, not materially but by the coherence, balance and self-sufficiency of its own particular system of volumes; by its plastic harmony, in short. In the glyptic art of Mesopotamia the separateness of its "space" had been particularly strong. Even if we consider the most "naturalistic" seals, like those of Pl. XXIV, there is a profound difference with Pl. XXXVII *f*, *g*, *i*, *j* which can most easily be expressed in saying that the figures of the older seals move in a space which is somehow different in quality from our own, while the Persian peasants, hunters and game move on our own plane, thereby appearing as if looked at through the wrong end of an opera-glass.

This difference is one of representation and not of aesthetic quality. The Persian seals, as works of art, are as perfect as the most linear of the Early Dynastic seals. There is complete harmony in both cases; but it should be realised that if the spatial representation of Pl. XXXVII *f*, *g*, *i*, *j* would have been of the same quality as was used in earlier times the space around the figure would appear as background and would be empty and the design unbalanced and aesthetically inadequate. The essential change which we observe is that "background" has become "space around" the figures. It denotes that we have left the field of Near Eastern art entirely and have entered the sphere of influence of the Greeks.

It has recently been argued[1] that the influence of the Greeks on Achaemenid art has been overrated, and that, in fact, archaic Greek sculpture derived some of its most characteristic features, such as the treatment of the garments, from Persian art. Persia's conquest of Ionia, and its influence in Greece through its support of the tyrants in several cities would adequately explain a parallel development of Greek and Persian art during the latter half of the sixth century.

The argument, if correct in this form, would merely necessitate dating

[1] Moortgat, "Hellas und die Kunst der Achaemeniden" (*Mitteilungen der Altorientalische Gesellschaft*, II, 1926).

such seals as Pl. XXXVII*f*, *g*, *i*, *j* to the fifth century, but it cannot be doubted that the new approach to the rendering of space is a Greek discovery. We can follow its progress step by step in Greece, not only in sculpture but also in vase-painting. In the East, on the other hand, it has never been understood, and even the artists of the Seleucids reverted to the older method, as the discoveries of Dura Europos prove.

But the cylinder seal did not survive in Hellenistic times; though a few cylinders may possibly have been cut in the third century, they were curios, not articles of common use. The stamp-seal had become increasingly common throughout the period of Assyrian dominance, and the history of the cylinder seals comes to a close with the magnificent specimens which retain the traditional shape, but are in spirit and conception part of the achievement of Hellas.

SECTION VI

THE DERIVATIVE STYLES OF THE ANCIENT NEAR EAST

CHAPTER I. THE EARLIEST GLYPTIC STYLES OF THE PERIPHERAL REGIONS

§ 34. THE PERIPHERAL CHARACTER OF NON-MESOPOTAMIAN GLYPTIC

IF WE HAD included stamp-seals in our survey, we should have needed to use the word "derivative" circumspectly. But it can be proved that the manu facture of cylinder seals beyond the Plain of the Two Rivers was in every case based upon Mesopotamian originals. In some cases, as in Egypt and Crete, the development soon outgrew its original dependence upon imported prototypes, but the comparative rarity of the cylinder and its disuse after some centuries, divide these countries sharply from the homeland of the cylinder seal. In Western Asia, on the other hand, the use of the cylinder seal was well established, by the end of the Fourth Millennium B.C., beside the stamp-seal, and remained uninterrupted. But its dependence on Mesopotamian seals is always noticeable, and with one exception the most flourishing periods of Syrian glyptic were those in which the Eastern influence was strongest. Mesopotamian expansion, either commercial or political, is very noticeable in Syria during the Jemdet Nasr period, the First Dynasty of Babylon and in Assyrian times, and though during the Assyrian empire the stamp-seal, which had been used elsewhere from the earliest times, was adopted in Mesopotamia also, and was ultimately to prevail over the cylinder, we notice even at that time an increase in the number of Syrian cylinder seals and in general a renewed vitality of Syrian glyptic art.

The one exception to the rule that the quality of Syrian glyptic is proportionate to the influence exercised by Mesopotamia occurs during the middle part of the Second Millennium B.C. The influence of the First Dynasty of Babylon had been throughout the Near East of immeasurable importance. When the centre collapsed under the onslaught of Hittites and Kassites, the cultural vacuum thus created was filled by indigenous elements. It was then for the first time that a truly distinctive Syrian glyptic came into being, dependent in its composition and in much of its subject-matter on the Babylonian tradition, but making increasing use of native material.

The term Syro-Hittite, with which this school is labelled, has proved dangerously misleading. It is the least of its disadvantages, that it implies a part-origin in Anatolia, though in reality the Hittites hardly used cylinder seals. Worse is the suggestion of independence from Babylonia which would be implied by any closer association with the Kingdom of Hatti.

To concentrate from the beginning on native characteristics of the Syrian cylinders blocks the way to their true interpretation. The so-called "Syro-Hittite" seals are a heterogeneous group—the most vital, it is true—within that large glyptic family which flourished all round Mesopotamia. The resemblance, for instance, between Syrian and Elamite cylinders has often been noted, and explained as resulting from a common racial strain in the population to the east and west of the Mesopotamian Plain.[1] But that view is untenable, since it requires some positive characteristics common to the seals of the two regions. As it is, the resemblances have a negative quality; they do not consist of true innovations in style or subject-matter, but rather of simplifications of Babylonian designs carried along obviously similar lines. Thus we find that in all the peripheral regions, and at all periods, the large surfaces, such as the bodies of animals, are covered with hatching (Pl. XXXIX*a*, *b*, *d*, *h*, *j*, *k*). This is an obvious translation of the modelling practised by the Mesopotamian seal-cutters into a simpler linear technique. In these and similar cases the resemblance between seals found at Susa and in Syria is due to the fact that both exemplify a provincial or even barbaric imitation of Mesopotamian designs; and indeed seals found in the Dyala region or at Assur or on the middle Euphrates often possess the same peculiarities.

It is of great importance to realise that the peripheral styles keep step with every development of Mesopotamian glyptic. This once understood, it becomes possible to enquire into the measure of expression which these border cultures attained in their glyptic art. Until the end of the Third Millennium B.C. native elements played no part at all. Then, as we have seen, there came a change, at least in Syria and Northern Mesopotamia. But even now the peripheral cultures asserted themselves in a most haphazard manner, and their manifestations remained mostly subsidiary to the themes which are directly derived from Babylonia. We notice changes in dress, equipment, or attributes of gods and men, superimposed upon a scene or scheme of composition which is derived from the south. Sometimes foreign motives, largely decorative, are added; rarely we find an action or combination of figures which is new and peculiar to the locality. With the passage of time these

[1] Moortgat, *Die bildende Kunst des alten Orients und die Bergvölker*.

native tendencies become more strongly marked, but we never find anything like the consistency with which Early Dynastic aesthetic mentality or Akkadian religion were reflected in the seals of their own periods and country.

Thus peripheral seals always retained their problematical character. In the absence of tradition we find incongruous combinations of figures, or of motives differing widely in origin or age. Eclecticism takes the place of discrimination, and a desire to escape technical difficulties often replaces the sense of style.

There is, of course, no precise line of demarcation between the peripheral methods and those which at each period we may call truly Mesopotamian. Transitional forms abound, but deviation from tradition becomes more marked the farther we get from the geographical centre. We have here, as far as possible, used seals of which the place of origin is known. We have, furthermore, only considered a seal to be produced in the periphery of Babylonia when it fulfils one or more of the following conditions:

(1) A rendering of a Mesopotamian subject at variance with its native treatment, either in details (such as the dress of individual figures) or in the composition as a whole.

(2) Subject-matter altogether unknown in Mesopotamia.

(3) Peculiarities of style or composition of a non-Mesopotamian character.

Thus, in contrast to our method in dealing with Mesopotamian seals, we put stylistic criteria not first but last. This is necessary in the case of material which is derivative, lacks consistency of style, and, in fact, often displays no more formal characteristic than extreme simplification (Pls. XXXIX*d*, *h*; XL*a*, *i*). Occasionally we find something more individual; the Cappadocian tablets show sealings with distinct qualities of composition, and the Syrian seals of the middle of the Second Millennium B.C. are often, as we have seen, peculiar in their modelling or cutting. In such cases our third criterion allows us to pass beyond the mere assertion that a seal is a peripheral product. Similarly, it is possible that purely stylistic features peculiar to a certain period of Mesopotamian glyptic may find a reflection, however barbaric, in neighbouring seals. The drilled holes of Pl. XL*b* recall the First Babylonian Dynasty (Pl. XXVI *d*, *f*), a dating of the seal's prototype which is confirmed by the appearance of the Bull-man as standard-bearer.

Our second criterion sometimes allows a more precise definition of the seal's origin. Phoenician designs of Aegean derivation, for instance, cannot be expected to occur on a seal of the Eastern borderland of Mesopotamia. We shall thus be able to divide and arrange a number of peripheral seals of the Second Millennium B.C. when they deviated considerably from their

Babylonian prototypes. It remains, however, essential, for a proper understanding of the development, that we should not lose sight of the provincial character of even these seals, and that we should be well aware of the implications of their dependence upon Mesopotamia. Therefore it is of great value to study the relationship between Mesopotamia and peripheral glyptic during an earlier period, when the material was less numerous and of a simpler nature in every respect. And it is with these earlier peripheral styles that we shall begin our survey.

§ 35. THE PERIPHERAL SEALS OF THE JEMDET NASR PERIOD

The power of expansion in the Jemdet Nasr period is proved by the distribution of the seal cylinders. Mesopotamian seals of this age reached Egypt and Anatolia, Troy and the Cyclades in the west; and the central Persian plateau in the east. In Egypt they gave rise to a native production of cylinder seals surviving all through the Third Millennium B.C. In Anatolia and, as far as we know, in Persia they did not exercise any lasting influence. But in Syria cylinder seals were regularly produced from the Jemdet Nasr period onwards. Elam, especially Susa, occupied a peculiar position in that its connections with Mesopotamia were at all times very close. It cannot therefore be taken as characteristic of Iran. We have actually illustrated seal designs from Susa (Pl. IV*g*, *i*, *j*, *k*, *l*) together with those of the Uruk period, because they are indistinguishable from those found at Erech, and there is no reason in this case to speak of a peripheral style, in spite of its preference for certain themes such as composite monsters (Text-figs. 7–10, p. 26). We have seen that it is occasionally impossible to separate the earlier impressions from indigenous productions of the Jemdet Nasr period, but the later Elamite seals display a character of their own (Pl. VIII *a*), and these represent therefore the earliest peripheral style found to the south-east of Mesopotamia.

It is possible that this style influenced Iran to a greater extent than we are yet able to estimate. Three cylinders were found near the south-eastern corner of the Caspian Sea, at Tepe Hissar (Damghan) (Text-figs. 69, 70).[1] One of these, with a chariot scene, is drawn in a straightforward linear style such as we find at all times and all points of the periphery of the cultural centre. Another shows a file of birds and quadrupeds which has no parallel in Mesopotamia. The third seal has evident connections with Elamite subjects of the Jemdet Nasr period. The division of the bull's body by a sharp line at the shoulder; the ample space between hindquarters and tail, the latter a lance-shaped

[1] Erich F. Schmidt, *Excavations at Tepe Hissar Damghan* (Philadelphia, 1937), p. 198, Fig. 118.

tassel; and the long hair of the animal's hocks, are all features recurring at Susa.[1] The cross is at home there too (Text-fig. 9), and the curious design on the right recalls the Inanna symbol of the Mesopotamian seals (Pls. III *a*; V *c*).[2]

Text-fig. 69. Seal from Tepe Hissar: chariot scene.

Text-fig. 70. Seal from Tepe Hissar: cattle and standard.

In Syria one isolated cylinder seal has appeared in a very early context at Tell Chagar Bazar.[3] It is a small stone roll, with four figures, presumably human but so coarsely drawn that one cannot speak of a style at all. Its age is not absolutely certain, and we cannot base any inferences on this problematical little object.[4]

Dr C. W. McEwan's excavations for the Oriental Institute of the University of Chicago have given us for the first time a chronological framework for Syrian archaeology.[5] The fourteen successive layers distinguished at Tell Judeideh are linked by various observations to Mesopotamian and

[1] Division of body: S. 302, 303. Shape of tail: S. 303, 337, 340. Hair at hocks: S. 281, 284.

[2] The fact that the cylinder reflects the Mesopotamian style of the Jemdet Nasr period does not vitiate the view that the layer in which it was found (Hissar III) would be contemporary with the Early Dynastic period, a view which seems to me the most probable though definite evidence of date is lacking. It is characteristic for peripheral regions that styles which are superseded in their homeland continue in use until a new wave of influence from the centre displaces them.

[3] *Iraq*, III, Pl. I, 5.

[4] The uncertainty is due to the fact that we cannot estimate the length of time during which Tell Halaf ware (with which this cylinder was found) was used in its native country. Its origin goes back as far as the earliest Mesopotamian wares, since the Samarra and Al 'Ubaid wares, of Iranian affinities, used by the earliest settlers in the south, only gradually penetrated into Northern Mesopotamia, where Tell Halaf ware prevailed. But there are no means of deciding when the manufacture of Tell Halaf ware was discontinued in Syria. Its use may overlap all or part of the Uruk period in Mesopotamia. Even the work of the Oriental Institute (see next note) leaves uncertainty at this point. The stratification at Tell Chagar Bazar is not continuous and the gaps between levels V and VI may affect the position of this cylinder in VII; in any case it makes comparison with the clear evidence from Tell Judeideh impossible. See *Iraq*, III, 8, 16 and Fig. 2.

[5] *American Journal of Archaeology*, XLI (1937), 10 ff. I am indebted to Dr McEwan for permission to study and use his unpublished material, and both to him and to Mr R. Braidwood for much detailed information on these important discoveries.

Palestinian strata. Stamp-seals, or at least engraved pendants which may or may not have served for this purpose, were found—as at Susa and Tell Arpachiya—in the deepest strata as well as in all subsequent layers. But from level XII onward, cylinders appeared bearing indubitable traces of their relationship to Mesopotamian glyptic of the Jemdet Nasr period. First, at the bottom of layer XII (Pl. XXXVIII *a*) there are geometrical motives reminiscent of the glazed steatite seals of Pl. VI *e–j*;[1] a little higher, in the upper part of layer XII and the bottom layer of XI (Pl. XXXVIII *l*) we find counterparts of Pl. VIII *c–f*.

Other types of contemporary Mesopotamian seals occur amongst cylinders found at Chatal Huyuk by McEwan (Pl. XXXVIII *f, j*) or bought from dealers in Syria. The popularity of the drilled circle with its centre is pronounced (Pl. XXXVIII *e, g, l*),[2] but we also find, in Syria and at Sialk in Persia, the characteristic "eye" motive (Pls. XXXVIII *h*; VII *b*; VIII *a, j, k*).[3] From Chatal Huyuk comes a Syrian version of the shrine and its sacred herd (Pl. XXXVIII *j*). It is instructive to compare this with the true Mesopotamian examples (Pl. VII *d–k*) and thus to realise its divergence from the original rendering. An exact parallel is the Syrian version (Pl. XXXVIII *i*) of the geometric designs of Pl. VI *e–j*.[4] Yet the difference is not sharply definable and it is clear that in some cases the distinction must be difficult to make. We have seen, for instance, that two-handled jars are preserved on seals from the Uruk period, but that it is only in the Jemdet Nasr age that they are shown in the hands of small pigtailed figures, who seem to be cleaning or perhaps even making them (Pl. XXXVIII *c* (left), *d, f*). The fringed piece of material occurs on such seals from Sialk and Tell Basher, as well as on our Pl. XXXVIII *f* from Chatal Huyuk. There is a close resemblance between all those seals, found either to the west[5] or east of Mesopotamia, and others discovered in the Plain[6] or to the south-east, at Susa.[7] Or, to follow up another indication, a rosette of dots can be traced

[1] The cylinder of Pl. XXXVIII *a* is of a different shape, namely a heavy limestone roll with concave sides, but this variety occurs also in Mesopotamia at Khafaje and Tell Agrab.

[2] See also *Hittite Seals*, 26, 38; and Text-fig. 5 on p. 56, loop-bored; and in the east, at Susa, S–280, 281, 283. Louvre, A–115 closely resembling our Pl. XXXVIII *l* is therefore probably a peripheral seal.

[3] Also *Hittite Seals*, 39.

[4] Also *Hittite Seals*, 48.

[5] Also *Hittite Seals*, 31, 32.

[6] Heinrich, *Fara*, Pl. 67*g*; or *Hittite Seals*, 25, which is a peripheral rendering of two pieces of the fringed material hanging from a vase. This is more clearly shown on a seal of the Baghdad Museum (I.M. 14242), which is presumably Mesopotamian. See also *Mémoires de la Délégation en Perse*, XVI, 204.

[7] *Mémoires de la Délégation en Perse*, XVI, 216, 218, 221.

from Khafaje[1] to Sialk[2] and Susa[3]. The modelling of the figures of Pl. XXXVIII *h* closely resembles the typical rounded forms of Pl. III *c, d, e*.

Thus it is clearly not always easy to distinguish the peripheral seals of this time from those made in Mesopotamia and exported. Seals bought in Syria are inconclusive in this respect, since they may be exported from Iraq in modern times.[4] But there are obvious anciently exported seals known from regular excavations. From Tell Chagar Bazar comes a fragment of a true glazed steatite seal with a geometric pattern,[5] and from Alishar[6] and Troy[7] stone specimens of the same class.

One type of seal, which belongs certainly to the peripheral regions, is only known to us from impressions on pottery, perhaps because the seals themselves were made of wood (Pl. II *o*). This has at least been suggested with much probability by M. Dunand, who discovered specimens at Byblos and noted the sharp edges and flat surface of the engraved figures.

Their date is difficult to establish. Cylinders were never used in this way in Mesopotamia, and the impressions do not, in fact, resemble any seals from Iraq. As with all peripheral products we must ask, therefore, to which Mesopotamian class of seals these impressions show the closest similarities. The evidence in favour of an Early Dynastic date has been fully published in connection with the Megiddo specimen.[8] The strongest argument was the use of animal heads (such as appear in Pl. XI *e*) as sole motive, a usage paralleled by stratified seals from Tell Asmar. Another theme[9] at Megiddo is the placing of goats *tête-bêche*. The closest parallel to this occurs on seals from Susa.[10] These may be of the Jemdet Nasr period, but of that we cannot

[1] *Oriental Institute Communications*, No. 20, p. 36, Kh. V/308.

[2] *Revue d'Assyriologie*, XXXIX, 116. [3] *Mémoires de la Délégation en Perse*, XVI, 102.

[4] But when they are bought at small villages, like *Hittite Seals*, pp. 33, 36, the chance that they were found nearby and are therefore not recent but ancient exports from Mesopotamia, is very great.

[5] *Iraq*, IV, Pl. XIV, A, left bottom corner.

[6] Kurt Bittel, *Praehistorische Forschung in Kleinasien*, p. 80 and Pl. IX, 14. Cf. As. 33-715.

[7] Hubert Schmidt, *Katalog Schliemann Sammlung*, 8868.

[8] Engberg and Shipton, *Notes on the Chalcolithic and Early Bronze Age pottery at Megiddo* (Chicago, 1934), pp. 31–39. Two further impressions were published in the *Quarterly of the Palestine Exploration Fund*, 1934, pp. 90 ff.

[9] The floral motive remains unique and the animal file cannot be limited to any period in Mesopotamia. Even in its specialised form of beast of prey alternating with ruminant it occurs as early as the Second Early Dynastic—and as late as the Akkadian—period.

[10] The seals from Susa are: S–250, 251, 252 and 282. The last is likely to be of Jemdet Nasr date because of its close relationship with S–281 and 283 (cf. on Pl. XXXVIII *g, l*); none of these seals shows the close interlocking of the designs which is characteristic of the Megiddo example. The latter rather recalls in this respect the Brocade style.

be sure; for these types do not occur on proto-Elamite tablets, and the resemblances with Mesopotamian seal designs are not very pronounced, because here we are dealing again with peripheral seals. We can only say that the *tête-bêche* arrangement is not usual on Mesopotamian cylinders of the Jemdet Nasr period, but is one of the commonest devices of the Brocade style (Pl. IX) and survives in the roughly-cut Early Dynastic types.[1] Its occurrence is therefore in favour of an Early Dynastic date.

This is corroborated by evidence from Byblos where eight of these impressions were found.[2] One of them (5684) shows a double fore-quartered animal resembling the Elamite friezes (Pl. XXV *b*). Others are identical in style with the Megiddo and Jericho examples,[3] some use a *tête-bêche* arrangement of lions and ruminants, others again show a man and a bull cut in a most primitive linear style (4512). The importance of the specimens from Byblos is their stratigraphical position; they are dated to the early part of the First Early Bronze age, contemporary with the First–Third Dynasty in Egypt, and belong, therefore, in terms of Mesopotamian chronology, to Early Dynastic times. And these Byblos specimens cannot be separated from those found at Megiddo and Jericho. An impression on a potsherd found by Mr Mallowan at Tell Mak in the Khabur Valley also shows a human figure and animals which suggest an Early Dynastic rather than a Jemdet Nasr prototype.

Recently, however, an impression has been discovered on some potsherds from the XIIth layer of Tell Judeideh.[4] The pattern consists merely of scrolls, but they resemble those of the potsherd with impression from Susa (Pl. II *o*) and another of unknown origin.[5] In the same layer at Tell Judeideh a stamp-seal[6] was found with practically the same fourfold spiral as we see in Pl. II *o*. Now layer XII at Tell Judeideh is contemporary with the Jemdet Nasr period in Mesopotamia. Another impression on pottery, found in Transjordan, has also a geometrical design, possibly an imitation of one of the geometric steatite seals, but the similarity is not very close.[7] The specimens from Susa and Tell Judeideh date probably from the Jemdet Nasr period.

The most likely assumption seems to be, therefore, that the custom of

[1] Kh. III/542; Heinrich, *Fara*, Pl. 48 *a*.

[2] I am greatly indebted to M. Maurice Dunand for full details regarding this material which is being prepared for publication at the time of writing.

[3] Sellin and Watzinger, *Jericho*, p. 97, Fig. 66.

[4] X–2791; X–2974.

[5] *Revue d'Assyriologie*, XXIX, p. 106.

[6] X–3290.

[7] *Zeitschrift des Deutschen Palaestina Vereins*, XL (1917), 170, Fig. 3.

impressing pots with seal cylinders arose in the countries bordering Mesopotamia in the Jemdet Nasr age and was continued during the Early Dynastic period.

There are also two modes of suspension which seem only to have been used in the periphery of Mesopotamia. At least they have not, so far, been found in Mesopotamian excavations and they are common among the seals from Syria. One is the "loop-bore" of Pls. I *c* and XXXVIII *c, j, k*; the other the square pierced loops of Pls. I *e* and XXXVIII *e*. The black seal was found in level XII of Tell Judeideh, the steatite cylinder is in the Ashmolean Museum at Oxford and forms part of a group of Early Cycladic objects from Amorgos. In the museum of Aleppo a series of seals of black stone[1] showing this square loop, as well as "loop-bore", display patterns resembling Pls. XXXVIII *e, g*. There can be no doubt that these seals originated in the Jemdet Nasr period, and that one of them was imitated in Amorgos; it seems to occur in a very early Cycladic context and is a valuable proof of the early date at which Cycladic civilisation was established.

Thus our evidence suggests that Mesopotamian influences asserted themselves in Syria for the first time as part of the great movement of expansion which brought "Jemdet Nasr" tablets and seals to Sialk in Central Persia, as well as to Elam, Anatolia, the Cyclades and Egypt.

§ 36. THE PERIPHERAL SEALS OF THE THIRD MILLENNIUM B.C.

Peripheral seals of the first half of the Third Millennium B.C. are much less numerous than those of the Jemdet Nasr period. They are also of a different character. The Mesopotamian and the peripheral seals of the earlier age are often equal in quality, as we have seen (Pl. XXXVIII *b, c, d, f, h*). In Early Dynastic and Sargonid times such seals of neighbouring countries as we can recognise show merely bungled versions of Mesopotamian themes. The lion crossing the owl-like human-headed bull on Pl. XXXIX *b* is drawn with his face seen from above, as is usual in Mesopotamia at this time, but his gesture is meaningless, since he finds no prey. A large dagger inappropriately takes its place. This type of weapon occurs in the Royal Tombs at Ur; so does the dagger of Pl. XXXIX *a*, a seal from Senchirli, where it is the only motive copied precisely from a Mesopotamian original. The Bull-man and the crossed animals, though obviously modelled on Early Dynastic motives, are different in every detail from their prototypes. The same applies to Pl. XXXIX *e*, where the man seems to hold a mace or war-axe and a

1 Numbers visible through the glass include 1468, 1470, 1473.

scimitar; nevertheless, it is most probably based on Early Dynastic designs, and Pl. XXXIX*c* might even be an imported Mesopotamian seal. Pl. XXXIX*d*, *h*, however, are so much simplified that it is almost impossible to define their affinities. Since the motive of a lion following a ruminant is very common on the simpler Early Dynastic and Sargonid seals, there is some likelihood that it belongs to this age; but it may be older, or again much later.[1]

Text-fig. 71, reconstructed from seal impressions,[2] is a seal from Susa with very peculiar features. Not only are deities mounted on animals; that occurs occasionally in Mesopotamia too (Pl. XXII*d*, *e*); but the rendering of crescent and star are alien and the human-headed scorpion,

Text-fig. 71. Impression from Susa.

the griffin and Bull-man of the upper register are akin to the monsters so common on Elamite seals of an earlier age. The two figures attacking the lion in the lower register resemble Early Dynastic rather than Akkadian designs.

The cylinders of Pl. XXXIX*f*, *g* are peripheral renderings of the Akkadian period; for the first this is at least probable, because the drinking tubes of Pl. XXXIX*f* seem to have been misunderstood; the star is rendered in a un-Mesopotamian way; the crescent standard and the bird do not occur like this on true Akkadian seals. The standard, in fact, is the result of a gratuitous connection between the crescent often used as filling of the space between the two figures,[3] and the large jar containing the beverage. Thus this last feature is also misunderstood by the cutter of Pl. XXXIX*f*. But the heads of the two gods are drawn exactly in the Akkadian manner (cf. Pl. XVIII*e*).

[1] Other seals which may be possibly imports from Mesopotamia are: *Hittite Seals*, 2, 4; Weber, 427 (Jerablus); peripheral seals inspired by Early Dynastic seals are *Illustrated London News*, 27 March 1937, Fig. 15; *Hittite Seals*, 1, 7, 8, 10, 14; Weber, 422 (Jerablus); uncertain is Weber, 545.

[2] See photographs of S. 462 in Delaporte, Pl. 45, 11, 12.

[3] Ur, 141, 142; Brussels, 448; Gawra, 66; and many from Tell Asmar and Tell Agrab.

The cylinder of Pl. XXXIX*g* is a typically confused rendering of the Sun-god in his boat, as we see it on Pl. XIX*e, f*. The boat with human-shaped prow has acquired legs and become a dragon, but the three motives which always appear in this context, the plough, the pot and the quadruped, are present: the animal is in front of the "boat", the plough is above the front of the "boat"; and the pot, together with a bird, is inside. We recall that a bird often occurs in the Mesopotamian versions of this scene.

The frieze of Pl. XXV*b* and the Guti cylinder, Pl. XXV*a*, are also examples of peripheral schools of glyptic art of the Third Millennium B.C. They differ from the seals, Pl. XXXIX*a–h*, which are merely bad imitations of Mesopotamian designs. In Pl. XXV*a, b* the deterioration is canalised, a certain selection, a positive quality in other words, becomes manifest, and to this extent these seals characterise their makers. The Guti seals render exclusively, as far as we know, scenes of worship, and the style of drawing is strictly linear but vigorous. The frieze of Pl. XXV*b* is a new creation from Mesopotamian materials. Its occurrence at Susa, Tell Asmar and Assur makes it difficult to establish its homeland. It demonstrates, in any case, that the surrounding regions sometimes possessed a limited inventiveness and independence which took them beyond the mere copying of Mesopotamian examples.

CHAPTER II. PERIPHERAL GLYPTIC FROM 2000 TO 1700 B.C.

§ 37. THE PERIPHERAL SEALS OF THE FIRST BABYLONIAN DYNASTY

(*a*) *Introduction.*

The Third Dynasty of Ur exercised considerable influence throughout Western Asia. Yet there are no peripheral seals which can be specifically assigned to this period. This deficiency is probably due to our inability to distinguish seals made during that time in Syria or Elam from seals made after the fall of Ur in Mesopotamia. We have seen that the Isin-Larsa period marks a decline in glyptic art. The repertoire being confined to the simple presentation scene with an inscription, there is no means of distinguishing a mediocre version of this subject executed, for instance, on the Upper Euphrates under Shulgi, from an average rendering of the same subject owned by an Amorite in Larsa one hundred years later; and in fact the seals of Pl. XXVI *a*, *b*, *c*, found in layers dated to the Isin-Larsa and Hammurabi periods at Tell Asmar and Ishchali, show all the characteristics of peripheral seals; the simplification of technique, the confusion of details of dress or even of the subject-matter. In Pl. XXVI *b*, for instance, the deity who is approached is either omitted, or, if the figure with the panther-headed scimitar stands for a god, he is drawn facing the wrong way.

The enrichment of the repertoire under the First Babylonian Dynasty was fully reflected in the glyptic of the surrounding regions. But the distinction between Mesopotamian and peripheral seals is more than ever fluid at this period. The curious position of the regions bordering on Babylonia is shown by the seals of servants of Shamsiadad I of Assyria, a contemporary of the early part of Hammurabi's reign. Three of these are in the purest Babylonian style. On one[1] a Bull-man followed by the interceding goddess, offers a bird to Shamash; in the field appear two goat-fish and a hedgehog. Two others[2] show a simplified scheme, one male god, two interceding goddesses, but again in faultless Babylonian style. Another servant of the same king owned a peripheral seal.[3] A god with his foot on a mountain holds a mace with two panther heads. The worshipper is followed by an interceding goddess whose crown has become a pointed "Hittite" cap, though the horns are still just visible. The worshipper wears a large round turban—as in Pl. XLI *b*—and while the balance appears in the field, a large

[1] A–359. [2] Bibliothèque Nationale, 216; and *Revue d'Assyriologie*, x, 89.
[3] A–284.

fish, of a type not normally shown on Babylonian seals, is probably a misunderstood goat-fish. The filling motives of Pl. XXVII *e, g, i, j* appear also. There is a slight muddling of characteristic features which points to a peripheral production.

Thus it is clear that in Assyria peripheral and true Mesopotamian seals were used side by side. With distance we should expect the purely Mesopotamian seals to diminish in proportion to the native peripheral products, and the sealings on Cappadocian tablets prove this assumption to be correct. But we are not so much concerned with their geographical distribution as with the possibility of distinguishing between them.

(*b*) *The Treatment of Mesopotamian Themes.*

Let us, to begin with, recall the three criteria by which we can recognise peripheral seals, and then take as our standard for Mesopotamia the glyptic illustrated by Pls. XXVI *d–l* and XXVII–XXX, which we have shown to be purely Mesopotamian. We contrast with these Pl. XXXIX *i–r* as contemporary peripheral seals, and we shall discuss some of the figures in detail, so that the argument may serve as an example of the manner in which such pieces should be treated. The seals of Pls. XXVII–XXX are chosen as representative of purely Mesopotamian usage in the rendering of individual figures and in their grouping or composition. Now compare Pl. XXVI *f* with Pl. XXXIX *o*. The Babylonian seal is made distinctive by a feature confusing the representation—namely by the placing of some of the figures upside down. But each person retains his character; Shamash is clearly identified, the two figures in front are both dressed in the normal Babylonian manner and both assume an attitude usual with worshippers. The next figure is the "anonymous god" with the mace, whom we feel inclined to interpret as a statue of the king. The figure on the left-hand edge is a curious compound—a worshipper if we hold the seal in the way in which we have printed it, but apparent as the interceding goddess, with the traditional pose correctly indicated, when the cylinder is reversed. In Pl. XXXIX *o* the relations of the figures are entirely confused: the two large figures which are standing normally, and the two small ones which are upside down, all wear the crown of divinity, as the other two pairs wear the turban. Yet the pairs of small figures all seem intended to represent worshippers in front of a god. The scene is best explained as an imitation of some such design as Pl. XXVI *f* by a seal-cutter who did not understand the meaning of the figures in the original.

Now compare Pl. XXVII *k* with Pl. XXXIX *i*. The former seal, from Ishchali, is coarsely engraved, but the details of all the figures are precise and in accordance with Babylonian tradition. In the other seal, the worshipper and the enthroned god seem at first sight correctly rendered, though the head-dresses are somewhat curious and the manner in which the cover of the throne is indicated seems unusual. But the motive of the flowing vase is misunderstood. One should expect a pot in the hands of the figure if the recipients of the outflow are introduced on so large a scale, for these can be dispensed with as many cylinders prove, but the vase in the hands of the figure represents the source of water in general and is, in fact, the most important feature of the motive. Moreover, the figure on the left is obviously a bungled rendering of Ishtar, the only deity who appears regularly in full-face (Pl. XXVIII*j* is exceptional). On Babylonian seals she assumes a distinctive pose and carries certain emblems, but in Pl. XXXIX*i* there are no attributes and the crown assumes an extraordinary shape.

A very similar seal was actually found at Telloh (Pl. XXXIX*k*). We must nevertheless consider it peripheral and therefore an importation. The face of the hero with long locks is identical with that of the Water-man of Pl. XXXIX*i* and the drill-holes in front of the lion are like the "vases" of the other seal. The lion, dragon and seated antelope form in all details an exact rendering of a common Mesopotamian group of which Pl. XXIX*e* gives a somewhat different example. Pl. XXXIX*k* is rendered however in a curious hatched manner, so that our third criterion (style) must also be applied. The Bull-man wrestles with a hero who is not naked—as always in Babylonia—and both are drawn with a hatched line which resembles the border of garments, but is no doubt a misinterpretation of the usual shawl with a fringe on one side. And our second criterion (foreign subject-matter) applies to the small figure who wears a curiously pointed cap which is decidedly un-Mesopotamian, and occurs in Cappadocian and late Syrian seals. The head-dress of the other small figure might be explained as a mis-drawn turban of the ordinary type; but this is doubtful. It is clear that this cylinder found in the very heart of Southern Mesopotamia must have been produced somewhere outside Mesopotamia proper.

The excavations at Susa yielded a whole series of seals which are peripheral renderings of Babylonian designs. Even the conventional panel "Shamash and Ay" appears among them (Pl. XXXIX*l*) as well as the lion-headed demon of § 27*g* (p. 174) (Pl. XXXIX*q*), the bow-legged dwarf and others.[1]

In all these cases we find our first and third criteria applicable.[2]

[1] S–492–517; *Revue d'Assyriologie*, XXIV, 17, and XXV, 176.

[2] Other peripheral renderings of Mesopotamian designs are: A–865, 867, 870, 875, 885; D–119, 124, 125; Bibliothèque Nationale, 244, 245, 246, 259, 263, 264, 268, 270, 432, 433.

(*c*) *Foreign Themes.*

The second criterion, the appearance of non-Mesopotamian subject-matter, is important in establishing the foreign or peripheral character of a seal, but gives very little indication as to its age. For instance, we do not find in Mesopotamia the figure of an animal supporting a shrine. In Syrian temples some such arrangement seems to have been customary. We have collected in Pl. XL*a*, *b*, *e*, *f* four versions which present this motive in widely differing styles.[1]

The fullest rendering, in Pl. XL*e*, shows a naked goddess standing in a shrine upon the bull; in Pl. XL*b*, *f*, the shrine is empty; Pl. XL*a* gives a rough rendering of the complete theme. It may be the oldest of the four seals, not because of its primitive style, for this straightforward delineation of a theme may occur, of course, at any time and contains no evidence as to age. But the design includes two men drinking through reeds, a common motive on Early Dynastic seals, which is very unusual in Syria and Cappadocia.[2] The normal version there is that of Pl. XL*d*, *f*, a man sitting alone and using a curved metal tube, not, as is usual in Mesopotamia, reeds descending straight into the jar. This type is also known on Early Dynastic seals (Pl. XIV*f* from Kish) but is as rare there as is the pair of drinkers in the north. Perhaps Pl. XL*a* was thus made under influence of an Early Dynastic or Akkadian seal design, and it would in that case be older than the others. For the drill-holes of Pl. XL*b*, and the occurrence of the Bull-man as standard-bearer prove this seal to be the reflection of a design of the First Babylonian Dynasty. The same applies to Pl. XL*d*, *f*, both of which show the arm of the balance in the field and the tasselled cloak which as an attire of male gods already becomes rare under the First Babylonian Dynasty. Pl. XL*e* belongs to the same period and reflects the First Syrian style which we shall presently discuss. The throne and dais of the god, and his appearance, are faithful copies of Mesopotamian prototypes (cf. Pl. XXVII*a*) and so is the sun-disk above the crescent. But the cup held by the god and the three figures in front of him are all un-Mesopotamian.

It is curious that the drinker of Pl. XL*f* should be associated with the bull carrying the shrine. The tasselled robe suggests that he is a god, and thus the peripheral renderings of this scene are sharply distinguished from the Early Dynastic prototypes of Pl. XV*a*, *c*, *f*, at least iconographically. It is true that even those represented in all probability a religious feast, a scene, perhaps, in which certain gods were impersonated. On the peripheral seals we find, however, a single drinker, clad in a robe not normally worn by men,

[1] Another version: Bibliothèque Nationale, 274.

[2] Weber, 418.

and sometimes connected with a bull which either supports a shrine, or is placed in it as chief object of worship (Pl. XL*k*).[1] In connection with the drinker we also notice a piece of furniture unknown in Mesopotamia. It is a small table piled high with cakes or loaves (Pl. XL*d*).[2] The same table appears in Pl. XL*c*, which gives the impression of an Early Dynastic seal because of the shape of the head of the seated figure. This impression is probably erroneous; the so-called "bird-headed" figures on Early Dynastic seals derive their peculiar appearance from the fact that the eye is left as a large hole surrounded by the contour of the head (Pl. XV). They never show, as in Pl. XL*c*, a drilled pupil. The lion is also drawn in a non-Mesopotamian fashion, and the rendering of the harp (if it is one) is so confused that one cannot say whether the seated or standing person is holding it, and would not be expected on Mesopotamian seals. It is only the stool with the crossed legs which connects this seal with Akkadian or other specimens from Mesopotamia, and that evidence is offset by the table with loaves which is so common on peripheral seals of about 1900 B.C. Once more we find that roughly engraved peripheral seals are wellnigh undatable.

We have again discussed some seals in great detail to illustrate the peculiar difficulties with which the peripheral styles confront us, and, in the present instances, especially to show features of the non-Mesopotamian cultures. These can be figured on the seals without disturbing in the slightest degree the peripheral character of the design or imparting originality to it. The composition of these seals is based on a Mesopotamian pattern, and such evidence as to age which we have been able to discover is obtained by comparison with Mesopotamian characteristics.

A number of "foreign features" remain to be discussed; the bull supporting a cone, being adored, or placed in front of an offering-table (Pl. XL*l*, *n*, *o*), the chariot with four horses (Pl. XL*m*, *n*), the four little men (Pl. XL*n*) are all unknown on Mesopotamian seals. We shall find, however, that they are most common in that particular group of peripheral glyptic which we will describe in § 38. Another motive of foreign affinity is the god mounted on an animal. It is true that the Weather-god appears in this fashion from Akkadian times onwards (Pl. XXII *a*, *d*, *e*). But he seems, indeed, closely related to the West, and a design like that of Pl. XL*j* is in any case proved to

[1] So also Ward-Morgan, 173. It is, of course, quite possible that both reflect the same group of beliefs, Pl. XL*l* omitting the temple in which the bull and its load are placed, and Pl. XL*e* figuring the temple but omitting the shrine and the goddess implied by the bull.

[2] Also shown in Ward-Morgan, 148, and with much detail in De Genouillac, *Céramique Cappadocienne*, I, Pl. B, 3—the Akkadian (or Guti) seals generally show a table with crossed legs; Musée Guimet, 26; Bibliothèque Nationale, 52.

be peripheral by its style, which resembles Pl. XXXIX*k*, *n*. The scene is much confused; not only do the two Weather-gods appear above lions, but also the two worshippers, though they do not stand in the same attitude as the gods. Similar seals are known, but none from regular excavations, though a Cappadocian sealing shows something similar.[1]

It remains to reject emphatically the claim that certain other motives, commonly so considered, prove the peripheral or foreign origin of the seals upon which they occur. These truly Mesopotamian designs, often decried as Syrian, are: the twist or *guilloche*, the hand-emblem, the human head, and finally the series of small objects placed one above the other.

The *guilloche* is at home in Mesopotamia from Early Dynastic times onward. Its rare occurrence on extant monuments may reflect continuous use in arts unknown to us because they dealt with perishable materials, such as wool, leather or paint. Thus wall-paintings of the period under discussion have recently been discovered for the first time in a palace at Mari, and there a running spiral pattern decorated a throne-base.[2] The *guilloche* must have been similarly used. It occurs not only on Early Dynastic monuments but also repeatedly on purely Babylonian seals (Pls. XXIX*l*; XXX*e*).[3]

The hand as an emblem occurs on Pls. XXVIII*k*; XXIX*k* and XXX*a* and in Text-fig. 42.[4] None of our criteria of peripheral manufacture applies to these, and the occurrence of Marduk's symbol on one of them corroborates Babylonian origin.

The human head occurs also on Pls. XXVII*f*, XXIX*a*, *h* and XXX*a*, and the vertical rows of small motives on Pls. XXVII*d* and XXIX*h*, and on similar purely Babylonian seals.[5] We may admit that in Syria these motives become rather popular, but they cannot serve as indication of Syrian influence in Mesopotamia. Moreover, those who maintain the western origin of these designs must indicate a Syrian glyptic style preceding the period with which we are dealing. Of the existence of such an early Syrian school with a character of its own there is no trace whatever.

It has been maintained in a general way that from the Third Dynasty of Ur onward, western elements penetrated into Mesopotamia and that these affected glyptic art. If this were so, the second criterion upon which we rely

[1] A–872, 873. On A–876 a row of gazelles appears below; the peripheral character of the seal is less pronounced but probable. The Cappadocian impression is Clay, *Letters and Transactions from Cappadocia*, Pls. LXXXI*d*, LXXXIV*d*.

[2] *Illustrated London News*, 31 October 1936, p. 762, Fig. 9.

[3] Also A–877; *Journal of the American Oriental Society*, 1907, p. 140, No. 7.

[4] Also Musée Guimet, 51.

[5] A–387; Bibliothèque Nationale, 249.

would be invalidated, and, indeed, it would in that case be wellnigh impossible to distinguish between Mesopotamian and peripheral seals, and we should have to abandon all hope of progressing beyond the vague and confused view of the history of seal design which at present prevails.

But the assumption cannot be substantiated and seems inherently improbable. The presumably western motives did not appear before the First Dynasty of Babylon, when the expansive force of Mesopotamian civilisation was such as to make derivation most unlikely.[1] It was towards the end of the Dynasty, in Kassite times, when Babylon had suffered attack and the Hyksos dominated Egypt, that Syria became a centre of radiation. Of this we have ample proof. On a tablet sealed in the reign of Ammizaduga we see a pair of winged sphinxes, Phoenician creatures; and Adad bestriding two mountains, as in Text-fig. 40 (p. 163), is probably a design influenced by Anatolian or Syrian representations. But to presume that western, Syrian, civilisation similarly influenced Mesopotamia at an earlier age seems to militate against historical probability.

As regards the seal cylinders, we note, then, a complete absence of an individual Syrian style previous to the First Dynasty of Babylon from which the supposed foreign elements could be derived, nor do our criteria force us to this assumption. If, however, we abandon those criteria, there is no known means by which to disentangle the problems with which we are confronted.

The decision in particular cases may be difficult. The disintegration of the design under the last reigns of the Dynasty are apt to cause confusion. The horned crown, for instance, may easily be represented in a manner recalling the pointed "Hittite" cap[2] (Pl. XXX*d, f*). On the whole it would be unwise to claim for any seal a foreign or even peripheral origin to which two of our three criteria, or the second in an indubitable manner, cannot be applied.

It is clear that in the catalogue of various collections a considerable number of seals are labelled as "Syro-Hittite" which we cannot even consider peripheral, still less foreign to Mesopotamia. The variations of quality, technique and design in Mesopotamia were, in fact, greater than is often realised.

[1] Interesting new evidence regarding the expanding movement towards Syria under the First Babylonian Dynasty is supplied by the texts from Qatna and Ras Shamra. See G. Virolleaud, *La Légende Phénicienne de Danel*, p. 10, and *La Légende de Kéret*, pp. 22 f.

[2] De Clercq, 116; Bibliothèque Nationale, 430; Musée Guimet, 123.

§ 38. THE SEALINGS OF THE CAPPADOCIAN TABLETS

Among the peripheral seals of the First Babylonian Dynasty one group is particularly well known. About 2000 B.C. traders from Assyria inhabited, in eastern Cappadocia, near Caesarea, a self-governing colony comparable with a settlement of the Hanseatic League.[1] The business archives of various firms have been discovered and the sealings on their tablets amount to several hundreds. They are widely scattered through various museums, and largely unpublished, though a special study devoted to them will appear shortly.[2] But sufficient is known to enable us to make a fairly accurate estimate of their affinities.

Kanish—the ancient settlement now covered by the Kultepe—accommodated a population of varied extraction. The personal names show that Mesopotamians were mingled with natives from Syria and Anatolia. It is all the more curious that the cylinders show throughout a foundation of Mesopotamian tradition. Very rough seals were found, indeed, together with specimens evidently of Mesopotamian manufacture, but these two extreme groups are insignificant beside the majority which show designs of Mesopotamian origin, modified to a lesser or greater degree as regards style or subject-matter.

It is particularly with the north of Mesopotamia that Kanish was in contact. The colony was founded by the city of Assur which retained a position of suzerainty. Since Assur was somewhat distant from the centre of Mesopotamian culture, we should expect its seals to be peripheral in style, but we have seen, in dealing with cylinders of servants of Shamsiadad I, that the evidence on this point is equivocal. Two impressions from Assur (Text-figs. 77, 78, p. 250) are of a more definite character. The one is a peripheral seal, peculiar in that three figures wear tasselled robes in place of the ordinary fringed shawl, and the attendant of the king or god wears a pointed "Hittite" cap. The other seal resembles in its style of drawing, especially the edging of the robes, peripheral seals of the type of Pl. XXXIX*k*, *r* and Pl. XL*j*, while the animals' legs have affinities with certain Cappadocian seals (Pl. XL*l*). Neither could be mistaken for a sealing of the Cappadocian tablets, but they

[1] See on this settlement and the problems connected therewith: Sidney Smith, *The Early History of Assyria*, Chap. X, and Landsberger, *Assyrische Handelskolonien in Kleinasien aus dem dritten Jahrtausend*. For the sealings also Moortgat, *Die bildende Kunst des alten Orients und die Bergvölker*, Chap. I.

[2] From the hand of Mr E. B. Reilly, to whom I am much indebted for acquainting me with some of his unpublished material.

agree in this with the Cappadocian group, that they are dependent upon Mesopotamian glyptic of the late Isin-Larsa period and of the Dynasty of Hammurabi.

While substantiating this statement we must dispose of the isolated evidence provided by the seal impressions of a servant of Ibisin, the last king of the Third Dynasty of Ur, which occurs on one of these tablets.[1]

Text-fig. 72.

Text-fig. 73.

Text-fig. 74.

Text-fig. 75.

Text-fig. 76.

Text-figs. 72–76. Cappadocian sealings.

On the same tablet there are five more impressions, and these agree with the bulk of the others in containing motives which are not used on the seals of the Third Dynasty of Ur. The most unequivocal evidence in this respect is provided by the Bull-man as standard-bearer (Pl. XL*n* and Text-fig. 74).[2] On the other hand, we may not date the prototypes of the Cappadocian tablets too late in the First Babylonian Dynasty, since large numbers show the drill-holes which were introduced as distinctive markings in the last part

[1] A–851.

[2] De Genouillac, *Céramique Cappadocienne*, I, Pl. B, 3; A–851; Newell, 284; Louvre, *Tablettes Cappadociennes*, III, 3, impressions Nos. 4, 23, 25, 51.

of the Isin-Larsa period (Text-fig. 73, and compare Pl. XXVI*d, f, h*).[1] A date of round about 2000 B.C. for the Cappadocian tablets, or, in other words, before the accession of Hammurabi, would well agree with the evidence of the seals and not conflict with the epigraphical evidence which proves the script of Kanish to be based on that of the Third Dynasty of Ur; it is also consonant with the mention of Sargon II of Assyria on some of the tablets. Beside the drill-holes and the Bull-man standard-bearer we find other motives on the Cappadocian tablets which could only be expected in a peripheral style dependent on the glyptic of the First Dynasty of Babylon or the end of the Isin-Larsa period. Such are the various filling motives like the monkey (Pl. XL*o*, Text-fig. 75); the human head (Text-fig. 72, and Pl. XL*m*); the bow-legged dwarf (Text-fig. 75); the arm of the balance (Text-figs. 73, 74); the hero throwing an animal as in Pl. XXIX*e*.[2] The Weather-god holding the bull upon which he is standing by a rein (Text-fig. 72) cannot safely be derived from such seals as Pl. XXVII*j*, since the association of Weather-god and bull is not proved for Mesopotamia previous to the First Babylonian Dynasty and may well have been derived from Syria, where this motive was always prevalent.

On the other hand, it is remarkable that even the crossed animals (Text-fig. 76; cf. Pl. XXV*g*; XXVI*h*), the human-headed bulls,[3] the heroes and Bull-men attacking beasts (Pl. XL*h*; cf. Pl. XXVI*g*), recall the Babylonian rather than the Akkadian designs. If in Pl. XL*h* the nude hero on the right might equally have an Akkadian prototype, the crowned hero on the left, and especially the bull attacked by a lion or dragon, are only explicable on the basis of Babylonian glyptic.[4]

The occasional survival of an Akkadian motive counts little against this solid mass of evidence; and even the rendering of Ea on a Cappadocian sealing[5]

[1] Also A–849; A–851; Bibliothèque Nationale, 261; Weber, 179; Clay, Pls. LXXXI*d*, LXXXII*a*, *c*, LXXXIII*a*; Lewy, *Die Keilschrifttexte aus Kleinasien*, 333 B (*a*), 342 B, 293 B. Louvre, *Tablettes Cappadociennes*, III, 3, impressions Nos. 10, 15, 59, 60, 74.

[2] Louvre, *Tablettes Cappadociennes*, III, 3, sealing No. 21.

[3] De Genouillac, *Céramique Cappadocienne*, I, Pl. A, 2; Clay, *Letters and Transactions*, Pl. 81*b*. Sidney Smith, *Early History of Assyria*, Fig. 15*b*. Louvre, *Tablettes Cappadociennes*, III, 3, impressions Nos. 34, 37, 38, 40, 81, 86, 87. Lewy, *Die Keilschrifttexte aus Kleinasien*, 275 B (*a*), 282 B (*a*); Weber, 179=Moortgat, Fig. i, is especially interesting, since between the human-headed bulls appear the drill-holes which confirm the post-Akkadian date. See also Lewy, *loc. cit.* 293 B.

[4] See our Pl. XXIX*e*, *m*, and for the bull especially the post-Akkadian seal Weber, 101. See also the typical deformations of monkey, double scimitar, the lion attacking a seated gazelle, all stock motives of Babylonian glyptic, in A–840.

[5] A–847.

which recalls Akkadian examples like our Pl. XX*f*, is shown by the combined sun-disk and crescent to be a Babylonian and not an older, Akkadian, derivation. A new possibility of the survival of motives for which we have not yet post-Akkadian examples has recently come to the fore. We have seen that in a palace at Mari, on the Middle Euphrates, wall-paintings were recently discovered with subjects identical with contemporary seals. From a similar source the Cappadocian sealings may have derived subjects known in Akkadian times but not, as it happens, preserved on monuments of the end of the Third Millennium B.C. Ea in his boat is one such subject, Ea attended by Usmu[1] another. The realistic design of a palm tree[2] actually recurs in a painting at Mari. On the other hand, it is quite possible that the proved revival of Akkadian motives in Babylonian glyptic embraced a greater variety than happens to be found in the extant seals. However that may be, there is no reason to assume a direct link between Akkadian and Cappadocian glyptic. It is true, that quite often the design of a human figure, such as Pl. XL*l*, recalls simplified Akkadian renderings like Pl. XX*a*, *f*, but here we have merely the converging results of two independent processes of simplification.[3] In addition to Babylonian motives we also find the combination and spacing of large and small figures, often clear reminders of Babylonian usage (Text-fig. 73).[4] Finally, some impressions on Cappadocian tablets were clearly made by seals of Babylonian manufacture.[5]

Such considerations establish the affinities and the date of these sealings. We have now to consider whether the Cappadocian seal impressions

[1] *Liverpool Annals*, I, Pl. XVIII, 11, 12. Mr Reilly has kindly informed me that the original clearly shows a two-faced god, and that some unpublished sealings also depict him, but beardless.

[2] De Genouillac, *Céramique Cappadocienne*, I, Pl. C, 1; Louvre, *Tablettes Cappadociennes*, III, 3, Pl. 230*i*.

[3] It is inadmissible to consider this type of drawing distinctly Cappadocian (Moortgat, *Die bildende Kunst des alten Orients und die Bergvölker*, p. 21). It occurs not only on Akkadian seals but also at Susa, or on a seal like Pl. XL*j*, which is stylistically related to Pl. XXXIX*h*, *r*, and may have been made anywhere in the periphery of Mesopotamia.

[4] Clay, *Letters and Transactions*, Pl. 81*b*; Lewy, *Die Keilschrifttexte aus Kleinasien*, 333B (*a*), 370, 382, 414; Louvre, *Tablettes Cappadociennes*, III, 3, impressions Nos. 15, 16, 53, 54.

[5] De Genouillac, *Céramique Cappadocienne*, Pl. B, 2; Lewy, *Die Keilschrifttexte aus Kleinasien*, 342B; Clay, *Letters and Transactions*, Pl. 83*a*, *c*. Probably also Louvre, *Tablettes Cappadociennes*, III, 3, impressions Nos. 69–72. It is on a Cappadocian tablet that we find one of the boldest innovations of the style of the First Dynasty, namely the figuring of a seated and a standing god in full front-view (A–847, Pl. 125, 5*a*). Experiments in perspective drawing were evidently made at the time in Mesopotamia (*vide* Pl. XXIX*a*); there is no doubt that the top impression of A–847 is purely Babylonian.

possess peculiarities which distinguish them from contemporary peripheral glyptic.

Distinctive features do, in fact, exist, and it is on the strength of these that we have considered Pl. XL *l–o* as belonging to Cappadocian glyptic.

In dealing with the peculiarities in the subject-matter of the non-Babylonian seals we must be more than ever on our guard against insufficiently founded interpretations. To refer these designs to Mesopotamian texts is not permissible, and all that we know of Anatolian religion belongs to a period 600 years later than the Cappadocian tablets, by which time many new influences were at work. Thus we are more than ever compelled to confine ourselves to the phenomenal side of the new designs. Nevertheless, we have to admit the possibility that certain changes in traditional Mesopotamian designs denote a change of meaning, whether or not we are able to grasp their significance. There is no doubt that the group on the right of Text-fig. 72, a man destroying a bull, descends via seals like Pl. XXIX *a* from Akkadian times. It may possibly, however, have acquired a meaning which it never possessed in Mesopotamia, where its value was purely decorative, its original meaning already having been lost by the end of the Second Early Dynastic period. On the Cappadocian seal of Text-fig. 72 the victor holds a dagger; does this mean that the scene was interpreted as a sacrifice? A comparison with Pl. XL *o* suggests it. Similarly the god treading upon a human victim is doubtless related to the Mesopotamian deity discussed in § 26 (*h*), p. 168. There was some evidence, as we have seen, for an identification with the Sun-god. The saw shown in his hands in Text-fig. 75 and on other Cappadocian sealings[1] agrees with this Mesopotamian tradition. It is nevertheless possible that local seal-cutters occasionally used this figure for their own ends. Thus it has been supposed that the god on the right in Text-fig. 72 who holds an axe in one hand and both lightning and a spear in the other, and who appears in other impressions of the same seal to be killing a man upon whom he treads, is making a human sacrifice in order to end a drought.[2] This ingenious interpretation is based on several unproved assumptions, and its correctness cannot be tested. It is a fact that the use of a spear is a new feature, and parallel with that of the dagger in Pl. XL *o*, but that fact alone cannot justify so elaborate a hypothesis. The least objectionable of its implications is that Ea, derived from Mesopotamia and figured on the

[1] De Genouillac, *Céramique Cappadocienne*, I, Pls. A, 4, B, 2. *Ibid.* A, I, shows the god with the saw stepping on to a mountain; also Louvre, *Tablettes Cappadociennes*, III, 3, impressions Nos. 7, 8.

[2] Dussaud, *La Lydie et ses voisins*, pp. 41 ff., especially p. 55.

Cappadocian sealings with his attributes including the goat-fish, became in Anatolia a dispenser of rain. This reinterpretation of the god's character was natural enough in his new homeland, and, in fact, an evident dispenser of rain appears on the Tyszkiewicz cylinder (Pl. XLIII *o*), and in Text-fig. 92 (p. 285), and that god is still served by Ea's two-faced herald Usmu. It is true that those Hittite seals are several centuries later but are certainly part of the same glyptic tradition.

On the whole, local beliefs find a less detailed expression; they are noticeable in the substitution of a Weather-god for the deities worshipped in Mesopotamia or in the depicting of ritual equipment not found on Mesopotamian seals; thus we have noted an ordinary Mesopotamian presentation scene with the table with loaves added.[1] Even on the seals just discussed the enthroned Water-god from the south is flanked by two Weather-gods, the type of deity predominant in Syria as well as in Anatolia. In Text-fig. 80 (p. 251) the Weather-god identified by the axe which he shoulders has become the main figure, appearing enthroned and receiving libations. The main group reflects a Mesopotamian pattern, but is translated into the sphere of western (Syrian and Anatolian) beliefs. The motives filling the field are obviously of local invention.

Other modifications of Babylonian designs consist of an elaboration of actual detail, and here most probably a typically Anatolian idiosyncrasy is expressed.[2] In the midst of these local designs detailed Mesopotamian groups sometimes incongruously survive. So we find, for instance, a god enthroned upon two human-headed bulls, a very complete rendering of Shamash, such as we saw in Pl. XXVI *k*. But in Cappadocia the god is not characterised as a Sun-god and one of his supporters has lost the distinctive horns, while the saw is held by another figure standing upon a lion.[3] In Pl. XL *o* we see in front of the bull a curious table bearing an offering and beneath it a man cutting the throat of a goat, presumably for sacrifice, while the next large figure holds a stave or wand, sculptured at the lower end in the likeness of a gazelle's head.

Elsewhere we find offering scenes or libations depicted in great detail (Text-fig. 80).[4] In addition to such designs, which can still be considered as

[1] Clay, *Letters and Transactions*, Pl. LXXXI *d*.

[2] Moortgat, *Die bildende Kunst des alten Orients und die Bergvölker*, observes that the difference between the Hittite (Anatolian) reliefs and those found in Syria is just this, that the latter often reproduce secular scenes (hunting and war) and the former exclusively ritual performances.

[3] Clay, *Letters and Transactions*, Pl. LXXXI *d*.

[4] This figure appears better in the photograph in De Genouillac, *Céramique Cappadocienne*, I, Pl. C, 3; *ibid.* 4; also *ibid.* B; Clay, *Letters and Transactions*, Pl. LXXXV *d*; Lewy, *Die Keilschrifttexte aus Kleinasien*, 292 B (*b*), 313.

more or less complete modifications of Mesopotamian prototypes, there are others which seem entirely original, and which may consequently be distinctive of the settlement of Kanish.

One of these is the chariot scene of Pl. XL*m*, *n*. Chariot scenes are not depicted on Mesopotamian seals after the Early Dynastic period, with the exception of the chariot of thunder (Pl. XXII*a*) in Akkadian times. The Cappadocian sealings show a chariot with a front part resembling the earlier Mesopotamian examples but with the driver seated and drawn by four horses or asses.[1]

Another Cappadocian theme is an animal generally considered to be a bull, which is an object of worship (Pl. XL*l*, *n*); a pyramidal erection often is shown on his hindquarters, on which a bird is perched. The bull may take the place of an anthropomorphic god in scenes of adoration where he stands before a table heaped with loaves (Pl. XL*n*; Text-fig. 76).[2] It also appears however as adjunct to a deity.[3] The animal is often placed upon a dais, and whether he has any connection with the ritual figures of bulls discussed on p. 238 in connection with Pl. XL*a*, *b*, *e*, *k* remains uncertain. He appears again to be mounted on a dais or platform above crossed beasts (Text-fig. 76), which may represent a decoration on the sides of the dais, similar to that of the throne in Text-fig. 38 (p. 143). We should not have used this realistic interpretation instead of the customary explanation of the crossed animals as stop-gaps, but for the fact that in one case two human beings appear on the side of the dais and require some such explanation as here given.[4]

The mere mounting of a bull figure on a dais or its use as adjunct of a god, or any of its appearances in Pl. XL, do not point to Cappadocia to the exclusion of other peripheral regions. But the bull figure with the pyramidal erection on his back has always been considered as pre-eminently characteristic of Kanish. We find it, however, recurring on two seals (Pl. XLI *a*, *m*) which are certainly not Cappadocian, and one of which was actually found in regular excavations at Byblos. Besides the bull this also shows the little offering-table of the Cappadocian seals, but its style is entirely different.

[1] Also De Clercq, 286; Newell, 282, 284; A–954; Meyer, *Reich und Kultur der Chethiter*, Figs. 43, 44; Ward, 976, 977; *Liverpool Annals*, I, Pl. XVII.

[2] Weber, 252; Ward, 968, 971, 972, 973; *Liverpool Annals*, I, Pl. XVII; Bibliothèque Nationale, 271; Newell, 283; Meyer, *Reich und Kultur der Chethiter*, Figs. 43, 44. De Genouillac, *Céramique Cappadocienne*, I, Pl. A, 4; and Louvre, *Tablettes Cappadociennes*, III, 3, sealing No. 8, shows the platform as a kind of structure on which two people are seated.

[3] Bibliothèque Nationale, 260.

[4] De Genouillac, *Céramique Cappadocienne*, I, Pl. A, 4.

There is no reason to be astonished at the occurrence of Cappadocian themes elsewhere; we have already met the table heaped with loaves on seals from non-Cappadocian parts of the Mesopotamian periphery (Pl. XL*c*, *d* and § 37, p. 235). We have separated those features in the Cappadocian repertoire which are without parallel in Mesopotamia, but the native civilisation of Kanish was certainly part of a larger cultural province, whose extent we are at present unable to gauge. It has not been noted before that the curious ritual figure of the bull belongs to this larger province, though that is clear now we find it on a seal from Byblos which is shown by its style to be made outside Cappadocia. There are two other motives which occur on the Cappadocian tablets and not in Mesopotamia, but which are to become popular in the Syrian seals of a later age. One is the group of four running men, often accompanying the chariot as in Pl. XL*n*, but sometimes figured by themselves; the other a goddess withdrawing her garments (Text-fig. 75).[1] In Mesopotamia the myth of Ishtar's descent into the nether-world, where she is required to leave some article of dress or adornment at each of the seven gates, would explain the design, but the fact that this representation is only found in peripheral regions makes it uncertain whether a Babylonian myth is at all relevant. It is quite possible that the character of the goddess of fertility is indicated by the gesture without any mythological implication. Occasionally an undraped female figure appears, differing from the naked woman of the Babylonian seals in that she is never placed on a dais and not shown with her head full-face, but in profile.[2] Consequently her affinities remain obscure. We may also recall here the drinker with the vessel and drinking tube from Pl. XL*d*, *f*, which belongs to the Cappadocian as well as to the Syrian repertoire, the last-named instance being found at Tell Judeideh.

Resuming our enquiry into the distinctive features of the Cappadocian sealings, we may say that they show a tendency to replace various Mesopotamian deities by Weather-gods, and that a chariot scene, ritual bull's figure, an unveiling goddess and a group of four running figures frequently occur. These cannot be considered entirely distinctive of the Cappadocian sealings, since they occur in Syria too. An analysis of the subject-matter has, however, established the distinction between Cappadocian and Mesopotamian glyptic. To determine in the same way the individual character of the Cappadocian seals among the large mass of peripheral glyptic we must now consider their style.

[1] Also Clay, *Letters and Transactions*, Pl. LXXXII *e*.

[2] De Genouillac, *Céramique Cappadocienne*, I, Pl. A, 4; Louvre, *Tablettes Cappadociennes*, III, 3, impressions Nos. 12, 13, 16.

A number of the Cappadocian seal impressions are not in any way peculiar. But in certain cases their style has a character of its own; one might say that the designs seem as if laid out on squared millimetre paper (Pl. XL*g*, *h*, *l*, *n*, *o*). There is nowhere any trace of modelling; the figures are purely linear, and they assume angular shapes. The design as a whole often appears to be built up from several square or oblong blocks, each of which is formed by a group of figures, each of these being again divided into bands by parallel lines or hatching. Even the sun appears now as a combination of four hatched quadrants (Pl. XL*o*). An excessive use is made of small ornaments which fill the interstices between the large figures. Even

Text-fig. 77. Seal from Assur.

Text-fig. 78. Seal from Assur.

cylinders which show a much less distinctive character than those just referred to often display in the squared grouping of subsidiary motives a similar tendency.[1]

It is most probable that this style was local. The provenance of none of the actual seals is known, but Kultepe has been plundered for many years by the natives and the cylinders may easily be derived from their diggings. Such cylinders as Pl. XL*l*, *o* and Text-fig. 81, which combine the stylistic features and the subject-matter common on Cappadocian tablets, were most likely found at Kultepe in illegal excavations.[2] On the other hand, it is likely that a seal closely resembling Pl. XL*l*, but found at Susa,[3] reached Elam as a result of trade, and belonged originally to a merchant from Kultepe. But

[1] De Genouillac, *Céramique Cappadocienne*, Pl. B, 1; Clay, *Letters and Transactions*, Pls. LXXXI *a*, *b*, LXXXII, LXXXIII *b*, LXXXIV *g*.

[2] The seal of Text-fig. 81 was bought at Smyrna fifty years ago. Its style is purely Cappadocian, but its subject is unparalleled amongst published impressions. Mr Reilly tells me, however, that a lyre-player, seated in front of a larger figure, occurs on an unpublished tablet-sealing from Kultepe found by Hrozny. It is curious to see it recur in Anatolian glyptic a thousand years later in Pl. XLV *c*, a seal found at Tarsus.

[3] *Revue d'Assyriologie*, XXVII (1930), 189. Similarly A–872, A–873 are probably Cappadocian because of these close resemblances with Louvre, *Tablettes Cappadociennes*, III, 3, impression No. 30.

we cannot be certain of seals which resemble these impressions either in subject-matter or style alone. And in the case of seals showing Adad mounted upon a bull, in the manner of such Mesopotamian seals as Pl. XXVII*j*, there is no reason to ascribe them to any one peripheral region.[1] For it seems that the style of the majority of Cappadocian sealings does not differ from that generally prevailing in the periphery of Mesopotamia (cf. Pl. XXXIX*i* and Text-figs. 77, 78, from Assur). We have already seen

Text-fig. 79.

Text-fig. 80.

Text-figs. 79, 80. Cappadocian sealings.

that there is no demonstrably closer connection between the Cappadocian sealings and the seals from Assur, than there is with any other peripheral region. Increased knowledge of Assyrian glyptic may, of course, reverse this statement, and it is curious that a very rough cylinder from Assur finds, indeed, a parallel at Kultepe.[2] Other rather coarse seals like Pl. XL*i*[3] are likely to be local imitations of peripheral seals of the type of Pl. XXXIX*h*.[4] Others again, such as Text-fig. 79,[5] suggest local manufacture by their freedom from Mesopotamian traditions in all but a few details.

The value of the Cappadocian sealings rests not a little upon their ability to show us a somewhat extensive selection of designs used at a single peripheral settlement. The extraordinary result of the mixture of Mesopotamian and local motives is instructive, and has exemplary value. It proves that in such a case the outcome is entirely unpredictable. Careful works like Pl. XL*g* are nevertheless, from the Mesopotamian standpoint, cases of extreme disintegration, where of the original ritual scene nothing but the seated god remains.

Text-fig. 81. Seal from Smyrna.

[1] Bibliothèque Nationale, 244, 245, 246; Lewy, *Die Keilschrifttexte aus Kleinasien*, 280 B (*a*).

[2] Weber, 38, and Musée Guimet, 128.

[3] So also A–847 (Pl. 125, Fig. 5*a*, bottom) and A–850.

[4] See Bibliothèque Nationale, 263, 432, and also one of impressions on A–517, dated to Sinmuballit's reign; also the lion on A–881, certainly a Cappadocian seal.

[5] Similar sealings are: Louvre, *Tablettes Cappadociennes*, III, 3, impressions Nos. 91–5.

§ 39. THE WESTWARD EXPANSION OF THE FIRST BABYLONIAN DYNASTY, AND THE FIRST SYRIAN GROUP

The western neighbours of Mesopotamia came under her influence no less than those in the north. The rule of the First Babylonian Dynasty marked a period of great commercial expansion. Seal cylinders of Babylonian manufacture are found all through the Near East not only in Syria and Palestine, but also in Crete and in Egypt; indeed a bilingual cylinder was found in Memphis with hieroglyphs set beside Babylonian cuneiform script. Egypt, however, has appeared more deeply involved in Asiatic affairs than was thought probable only a few years ago. The excavations at Byblos and Qatna have shown that the Pharaohs of the Middle Kingdom took an active interest in Syria. Thus the Levant, trading with its own hinterland as well as with the great power of Africa, knew much prosperity at the beginning of the Second Millennium B.C. For the first time it assumed on a considerable scale its henceforth traditional role as intermediary.

It is at this time, shortly after 2000 B.C., that we must place the birth of Phoenician art, that curiously hybrid product, created by the dexterity and love of magnificence of a population devoid of plastic genius, but impressed by the works of art with which it became acquainted. Whoever approaches Phoenician work already steeped in the traditions of Egypt and Mesopotamia will be repelled by the vulgar disregard for suitability with which divine figures and symbols are jumbled into gaudy patterns. Occasionally we recognise in this mass of abused derivatives an original idea, which then refers to religion, a field where Syria at all times displayed originality, and that in a prodigious fashion. Religious concepts of an original nature found occasional expression in Phoenician art, but it seems that these people, Hebrews and Phoenicians, did not turn naturally—like the Egyptians, for instance—to pictorial expression. To them the poetic word was congenial. It has become a commonplace to point out the discrepancy between the Old Testament considered as a work of literature, and anything that Palestine has produced in the way of material culture. But a similarly glaring discrepancy exists between the Ras Shamra poems and the totality of Syrian or Phoenician art.

The first centuries of the Second Millennium B.C. certainly did not favour the development of anything original in Syria. The country was swamped by the products of the three surrounding centres of civilisation, works excelling in sureness of conception and quality of execution. From Mesopotamia came woven stuffs, carpets and other perishable materials and presumably works of art in metal, which were also imported from the Aegean, as we now know from discoveries in the tombs of the rulers of Byblos. Each of these princes was, moreover, the recipient of valuable pectorals, vases and other objects sent as presents by Pharaoh, and Egyptian influence reached much farther inland than is often supposed. The daughter of Amenemhet II sent gifts to the temple of the Babylonian Moon-goddess Ningal at Qatna—the elements thus combined in a sanctuary on the Orontes correspond exactly to such seal designs as we illustrate in Pls. XLI, XLII. The royal gifts were, of course, concomitant to much commercial and personal intercourse, which brought to the Syrians knowledge of Egyptian arts and crafts; and it is, in fact, in the period preceding the Hyksos invasion of Egypt that recent excavations have disclosed the first emergence of Phoenician art, in which derivations from Mesopotamia, Egypt and the Aegean are inextricably mingled.

Excavations have hitherto failed to illuminate the history of Syrian glyptic during these centuries, and if we assign the seals of Pl. XLI *b–l, o* to a First Syrian group, which we date between 1900 and 1700 B.C., that classification is a matter of inference only. Nevertheless, we make it with considerable confidence, since these curious works could hardly have been produced at any other time. It is evident that they belong to the periphery of the First Babylonian Dynasty; they share with many Mesopotamian seals of the period (Pls. XXVI–XXIX) a design in which a main theme, of a ritual nature, is accompanied by various subsidiary motives. While, however, the main theme of these Syrian seals agrees with its Babylonian prototypes to a surprising degree, the subsidiary motives are as clearly alien to Mesopotamia.

Let us, first of all, consider the thoroughness with which Mesopotamian usage is reflected. We find Ea, for instance, accompanied by his two-faced attendant Usmu (Pl. XLI *c, f, h*). We find a priest pouring libations over a branch mounted in a terracotta stand, a scene which tallies in every detail with those found at Tell Asmar and other sites in the Plain (Pl. XLI *i*; Text-fig. 38, p. 143). The divine couple of Pl. XLI *c*[1] is a rare subject, but finds a parallel in a cylinder from Ishchali. Other points of agreement, such as the garments of the gods, the shape of their thrones, the recurrence of certain filling motives (monkey, arm of the balance, sun-disk and crescent), might be explained by the survival of some Babylonian seals; but the correctness in detail of the groups which I have just enumerated has another significance. They prove intimate and contemporary knowledge of Babylonian myth and ritual. In other words: these seals must have been made while Babylonian

[1] So also, probably, Ward-Morgan, 205, and our Text-fig. 82.

civilisation stood unimpaired and found adequate expression in its statuary, its wall-paintings, its glyptic art and in the temples throughout its dependencies. It is this argument that compels us to date these cylinders before the profound upheaval which shook the civilised world in the eighteenth century B.C. Then the Hittites invaded the Plain and sacked Babylon. Kassites, uncivilised mountaineers, established their rule on its ruins; mixed Anatolian and Syrian hordes overran Egypt and dominated it for a century and a half under their "Shepherd Kings", as Manetho explains the term "Hyksos".[1] The detailed rendering of Mesopotamian myths and ritual on Syrian seals is inconceivable during the time when the Kassites ruled a reduced and uninfluential realm. We know, moreover, the disintegrated glyptic style of this period (Pl. XXX*c–f, h, j*), and the Kassite and Mittanian styles which succeeded it, and none of these would fulfil the requirements of a prototype of the Syrian seals of Pl. XLI.

Text-fig. 82. Divine couple.

Text-fig. 83. Contest with lion.

The cylinders which we gather into our First Syrian group possess, in fact, a number of distinctive qualities. They combine, as we have seen, a central theme that is purely Babylonian with by-work of a foreign nature. Many of them have also this peculiarity in their composition, that they place their main theme between two twists or *guilloches* (Pl. XLI *c, f, i*). Alternatively, they divide the whole or part of the cylinder surface in two parts by a horizontal *guilloche* and effect a decoration in the manner of such Babylonian seals as we illustrated in Pl. XXIX*m*, and which sometimes, even in Babylonia, have the two registers thus separated. In Pl. XLI *h* Ea is figured above the twist, and before him is Usmu, beardless, contrary to Babylonian usage, but followed by Babylonian-looking worshippers. Below the twist we see curious Phoenician monsters. In Text-fig. 82 we find purely Babylonian figures in the divine couple and the suckling cow (Pl. XXVI *i, l*) and the two winged dragons below the *guilloche*. But above it we see on the left a kneeling sphinx, and then two of the bird-headed demons of Pl. XLI *k, l*.

[1] Allbright has given evidence that the conquest of Egypt is likely to have taken place soon after 1740 B.C. The fall of Babylon is mostly dated to 1758 B.C. (see *Journal of the Palestine Oriental Society*, XV (1935), 226).

Finally, we see in Text-fig. 83 only the winged dragon as deriving from the Babylonian repertoire. Several other seals of this type are known. Pl. XLI *d*, found at Chatal Huyuk, belongs to the same group of seals but presents a rather provincial version. The drinker in the lower register (cf. Pl. XL *k*), the arm of the balance and the goat looking backwards betray its dependence on examples of the Hammurabi period. The division into two registers shows a simplification of the twist pattern which is in keeping with the generally provincial character of this seal.

A less sharply defined, but corresponding, scheme of composition appears in Pl. XLI *g*. The main theme, a presentation scene, is rendered on a small scale, not between twists but above a decorative group of two antithetical winged griffins. A similar group, consisting of sphinxes, appears on an impression dated to the reign of Ammizaduga.[1] I do not know of any truly Babylonian seal which retains the age-old presentation scene while reducing it to a small seal design; especially curious is the appearance of the owner of the seal outside the main theme, drawn full-scale and markedly foreign in dress and coiffure. I would hazard a guess that here the main theme, the presentation, complete with a decorative dado, was copied from some such wall-painting as those discovered in the palace of Mari (a peripheral site), while the hero, bull and monkey on the left are derived from current Mesopotamian glyptic. A similar case is presented by Pl. XLI *b*, which according to criteria described above (p. 226) could not be considered peripheral but for the dress of the worshipper. Yet we note a certain unconventionality in the rendering of the deity. Since a scroll-border was painted on a throne-base of the palace of Mari, we may postulate a similar origin for the *guilloche* of Pl. XLI *b*; and the two kneeling men with flowing vases would be subsidiary statues, flanking the temple entrance or the main statue, of a type we know well from Early Dynastic as well as from Assyrian times.[2] A similar freedom prevails in the rendering of Amurru in Pl. XLI *e*. Both the curved stick and the goat appear as his attributes in Mesopotamia (Pl. XXVIII *b*, *e*, *f*), but the way in which they here are made into a symmetrical pattern is un-Mesopotamian.[3]

Antithetical groups are, in fact, frequent in these Syrian seals (Pl. XLI *f*, *g*, *j*), but they never take the chief place in the design, as they do in Mitannian and later Syrian glyptic. Nor does the artificial "sacred tree" appear in the "First Style". The two goats flanking a palm tree in Pl. XLI *f* are a stock

[1] A–570. [2] Gordon Loud, *Khorsabad*, I, 98 ff.; Text-figs. 107–12.

[3] The weapon appearing behind this god recurs in two other seals which may be placed in the first group—our Pl. XXXIX *p* and Ward, 932, 1017.

theme of Syrian and Palestinian decoration from time immemorial, and also occur in Mesopotamia (Pls. XVII *h*; XXVI *l*). But in Mitannian glyptic the "tree of palmettes" makes its appearance. There is yet another contrast with the later Syrian seals in that monsters, too, are sparingly used in the first group. Beside local versions of the winged lion-demon (Pl. XLI *h*; Text-fig. 82, p. 254) and the winged dragon of contemporary Babylonian seals, we find a crested bird-headed monster, either four-footed (Pl. XLI *f*, *g*) or semi-human, and then kneeling in a characteristic attitude (Pl. XLI, *k*, *l*). There are also winged sphinxes, with traces of the ribbed wig and the uraeus which are appropriate to them in Egypt (Pl. XLI *j*). The large bird of Pl. XLI *i* evidently imitates the great vulture or falcon which often forms the upper part of Egyptian designs and occurs, in fact, in this function in the pectorals which successive Pharaohs gave to the princes of Byblos. The human-headed sphinxes on Pl. XLI *o* derive ultimately from the same source, as does the Crux Ansata; but this hieroglyph is as badly bungled as the figure which follows the worshipper and wears the Babylonian tasselled robe but not a crown; note, however, the delightful characterisation of the sacrificial kid with its dangling legs.[1]

From the mention of the antithetical group on the preceding page, we have been concerned with the subsidiary motives of the Syrian seals of the First Style. These, in contrast with the main groups, are preponderantly of a non-Mesopotamian character. They are evidently meaningless designs which fill available spaces pleasantly, and by analogy with that we observe in later times, we should expect them to be used as freely by joiners, goldsmiths and other craftsmen as by the seal-cutters. In addition to these motives which we have already mentioned, there is the characteristic group of the lion pawing at a passive antelope (Pl. XLI *j*) which recurs, though somewhat changed, on later seals. Rows of human heads also supplied a useful means of filling space (Pl. XLI *d*, *e*, *k*); they had been used in Cappadocia for the same purpose (Pl. XL *m*). The nature of these winged lions or sphinxes, with or without uraeus, combined with antelopes or trees, strongly recalls the ivory and metal work of the Phoenicians. I have no doubt that the subsidiary motives which we have discussed are indeed derived from workshops in the Syrian coast towns. Whether the seals on which they occur also belong to that area is doubtful. The seals, as legal instruments in the hands of merchants, in any case belong to that sphere of Syrian life in which Babylonian influence was paramount. If they show a peculiar division of affinities—main themes directly derived from Mesopotamia while the sub-

[1] Ward, 858 seems to be closely related to this seal.

sidiary motives are Phoenician—we may explain this in two equally satisfactory ways, either by assuming Babylonian usage to be normal even with the merchants in the harbour towns, or by admitting the use of Phoenician jewellery, furniture and so on in the Syrian hinterland.

In any case we should be clear in our minds as to the inadequacy of our distinctions. The seals of Pl. XLI *b–l* and their homologues, which we classed together as a First Syrian group, form indeed a somewhat homogeneous series. But it is evident that they do not represent the whole of Syrian glyptic of the nineteenth and eighteenth centuries B.C. In the first place a goodly number of Syrian seals must in this period of strong Babylonian influence have been of the peripheral style of § 37 *b*, p. 236, which makes it impossible for us to recognise them as Syrian at all. Moreover, Syria is a highly complex conglomerate of mountainous regions and plains, trading centres and desert. It is quite unlikely that at any one time a single school of art held sway throughout the land. If we state with a certain amount of justification that the seals of Pl. XLI *b–l* are Syrian and were made between 1900 and 1700 B.C., we may be equally certain that very different seals were made in Syria during the same period. In some cases these may be recognised. The design of Pl. XLI *a*, for instance, was certainly made before the period of the migrations; that is shown by the intimate correspondence of many of its motives with seals of the First Dynasty of Babylon. The seated figure holding a cup, the monkey, the sun and crescent, the arm of the balance and the hero swinging a lion (cf. Pl. XXIX *e*) are all copied from those seals. The calf with a branch on its back evidently belongs to the bull cult of the Cappadocian sealings. There is no reason to claim this motive as a derivation since the ritual custom reflected on the Cappadocian seals may have had a much wider distribution in Syria and thus may find independent expression in different localities. We have in fact a version from Byblos (Pl. XLI *m*) which differs so thoroughly from both Pl. XLI *a* and the Cappadocian sealings in style, that we must assign it to yet another place of origin. It was found in a jar with many other objects, among them the seal of Pl. XLI *n*, a typically Syrian seal such as occurs at all periods without noticeable differences; in fact the subject is so simple and the execution so coarse that there is no scope for any distinction of time or locality.[1]

To return to Pl. XLI *a*, there remain two figures which are unrelated with

[1] The deposit was dated by Montet, *Byblos et l'Égypte*, pp. 127 ff., to the end of the Egyptian Old Kingdom, which seems impossible (see Frankfort, *Studies in Early Pottery of the Near East*, II, 149, note 5). Subsequent discoveries by M. Maurice Dunand suggest the Thirteenth Egyptian Dynasty or the beginning of the Hyksos period as the most likely date.

the Babylonian as well as with the Cappadocian seals. The woman on the extreme left appears to be a Phoenician (cf. Pl. XLI *r*). And the curious bearded sphinx crowned by a snake which is meant for the royal uraeus of Egypt is certainly also a product of the coast towns. It recurs several times, for instance in Pl. XLI *j*.[1]

In addition to all this we see that the worshipper approaching the seated deity drags two snakes along with him. There we have almost certainly a mythological rather than a ritual representation, and we are entirely unable to explain it. It is worth once more insisting on the danger of applying what little knowledge we have of Syrian religion to any of these seal designs. Syria has at all times been incredibly prolific in religious beliefs, each of which may or may not find acceptance over a somewhat extended area. The Ras Shamra texts have shown us how specialised certain myths could become; they have, once and for all, discredited the custom of explaining Syrian seals by reference to Hittite texts.

Resuming, we may state that the peripheral glyptic of the nineteenth to seventeenth centuries is characterised by dependence on the style of the First Babylonian Dynasty, the seals notably retaining the Babylonian custom of depicting a main theme of a ritual nature, together with a number of irrelevant subsidiary motives. Syrian seals of this period rendered the main theme with a faithful adherence to Mesopotamian standards, but used as subsidiary motives Phoenician designs of a mixed nature, occasionally with Egyptian affinities. In addition to the Syrian seals of the First groups, other styles were simultaneously in use, but for the moment they evade recognition.[2]

[1] Also Newell, 310.

[2] Other seals of the First Syrian group are:

Ward, 858, 1024, which are of the type of our Pl. XLI *o*.

Ward, 932, 1017, which have, like Newell, 312, the axe or scimitar of Pl. XLI *e*.

To Pl. XLI *h* and Text-figs. 82, 83 belong *Hittite Seals*, 152, and Newell, 312, 314, in which we find a similar mixture of Babylonian and Syrian motives and a *guilloche* so much simplified as to approach Pl. XLI *d*; A–942; a closely related seal to those here quoted, where however the demon of Pl. XLI *l* is repeated several times; A–946; Newell, 342.

Ward, 1031, and Bibliothèque Nationale, 280, belong to this period (cf. Pls. XLI *h*, XL *m*).

Hittite Seals, 165 resembles in style of cutting Pl. XLI *f*, but here the two *guilloches* occur as border to the whole.

Further: A–902; *Hittite Seals*, 171; Newell, 332, 340. Bibliothèque Nationale, 454 is interesting, showing a Sun-god enthroned between two *guilloches*, as in Pl. XLI *c*, *f*. The sun is indicated by a dotted rosette, and another Sun-god holds the staff with globes and stands with his foot on a mountain consisting of drilled globes. In other words, seals of the last part of the Hammurabi Dynasty (Pl. XXX *c–f*) are imitated, but the seal in question is much more carefully executed. Its foreign character appears in the composition and in the bungling of the inscription.

CHAPTER III. PERIPHERAL GLYPTIC FROM 1700 TO 1200 B.C.

§ 40. PALESTINIAN CYLINDERS OF THE HYKSOS PERIOD

The great migrations of the middle of the eighteenth century decisively affected the relationship of Syria with her neighbours. Taking Egypt first, we note a much closer connection than in the past. Whether or not the Egyptian trade of the Syrian ports maintained its volume during the dominance of the Hyksos, parts of Syria were actually united with Egypt under one rule, and however transient this combination may have been, within its boundaries Egyptian influence became the leading factor in the development of the arts. Egyptian motives were more or less correctly copied where Babylonian themes had previously been used by the seal-cutters. The cylinder of Pl. XLI *p* was found at Tell Beit Mirsim in Palestine, in layers assigned to the early part of the Hyksos period.[1] Its cuneiform signs, believed to denote "the god Nabu", the little monkey and the *guilloche* of Pl. XLI *e* are derived from Mesopotamia, for the rest Egyptian motives prevail. The correctness with which the sun-disk and crescent and the two Bull-men of Pl. XLI *r* are drawn has led me to place this cylinder also in the Hyksos period, which finds prototypes in the Bull-men standard-bearers of the First Babylonian Dynasty. The fanciful cartouche which they support in Pl. XLI *r* finds parallels on other seals of this class.[2] One of these has erroneously been ascribed to a King Khendy of the First Intermediate period;[3] another[4] shows, beside the cartouche, a cuneiform inscription in which the personal name of the owner is bungled, but the conventional phrase "beloved of Adad" is legibly copied from a Babylonian original. This inscription is a parallel to the Bull-men of Pl. XLI *r* as an indication of date. Both features betray direct contact between Mesopotamia on the one

[1] Allbright, *Journal of the Palestine Oriental Society*, XV, 215. Also Alan Rowe, *Catalogue of Egyptian Scarabs in the Palestine Museum*, pp. 237 f. (S–11). The stratum in which the seal was found extends from the second half of the eighteenth to the end of the seventeenth century B.C.

[2] Seals of this class are: Rowe, *loc. cit.* p. 235 (S–7), assigned on stratigraphical grounds to the early part of the Hyksos or earlier periods; and Newell, 318; Bibliothèque Nationale, 485; A–906.

[3] Petrie, *History of Egypt*, I, 123, a view which I endorsed some twelve years ago in the *Journal of Egyptian Archaeology*, XII, 92. The correct interpretation was given by Allbright, *loc. cit.* p. 217, note 73, earlier assignations to "Syro-Hittite" glyptic of the Second Millennium B.C. being too vague to be useful.

[4] A–906.

hand, and, on the other, the region where the seal was made, and where Egyptian influence was strong. It seems unlikely that such direct contact as may have taken place during the Kassite period could have had this effect in the field of the arts. Contrast the pair of Bull-men on a later seal, of the Second Syrian group.[1] But the date of Pl. XLI *r* is less well established than that of the other seals just mentioned which are related to the stratified example from Tell Beit Mirsim.

§ 41. THE SECOND SYRIAN GROUP (1700–1350 B.C.)

(*a*) *General Considerations.*

The larger part of Syria remained outside the Egyptian empire, and was subjected to various influences as a result of the migrations. Neither Egypt nor Babylonia, weakened as she was by the Hittite and Kassite invasions, exercised such influence. The art of Syria, left to itself, did not disown its Babylonian heritage, but since it received no fresh stimulus from Mesopotamia, the traditional repertoire was required in its turn to supply prototypes, and the successive copies drifted farther and farther away from their original conception. It is mainly by this rendering of Babylonian motives at second-hand that we can distinguish the Syrian seals made after the Hyksos migration from those antedating it. We can thus recognise a number of late seals which we call the Second Syrian group.

In the seals of the First group we found sets of Mesopotamian figures, correct in attributes and action (Pl. XLI *c*, *e*, *f*), or they appear in variety (Pl. XLI *g*, *h*). In the Second Syrian group we find that only isolated figures of the Mesopotamian repertoire survive, and they often show curious modifications. There is, moreover, a change in the subsidiary motives, in that those which played a subordinate role in the First group are now apt to play a dominant part in the design. Finally the composition changes. The seals of the First group often reflected a Mesopotamian scheme; the Second group no longer embodies such survivals. While, for instance, in Pl. XLI *i*, *j–l* the interceding goddess stands before the chief deity, as on Mesopotamian seals, we notice that in Pl. XLII *i* both figures have been made subservient to the "sacred tree" with the winged disk; and in Pl. XLII *h* the worshipper and the interceding goddess are separated by a large mass of design which it merely serves to frame on either side.

The transition from the First to the Second group is gradual and the decision as to whether a seal should be placed before or after the migrations

[1] Bibliothèque Nationale, 485.

may often seem arbitrary.[1] But we are not solely dependent on the state of preservation of Babylonian motives when enquiring into the age of Syrian seals. It is often possible to discover detailed resemblances, recurring characteristics, which connect various seals with others, the age of which cannot be in doubt. By drawing together a series of such resemblances we may isolate a number of seals as belonging to the period under review, though some uncertainty cannot be avoided until we are able to dispose of a large series of stratified specimens. Moreover, our treatment of Syria as a unit is a mere makeshift. We are unable to separate the various cultural provinces into which Syria must have been divided in the Second Millennium B.C. as it is to-day, but we can at least be certain that we are dealing with an imaginary entity, when speaking of Syria as a region in which a more or less homogeneous culture, and a simple unilinear stylistic development, in glyptic or any other art, can be observed. Pls. XLII–XLIV show contemporary designs, and with greater knowledge we should be able to bring together an even more heterogeneous collection. In fact we do not postulate the existence of a Syrian glyptic *style*. But we have attempted to collect a certain number of seals which form a group in the sense that they are interrelated by a fairly close network of similarities in style or subject. Any one of these features may have come into use before 1700 B.C.—with some examples that is demonstrably the case—and several survived beyond the later limit of our period. Nevertheless, their combined appearance points consistently to the period between about 1700 B.C. and about 1350 B.C. There is in any case a greater likelihood that our incomplete knowledge leads us to exclude seals which were made and used somewhere during this period, than that we have included seals which do not belong here.

As regards interpretation, the emancipation of Syrian glyptic from the Mesopotamian repertoire in its principal motives confronts us with a richness which we are for the moment unable to exploit. Anyone who has followed the attempts of a number of ingenious scholars to define the character of the several gods mentioned in the texts of a single small harbour-town, such as Ras Shamra, will realise the impossibility of deciding whether in any given case a goddess on a seal of unknown provenance should be called Asherat,

[1] Bibliothèque Nationale, 488 is instructive. The composition is that of the First group (cf. Pl. XLI *c*) and the sun and crescent with the short wings are generally early too. But not a single motive retains its Mesopotamian form, except the interceding goddess. Therefore the seal belongs to the Second group, but it confirms that many designs of that group gradually developed out of the First. The seal of our Pl. XLIV *i* similarly retains the method of enclosing its main theme in two *guilloches*, but the motives are Syrian in all their detail.

Ishtar, Anat, Qadesh, Elat, or by yet another name. And it has been pointed out[1] that the pictorial renderings are even more confusing than the texts because they influence each other independently. Thus the texts show that Egyptian gods were not worshipped at Ras Shamra, and yet not a single representation of a deity has been found which does not exhibit Egyptian features in attire or attributes. We must needs therefore be satisfied to speak of Weather-gods, gods of fertility and so on, or, in other words, to refrain from endeavouring to penetrate beyond the phenomenal side of our subject, until such time as certain representations can be shown to be characteristic of certain localities, and may therefore be interpreted in terms of local mythology. A first attempt in this direction has been made here with the seals of Mitanni.

The Second group of Syrian seals is more numerous than either its predecessors or those that follow it. The period from 1700 to 1350 B.C. represents the most productive period of Syrian glyptic art. Before that time many seals used in Syria were of the peripheral Babylonian type, while subsequently the innovations of the Second group seem to have been repeated. While local invention was at its height, local variations must have occurred; they must have been strengthened by the religious particularisation which at all times distinguished Syria, and counteracted by the abundance of trade connections and the eclecticism of the Phoenician craftsmen. However that may be, we are only able now to isolate one group of East Syrian cylinders, made within the Kingdom of Mitanni. These cylinders do not contrast with examples produced elsewhere at the time, but only show distinctive peculiarities of style and subject. And since one of them is dated, they supply a valuable anchorage for the floating comparisons by which we must establish the individuality of our complex Second Syrian group. This dated cylinder impression is shown on Pl. XLII*a*. It is the seal of King Shaushattar of Mitanni.[2]

Out of the turmoil of the migrations a temporary power arose in the North Syrian plains. Its centre was the Khabur valley, and the polity which formed there was of an artificial and ephemeral character. Unity was enforced on the native population by a minority of warlike immigrants, speaking an Indo-

[1] R. Dussaud, *Revue de l'Histoire des Religions*, 1931, p. 372; Götze, *Kulturgeschichte Kleinasiens*, pp. 122–38.

[2] See Richard F. S. Starr, *Nuzi*, II, Pl. 118, I—our photograph illustrates a plastic reconstruction made up by the Field Museum of Natural History at Chicago and kindly put at my disposal by Prof. Robert H. Pfeiffer of Harvard University, who published the tablet upon which it occurs.

European language and worshipping Indra, Varuna and other Indo-Iranian gods.

The precise date of the establishment of this kingdom of Mitanni is uncertain. It went down before the onslaught of the Anatolian Hittites when Egypt, under Akhenaten, failed actively to intervene in the affairs of Asia. The consequent elimination of Egyptian influence for about a generation from Palestine, and permanently from Northern Syria, marks another turning-point in Syrian history. We have, therefore, taken 1350 B.C. as the later limit of the period with which we are concerned.

Shaushattar ruled about a century before that date. The features of his sealing (Pl. XLII *a*), which seem peculiar to his country and determine the Mitannian style, will be discussed in § 42. We shall here consider it exclusively from the point of view of Babylonian and Syrian similarities, being first occupied, not with what distinguishes it, but with what links it to other seals. These features are numerous enough to enable us to build up around them our Second group of Syrian seals.

(*b*) *The Foreign Affinities of the Second Syrian Group.*

It is, then, striking to notice the independence of Shaushattar's sealing from Babylonian tradition, an independence which at first sight seems complete. Instead of a design ordered in one or two horizontal friezes, we find a variety of figures spread over the whole surface, and some of the separate groups, as also their general arrangement, form a symmetrical pattern.

Considering the motives separately, we note only one which has undoubted connections with older Mesopotamian glyptic; the head with long locks to the left of the winged disk (cf. Pl. XXIX *h*). The figure on the right of the disk may represent the interceding goddess in Mitannian dress. The winged being dominating two lions does not resemble any Mesopotamian figure, but the two combatants with pointed caps may be inspired by such groups as are depicted in Pl. XXIX *a*.

We note, furthermore, the complete absence of links with contemporary Babylonian, i.e. Kassite, glyptic. Such connections as exist are with the seals of the First Babylonian Dynasty, and these are so feeble and the motives so distorted that we must assume them to be derived from native Syrian tradition, in which they had lingered. Here then we have the rendering of Babylonian motives several times removed, through the intermediary of earlier Syrian derivations which had already diverged from the original designs. In the case of Mitanni it is not geographical distance but distance in time alone which can account for this thorough modification. And if we find Syrian seals like Pl. XLII*g*, *i*, *j* in which Babylonian tradition is more clearly preserved, we are inclined to date them before Shaushattar's reign, or, in other words, between 1700 and 1450 B.C. We cannot dogmatise on this point because it is possible that in well-established Syrian cities Mesopotamian tradition was more highly valued, and more closely adhered to, than in the newly founded capital of Mitanni.

There can be no doubt that the seals just quoted are contemporaneous with the Mitannian kingdom. The winged sun-disk supported by some elaborate pole is the most distinctive trait of Mitannian glyptic. It is taken over on Pl. XLII*k*, where it is placed in the hands of two Bull-men who usually hold the simple sun-standard on Babylonian seals of the Hammurabi Dynasty. It appears again in Pl. XLII*i*, where Babylonian motives are in evidence. These two seals clearly recall those of the First Syrian group in their well-executed *guilloches* and the precise detail of the Mesopotamian motives, and thus there is some additional likelihood that they antedate the fourteenth century B.C. The squat figure of a lion in Pl. XLII*i* is characteristic of some other seals[1] which can thus be approximately dated. This squat lion somewhat resembles the one in the upper part of Pl. XLII*m*. The birds upon the bulls in the lower part confirm its affinity with the second style (cf. Pl. XLII*g*, *h*, *j*), the extraordinary wheel of interlocked men with water-pots, which at first sight seem to suggest an earlier date, confirms by inference the later ones, since neither the human wheel nor the wrestlers on Pl. XLII*n*, can be derived from Mesopotamian glyptic of the Hammurabi period. These designs go back to Early Dynastic prototypes (see Pls. XI*d*; XIV*h* and Text-fig. 22, p. 53).[2] Ancient seals, as we have noted, are continually discovered in Mesopotamia and Syria. They may be reused from time to time, but they can only influence glyptic art in periods of ebbing inspiration. They affect, for instance, neo-Babylonian but not Assyrian glyptic. During the existence of the first Syrian style when Mesopotamian designs were accepted as normal for all but subsidiary motives in Syria, the introduction of archaic motives would be unlikely, but after the waning of direct Babylonian influence in Syria, it is quite comprehensible that they were copied from seals accidentally discovered or from other fields of art.

The limitations of the material available to us can never be exaggerated; we are dependent upon imperishable remains only; we possess but a fraction of the goldsmiths' and ivory-cutters' products and none of those of the

[1] Newell, 334; Boston, 98–102; *Hittite Seals*, 178; Ward-Morgan, 221.

[2] Another human wheel: Ward, 706, probably also belonging to the Second Syrian group.

weaver, embroiderer, leather-worker or cabinet-maker. We shall have occasion to bring forward in the Epilogue some evidence of the value of textiles as a depository of pictorial tradition, and from most unexpected quarters reminders of the deficiency of our knowledge are apt to issue. Recent discoveries in a palace-kitchen at Mari, dating to Hammurabi's time, produced a set of forty-seven pudding-moulds of baked clay. One of them actually showed the human wheel of Pl. XLII *m*, which is entirely unknown in Mesopotamia proper, in glyptic or other forms of art, after the Early Dynastic period.[1]

Other seals in which Babylonian influence is stronger than in Shaushattar's seal, but less precise than in the seals of the First Syrian style, are illustrated in Pl. XLII *g*, *j*. These also show a strong Egyptian element, though much confused in true Phoenician fashion, where, for instance, the sphinxes in both seals are made to tread upon snakes, the Egyptian symbols of royalty; or the crowned god of Pl. XLII *g* is made to hold a bird, no doubt his attribute, in the hand. Another Syrian cylinder shows however a ritual purification rendered as on the Egyptian Temple reliefs.[2] The fine lion of Pl. XLII *g* shows that several cylinders with rows of well-drawn animals should be assigned to the period under discussion.[3] These, then, are seals which exhibit better preserved survivals from the Babylonian repertoire than that of Shaushattar and therefore possibly antedate his reign. It remains now to consider the Babylonian motives which Shaushattar's sealing seems to imitate and which may have parallels on contemporary Syrian seals. The head with long locks shown front-view is not rare. It occurs on a sealing from Sinmuballit's reign[4] and on some cylinders (Pl. XXIX *h*)[5] which show no sign of being even peripheral; but one of these[6] and also our Pl. XLII *d* contains in the inscription non-Semitic, presumably North Syrian (Hurrian), names. It would be interesting to inspect the original of our Pl. XLII *d* with a view to establishing whether the Crux Ansata, the face and the line above it were engraved at a subsequent date. For at Tell Judeideh a late seal of the Hammurabi Dynasty,[7] of the type of our Pl. XXX *c–f*, with Amurru and Shamash, has been subsequently engraved with the face and the Crux Ansata, and the association is here explained: the face which on the Baby-

[1] *Syria*, 1937, Pl. XII, 2.

[2] Brett, 88.

[3] *Hittite Seals*, 183; Newell, 299, 347.

[4] A–518 (Pl. 113, 46, second sealing).

[5] A–385; Bibliothèque Nationale, 166; Prinz, *Altorientalische Symbolik*, Pl. XI, 1; Ward, 212.

[6] A–385; Jahzi-hadnu, son of Baria, servant of Himdia. Pl. XLII *d* is, according to Delaporte, "Halilum, son of Pashdia, servant of Ramman".

[7] Z–839.

lonian seals was clearly a male head with a curling beard has here become the head of the Egyptian goddess Hathor, and as such it appears on some other seals of undoubted Syrian manufacture (e.g. Pl. XLIV*n*).[1] One of these (Pl. XLII*l*) shows a remarkably vivid hunting scene, in which the griffin, who is so popular in Syria as mere decorative filling (Pl. XLI*f*), takes part. Related seals may well be roughly contemporaneous, two of these[2] being of special interest: one (Pl. XLIV*b*) is in spirit so Aegean—free of conflict and full of life—that one suspects influence from that quarter. The other with vividly drawn animals (Pl. XLIV*a*) suggests an Asiatic Artemis, but the hunter is probably male. If the tasselled quiver which he wears should prove to be distinctive we should meet him again on Pl. XLIV*e*[3] killing an adversary. The style of the latter seal is not characteristic, but the former is connected by the antelope and the jumping calf with the seals we have considered as belonging to the Second Syrian group, and on the other seal the victor is again accompanied by animals. There he wears a horned helmet, the Syrian equivalent to the divine crown of Babylonia. In Pl. XLIV*a* he has a curious coiffure which is also shown elsewhere and can be an indication that some other cylinders belong to the Second group. To realise this we must return once more to Shaushattar's sealing (Pl. XLII*a*).

The second motif, which seemed to go back ultimately to a Babylonian theme, was the domination of a lion by a heroic figure. Let us remember that in Mesopotamia this group does not include any deities. The beasts are subjected either by a Bull-man or by a nude heroic figure, neither of whom possesses the attributes of divinity. The victorious combatants in Pl. XLII*a* wear curious helmets, with a rim-piece in front and a triple crest; there is no reason to connect this with the horned crown of the Mesopotamian gods, nor with the spiked and horned helmet of the Syrian and Anatolian gods (Pls. XLIV*h*, *l*; XLV*d*, *f*). It is more likely that the nude hero is here rendered in a manner appropriate to Mitanni, in other words with the equipment of a Mitannian nobleman. And this surmise is shown to be correct by the exceptionally interesting seal of Pl. XLII*c*. For here we see the same figure attacked by two others, who are most emphatically human. They are, in fact, well characterised by their dress and coiffure as Syrian Semites, the one an Amorite of the Egyptian tomb paintings, the other a turbaned inhabitant perhaps of the Euphrates valley, since his dress is well known at Mari. We have here apparently an incident enacted of one of the

[1] *Hittite Seals*, 182, 185; and De Clercq, 235 *bis*, if it is genuine.

[2] Similar groups on Bibliothèque Nationale, 463.

[3] Cf. *Archiv für Orientforschung*, XI, 2.

numerous conflicts between the Mitannians and their neighbours, in which two Syrians succeed in disposing of one of the foreigners, a feat commemorated on the seal of one of the victors.

The same helmeted figure once more appears attacking a lion,[1] but in contrast with Shaushattar's sealing the association with the old Akkadian motives is entirely lost; on the contrary, the subject has all the appearance of a secular hunting scene, such as became usual in Persian times. The date of this seal is well established by a winged disk and pillar closely resembling Pl. XLII *e*. The helmeted man is assisted by another whose coiffure is somewhat doubtful, since it is placed on the very edge of the impression.

In Pl. XLII *c* we see furthermore two little men in conflict, and distinguished by a curious projection from their head-dress, which may or may not be a simplification of the helmet of the larger figure. In any case they recur in this form on certain other seals. In Pl. XLII *f* they form, apparently, the suite of a Weather-god of Hittite appearance, who holds a mortal by the hair. On other seals[2] they follow a chariot. They also occur in groups of three[3] or even singly.[4]

These small figures already occur on Cappadocian sealings (Pl. XL *n*) following a chariot as in Syria, where this is the commonest of their functions (Pl. XLIV *f*).[5] Sometimes, as we have seen, they form the suite of a god (Pl. XLII *f*; XLIV *c*) or of a seated personage,[6] and once even of a man riding a camel.[7] At other times they serve merely as stop-gaps.[8]

In some instances, as in Pl. XLII *c*, *f*, they appear with a curious head-dress resembling closely the hunters' on Pl. XLIV *a*, which, by this chain of connections, is linked as we have seen with the kingdom of Mitanni. Whether he is a man or a god remains to be discovered.

The "galop volant" of the antelope accompanying the hunter of Pl. XLIV *a* and appearing on such seals as Pls. XLII *l*,[9] XLIV *b* and the seals quoted in connection with them, belongs to the last part of the period of two and a half centuries which we are discussing here. This seems not only likely on general historical grounds, since Aegean art influenced the littoral of the Eastern Mediterranean with particular intensity

[1] Ward-Morgan, 225; the drawing in Ward, 1023, is quite incorrect in rendering the man's head-dress, for in the photograph the triple crest is visible.

[2] Bibliothèque Nationale, 479, and *Journal of Egyptian Archaeology*, VIII, Pl. 24, No. 10.

[3] A–924. This seal may belong to the First Syrian group.

[4] Palestine Museum, 8914, with four spirals, lions and winged sphinxes.

[5] *Hittite Seals*, 167; Newell, 343; De Clercq, 287.

[6] Qd, 11; A–901.

[7] A–904.

[8] Newell, 311; Brett, 97.

[9] This cylinder was actually bought in the Syrian village of Mumbidj.

immediately after the fall of Knossos when emigrants from Crete seem to have settled in many places; it also follows from a consideration of Pl. XLII *h*, where we find a finely drawn bull and the bird of Pl. XLIV *a* (here characterised as the royal and divine emblem of Horus). Now that seal can be accurately dated, it seems, to the latter half of Akhenaten's reign. The small figure appearing under the winged sun-disk shows the extraordinarily bulbous skull of the royal princesses at Tell el Amarna, a physical peculiarity which the courtiers imitated, as is well known, whenever they had themselves portrayed. It is curious to find that a Syrian, perhaps one of those who championed the Egyptian government though obtaining little support, has depicted one of these royal children. We must not forget, however, that there were marital ties between the courts of Mitanni and Egypt for three generations, and that this implied the emigration of large Syrian retinues to Egypt and much travel to and fro. However this may be, there is no denying that the little figure of Pl. XLII *h* accompanied by a Horus falcon under a winged sun-disk, and perhaps worshipped by the Syrian on the left, displays a skull which is quite abnormal but which appears habitually in the art of Tell el Amarna, especially in the case of the royal princesses who are figured naked. In the cylinder we should then have an example of the Second Syrian style at the very end of the period considered here.[1]

These, then, are the seals which direct or indirect connections with the sealing of Shaushattar seem to assign to the centuries between the Hyksos and the Hittite conquests of Syria and Palestine.

(*c*) *The Syrian Themes of the Second Group.*

So far we have considered the Syrian seals in relation with Mesopotamia and Egypt. A considerable number, however, contain as their main subject motives not derived from these countries. Several of these have already been observed in the sealings of the Cappadocian tablets. Others resemble figures on Hittite reliefs. Considered by themselves these native Syrian themes cannot be dated, but they are often associated with subsidiary matter which contains criteria of age.

In all peripheral seals the personal appearance of figures is apt to be

[1] Another possible reflection of Akhenaten's reign may be seen in a seal (A–937) which is unfortunately damaged but belongs to the Second group, if we may judge by the large Hathor head and by the lion pursuing an antelope. The rest of the design contains two boats. Above them the winged disk appears with two hands, each holding a "sparkling ring" such as Ishtar holds on the Assyrian seals of Pl. XXXIII. The whole design of the cylinder is exceptional, and the development of the Assyrian designs which we have discussed has no point of contact with this unique Syrian echo of Akhenaten's religious innovation.

modified to agree with local fashions (e.g. Pl. XLI *b*). It is difficult to specify such characteristics on the basis of the miniature renderings of the seals. There is evidence available from the wall-paintings of the palace at Mari which requires further study. It shows that the head-dress of Pl. XLI *b*, for instance, may well be characteristic of the region of the middle Euphrates. We notice, furthermore, a tendency to depict shawls and garments with heavy borders, often projecting as if they were made of heavy material, or rolled backward over the shoulder (Pls. XLI *r*; XLII *e, f, h*; XLIV *g, h*). A square horned crown (Pl. XLIV *g, h, j, n*) is as characteristic of the goddesses as the dervish cap or the spiked helmet of the gods. But numerous other fashions are also shown; the cap topped by a bird of the right-hand figure of Pl. XLIV *h* may be connected with the ritual there depicted; the figure on the left seems to represent a purely Phoenician fashion, resembling, but not identical with, that of Pl. XLI *r*. Features of Egyptian and Mesopotamian attire more or less correctly imitated also occur in all conceivable combinations on these seals.

Some definite information may be derived from the appearance of certain Weather-gods. The high caps of Pl. XLII *f* find their nearest parallels nowadays in the Gebel Sinjar and may therefore well denote a purely Syrian deity; the god who faces the interceding goddess on Pl. XLII *k* recalls by his helmet, long hair and kilt the figure at the entrance of the Palace of Boghazkeuy. On other seals he wears the curved sword. We now know how to interpret his pointed helmet, since an ivory statuette from Nuzi shows it to be of the same shape as the Assyrian kings' crown, with the two horns, the Babylonian emblem of divinity, laid along its sides and a spike projecting from the top.[1] His presence at Nuzi proves that his worship precedes Shubbiluliuma's conquest of Syria, and that we cannot therefore consider him a Hittite god, or date the seals upon which he is depicted after that event. This, in any case, would be difficult with seals such as Pl. XLII *k* or others which repeat the composition of Babylonian seals with some precision,[2] or where a Babylonian goddess complete with flowing vase, sprouting plant and fishes is associated with him,[3] or where he appears under a winged disk of the type of Pl. XLII *i, k*.[4] In the last-named instance he holds the rein of a crouching bull-calf, as on Pl. XLIV *l*, and one seal of this type has actually been found at Beisan in layers dated to the reign of Amenhotep III.[5] These

[1] Starr, *Nuzi*, II, Pl. 101.

[2] Meissner, *Beiträge zur altorientalischen Archaeologie*, p. 24, Fig. 16.

[3] A–914.

[4] Bibliothèque Nationale, 495.

[5] Alan Rowe, *Topography and History of Beth Shan*, Pl. 36.

instances of his occurrence antedate Shubbiluliuma, but most of them are without indication of age.[1] It would be exceedingly rash to name this or any other divinity on the Syrian seals.[2] He is a Weather-god, and Text-fig. 86 suggests that he is identical with a Weather-god bestriding mountains.[3]

Text-fig. 84. Mountain-gods.

In several cases he is accompanied by a goddess who exposes her nakedness either by drawing her garment aside (Text-fig. 85) or by raising it (Pl. XLIV *d*). In Text-fig. 86 she is mounted on a bull the rein of which is held by the god. We have already met this goddess on the Cappadocian sealings (Text-fig. 75, p. 243) and have expressed doubt as to whether the myth of Ishtar's descent into the nether-world would be relevant in dealing with a

Text-fig. 85. Various deities.

Text-fig. 86. Various deities.

subject belonging to the peripheral civilisation. One seal (Pl. XLIV *d*), where the goddess appears under a canopy set with wings, feathers or plants, recalls the Akkadian renderings of Ishtar's descent into the nether-world to free Tammuz (Pl. XXI *a*); and we know a rendering of the First Babylonian Dynasty of this theme, which would bridge the gap in time. There is, then, at least the possibility of interpreting the subject in this way. But the same goddess is shown embraced by a god in Pl. XLI *c* (see §25 (*j*), p. 169). To name the goddess Ishtar would account for all these scenes. In any case the gesture of the goddess has become a mere means of identification in Syria, a kind of attribute with which she is depicted whether or not it is appropriate to her circumstance. Thus she is placed in this attitude upon a bull (Text-fig. 86),[4]

[1] A–916, with two griffins holding the pillar of heaven of Pl. XLII *e* but crowned with the moon and crescent emblems; A–917, with the winged disk, and De Clercq, 281; Newell, 324, 327; Bibliothèque Nationale, 494; *Illustrated London News*, 16 June 1934, p. 979 (Gaza).

[2] See above, p. 262, note 1, and Götze, *Kulturgeschichte Kleinasiens*, p. 125.

[3] Also Newell, 303; Ward, 883.

[4] Ward, 913–916; A–930.

or under a winged canopy which may symbolise the earth with its vegetation,[1] or she replaces the interceding goddess in a presentation scene,[2] or she is the object of adoration.[3]

Sometimes a goddess is enthroned upon a bull in the normal way;[4] sometimes she is winged.[5] The question therefore arises whether she is identical with a winged nude female figure who often carries hares or other game by the hindlegs, but is once depicted with human victims[6] in this position. Her earliest appearance seems to be on a cylinder in the style of the Kirkuk sealings, but so closely connected with the late style of the First Babylonian Dynasty, that we must place it before 1500 B.C.[7] She also occurs on Mitannian seals.[8] A male winged god occurs in a similar position in Pl. XLIV *l*[9] and also in seals of a later group (Pl. XLV *g*), but also shown without game;[10] in several instances it is impossible to say whether the god or the goddess is depicted.

The naked goddess under the canopy once occurs associated with the axe of Pl. XLI *e*, on a seal which should also, on other grounds, be assigned to the First group.[11] This canopy occasionally shelters two other figures, one a naked squatting woman,[12] the other a personage—sometimes winged—whose legs are interlaced in a curious way (Text-figs. 87, 90).[13] Occasionally a double shelter appears (Pl. XLIV *k*).[14] Whether this is derived from the jets of water as in Pl. XLIV *j* or from the Egyptian figure holding two "yearsticks" and signifying eternity,[15] or whether it merely reproduces the decorations of a statue base as a Cappadocian sealing suggests,[16] remains uncertain.

Text-fig. 87. Two-headed and crosslegged figures.

[1] Ward, 930. [2] Ward, 918; Boston, 99, 353. [3] *Hittite Seals*, 170.

[4] A–927. [5] *Hittite Seals*, 172; Bibliothèque Nationale, 453.

[6] A–932. [7] Brussels, 518.

[8] Newell, 361, 364; Furtwängler, *Antike Gemmen*, III, Pl. I, 16; Ward, 986, 1003.

[9] Also Ward-Morgan, 176.

[10] Newell, 322, 324, 325, 327 (or are these the goddesses?). Bibliothèque Nationale, 490, 497; *American Journal of Archaeology*, II, Pl. IV, 15.

[11] Ward, 932. [12] Brett, 91; *Hittite Seals*, 173; A–931.

[13] Also on a boundary stone: L. W. King, *Boundary Stones*, Pl. 30.

[14] Ward-Morgan, 245, 247; Ward, 934, 936; De Clercq, 245.

[15] These occur, for instance, on pectorals of the Middle Kingdom which were sent to Syria as gifts to local princes, e.g. Steindorff, *Kunst der Aegypter*, p. 292.

[16] De Genouillac, *Céramique Cappadocienne*, I, Pl. A, 4.

Apart from the goddess discussed in the foregoing lines, there appears a naked woman dispensing streams of water (Pl. XLIV *i*),[1] the action taken on Babylonian seals by a naked male figure which is also found in the Second Syrian group (Pl. XLIV *i*, *m*).[2] Another frequent theme on these Syrian seals consists of two people facing each other and either drinking from cups (Pl. XLIV *k*)[3] or filling their jars from a flowing vase (Text-fig. 85),[4] or facing a table heaped with loaves.[5] Other characteristic Syrian motives such as the row of running men (Pls. XLII *f*; XLIV *c*, *f*), who, like the griffin, lions, sphinxes, but also like the feasters, always occupying a subordinate position, have already been mentioned.

Another curious feature on Syrian seals is the bull's head which appears in the field of Pl. XLIV *c*. Whether this is derived from the Aegean is questionable; rhyta in the shape of bulls and bulls' heads are very common both in Anatolia and in Syria. The bull's head appears also in the frescoes at Nuzi, which are contemporary with the seals under discussion. On seals it is fairly common[6] and it survives into the next period.

Some designs show a certain creative activity on the part of the Syrian seal-cutters. The adoration of the "sacred tree" in Pl. XLIV *h*, or the epiphany of the gods in Text-fig. 84, present subjects of the greatest interest. We have not attempted to explain them nor any other subjects of the Syrians. They certainly deserve detailed study; but if material illuminating the meaning of these scenes has already been discovered, it is certainly not available for an archaeologist.

A number of seals not mentioned in the text belong to the Second group.[7] Others may well be contemporary, though we are as yet unable to prove it and they are therefore omitted here.

It is obvious that the manufacture of seals of the various types here discussed did not suddenly come to an end about the middle of the fourteenth century B.C., and at all times we have to reckon with a continued use of seals of a former age. But the seals of Pls. XLII–XLIV may be considered

[1] So also A–896, 914.

[2] Also A–897, 899; Ward, 836. A–895 shows this creature with bull's ears, perhaps a typically Syrian confusion of Bull-man and hero, such as we shall note in connection with Pl. XLII *b*.

[3] Bibliothèque Nationale, 451.

[4] A–897, 907.

[5] De Clercq, 245; Ward, 826, 915; A–932.

[6] Bibliothèque Nationale, 488 (one of the earliest seals of the Second group); Newell, 302; Brett, 86; A–919.

[7] *Hittite Seals*, 176, 178; Newell, 300, 311, 316, 317, 321, 331, 346, 349; Boston, 52–99; Brett, 86, 88; Bibliothèque Nationale, 446; Ward, 899; Qd, 11.

characteristic of the period comprised between the Hyksos migration and the Hittite conquest of Syria. What was new in, and therefore characteristic of, the subsequent age, is combined in a Third group of Syrian seals.

§ 42. THE SEALS OF MITANNI

(a) *The fully-grown Mitannian Style* (1500–1350 B.C.).

The glyptic style of Mitanni presents a collateral development. The First, Second and Third Syrian groups are continuous. But in the north-eastern Plain, and as far east as Kirkuk, a somewhat special development took place, already studied from a Mesopotamian angle in § 29 (p. 182), where its origin escaped us. We now recognise that a mixture of Mesopotamian and Phoenician motives accounts at least for its subject-matter. Looking back to Pl. XXXI *a, c, d* and Text-figs. 44–54, pp. 183–4, we perceive that various peculiarities of these seals, such as the placing of the *guilloche* and the nature of the subsidiary motives, are in accordance with Syrian usage before and during the Hyksos period. In other words: these foreign features derive from the First Syrian group. It is only natural that cylinders made in Mesopotamia should retain Mesopotamian features longer than was usual farther to the west; and that the main themes of the sealings from Kirkuk should therefore conform more closely to the glyptic tradition of the First Babylonian Dynasty than the contemporary "Second group" in Syria. For this very reason they do not give a good impression of the actual achievement of the Mitannian seal-cutters.

The sealings of the Kirkuk tablets are moreover popular products of Mitannian art. There are but a few documents of a higher order, and these do afford some indication of its true quality. One is the sealing of King Shaushattar (Pl. XLII *a*), the other a fine cylinder found at Tell Chagar Bazar in the Khabur valley, the very centre of Mitanni (Pl. XLIII *m*).

These designs have in common a free treatment of the surface. In Mesopotamia the space to be decorated was always considered as a narrow band which just accommodated the tallest figures. If the seal was divided into two registers, each division was treated in the same way as a narrow frieze. Thus composition became largely a problem of horizontal spacing. On the Mitannian seals this was otherwise; the vertical composition is here as complicated as the sideward spacing and the result in Pl. XLIII *m* is highly satisfactory. The design is strictly symmetrical, and there is neither over-crowding nor an awkward filling of open spaces. In Pl. XLII *a*, symmetry is less strictly maintained, though it obviously was desired. The inequality of the lowest row of figures probably occurred in the making of the impression and would not have appeared on the original cylinder. There is not, however, a single axis to the whole design, since the large winged figure stands to the left of the sun-disk and its support. Nevertheless, the equilibrium achieved is quite ingenious. It is clear that the non-Mesopotamian portions of the designs from Kirkuk, such as the right halves of Text-figs. 51, 54, p. 184, are treated in exactly the same manner as Pls. XLII *a* and XLIII *m*. But this freer method of composition requires more skill than the simple designing of friezes, which always derives coherence from the use of the upper and lower

Text-fig. 88. Seal of a king of Hanigalbat.

limit of the cylinder as a support of the pattern. And thus we see that in the very widely spread popular form of Mitannian glyptic (Pl. XLIII *c–h*), the frieze design again prevails, or the surface is divided by horizontal lines into narrower friezes. But clumsy versions of the free-field style are sometimes found (Pl. XLIII *d*, *k*). It is adequately applied in the royal sealing of Text-fig. 88, found on a letter sent by the King of Hanigalbat to the Hittite King at Boghazkeuy.[1] Unfortunately the top is lost, but we notice a deity mounted upon a lion and various figures—antelopes, kids, bird-footed monsters—grouped antithetically beside a "sacred tree" but freely spaced in the height of the cylinder surface. The sealing is dated to the period 1380–1280 B.C., and Hanigalbat is either a region bordering on Mitanni,[2] or another

[1] K. Bittel in *Mitteilungen der Deutschen Orient-Gesellschaft*, LXXII, 19; Bittel and Güterbock in "Boghazkeuy", *Abh. Preuss. Akad.*, Phil.-Hist. Kl. 1925, p. 43 and Pl. 28, 5. Other Mitannian seals showing the free scheme of composition are Ward, 711, 1015*a*.

[2] Sidney Smith, *Early History of Assyria*, pp. 247 ff.

name for Mitanni.[1] The sealing is too much damaged to serve as a basis for classification, but enough is preserved to show its relationship with Pls. XLII *a* and XLIII *m*.

The subject-matter of the Mitannian seals has already been to some extent discussed in an earlier chapter, since the middle Assyrian seals cannot be understood without their Mitannian antecedents, and the Second Syrian groups cannot be determined without reference to the dated sealing of Shaushattar. To do justice to the Mitannian seals we should have to state here again what was said in §§ 31 and 41, pp. 194, 260. We shall, therefore, merely insist on one circumstance which is easily overlooked when treating Mitannian seals in isolation. The kingdom of Mitanni was founded some time after the passing of the great migrations of the eighteenth century B.C. Its existence can only be proved from the sixteenth century B.C. onward. It is therefore comprehensible that all the elements of the Syrian repertoire—hares, birds, griffins and so on—as well as the Egyptian features, such as the large vulture of Pl. XLIII *m*, appear on purely Mitannian seals. The most important new feature, and one for which we may probably credit the Mitannians, is the introduction of the winged disk and its support. We have already referred to the Vedantic texts which mention the pillar supporting heaven, and the evidence which shows that the outstretched wings were, in fact, interpreted in Western Asia as representing the firmament and not as attributes of the sun (§ 31 (*e*), p. 205). In Mitanni one pillar is depicted, in Anatolia two (Text-fig. 89). We have also seen that the Egyptian examples influenced Asiatic renderings in various ways, first of all by supplying the motive of the winged disk, next by leading to certain modifications in the Mitannian and Hittite designs in which the Egyptian interpretation of winged *sun*-disk cut across the symbolism of the sky. A third factor of confusion was supplied by the ritual connected with the "sacred tree". There are but few seals on which the winged disk is definitely represented as supported by a pillar (Pl. XLII *a, e*). More common is the modification shown in Pl. XLII *i*, where the pillar has acquired vegetal features.[2] Now this agrees very well with the views we have propounded here. The Indo-European ruling class of Mitanni was rapidly absorbed by the native population. If they introduced the Indo-Iranian idea of the pillar supporting heaven, it would be natural for the mass of the

Text-fig. 89.
Hittite royal name.

[1] Götze, *Kulturgeschichte Kleinasiens*, p. 57, note 4.

[2] Qd, 6; Bibliothèque Nationale, 468.

population to interpret the pictorial expression of this alien conception in terms of their own beliefs. The Asherah, the "bedecked maypole", which was so conspicuous an element of the most important religious festival of the year,[1] showed obvious affinities with that other ornamental pole which designated the "pillar of heaven"; and the gradual absorption of the Indo-European immigrants by the North Syrian (Hurrite?) population finds its correlative in the interpretation of the "pillar" of Pl. XLII *a*, *e*, as the "sacred tree" of Pl. XLII *i*, *k*. The transformation is complete on the impression from Assur in Text-figs. 54, 59 (p. 184, 187), where the supporting pillar has become an entirely detached "sacred tree". Similarly the "sacred tree" appears without the winged disk on the sealings from Kirkuk or on other Mitannian seals (Pl. XLII *b*; Text-figs. 44, 46, 48, 49, p. 183). It seems clear, then, that the association of the "sacred tree" with the disk was a result of the assimilation of the alien conception of the "pillar of heaven" with the autochthonous ritual object, the "sacred tree", just as the winged disk was in middle Assyrian times transformed into a symbol of the indigenous god Assur.

It is interesting to note that it was the notion of the "pillar of heaven" which was eliminated by these transformations, but that the outstretched wings retained their validity as a symbol of the sky in Assyria, as we have seen. The characteristic Assyrian device of rendering the "pillar"—meaningless to the Asiatics—by Atlantid figures (Pl. XXXIII *e*, Text-fig. 57, p. 187) is only once found on a seal, Text-fig. 90, which is most probably Mitannian. In Syria the powerful influence of Egypt, as we saw, caused confusion. It is no doubt due to the example of the winged sun-disk of Egyptian monuments that the Mesopotamian sun and crescent emblem occasionally, in seals of the First Syrian groups (Pl. XLI *c*),[2] acquires short wings. Sometimes the winged disk actually becomes a bird, the falcon of Horus.[3] It may be for the same reason, namely confusion with the Egyptian sun-symbol, that the supporters of Pl. XLII *b* hold a stool underneath the disk[4] instead of touching the tips of the wings as they do on Assyrian

Text-fig. 90. Cross-legged figure supporting sky.

[1] See above, p. 205, § 31 (*e*) (i).

[2] Also of the Second group, e.g. A–927; Bibliothèque Nationale, 461.

[3] De Clercq, 245; less precise Bibliothèque Nationale, 496. Cf. the Mut-vulture, Pl. XLIII *m*.

[4] It occurs again in a Mitannian seal in V.A. 508 (Weber, 258), and on two Assyrian

seals. On the other hand, the stool may replace the original pillar, but in any case its introduction confuses the symbolism of the outstretched wings as sky, which the use of supporters (seen in Text-figs. 56–59, 65–68 and Pls. XXXIII *e*, XXXIV *b*) had preserved. How little this symbolism was understood in Syria appears from a cylinder[1] which shows the two figures with the stool of Pl. XLII *b*, but the winged disk has become a row of rosettes as on Pl. XLIV *g*, *h*.[2] An alternative transformation took place under Mesopotamian influence, which assimilated the winged disk to the sun-standard which had been in use in Babylon since the First Dynasty of Babylon and occurs more than once on Kirkuk sealings (Text-fig. 44, p. 183). It may be due to the influence of this standard that the disk supported by the outstretched wings on Mitannian and Hittite monuments was decorated with a star. In any case the two supporters of the sky (Text-fig. 59, p. 187) and the two Bull-men holding the standard in Pl. XLII *k* and Text-fig. 44 are actually combined on a cylinder found at Tiryns (Pl. XLII *o*),[3] where the wings with superimposed disk rest on a pillar held by two Bull-men. This seal is so intimately related with our Pls. XLII *b* and Pl. XLIII *i*, that the curious coiffure of the supporters in Pl. XLII *b* may well be a humanised reflection from the old Mesopotamian monster; anyway it appears intact on Pl. XLII *k*, where the standard, or the pillar of the sky, has become a "sacred tree". On other seals, sometimes Mitannian but generally of the Second or Third Syrian group, the pillar is retained, but the wings have been omitted and thus a new type of sun-standard is evolved (Pl. XLIV *k*).[4]

It may be useful to summarise once more the various factors which influenced these North Syrian designs.

(1) The winged sun-disk of the Egyptian monuments, a symbol of the most impressive monarchy known to Western Asia in the Second Millennium.

(2) The Indo-European conception of a pillar supporting the sky, which was pictorially expressed by means of the outstretched wings supported on

seals: Bibliothèque Nationale, 364, and Ward, 1100. And furthermore on the reliefs from Tell Halaf (English ed. Pl. VII *b*), where the Bull-men hold a stool.

[1] B.M. 102686; *Hittite Seals*, Fig. 71 on p. 68. This seal is especially important because it was bought near Carchemish on the western outskirts of Mitanni. It contains, besides the figures with the stool of Pl. XLII *b*, the male figure and the interceding goddess of Pl. XLII *i* with identical costume, and thus confirms once more the close affinities between the various seals which we classify as Mitannian and the contemporary Second Syrian Group.

[2] Similar rosettes on Newell, 341, 353; Ward, 1015 *a*, which is Mitannian.

[3] Unfortunately the seal formed part of a hoard embracing objects of different ages.

[4] Bibliothèque Nationale, 466, 467; A–916; Newell, 288.

one or two pillars, and surmounted by a disk, a motive which, for the reason just given, offered peculiar attractions to the Hittite and Mitannian kings.

(3) The Mesopotamian sun-standard, which influenced the rendering of the sun by a disk with a star, and also the further development of the motive, by suggesting a familiar interpretation.

(4) The immemorial North Syrian ritual connected with the "Asherah" or "sacred tree", which offered another interpretation and development of the design.

We have so far only dealt with high-class specimens of Mitannian glyptic. But it is evident that many seals of inferior quality must have been in use in Mitanni, and there are obvious connections between Pl. XLII *b* and Text-fig. 88 on the one hand, and Pl. XLIII *a, d, i* on the other. Nevertheless, the Mitannian character of these less well executed seals of stone cannot well be substantiated before we have studied that large class of Mitannian glyptic best known in the form of seal impressions on tablets from the neighbourhood of Kirkuk. It will then be clear that the official style of Mitanni is founded upon a widely spread popular production, mainly of glazed cylinders, which preceded the formation of the finer Mitannian style.

(*b*) *The Popular Style of Mitanni* (1700–1200 B.C.).

The seal of Pl. XLIII *m* was found in the heart of Mitanni, and the sealing of King Shaushattar is naturally characteristic of the glyptic art of his reign. Besides these two documents we possess a number of Mitannian sealings on "Kirkuk tablets" (Text-figs. 44–54, pp. 183–4) which were made on the spot and show, therefore, a greater dependence on Mesopotamian design than was usual in the more westerly part of the kingdom. But if we allow for this peculiarity, it appears that these seal impressions share their characteristic designs and well-marked technical qualities with others, found as far east as Tepe Giyan, in Persia, and all through Syria and Palestine as far to the south as Gaza. The type of seal, which was so widely used, was generally made of glazed steatite and sometimes of faience; its design is simplified in a characteristic manner, which is largely determined by the use made of the ordinary and the tubular drill. The *guilloche* becomes a series of concentric circles, with or without tangents (Pl. XLIII *b, c, i*). The animals show characteristic drill-holes at the tips of nose and tail and at the joints, and the tubular drill is often used to mark the eye.

It would be a mistake to consider these seals as disintegrated products of a Mitannian style of the quality of Pls. XLII *a*, XLIII *m*. Both types are contemporaneous, as is proved by the occurrence of Shaushattar's sealing on a "Kirkuk tablet" from Nuzi, where the sealings of Text-figs. 44–49, p. 183, were also found. The relationship is exactly the reverse, for the Kirkuk sealings agree in their technique with the last cylinders of the First Babylonian Dynasty. We have already seen that seals of the type of Pl. XXX *b–f* continued in use after the Hittite attack on Babylon, and that the new Kassite style, not datable before the fifteenth century, was developed on the basis of such seals as Pl. XXX *h*, *j*, which represent the last stage of Babylonian glyptic of the Hammurabi Dynasty. We have also argued—and Pl. XLIII *b* adds further evidence to this effect—that the Kirkuk seals are based on exactly the same foundation. In contrast with the seal of Pl. XXXI *a*, the whole design of Pl. XLIII *b* seems to be made in one. The symbol of Marduk, the head and the goat-fish belong to the Babylonian repertoire, as does the very debased rendering of the interceding goddess; the rest of the design is Mitannian, and the text gives a non-Semitic name (Awilia) for the owner.

It is, therefore, clear that the popular style of the Kirkuk sealings is not a degenerate form of Mitannian craftsmanship, but that, on the contrary, the hitherto rarely found Mitannian seals of high quality are the contemporary flowering of an established and more widely distributed school.

On the other hand, the innovations of the best Mitannian seal-cutters, both in subject and composition, were bound eventually to affect the popular style of the region. Thus Text-figs. 53, 54 (p. 184) and Pl .XLIII *h* show the winged disk and "pillar of heaven"; Pl. XLIII *d* shows a break with the habitual frieze, and exemplifies a type of composition using height and width equally.

This popular style is found far outside the boundaries of Mitanni. Pl. XLIII *j* was found at Tepe Giyan in Persia;[1] it also occurs in Cyprus.[2] In Palestine it is exceedingly common, occurring at Beisan in strata assigned to the reigns of Thotmes III;[3] at Tell ed Duweir (Lachish) (Pl. XLIII *f*, *h*), in a temple which existed from the reign of Amenhotep III down to that of Ramses II.[4] It is also found at Megiddo,[5] Tell Abu Hawam,[6] Balata,[7]

[1] Contenau et Ghirshman, *Fouilles du Tepe Giyan*, Pl. 38, Nos. 1, 4.

[2] Murray, Smith and Walters, *Excavations in Cyprus*, Pl. V, 53, 425; Gjerstadt, *Swedish Cyprus Expedition*, I, Pl. 150, No. 14; very interesting is Pl. 76, No. 87, three adorers (not unlike our Pl. XLIII *f*) and a lyre-player before an enthroned figure.

[3] *Museum Journal*, 1929, p. 42.

[4] I am indebted to the late Mr J. L. Starkey for this information. See *Illustrated London News*, 6 July 1935. A seal resembling Pl. XLIII *f* was found at Chatal Huyuk, and another bought at Jaffa (Nies-Keiser, *Hist. and Religious Texts*, Pl. 7, 4).

[5] Palestine Museum, I–3575.

[6] Palestine Museum, 34–186.

[7] Palestine Museum, I–742.

Tell Zakariya[1] and Gezer.[2] At Chatal Huyuk and Tell Judeideh (Pl. XLIII*e*, *g*) this style occurs together with Mycenean pottery[3] as it does at Ras Shamra. It must therefore have remained in use during most of the thirteenth century B.C. In Palestine (and in Persia, for that matter) the repertoire is much poorer than at Kirkuk, not only because Babylonian motives continued in use in the last-named place, but also because the Mitannian innovations were adopted there.

The distribution of these seals makes the term Mitannian seem rather inappropriate, since the kingdom of Mitanni did not at any time include all these regions, and since these seals continued to be used for some time after the collapse of Mitanni. I have considered the term Hurrian as an alternative, since the Hurrians spread into Palestine during the migrations and certainly formed the bulk of the populace in the Mitannian kingdom. Yet these seals can hardly be considered as manifestations of a peculiar mentality, as regards either subject-matter or style. Their repertoire consists of a very limited selection of derived motives and these are executed in a specialised technique which made mass-production—in the limited sense to be given to this term when applied to the ancient world—possible. In other words: it does not seem that the Hurrians migrating during the Hyksos movement took these seals with them and continued their manufacture, but rather that at a later time, perhaps since the end of the sixteenth century, they were more and more widely exported or imitated; in fact it seems unlikely that any of the characteristic glazed specimens can be dated to the time of the migrations.[4] Moreover, the fact that they were sought after may to some extent be due to the prestige of Mitanni; certainly all that was new in these "Hurrian seals" was more clearly, and on a much higher level, present in the Mitannian seals discussed in the preceding pages. Finally, there is no reason to assume that they had always been made where they were used. Their distribution resembles that of another group of glazed ware, namely vessels in the shape of animal or human heads. These have been found at Enkomi in Cyprus, at Ras Shamra, at Assur and at Tell Abu Hawwam in Palestine. Now we know that the glazed seals of the popular Mitannian style were used and made in Mitanni, and astonishing works of plastic art in glazed ware were discovered in the temple of the Mitannian city of Nuzi. The wide distribution of the seals, as well as that of the vases, may well be due to the widely ramifying trade of a renowned centre of glazed ware manufacture.

[1] Palestine Museum, I–742.

[2] Macalister, *Gezer*, III, Pl. 114, and others.

[3] Information kindly supplied by Dr C. W. McEwan.

[4] Since traces of Kassite occupation occur at Khafaje, Speiser's earlier dating of the cylinder in *Bulletin of the American Schools of Oriental Research*, No. 68, p. 12, Fig. 5, is not justified.

For all these reasons I have preferred to avoid the designation Hurrian, with its implication that we have in these seals something as distinctive in the field of art as the Hurrians represent in the fields of language and religion. In considering these glazed seals as the exponents of a popular Mitannian style, we suggest a limited scope for their adoption in Syria; and, indeed, at no time were seals of this type exclusively in use. There was always a more general "Syrian group" flourishing along with the Mitannian seals.

We are now in a position to judge a number of seals which combine features of the Second Syrian with the popular Mitannian style. These are mostly made of stone. Pl. XLIII *i* is instructive.[1] The animals on the right are in design and execution similar to those on the Kirkuk tablets (Text-figs. 50, 51, p. 184). The Babylonian motives on the left are well removed from their prototypes; a comparison with Pl. XLII *i* shows that a progressive disintegration was consistently at work; the figures on the two seals stand in the same mutual relation as the *guilloche* on the one with series of tubular drillings on the other. Note also that the nude woman in Pl. XLIII *i* shows the head in profile, which is never the case on Babylonian seals. But she has already occurred in that attitude on Cappadocian sealings and recurs on Pl. XXXI *d* and on Pl. XLII *b*, where in addition to the concentric circles we find, horizontally drawn, the same naked figure and an interceding goddess. Below are two goats beside a "sacred tree", as on the Kirkuk sealings (Text-fig. 49, p. 183). The figures supporting the winged disk on a stool represent the nude hero of the Babylonian repertoire, or, rather, an anthropomorphised Bull-man, for the curious manner in which the head is drawn recalls a cylinder found at Tiryns (Pl. XLII *o*), where similar figures have tails as if Bull-men were intended. The various peculiarities of these seals and of Pl. XLIII *a*, *d*, *l* speak strongly for a Mitannian origin. The antelope and sphinxes of Pl. XLII *b*, *o* recurs in Pl. XLIII *i*. Pl. XLIII *l* shows the same stool as Pl. XLII *b*, but now used by a drinker; griffins, antelopes and rosettes substantiate the connection with Pl. XLIII *i* but the main theme, as well as the hunting scene, form a prelude to the Assyrian seals, where purely secular scenes of this type are known.

In this respect our cylinder corresponds with Pl. XLIII *a*, another seemingly secular scene, a royal audience. It must be admitted, of course, that the possibility that gods are depicted exists. The subsidiary groups contain almost every combination of man and animal known to glyptic art:

[1] This and its homologues are already named Mitannian in R. Heidenreich's dissertation: *Beiträge zur Geschichte der Vorderasiatischen Steinschneidekunst*, a work in which some penetrating analyses are combined with quite untenable views, the latter partly explicable by the paucity of dated material at the time of its publication.

a small figure holds a dead buck by the hindlegs while guiding a humped bull by the horn; behind the latter a kneeling figure carries a goat or antelope on his shoulder, and underneath two variants of the subjection of beasts appear. The cylinder was found at Alishar in Anatolia, but it is closely related to such seals as Pls. XLII*b*, *o*; XLIII*i*, in some of its motives as well as in the combined use of drill and graver.

Another cylinder,[1] intimately resembling those which we have discussed, shows the goats and "sacred tree" of Pl. XLII*o*, the lion pawing an antelope of Pl. XLIII*i*, but mounted upon him a male deity, and in front a nude winged goddess holding a hare by the hindlegs, and furthermore the face with its long locks of Pl. XLI*a* and Text-fig. 44 (p. 183), connections which once more stress the Mitannian character of the closely interrelated groups of seals, though the face is, as we have already seen, derived from the glyptic of the First Babylonian Dynasty. Other motives of the same origin are the monkey of Pl. XLIII*i*, the arm of the balance of Pl. XLII*b*, the sun and crescent of Pl. XLIII*l*. The more striking is the complete absence of truly Egyptian features such as the Crux Ansata or Egyptian attributes of gods at a time when Egypt was politically most closely allied with Mitanni. But it is trade, not politics, which influences an artistic repertoire and the Mitannian territory had, after all, for many centuries been dependent upon Mesopotamian culture. The lack of Egyptian features in Mitannian glyptic confirms the surmise that they entered the Syrian repertoire through the Phoenician ports, and the sphinxes of the Mitannian seals bear clear traces of this origin.

The ultimate dependence of Mitannian glyptic on Mesopotamia even becomes manifest in the restricted selection of purely Syrian motives by the Mitannian seal-cutters. The goddess withdrawing her robes is absent from Mitannian seals, and the naked woman of Pls. XLII*b*, XLIII*d*, *i* is related with the full-face naked woman of Babylonian glyptic. The Weather-gods, so common in Syria, do not appear on Mitannian or Kirkuk sealings, while the god holding the staff with globes, of the late Babylonian seals, is retained (Pl. XXX*c*, *d* and Text-figs. 46, 50, pp. 183, 184). The Syrian chariot scene is, again, absent from the popular Mitannian style.

On the other hand, we find traces of the free mode of composition, introduced

[1] Furtwängler, *Antike Gemmen*, III, Pl. I, 6. In addition to those mentioned, the following may be considered Mitannian seals: Dussaud, *La Lydie et ses voisins*, Pl. IV, 4; Newell, 289–296, 357, 364; De Clercq, 397 *bis*; Bibliothèque Nationale, 468, 469, 470, 472; Ward, 711, 986–991, 996, 1002, 1003, 1015*a*; *Hittite Seals*, 231; A–910, 945, 952; Ward-Morgan, 168, 176; Brett, 107; Murray, Smith and Walters, *Excavations in Cyprus*, Pl. IV, 299, 606, 607.

by the leading Mitannian seal-cutters, also in the popular Mitannian style. Though on most of its seals the main figures are again made to occupy the full height of the cylinder while the subsidiary motives are arranged in two registers, these are occasionally (Pl. XLIII *d* and Text-figs. 51, 52, p. 184) more or less clumsy attempts to apply the scheme of composition so skilfully used in Pl. XLIII *m*. This use of a distinctively Mitannian scheme of composition is rare, and the subject-matter of these seals is not entirely distinctive either. Yet they form a clearly recognisable class among peripheral seals, and others can without hesitation be grouped with them and thus assigned to Mitanni.

It is quite obvious for instance that the figures added to the original Babylonian design of Pl. XXXI *a* (see p. 154 above) are derived from the same school to which the seals of Pl. XLIII (and especially *i*, *k*, *l*) are due. Pl. XXXI *d* is another example of similar work. The most distinctive feature of these popular Mitannian seals is, in fact, their technique, the peculiar combination of drills and graver in building up the design, the small holes marking the snouts of antelopes and lions, the crests of griffins, the joints of all animals, the tubular drillings that mark their eyes, and the concentric circles imitating the *guilloche*; also the cylindrical shapes of the human figures scooped out with the graver after having been outlined by a series of drill-holes, characteristics which these cylinders share with the commoner contemporaneous seals of glazed ware. The same technical peculiarities are moreover noticeable in the late seals of the First Babylonian Dynasty (Pl. XXX *b–f*), and these seals are not merely comparable in technique with those from Mitanni, but there is a genetic connection, for as we have seen (§ 29, p. 182) the popular Mitannian style as exemplified by the Kirkuk sealings (Text-figs. 50–54; Pl. XXXI *a*, *c*, *d*) was based upon those Babylonian seals and derived its technique from them. But among the non-Mesopotamian seals the combination of work by drill and graver in the manner which we have described is characteristic of the popular seals of Mitanni.

Seals of harder stone cut in this manner are rare compared with the large quantity of seals of glazed steatite. And both classes combined are outnumbered by contemporary seals rooted in another tradition. For the Mitannian cylinders, it must be repeated, form merely a collateral development. Just as the Second Syrian style developed out of the First after the great migrations of the eighteenth century B.C., so also a Third Syrian style (§ 44, p. 288) grew on the basis of the Second, after the changes which mark the Tell el Amarna period in Western Asia.

§ 43. HITTITE CYLINDERS

Until 1933 no cylinder or cylinder impression had been found which could be called Hittite with much justification. Outside Kultepe seals and impressions were in any case rare, and at that site the seals were, as we have seen, peripheral Mesopotamian or Syrian works, of which it would be impossible to say whether they had been made in Anatolia or imported from Syria.[1] But one unusual impression from Boghazkeuy (Text-fig. 91) is probably

Text-fig. 91. Impression from Boghazkeuy.

Hittite because of the double-headed eagle.[2] The ancient impression is too much marred for the smaller motives to be recognisable; the god mounted on a beast wears the pointed Hittite cap of the rock-sculptures of Yasilikaya, now proved to belong to the new Hittite empire between 1450—more probably 1350—and 1230 B.C.[3] But gods on animals, and even the pointed cap, occur in Syria too, though mostly with a more rounded outline (Pl. XLII*f*), like the felt cap of Derwishes and Yezidis.[4] It is not unlikely, however, that the

[1] An interesting cylinder, related to the Cappadocian sealings, was bought at Smyrna, *Proceedings of the Society of Biblical Archaeology*, 1877, our Text-fig. 81 (p. 251). At Alishar were found: a fragment of a Mesopotamian cylinder of the Jemdet Nasr period (Bittel, *Praehist. Forschung in Kleinasien*, Pl. IX, 14); a magnificent Akkadian cylinder (our Pl. XXIV*b*; *Oriental Institute Communications*, No. 14, p. 47, Fig. 45); one fine Syrian cylinder of the First group, a number of peripheral seals dependent upon the glyptic of the First Babylonian Dynasty, but lacking distinctive features which would enable us to ascribe them to Anatolia to the exclusion of Syria (*Oriental Institute Communications*, No. 14, p. 47, Fig. 45, *c* 350 and *c* 200); one popular Mitannian seal (*Oriental Institute Communications*, No. 14, p. 52, *d* 1912); another (our Pl. XLIII*a*) and a number of seals too coarsely cut to be defined in any way (*Oriental Institute Publications*, No. VII, p. 43; No. XIX, p. 143). All these seals, with the exception of the Jemdet Nasr fragment, were found in layers dating between 1800–1200 B.C. and not datable with greater precision. Dr Hetty Goldman found at Tarsus a cylinder of the First Babylonian Dynasty belonging to Parishul, servant of Ninshubur; it shows the interceding goddess looking, not towards, but in the same direction as the enthroned deity, *American Journal of Archaeology*, XXXIX (1935), 541, Fig. 31.

[2] But see Bibliothèque Nationale, 463, which is purely Syrian.

[3] Bittel and Güterbock, *Boghazkeuy*, pp. 46–51.

[4] The two cylinders which I remember as showing the true Hittite shape of head-dress are *Hittite Seals*, 178, and Brett, 89. The latter may well be Anatolian, since there is no Syrian parallel for the confrontation of three deities on animals, with a few small filling motives.

two cylinders of Pl. XLIII *n*, *o* and Text-fig. 92 are also Anatolian, but these are from every point of view exceptional.[1] Their shape is a combination of the stamp-seal and the cylinder (Pl. II *n*), the shank of the former type of seal being put on top of the engraved cylinder which bears, in contrast with the cylinder seal, an additional design on its lower surface. That of Pl. XLIII *n* is apparently decorative, but in the case of Text-fig. 92 there are recognisable Hittite hieroglyphs. This speaks for an Anatolian origin, like the elaborate

Text-fig. 92. Cylinder with presentation scene.

rendering of a ritual procedure. We do not find this on Syrian seals, but it has been pointed out that the Anatolian reliefs are distinguished from those found in Syria by just this prevalence of the representation of ritual.[2]

The libation vessel held by the double-headed figure of Pl. XLIII *o* and the ewer placed before the dais are moreover types which are characteristic of the new Hittite empire;[3] and taken together with all this evidence, the fact that the seal of Text-fig. 92 was bought at Aidin, in south-west Anatolia, is not without significance.

Such resemblances to other seals as these two extraordinary objects reveal are confined to the Second Syrian group. Pl. XLIV *n* shows the only other occurrence of a god wearing a helmet with a crescent crest. Another seal, connected by all its motives with the Second Syrian group, shows the pointed helmet worn, in Pl. XLIII *o*, by the god preceding the Moon-god.[4] The fine

[1] Related is the eight-sided seal V.A. 3837, in Ed. Meyer's *Reich und Kultur der Chethiter*, Pl. IV, pp. 145 f., which shows isolated figures on the sides among which the double-faced god appears; the under-surface shows signs and a circular *guilloche*. Another seal in Berlin (Weber, 453) is a copy of the seals we are discussing here, and most likely a modern copy; in other words, a forgery, as Ronzevalles (see p. 286, note 1) and Opitz, *Archiv für Orientforschung*, VII, 113 ff., maintain.

[2] Moortgat, *Die bildende Kunst des alten Orients und die Bergvölker*.

[3] Bittel and Güterbock, "Boghazkeuy", Pl. 7, nos. 3, 4.

[4] Bibliothèque Nationale, 451; Heuzey, *Les Origines Orientales de l'Art*, p. 147, considered the two seals as closely related with Pl. XLI *h*, a comparison upheld by Ward, Contenau, Dussaud and Ronzevalles, but which seems doubtful to me. It is true that in Pl. XLI *h* a two-faced figure occurs, but in connection with Ea this is usual (cf. Pl. XLI *f*),

spiral border is without parallel in glyptic art, and so is the combination of two types of twists, though each occurs separately in Syria.

As to the subject, this has been much discussed.[1] The central feature on both seals is the introduction to a seated god of three approaching figures. The seated god is on both cylinders placed behind an elegant table; figures of lions support the table-tops[2] upon which are heaped offerings. In Pl. XLIII *n* the worshippers have to mount steps towards the platform where the main deity is seated. The introduction is effected by a two-faced figure, bearded in Pl. XLIII *o* and possibly also in Text-fig. 92.[3] The seated god in Pl. XLIII *o* holds a double axe and some curved sticks,[4] while an enigmatical emblem appears above his shoulder. In Text-fig. 92 his two-faced attendant holds the double axe. Behind the seated god of Pl. XLIII *o* appears a kneeling or collapsing figure with uplifted arms, which recurs in Text-fig. 92, though a second seated figure, perhaps the spouse of the chief god conceived as enthroned beside him, intervenes between the figures. The fish and the person with a flowing vase in Text-fig. 92 make it likely that the design represents a cloud discharging rain over this man with uplifted arms, especially as the two-faced introducing god supplies a connection with the Babylonian Water-god Ea, whom we have already seen, in native guise, on several Cappadocian sealings.

The extended figure holding a fish in front of or beneath the god's dais in Pl. XLIII *o* represents a swimmer. The god destroying a prostrate man is a stock motive of Babylonian glyptic (§ 26 (*f*), p. 166), and the Cappadocian sealings show that it was adopted in Anatolia together with other themes of the Babylonian repertoire. This makes it unsafe to connect it with the main motive of Pl. XLIII *o* or to assign to it a very special significance, which it would lack elsewhere. The victorious god, as well as the

though the absence of a beard is indeed curious, and distinguishes this seal not only from all Babylonian examples but also from Pl. XLIII *n*. On the other hand, a beardless two-faced figure appears on the Cappadocian sealings: p. 245, note 1. In any case the seal of Pl. XLI *h*, with its main Babylonian theme and its elaborate series of subsidiary Syrian motives, evidently fits into the First Syrian group, where the two cylinders discussed here would be entirely misplaced.

[1] The essential basis of any discussion is supplied by Ronzevalles who gives a number of enlargements of photographs of the impression taken with different lighting: *Mélanges de l'Université St Joseph, Beyrouth*, XII and XV. All drawings published hitherto are inaccurate in more or less important details.

[2] Ronzevalles sees in the table-top of our Pl. XLIII *o* a boat with rudder and tufts of plants at prow and stern.

[3] See page 245, note 1, for beardless two-faced figures occurring on the Cappadocian tablets.

[4] Compared by Ronzevalles with the lituus of the augurs at Rome.

goddess with robe withdrawn, appear for all we can say in Pl. XLIII *o*, as elsewhere, as isolated motives occupying the cylinder surface left over by the main theme. Whether the lion and bull are a clumsy rendering of the immemorial Mesopotamian groups of a beast of prey attacking a ruminant, or whether the bull is to be referred to the Weather-god and the lion to the goddess (Ishtar) must remain undecided.[1]

Lastly, there is a curious group inserted between the victorious Weather-god and the man under the rain-cloud in Pl. XLIII *o*. A helmeted figure lies on a table. Apparently it has two faces. On the right is a figure in a Mesopotamian cloak with a libation jug, on the left is a person with a knife or dagger. Three lines may indicate flames rising from the prostrate form, while the two-handled vessel below may be intended as the source or container of the fire, or, alternately, as the receptacle for the victim's blood. The animal heads in front perhaps represent rhyta, common in this shape in Anatolia; but since a gourd and a head of corn are depicted beside them, the heads may be those of sacrificed animals, the whole group perhaps showing an offering of first fruits or a similarly suitable sacrifice to the giver of rain, who thereby maintains the life of crops and flocks.

This scene has been variously interpreted. Contenau and Meissner have tentatively considered it to represent a cure by lustration and incantation.[2] The man on the left holds an arrow or dagger used in a kind of blood-letting which the texts mention in this connection. Ronzevalles has suggested that the seal shows a mythological scene, namely the castration of Uranos by his son El or Kronos, a myth preserved by Philo of Byblos and generally supposed to be dependent on Hesiod's Theogony; but the latter may have used ancient Oriental sources. Dussaud invokes Elijah's contest with the prophets of Baal (i Kings 18) and sees in our seal the sacrifice of a human victim to make rain.[3] These explanations remain entirely hypothetical, and Dussaud and Ronzevalles imply that all the elements of the design are connected, a possible and attractive but by no means proven assumption. All we can say with some degree of probability is that these two cylinders were made in Anatolia, under the influence of such Mesopotamian traditions as lingered in the Second Syrian group and perhaps, in Anatolia, though

[1] In Text-fig. 72 it is not the god mounted on a bull who spears the prostrate man.

[2] Contenau, *La Glyptique Syro-Hittite*, pp. 112–15; Meissner, *Beiträge zur altorientalischer Archaeologie*, pp. 21–4. Meissner rejects Contenau's interpretation as "a scene of judgment" without apparently having read Contenau's qualification that it would be a "jugement à la suite duquel le dieu accorde son pardon au coupable frappé de maladie", which is Meissner's own view.

[3] Dussaud, *La Lydie et ses voisins*, pp. 41–54.

not apparently in Anatolian glyptic, as an inheritance of the Assyrian trading stations. The fourteenth century is the most probable date for their production.

It is only the seal impression found at Boghazkeuy (Text-fig. 91) which we may call "Hittite" with full justification.

§ 44. THE THIRD SYRIAN GROUP (1350–1200 B.C.)

We have isolated a number of Syrian seals which are closely related to those of the First Babylonian Dynasty (First Syrian style, 1900–1700); we have discussed another group which is a local continuation of the earlier style and roughly contemporaneous with the Kingdom of Mitanni (Second Syrian group, 1700–1350); there is a Third group which belongs to the last part of the Second Millennium. We might expect this Third Syrian group to reflect influences received from two foreign centres: the Anatolian Hittites who at this time dominated Syria, and "Mycenean", i.e. post-Minoan Aegean culture, since Aegean settlers had founded colonies in Rhodes, Cyprus and in places along the Asiatic coast. But the Hittite domination of Syria, achieved by the destruction of Mitanni and the temporary elimination of Egypt, could not affect Syrian art to any appreciable extent, for the Hittites were artistically inarticulate and had originally derived most of their art forms from Syria. And such Aegean influence as is noticeable during this period was similarly unproductive; Minoan art had strongly influenced Syria at the beginning of the Second Millennium and again after the sack of Knossos, but during the period with which we are dealing it was already far gone in decline. The palace at Knossos had been destroyed in about 1400 B.C. and the very individual Mycenaean civilisation of the mainland was not so much creative in the arts and crafts which produce goods for export, as in such fields as architecture, for instance, which do not influence foreign regions. Thus "Mycenaean" civilisation was everywhere, except on the Greek mainland, thoroughly second-rate, and such seals as Pl. XLIV*b* cannot be dated after 1400 B.C., and are probably considerably earlier.

By the end of the fourteenth century B.C. Syrian glyptic was thus reduced to its own resources; and it shows indeed all the signs of inbreeding and disintegration (Pl. XLV).

In the south some good work was being done under Egyptian influence, for Palestine was recovered by Seti I and remained an Egyptian dominion until the "Peoples of the Sea" overran it. It is no doubt to Palestine or to one of the Phoenician cities (and possibly to a somewhat earlier period than that under discussion) that we must ascribe a cylinder like Pl. XLIV*q*, which shows an Asiatic prince in a thoroughly Egyptianised setting. In the time of the Nineteenth Dynasty the same influences prevail, but the execution is much poorer; we must probably date here the seal of a man from Sidon, Pl. XLIV*p*, which shows the Egyptian god Set, brought into prominence under that Dynasty.[1] The inscribed cylinder of Pl. XLIV*u* may still belong to the fourteenth century. It comes from Damanhur in the Delta and gives the name of a servant of Adad. The "sacred tree" is of a peculiar design, remotely resembling that on seals which are probably Middle Assyrian and contemporaneous with our Text-figs. 56–9.[2] The large cylinder of Pl. XLV*a*, from Beisan, shows Ramses II practising with bow and arrow on a target mounted on a stand composed of the figures of two bound captives. This motive was introduced into Egypt by the athletic son of Thutmosis III, Amenhotep II, whose sportsmanship is celebrated with much attention to detail: "he, when he shoots at a plate of copper, cleaves it as one does a clump of papyrus. He disdains all wood, as befits his strength.... This is the great plate of mined copper at which His Majesty shot, three fingers in thickness. The hero pierced it with many shafts, three handbreadths of them standing out at the back of the plate."[3] Similar seals, or the hunting scenes which decorated Ramessid temples, and furniture (such as the painted casket of Tutankhamen) influenced the seal designs of Syrian people also; Pl. XLV*b* shows a seal found at Ras Shamra; another from the same site portrays the same god and absurdly elongated figures of archers, with the folds of Ramses' robe of Pl. XLV*a* especially emphasised or rendered as tassels.[4]

The chariot scene of Pl. XLIV*f* was also Egyptianised (Pl. XLV*m*). The Palestinian cylinders of Pl. XLIV*s* from Balata, and Pl. XLIV*t* from Tell el Ajjul, are made of glazed steatite with an incised design, a technique used for Egyptian cylinders since the Middle Kingdom. Pl. XLIV*r*, from Bethel, is interesting in that it spells out the name of the goddess Astarte in hieroglyphs. But on the whole Egyptian influence did not so much affect the design of the Palestinian cylinders as it tended to oust cylinders altogether,

[1] A similar seal belonging to the son of the owner of Pl. XLIV*p* is De Clercq, 386 *ter*.

[2] Bibliothèque Nationale, 385. Sidney Smith reads the name of the owner Iakbu-bieda (or Iakba-biefa) servant of Adad, and dates the seal about 650–600 B.C. (*Journal of Egyptian Archaeology*, VIII, 207 f.). Allbright reads the name Yakub-eda and dates it to 1800–1600 B.C. (*Journal of the Palestine Oriental Society*, XV, 217, note). Our comparison points to an intermediate date, about 1200 B.C.

[3] Norman de Garis Davies, in *Bulletin of the Metropolitan Museum of Art*, Section II, November 1935, p. 51, and Schäfer in *Orientalistische Literaturzeitung*, XXXII (1929), 233–44.

[4] *Syria*, XII, Pl. III, left half lowest impression; *Enc. Phot. de l'art*, II, 84, No. 91.

replacing them by scaraboids and stamp-seals. Pl. XLIV*o* shows a seal from Tell Abu Hawam as an example of a common local style, without clear resemblances to any better known glyptic schools and devoid of internal evidence of date, so that it can only be dated by its context. Pl. XLV*h* from the same site was found in a later layer. It shows once more that the numerous crude seals, of which date and origin are unknown, must for ever remain problematical.

Yet Pl. XLV*h* has one feature which seems characteristic of this period. The dotted background produces the effect of a textile pattern and a number of seals which seem to belong to this period possess the same characteristic. It is, for instance, pronounced in Pl. XLV*e*, *f*, *l*—the designs are, moreover, florid and elaborate (Pl. XLV*c*, *d*, *i*, *j*), or consist of a number of unconnected and partly fragmentary motives, the disintegrated products of other designs (Pl. XLV*n*). Peculiar is the occurrence of animal-headed personages; it is interesting that the Mesopotamian tradition of the Bull-men standard-bearers seems to survive (Pl. XLV*f*) though the rendering is sometimes bungled.[1] The hunter in various guises, but always carrying an animal by the hindlegs, seems common (Pl. XLV*f*, *g*), and the bull's head occurs frequently (Pl. XLV*e*, *f*, *l*). Both these motives are also known at an earlier age in Syria.[2] The Cypriote seals belong to this class. It is quite likely that some were made in Cyprus,[3] and all along the Syro-Palestine coast Cypriote pottery was imported in large quantities, but until we have more dated material from the mainland it is impossible to distinguish the two schools, especially as Syrian products were regularly copied on the island. For instance, how are we to interpret seals like Pl. XLV*g* and *i*? Equivalents are found in Cyprus, showing the same elongated figures, the upright lion, the bull-mask;[4] but Pl. XLV*f*, inseparable from the others, was found at

[1] In De Clercq, 206, their standard has become a pair of snakes, one of which a bull-masked man holds beneath the sun and crescent emblem.

[2] A clear transition from the Mitannian style to the Third Syrian group is Newell, 361.

[3] John L. Myres, *Handbook of the Cesnola Collection* (Metropolitan Museum of Art, New York, 1914), p. 434, No. 4311, resembling our Pl. XLV*g* in style, seems to bear archaic Cypriote writing.

[4] Gjerstadt, *Swedish Cyprus Expedition*, I, Pl. 67, Nos. 3, 12, from the Bronze Age shrine at Ajios Jakovos. One of these bears a cuneiform inscription but the seal is certainly not Babylonian as is asserted on p. 357. The inscription is readable on the seal itself—and therefore reversed in the impression—and seems a gratuitous addition, due perhaps to a meeting between the owner and an engraver conversant with cuneiform. The text is tentatively translated as "Milataja, the prince". They are assigned by Gjerstadt to the fourteenth century. A similar seal from Enkomi is seen in Murray, Smith and Walters, *Excavations in Cyprus*, Pl. IV, No. 743.

Ras Shamra. A certain coarse type of seal (Pl. XLVI *r*) seems to occur mainly in Cyprus and is therefore probably of local make.[1]

The Third Syrian group is heterogeneous and ill-defined. If such seals as Pl. XLV *b*, *d*, *f*, *g*, *i* can with certainty be ascribed to one period, other seals are shown by their stratigraphical position to belong here.[2] But in the absence of clear-cut characteristics the danger of survivals being considered as typical of a later period than that in which they were made is particularly great; Pl. XLV *d* may be a case in point. The products of an age which achieves nothing new nor of its own invention are difficult to recognise. As earlier limit—which of course is fluid—we have taken the destruction of Mitanni in about the middle of the fourteenth century. As a later limit we may perhaps assign the migration of the "Peoples of the Sea", which destroyed Ras Shamra about 1200 B.C. and generally upset the situation in Syria. Some characteristic work must have been produced even after this event. The seal of Pl. XLV *c*, found at Tarsus and dated by its context to approximately 1000 B.C., is probably not a survival but was most likely made about that date. The motive of the lyre-player recurs in a vase-painting from Megiddo of the same period. But the seals from Chatal Huyuk and Tell Judeideh suggest that after the invasion of the Peoples of the Sea, Syrian glyptic became again a peripheral production in the strict sense. This time the Assyrian seals were imitated in Syria, and this continued up to Hellenistic times. Even quasi-Persian cylinders are found. But just as in Palestine Egyptian influences ousted the cylinder and encouraged the use of scaraboids, so Assyrian influence tended to further the use of conical and other stamp-seals in Syria.

[1] Examples, besides those in Cesnola's *Cyprus* which are given in drawing only, are: Murray, Smith and Walters, *Excavations in Cyprus*, Pl. IV, Nos. 8, 361, 690, 745; Gjerstadt, *Swedish Cyprus Expedition*, I, Pl. 150, 15, 16; II, Pls. 186, 17–21; 243, 20, 21; Schaeffer, *Missions en Chypre*, Fig. 44 and p. 81. Myres, *Handbook of the Cesnola Collection*, pp. 439 ff.

[2] Other seals which I would ascribe to the Third group are: Brett, 93; Newell, 328, 354, 355; Dunand, *Byblos*, 1822; A–955, 1191, 1193–6. Bibliothèque Nationale, 476, 477, 478.

CHAPTER IV. INDEPENDENT GROUPS OF CYLINDERS

§ 45. THE CYLINDERS OF EGYPT

The history of the cylinder seal in Egypt provides a classical example of the influence which one cultural centre of the Ancient Near East may exercise upon another. The cylinder seal was in practical use in Egypt all through the Third Millennium B.C., and its appearance was Egyptian in every respect (Pl. XLVI *h–k*). And yet there can be no doubt that in adopting the cylinder seal during the First Dynasty, Egypt followed a Mesopotamian example. But here, as in many other fields, the stimulus received in the course of contact did not lead to slavish copying; not a single Egyptian cylinder can be called an imitation of a Mesopotamian seal. Yet we know that at the time when Egyptian cylinders were first made, Mesopotamian cylinders had already been imported into the Nile valley. Thus they form part of that much increased body of evidence, which establishes beyond possibility of doubt that Egypt and Mesopotamia were in contact during the formative phase of Egyptian culture, and that the latter derived a powerful stimulus from impact with foreign conceptions at a time of heightened creative power.

Our increased knowledge of early Mesopotamian archaeology has not only added to the list of specific instances when the influence of Asiatic examples can be traced in the Nile valley, it has also revealed which precise stages of the two civilisations were involved in the process. The artistic motives and technical devices which Egypt derived during the late pre-Dynastic age and under the early kings of the First Dynasty, from intercourse with Asia, are now recognised as pointing consistently to the Jemdet Nasr period. This again agrees well with the independent evidence supplied by the tablets and cylinder seals of that age which are found in Persia, North Syria, Anatolia and even on the Cyclades, and which prove that the Jemdet Nasr period was an age of Mesopotamian expansion in all directions (§ 35, p. 277). The Mesopotamian cylinder seals found in Egypt thus fit perfectly into the picture of the times.[1]

[1] A comprehensive discussion of the evidence is contributed by Scharff, *Zeitschrift für Aegyptische Sprache*, LXXI, 89–106, to which can be added evidence from the latest discoveries at Warka (*Uruk Vorläufiger Bericht*, VIII, Abh. Preuss. Akademie, 1936, Abh. no. 13), which confirms Egyptian recessed building with sun-dried bricks as dependent on that of the Jemdet Nasr period in Mesopotamia. As to Scharff's synchronisms, I am

Only one of these is derived from regular excavations (Pl. XLVI *a*). It was found at Naqada in a tomb which, Sir Flinders Petrie kindly informs me, contained merely two pots beside this seal and its beads. Their types[1] date the interment to the latter part of the Gerzean or to the late pre-Dynastic period. The cylinder is a typical Mesopotamian specimen of the Jemdet Nasr age, as a comparison with Pls. VII *b*, VIII *a* will show. Some other cylinders belong to the same context. Pl. XLVI *b* shows a somewhat disintegrated version of the "eye"-motive combined with fishes, as is not unusual on Jemdet Nasr seals (Pl. VIII *a*). The material, moreover, is grey limestone, rare in Egypt, and for that matter, in Mesopotamia—except in the Jemdet Nasr period when it was common. This seal was bought in 1901 at Luxor before any Jemdet Nasr remains had been unearthed, so that it was most likely found in one of the numerous pre-Dynastic tombs which were being rifled by illicit diggers at that time. The same applies to another cylinder, bought at Luxor in 1911, of a design which can be matched by seals found at Fara and Telloh and covered with a blue glaze which is decidedly un-Egyptian.[2]

No cylinder made in Egypt can be proved to antedate the First Dynasty.[3] When they do appear they are of two types.

One of them is short and squat (Pl. XLVI *c*, *d*, *f*), a shape not known in Mesopotamia after the Jemdet Nasr period (Pls. I *e*, *j*; VIII *b*–*i*). No impressions of this type have been found in Egypt, and it is therefore likely that they served another purpose; since they are found in graves, they may well have been funerary amulets, especially as they often show a figure at a table loaded with loaves of bread (Pl. XLVI *d*, *f*), and this theme was the first to be depicted in the Mastaba tombs when reliefs were introduced—early in the Old Kingdom. A seal like that of Pl. XLVI *d*, with a figure sitting upon a bed and stretching his hand to the table of food, plainly

satisfied that his table should be simplified, and the Jemdet Nasr period (including Warka, II–III) made contemporaneous with the late pre-Dynastic period (Semainean) in Egypt. His view of the dependence of the Egyptian seal designs on those of Mesopotamia (pp. 102 ff.) does not quite tally with the one I hold to be correct, partly because the First Early Dynastic and the Jemdet Nasr periods could not be properly distinguished at the time of his writing.

[1] The types were B 53*a* and P 57*b*, with a range of Sequence Date 38–66 and 48–74 respectively.

[2] The glaze is deep dark blue. See Scharff, *Altertümer der Vor- und Frühzeit Aegyptens*, II, 99, No. 137. The best Mesopotamian parallel is found in H. de Genouillac, *Fouilles de Telloh*, Pl. 39, 1, 2. But also Heinrich, *Fara*, Pl. 69*b*.

[3] Childe, *The most Ancient East*, p. 101, erroneously ascribes the seal of Randall-MacIver and Mace, *El Amrah and Abydos*, p. 13 and Pl. VI, 6, to the pre-Dynastic age. It belongs to the latter part of the First Dynasty.

illustrates the exhortation of the ritual of the dead preserved in many variations of the Pyramid texts, in which the deceased is treated as a sleeper who is called to go to table.[1] "Ho, King Pepi!... Raise thee up! Arise! Sit down to thy thousand of bread, thy thousand of beer, etc."[2]

It is, on the other hand, quite obvious that the figure of Pl. XLVI *c*, seated upon a couch, resembles those of Pl. VIII *c*, *d*, *f* and these constitute the standard designs of just those squat Mesopotamian seals which are the most likely prototypes of the Egyptian cylinders. Then we notice once again the mechanism of Egyptian derivation, which did not consist in a mere imitation of foreign customs, but utilised certain suggestions for the expression of indigenous thought, or for some technical requirement which happened not yet to have found fulfilment.

Exactly the same argument applies to the second class of early Egyptian cylinders, namely those actually used as seals and known to us through their impressions. It is significant that their use in Egypt is the same as that prevailing in Mesopotamia throughout the Jemdet Nasr and Early Dynastic periods. They were employed to seal packages and jars containing stores or merchandise (Pl. XLVI *g* and Text-fig. 1). Occasionally the design of these Egyptian seals reflects the most common Mesopotamian animals in file, but this motive is rare[3] and the new device is so forcefully integrated into Egyptian civilisation, that the majority of these Early Dynastic seals do not show a trace of foreign influence. They are made, not as mere ornaments, but sensibly, as objects of daily use, from material never, to our knowledge, employed in Mesopotamia for this purpose, namely hard wood (Pl. XLVI *e*) and ivory. The notion of the cylindrical seal was borrowed; the realisation of the idea was entirely Egyptian. For the seal designs are the earliest existing examples of hieroglyphic writing (Text-figs. 94–98). They contain short inscriptions, as yet largely unintelligible, often consisting of a king's name with the titles of his officials.

[1] Kees, *Totenglauben und Jenseitsvorstellungen der Aegypter*, pp. 24 f., shows that these spells apply to conditions more primitive than those of the Old Kingdom, and, in fact, prevalent in predynastic times.

[2] After Breasted, *Development of Religion and Thought*, p. 132. As to the designs of these amuletic seals, it deserves notice that the symbol of the goddess Neith worshipped in Sais, in the Western Delta, frequently occurs (Pl. XLVI *c*). See Petrie, *Scarabs and Cylinders with Names*, Pls. I–V. The transcriptions and translations of the hieroglyphs appearing on these seals are purely conjectural.

[3] Scharff, *Altertümer der Vor- und Frühzeit Aegyptens*, II, No. 134; Petrie, *Royal Tombs*, II, Pl. XIV, Nos. 101–4, all, as Scharff points out, belonging to the early part of the First Dynasty. Also Ayrton and Coat, *El Mahasna*, Pl. XXVII, 1.

These cylinders of the First Dynasty differ not in principle but in quality from those in regular use during the Old Kingdom (Pl. XLVI *h–k*). The cylinders of the later reigns of the First Dynasty (Text-fig. 96) show a great advance in clearness and sense of composition when compared with the

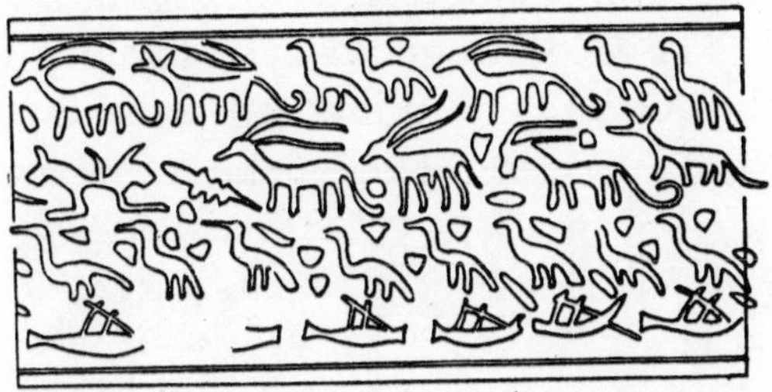

Text-fig. 93. Sealing from the tomb of Aha.

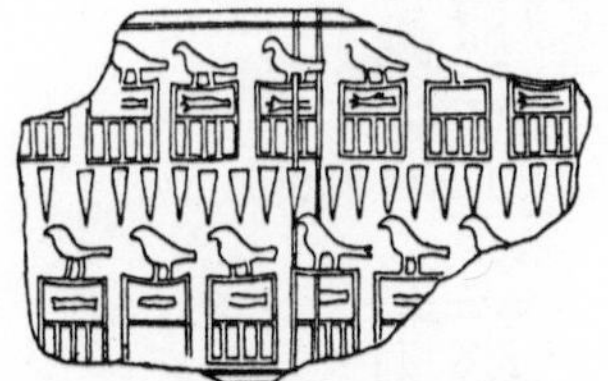

Text-fig. 94. Sealing from the tomb of Narmer.

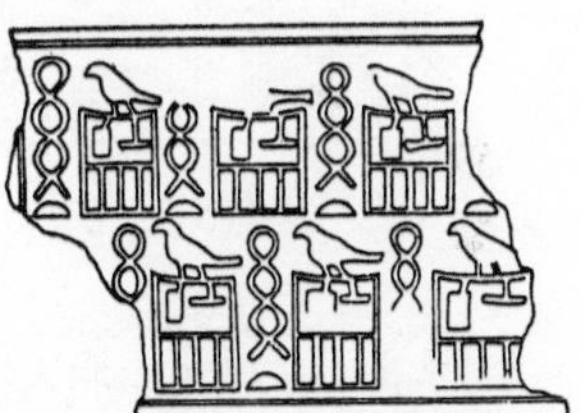

Text-fig. 95. Sealing from the tomb of Aha.

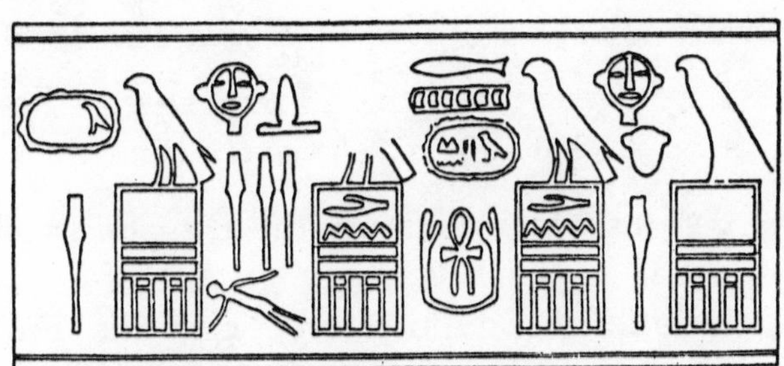

Text-fig. 96. Sealing from the tomb of Den.

earlier examples (Text-figs. 94, 95). In the seals of the Second Dynasty (Text-figs. 97, 98) this is carried still further, till the classical period of the Old Kingdom brings balance and clarity to perfection (Pl. XLVI *h–k*).

There is a group of cylinders of which it would be difficult to say whether they belong to the amulet class or to the seals. They show the squat shape of the first and the hieroglyphic inscription of the latter, though they lack royal names.[1]

[1] E.g. Petrie, *Scarabs and Cylinders with Names*, Pls. IV, V.

Already during the First Dynasty seals with purely decorative designs disappear. The cylinders are engraved with writing alone; if they are official, they give either the name of the king and the title of the officer but not his personal name, or they only name the office. The shape also differs considerably from that used in Mesopotamia throughout, and in Egypt during the First Dynasty. The Old Kingdom cylinders are tall tubes with very wide perforations (Pl. XLVI *i*). But it is especially the complete absence of

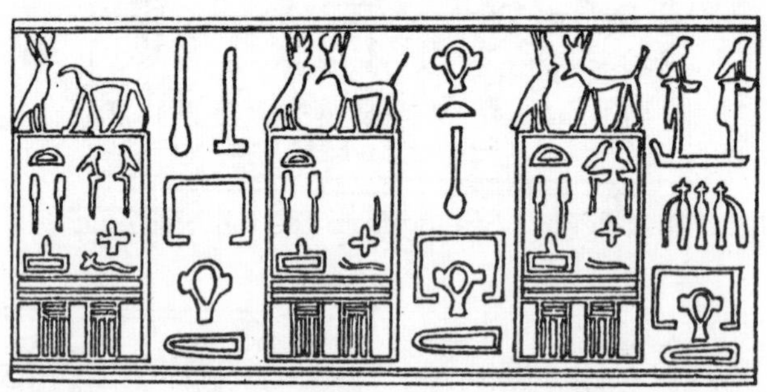

Text-fig. 97. Sealing from the tomb of Khasekhemuy.

Text-fig. 98. Sealing from the tomb of Khasekhemuy.

purely decorative designs which contrasts the Egyptian seals with those of Mesopotamia.

Decoration again entered Egyptian glyptic in the First Intermediate period (2300–2050 B.C.),[1] a time of confusion when the central authority, after the ninety-four years of rule of Pepi II, collapsed, Beduin overran the Delta and disaffection shook the unity of the country. Text-fig. 99 shows a cylinder originally cut for an official of Pepi I; on the space left over by the inscription a barbaric design is engraved, resembling in many details the patterns of the button-shaped stamp-seals which are found all through Egypt from the latter part of the Sixth Dynasty on-

[1] This event and all the difficult problems connected with it, including absolute chronology, has recently been much illuminated by Scharff in *Sitzungsberichte der Bayerischen Akademie der Wissenschaften*, Phil.-Hist. Abt. 1936, Heft 8.

wards.[1] These objects are unconnected with anything known in Egypt before the First Intermediate period. Their designs are on the other hand related with the stamp-seals of Syria and Crete.[2] The Egyptian examples are not on the whole importations, and Egyptian motives do enter into their decoration, but other elements of design and shape, and even the fundamental idea of using a stamp-seal, are of Asiatic derivation. There, again, the Egyptian adapted a foreign suggestion so thoroughly to his own usage that the fact of alien origin soon became entirely irrelevant. The earliest scarabs[3] show on their base engraved patterns resembling those of the "button-seals"; their shape is merely one out of several varieties of stamp-seals with animal-shaped handle and engraved base. It is perhaps fatuous to speculate why this shape should have been adopted to the exclusion of all the others, which do not survive the First Intermediate period.[4] What matters is that the Egyptians realised the practical advantage of using a small signet instead of the cumbersome roll as a seal, since they wrote on papyrus and not on clay like the Mesopotamians, and secured their documents and packages with sealings not larger than those which we employ.

Text-fig. 99. Seal of an official of Pepi I.

It is quite immaterial whether these "buttons" had been used as seals in Syria. Brunton has pointed out that even in Egypt many must have been amulets. But one actual impression of a "button-seal" is known;[5] and it can be proved, as we have seen, that these small engraved objects decisively influenced the Egyptian use of seals. The seal cylinder, practical for the safe-guarding of stores by sealing the mud-covering of jars and baskets, was also

[1] These have been fully discussed by Guy Brunton in *Qau and Badari*, I, 55–8. See also the many illustrations in Flinders Petrie, *Buttons and Design-Scarabs*. The drawing of Text-fig. 99 was kindly supplied by Professor Percy L. Newberry.

[2] See F. Matz, *Frühkretische Siegel*, pp. 30–8.

[3] Brunton, *Qau and Badari*, I, 56.

[4] The two most obvious explanations are, for the realist, the fact that the compact shape of the beetle made the seals less liable to be damaged when worn on the person or impressed on the clay, than the thin buttons or the stamp-seals of elaborate shape, like sitting men; and on the other hand there is a magico-religious relation between the beetle, symbolical of the Sun-god, propelling his ball of dung, and the application of a beetle-shaped seal to a small lump of sealing-clay.

[5] Brunton, *loc. cit.* Brunton prefers the term "seal-amulet" since many shapes occur beside the most common "button".

practical as a legal instrument in Mesopotamia where clay tablets were in use. In Egypt this secondary use of the cylinder was not so well correlated with the writing material; but it was not before the First Intermediate period that the introduction of the Asiatic "button-seals" brought about a change. And just as the early cylinders of Egypt possess a character of their own and do not strike one as imitations of Asiatic seals, so also the Egyptian stamp-seals are, on the whole, unlike the Syrian signets, and with the universal and exclusive adoption of the scarab shape they became a class *sui generis*.

The cylinder, being the prevalent seal form of Egypt at the time when the foreign influences made themselves felt, was also affected. In Text-fig. 99 curious outlandish motives have been added to the blank space of a seal of the ordinary Old Kingdom type. Eventually a number of cylinders were made which were entirely decorated with designs derived from the repertoire of the "button-seals". They are often merely barbaric versions of Egyptian designs (Pl. XLVI *l*, *m*, *n*). We notice two Seth-animals facing a Ded-pillar, an uraeus rising up in front, and beneath them an acrobat and a dwarf with a baboon, figures which are known from Egyptian funerary reliefs. Next comes the bee, in the shape of the hieroglyph with which the King of Lower Egypt is named; then follows a crocodile or lizard and above it a monogram consisting (as more detailed examples show)[1] of the head of the goddess Hathor as a centre, two foreparts of bulls below, and two squatting lions facing each other, above; the lions' forelegs are at the same time the horns of Hathor. This seal is also decorated on the two ends (Pl. XLVI *m*, *n*), a feature which recurs on a closely related Asiatic cylinder.[2] Several cylinders and "buttons" are known with designs of this type.[3] The monogrammatic

[1] *Zeitschrift für Aegyptische Sprache*, LXVII (1931), 95 ff.

[2] Ashmolean Museum, 21–1199; Matz, *Frühkretische Siegel*, p. 71, calls it Hittite but it was bought in Cairo. See Evans, *Palace of Minos*, IV, II, 506, note 3. Von Bissing, *Zeitschrift für Aegyptische Sprache*, LXXI (1935), 677, has erroneously considered this feature an argument against a Third Millennium date. It commonly occurs on seals of the First Early Dynastic period from Ur, Legrain, *Ur Excavations*, *Archaic Seal Impressions*, p. 8 and Plates, *passim*, and occasionally somewhat later as on a similar cylinder from Tell Agrab, or even somewhat earlier, as on the Syrian seal of the Jemdet Nasr period in Hogarth, *Hittite Seals*, pp. 5–6, Fig. 58.

[3] They were figured and discussed by Scharff in *Zeitschrift für Aegyptische Sprache*, LXVII (1931), 95–102, and *Altertümer der Vor- und Frühzeit Aegyptens*, II, pp. 95–7; he rightly rejects the view expressed by me some twelve years ago in *Studies of Early Pottery of the Near East*, I, 132. See further seals of this class in Petrie, *Scarabs and Cylinders with Names*, Pl. VI, Nos. 140, 147; Pl. VII, No. 174 and probably 163; Reisner, *Mycerinus*, Pl. 64*j*, *h*; Jéquier, *Les Pyramides des Reines Neit et Apouit* (Fouilles de Saqqarah, 1933), p. 33, Fig. 16. Brunton, *Mostagedda*, Pl. LX, 2, from a grave assigned to the 5th Dynasty, shows Egyptian motives only. The appearance of a cylinder with designs at that time may be explained by the sudden increase of amulets in the late Fifth Dynasty (Brunton, *Gau and Badari*, I, 74).

coalescence of signs is un-Egyptian, as is also the fact that these seals display a decorative design, as distinct from a decorative inscription; for such designs had not, as we saw, been used since the early years of the First Dynasty in Egypt (Text-fig. 93). Even on such cylinders as Pl. XLVI *l* most of the motives recall, more or less distinctively, hieroglyphic signs, but they are not, as far as we can say, used in the manner of writing-signs; once a badly written inscription appears separately amongst them.[1] These cylinders and the stamp-seals with which they are related were probably produced mainly in the Western Delta. The graphic combination of two foreparts of bulls occurs on a late pre-Dynastic palette, which can be shown to be derived from Lower Egypt, and the bee and Hathor head point in the same direction;[2] it was, indeed, at all times the Delta which was most exposed to foreign influence and immigration.

Text-fig. 100. Seal of Amenemhet III.

At the end of the First Intermediate period the cylinder seal had lost its predominance. It is impossible to say whether the cylinders with names of kings of the Twelfth Dynasty (Text-figs. 100, 101) were seals, amulets or ornaments. They somewhat resemble decorated beads, and a fourfold cylinder, such as Pl. XLVI *o*, *p*, *q*, cannot have been employed as a seal. The official seals, in any case, seem to have been signet rings, these at least being in use during the New Kingdom.[3] Cylinders with royal names of the Middle Kingdom, whatever their purpose, are not rare (Text-figs. 100, 101)—they were even found at Byblos,[4] but the scarabs exceed them in numbers.

A not inconsiderable number of Babylonian cylinders of the early part of the Second Millennium were imported into Egypt,[5] but they had no effect on

[1] Berlin, 15399 (Scharff, *Zeitschrift für Aegyptische Sprache*, LXVII (1931), 95, abb. 62).

[2] Scharff, *Zeitschrift für Aegyptische Sprache*, LXVII (1931), 99–102.

[3] Newberry, *Scarabs*, Pl. II.

[4] Dunand, *Byblos*, I, No. 1551.

[5] One of these in *Proceedings of the Society of Biblical Archaeology*, XXXIII (1911), Pl. LI. (1) is a Syrian version of an Early Dynastic cylinder; (2) is perhaps a Syrian or, more likely, a modern imitation and (3) is somewhat strange too and made of carnelian which is rarely used in Babylonian times. A group from Memphis was published in the *Journal of Egyptian Archaeology*, VIII, Pl. XXXIII, 2–5. Another set was found at El-Tud, *Illustrated London News*, 18 April 1936, pp. 682 ff., or *Archiv für Orientforschung*, XI, 182, Fig. 6. One of the seals from Memphis belonged to a man whose name in cuneiform reads "Shukur-ili son of Akkutahu". Mr Sidney Smith is inclined to accept Sayce's identification of "Shukur" in the man's name, with that of the Memphite god Sokaris, Shukur-ili being a theophorous name of a common type (Sokaris is my god). The scene is a purely Babylonian presentation scene, of the type used during the Third Dynasty of Ur or the early part of the Isin-Larsa period; the figures of the scene are conventional and cannot, therefore, be identified. But the following remarks of Mr Smith are well worth quoting, since the conclusion seems

local glyptic art. Some glazed cylinders with figures were incised in the Hyksos period (Pl. XLVI *t*, *u*), two naming King Khian.[1] In later times royal or private names were occasionally inscribed on a cylinder seal,[2] but

Text-fig. 101. Seal of Sebekneferu.

these strike us as mere curios. In Egypt the cylinder *seal* did not survive the invention of the scarab.

There is also an Egyptian peripheral style of which Pl. XLI *p*, *q* and Pl. XLV *a* may be considered examples, but for the most part Egyptian influence in Palestine affects, as we have seen, the details of designs which remain Babylonian in general arrangement and character. A curious early seal cylinder was found at Byblos; there the design consists entirely of hieroglyphs, but the provincial character of the work prevents our understanding its meaning.[3]

§ 46. THE CYLINDERS OF THE AEGEAN

The astounding richness of Cretan glyptic falls outside the scope of this book. The cylinders used from the Third Early Minoan period onward are not engraved on the circumference but on both ends, and the perforation does

inevitable. "Apparently the son of a Syrian, born and settled in Egypt, owns a Babylonian cylinder seal of good workmanship....The seal can only have belonged to a man who perpetually needed it for sealing legal documents written on clay, in other words to a man employed in constant trade with Babylonia or Mesopotamia. Was Shukur-ili actually the agent of some Babylonian firm?"

[1] The cylinders of Khian are figured in Newberry, *Scarabs*, Pl. VII, 7, 10. Others from the Hyksos period, *ibid.* Nos. 8, 9, 11–13; *Journal of Egyptian Archaeology*, VIII, Pl. XX, 3, 4.

[2] Newberry, *Scarabs*, Pl. VIII, 3, Amenhotep III and Tiy; *ibid.* 7, Seti I; Hall, *Catalogue of Egyptian Scarabs in the British Museum*, Nos. 2647–2649, Amenhotep III and Shabaka.

[3] Montet, *Byblos et l'Égypte*, pp. 61–8 and Pl. XXXIX. Probably made during the Old Kingdom.

not coincide with the axis but passes at right angles to it (Text-figs. 102–4). The design was stamped in the clay; and pyramidical, button-shaped or other stamp-seals were found along with these cylinders.[1] The signet remained the usual form of the Aegean seal.

The curious cylinder of green steatite (Pls. XXXVIII *e*; XLVI *v*) is an exceptional Aegean product. It represents an ordinary Syrian type (Pl. I *d*) and the design resembles that of a number of cylinders of the same shape in the Aleppo Museum. But the tangents of Pl. XLVI *v*, which seem to be a

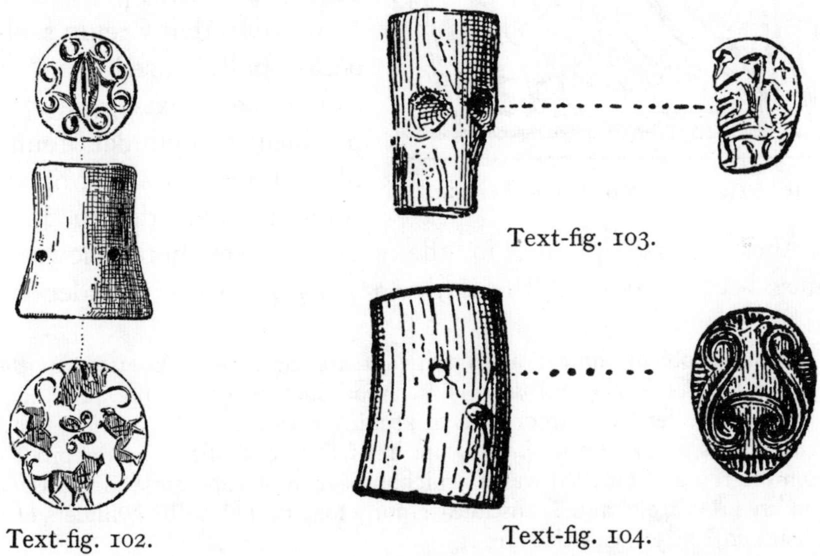

Text-fig. 103.

Text-fig. 102.

Text-fig. 104.

Text-figs. 102–4. Cretan cylinders (Text-fig. 102 from Porti, Text-figs. 103, 104 from Mochlos).

diffident attempt to convert the concentric circles into a spiraliform design, can only be explained by the assumption that the seal was cut on the island where it was found, and where the earliest population contained elements derived from the European mainland as well as immigrants from Asia; the first used spiral designs to decorate their pottery, and the concentric circles with tangents are the normal disintegration product of the spiral. It is an important document, for the excavation of Tell Judeideh shows that this type of seal did not remain in use in Syria after the Jemdet Nasr period. Amorgos, on the other hand, seems not to have been inhabited before or after the First Early Cycladic period. The cylinder thus confirms the view,

[1] The intricate network of affinities which connect these early Cretan seals with Africa and Asia has been studied in detail by F. Matz, *Frühkretische Siegel* (Berlin, 1928).

that the beginning of the Copper Age in Greece cannot be put much later than 3000 B.C.[1]

During the next period of Mesopotamian expansion, the First Babylonian Dynasty, a number of cylinders reached Crete, without, however, in the least influencing native glyptic.[2] A few Syrian seals were also found there,[3] but it was only during the latest phase of Minoan civilisation that Cretan seal-cutters occasionally used the cylinder form. In Text-fig. 105 we reproduce a cylinder found in a Mycenaean (Late Minoan III) context. The design is entirely Cretan, the papyrus plants, in the curious form here shown, having long since become part of the native repertoire. This cylinder is closely

Text-fig. 105. Seal from Hagia Pelagia.

[1] The various problems hinted at in the text are more fully discussed in the second volume of my *Studies in Early Pottery of the Near East*, especially pp. 42 ff., 49, 50. The evidence of the cylinder from Amorgos is in keeping with recent discoveries—see Winifred Lamb, *Excavations at Thermi in Lesbos*, pp. 210 f. The cylinder is better proof than the distribution of grey and mottled wares, which appear in Mesopotamia in the Uruk period, but were in use in Anatolia and Transcaucasia for a long period, while cylinders of this type fell into disuse in Early Dynastic times.

[2] Several seals found in the Aegean are either too much damaged or too coarse for it to be possible to determine their date or country of origin. The the first class belong *Annual of the British School at Athens*, XXVIII (1926–7), 262 and Pl. 19; Seager, *Mochlos*, Fig. 36, I and p. iii. To the second belong: *Ephemeris Archaeologike*, 1888, Pl. 10, No. 38 from Mycenae, and *Annual of the British School at Athens*, XXVIII (1926–7), 262 from Mavro Spelion. A cylinder from a late Mycenaean tomb at Ialyssos in Rhodes is evidently a peripheral Anatolian or Syrian seal (*Annuario*, 6–7 (1923–4), 127, Fig. 47). Babylonian seals, in the advanced style of the Hammurabi Dynasty are: Evans, *Palace of Minos*, I, 198, Fig. 146; only one male bearded figure and an interceding goddess; *ibid.* II, 1, p. 265, Fig. 158, of Apillim, son of Marduk "mu-Salim, servant of Nabu"; it shows sun, mountain and fringe of robes reduced to a series of drill-holes, as in our Pl. XXX*c–f*.

[3] A fine lapis lazuli cylinder set in gold found at Knossos is only published in drawings (Evans, *Palace of Minos*, IV, 2, Figs. 349, 350). It seems to belong to the First Syrian group, showing a sphinx, the griffin-demon of our Pl. XLI*h, l*, and the full-face (here drawn as a lion head) which is so common there. Unfortunately its stratification is not absolutely certain, but its proximity in the soil to an alabaster vase-lid inscribed with the name of the Hyksos King Khian (Fimmen, *Kretisch-Mykenische Kultur*, p. 170, note 1) and Sir Arthur Evans' statement (*loc. cit.* p. 425) that it was found near a deposit of the Third Middle Minoan period, tally well with its affinities with the First Syrian group.

related to Minoan frescoes and signets. The cylinder of Text-fig. 106 is less well executed, and cannot be dated; the same applies to two carnelian cylinders found in Eastern Crete, one showing an octopus, bull's head and plants, the other a series of dolphins.[1]

On other Cretan seals of this age[2] a curious monster appears, which was derived from the beneficial Egyptian goddess Taurt, and retained the hippopotamus head and crocodile tail.[3] We illustrate it on a cylinder discovered

Text-fig. 106. Seal from the harbour town of Knossos.

in Cyprus (Pl. XLVI *s*), which shows a number of Aegean motives with great clearness. It is found in circumstances which are inconclusive as to its age.[4]

The figure between the lions shows a Cretan contour, the lions with fore-feet on a concave support are known on Cretan seals as well as on the gate of the Acropolis at Mycenae. The antithetical birds and the griffin may be derived from Crete as well as from Syria, and while the head beneath one of the lions is taken from Syrian glyptic, the dolphin below the other belongs as certainly to the Aegean.

In Cyprus, from which the Asiatic mountains can be seen on clear days, Syrian cylinder seals were known and imitated. Pl. XLVI *r* shows a Cypriote seal with typical designs; they are coarse little objects. With the better cylinders it is at present impossible to separate those made in Syria

[1] Evans, *Palace of Minos,* IV, 2, Figs. 434, 435. *Ibid.* Figs. 338, 339, are hybrids and undateable.

[2] Evans, *Palace of Minos,* IV, 2, p. 459, Fig. 383, and *Annual of the British School at Athens,* VIII, 302, Fig. 18. The first shows two goats, recalling popular Mitannian seals (our Pl. XLIII *f*), a man pouring libations and a Bull-man of Asiatic affinities beside the Cretan demon and an obviously Cretan man.

[3] The literature on this demon is collected by Sir Arthur Evans, *Palace of Minos,* IV, 2, pp. 431 ff.

[4] C. F. A. Schaeffer, *Missions en Chypre,* p. 89.

and those made in Cyprus in imitation of such seals as our Pl. XLV*g*, *i*. But Text-fig. 107 shows a seal found in Eastern Crete as an example of the glyptic style coexistent with the Mycenaean pottery used throughout the Aegean and on the Syrian coasts in the thirteenth century. The winged disk

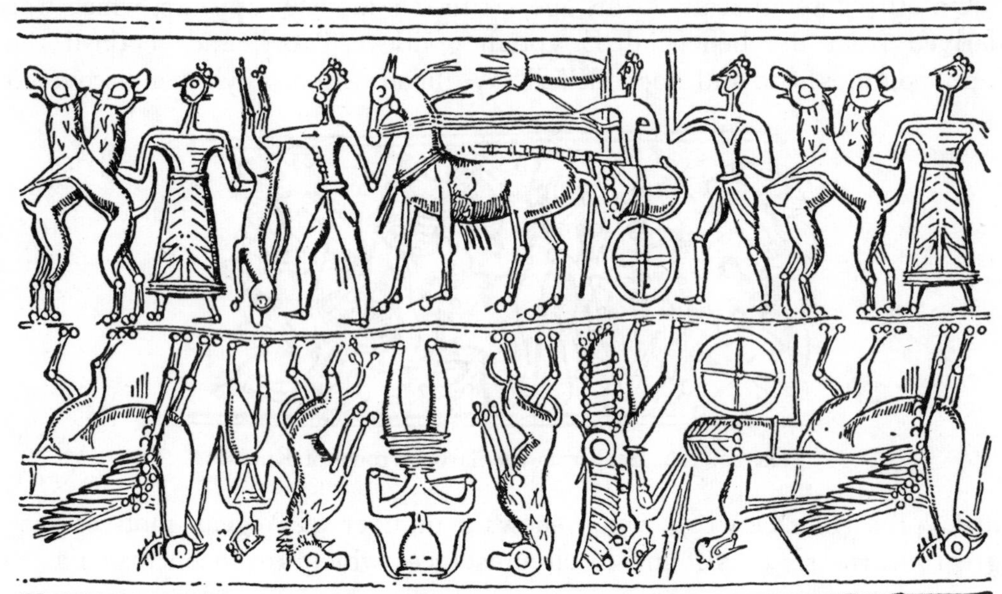

Text-fig. 107. Cylinder from Astrakous.

and the goddess holding a gazelle by the hindleg are derived from Syria, the squid in front of the charioteer from Crete; the chariots as we have seen are common in Syria, but also occur in Mycenaean frescoes and on the Mycenaean pottery from Cyprus. Products of this type[1] are the last representations of this ancient form of seal in the Aegean.

§ 47. THE CYLINDERS OF INDIA

The Indus civilisation used the signet, but knew the cylinder seal. Whether the five tall ivory cylinders tentatively explained as seals in Sir John Marshall's work were used for that purpose remains uncertain. They have nothing in common with the seal cylinders of the Near East.[2] In the upper layers of Mohenjo Daro, however, three seal cylinders were found.[3] The published specimen shows two animals with birds upon their backs, a snake

[1] Cf. A–1191.

[2] *Mohenjo Daro and the Indus Civilisation*, p. 371 and Pl. CXIV, 529–33.

[3] Ernest Mackay, *The Indus Civilisation* (London, 1935), p. 192 and Pl. M 10, 11.

and a small conventional tree. It is an inferior piece of work which displays none of the characteristics of the finely engraved stamp-seals which are so distinctive a feature of early Indian remains.

Another cylinder of glazed steatite was discovered at Tell Asmar in Iraq, but here the peculiarities of design, as well as the subject, show such close resemblances to the seals from the Indus valley that its Indian origin is certain (Text-fig. 108). The elephant, rhinoceros and crocodile (gharial), foreign to Babylonia, were obviously carved by an artist to whom they were familiar, as appears from the faithful rendering of the skin of the rhinoceros (closely resembling plate-armour) and the sloping back and bulbous forehead of the elephant. Certain other peculiarities of style connect the seal as definitely with the Indus civilisation as if it actually bore the signs of the Indus script. Such is the convention by which the feet of the elephant are rendered and the network of lines, in other Indian seals mostly confined to to the ears, but extending here over the whole of his head and trunk. The setting of the ears of the rhinoceros on two little stems is also a feature connecting this cylinder with the Indus valley seals.[1]

Text-fig. 108. Imported Indian seal from Tell Asmar.

A similar procession of animals, with a gharial placed above them, appears on a seal impression at Mohenjo Daro[2], and this and others of these impressions may well be derived from cylinders.

Three other seals found in Babylonia are also probably of Indian manufacture.[3] One of these, which comes from Ur, shows a Brahmani bull at its manger, a typically Indian subject. It has, moreover, grooves at each end "with the outer edges nicked, probably to be fitted with metal caps". Similar but deeper grooves occur on the seal from Tell Asmar, a feature decidedly foreign to Mesopotamia.[4] The seal from Ur shows, however, a scorpion beside the bull and that creature, so frequently depicted in Mesopotamia, occurs neither on the Indus seals nor among the signs of the Indus script. The design of the seal from Ur thus supports the view that Mesopotamian influence accounts for the use of the cylinder in India and its extreme

[1] *Oriental Institute Communications*, No. 16, p. 52.

[2] Sir John Marshall, *loc. cit.* Pl. CXVI, 14.

[3] De Clercq, 26, identified by Mlle Corbiau in *Iraq*, III, 100 ff.; and C. J. Gadd, "Seals of Ancient Indian style found at Ur", *Proceedings of the British Academy*, XVIII, Pl. I, 6, 7.

[4] In the Jemdet Nasr period, when the seal-cutters experimented a great deal, this peculiarity is also occasionally found (Pl. I*m*), but never, as far as I know, after that time.

rarity compared with the signet, a conclusion which is by no means invalidated by the dissimilarity of the designs in general. We have noticed the same divergence in Egypt and in Crete, where the introduction of the seal cylinder is demonstrably due to Asiatic influence. In Syria alone were found close imitations of Mesopotamian seals; in India, Egypt and Crete the mere suggestion that an engraved cylinder might be used as a seal was accepted, but put into practice with the independence characteristic of the Ancient Near East whenever foreign inventions were adopted.

The influence exercised by Mesopotamia on the Indus valley may be of a twofold nature. We have definite proof of commercial intercourse during the middle of the Third Millennium B.C., for in the private houses of the ancient city of Eshnunna (Tell Asmar) which were built during the Sargonid Dynasty we found not only the cylinder of Text-fig. 108 but pottery, beads, a stamp-seal and various pieces of inlay, all of Indian origin.

Carnelian beads with etched designs occur in both earlier and later contexts in Mesopotamia, namely in graves of the Third Early Dynastic and of the Isin-Larsa periods.[1] The Indian cylinder from Ur, which we have discussed above, probably belongs to the latter age.[2]

But signs of intercourse, or at least similarities of culture, are not lacking in earlier periods. The Indian remains cannot, unfortunately, be subdivided; they are homogeneous throughout and must be assigned to the second quarter of the Third Millennium B.C. At Tell Agrab in Mesopotamia, however, a steatite vase was discovered which belongs to the Second or First Early Dynastic period; it is entirely Mesopotamian in execution and in certain details of its design—such as the type of the human figure—yet it shows besides a building which shelters a Brahmani bull standing in front of its manger.[3] Later we discovered at the same site a similar design on a pot of "scarlet ware", a fabric only made during the First Early Dynastic period.[4]

[1] These beads have been studied by Dr Ernest Mackay in the *Journal of the American Oriental Society*, LVII (1937), 1–15; and by Mr Horace C. Beck, *Antiquaries Journal*, XIII (1933), 384–98, especially Pl. LXVI, Fig. 8, and p. 389.

[2] C. J. Gadd, *loc. cit.* p. 8. Sir Leonard Woolley's assignation of some tombs at Ur to the enigmatical "Second Dynasty" would affect us in so far as one of them contained an Indian stamp-seal, but as a matter of fact there is complete agreement with the evidence from Tell Asmar, since these "Second Dynasty" tombs belong to the period of Sargon of Akkad. See *Journal of the Royal Asiatic Society*, 1937, pp. 334 ff.

[3] *Illustrated London News*, 12 September 1936, p. 134, Figs. 10, 11. Mr Gadd, *loc. cit.* p. 8, note 2, points out that at Mohenjo Daro it is the short-horned bull and not the humped bull which is depicted with a manger; and on the pot from Tell Agrab quoted in the following note we see a short-horned bull tethered in a building, but here without a manger.

[4] *Illustrated London News*, 6 November 1937, Pl. I.

Finally, there is the seal of Pl. VI *c*, undoubtedly belonging to the Jemdet Nasr age, as its technique and the tree-and-mountain design make clear, and yet it depicts a monster which is unique in Mesopotamian art but well known in the Indus civilisation, a bull with an elephant's trunk.[1] On the other hand, a type of Bull-man reminiscent of Mesopotamia occurs at Mohenjo Daro.[2] It is just possible that here too we find traces of contact and trade of which no other evidence has come down to us, but this seems unlikely. Some years ago a more comprehensive analysis of the available material led to the conclusion that "an important element in the population of the two regions belonged originally to a common stock. We have noticed in discussing architecture and metrology, religious monuments and seal designs, that the suggestion of a common substratum for certain cultural traits in India and Mesopotamia has as it were been forced upon us by the various similarities which could not adequately be explained as being due to commercial intercourse, or to other factors active in the one period in which we have any knowledge of the Indus civilisation."[3] Since the seal cylinder was used in Mesopotamia from the Uruk period onwards, it may have spread throughout the cultural continuum which, in the Al 'Ubaid period, extended from the Tigris to the Indus, formed the homeland of the earliest settlers in the Mesopotamian Plain and was only destroyed by the progressive desiccation of the Iranian Highlands.

We do not know the rate of its progress. But if the seal cylinder belonged, together with a variety of other inventions, to the common stock of the Indus and Mesopotamian civilisations, then the discovery of earlier remains than any yet found at Mohenjo Daro, Harappa or Chanhu Daro should reveal a more extensive use of the cylinder seal in India.

[1] Marshall, *loc. cit.* Pl. CXII, pp. 377–81.

[2] Marshall, *loc. cit.* Pl. CXI, pp. 356–7.

[3] *Annual Bibliography of Indian Archaeology for the year* 1932 (Leiden, 1934), p. 11.

EPILOGUE

IT MAY be true that elsewhere glyptic art reflects the great works of contemporary sculpture and painting, but in Mesopotamia the situation is reversed. From Early Dynastic times decorative art in all its branches utilised the inventions of the seal-cutters. The great tableaux of the Assyrian royal palaces represent an entirely new artistic conception in the ancient world, but in the history of art these magnificent works remain isolated, except in so far as Persian glyptic carries their relative freedom westwards, to return, enriched an hundredfold in such works as shown in Pl. XXXVII *i*.

The applied arts, with glyptic art at their head, not only fully represented the artistic genius of Mesopotamia, but were the vehicle by which it influenced the outside world. In this respect the contrast with Egypt is apparent. The stone monuments of the Nile valley remained for the instruction of posterity, and the astoundingly rapid rise of Greek architecture and sculpture is partly explained by the fact that the technique of stone-work and a number of plastic formulae were ready to hand. But the monumental brick buildings of Mesopotamia disappeared in the successive sacks of Nineveh, Babylon and Susa. The legacy of Mesopotamian art was preserved in the living traditions of certain crafts, in the portable objects which trade had spread far and wide and in ancient works discovered by chance. We have recognised the importance of the last-named factor in dealing with Syrian and Neo-Babylonian cylinders. Engraved seals, indestructible, attractive and certain to come to light during the very process of decay which destroyed buildings and paintings, must have been—together with specimens of ancient metal-work—an important factor, though intermittent, in the revival of ancient artistic conceptions.

The main depositories of tradition were those workshops which produced the woven stuffs for which Mesopotamia was famous at all times. It is well to realise how far-reaching was this transmission of artistic motives by means of textiles. An embroidered shoulderpiece of the garment of an Assyrian king (Text-fig. 109), transmitted in a relief, contains the following groups: a kneeling figure, winged, holding by each hand a lion which attacks a bull; winged genii flanking a "sacred tree" with pail and "cone"; a four-winged crowned demon, *passant*; and two winged bulls with averted heads flanking a "sacred tree". In addition there are three different borders with vegetal designs, palmettes, cones, etc.[1]

[1] Perrot et Chipier, *Histoire de l'Art dans l'Antiquité*, II, 772.

The contribution of the Ancient Near East to the common treasury of western art may, without too great a sacrifice of truth, be resolved into the following formula: while Egypt invented plant design, Mesopotamia subjected

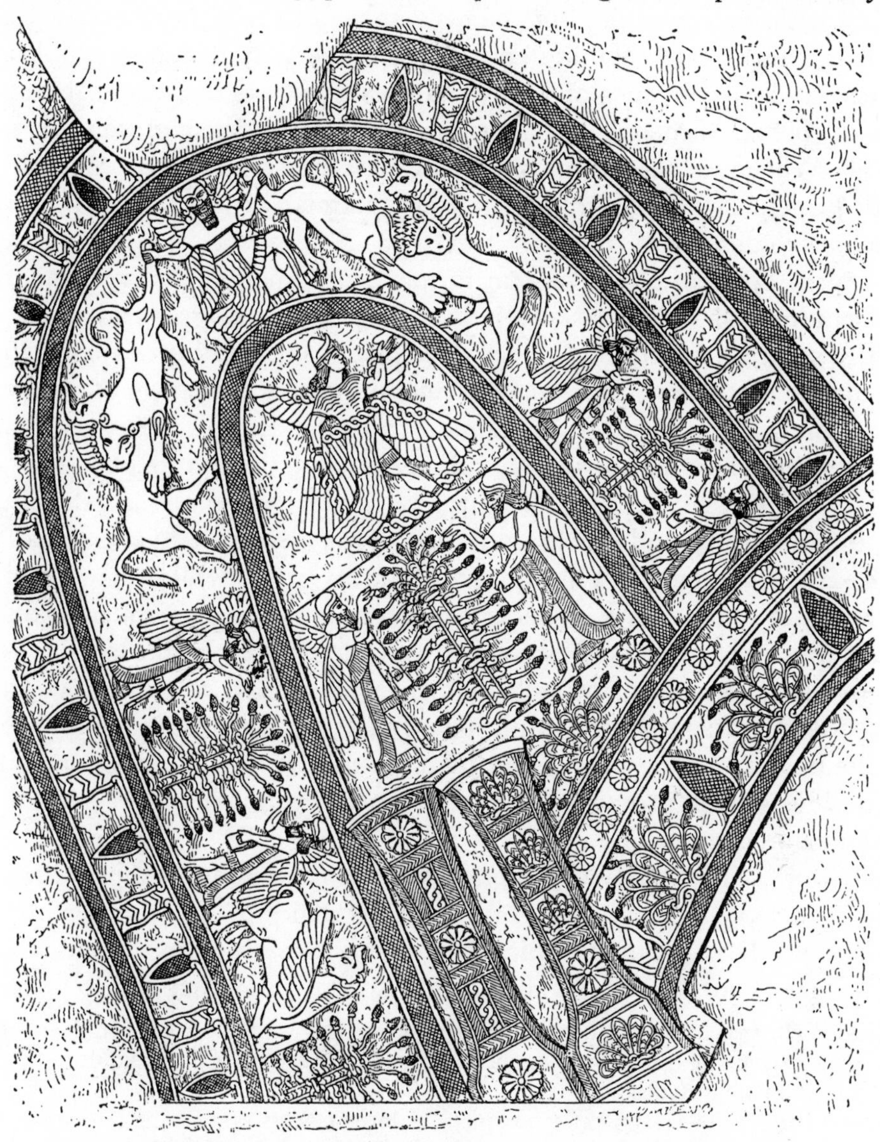

Text-fig. 109. Embroidery on the garment of an Assyrian king.

the animal kingdom to art. And this conquest was of a twofold nature, the one decorative, the other imaginative. In Mesopotamia, for the first time, animal shapes were used not for what they represented but as pure decoration (Pl. IV*e*, *f*, etc.). In the second place, creatures were conceived which had no physical existence but which were so vividly imagined that they could take their place among the images of nature (Pls. VI, X, XXXII, XXXV, XXXVI, XXXVII) and have proved convincing to generations, sharing nothing with their creators but the acceptance of these monsters.

It is by this fantastic fauna that Europe's artistic indebtedness to Asia can be traced. The occurrence of Mesopotamian monsters in European art is by itself, of course, of merely antiquarian interest. But their presence is symptomatic. Whenever they appear in numbers they signify the revival of an artistic principle which triumphed in Mesopotamian art, namely the autonomy of decorative design.

Even the application of vegetal forms to ornamental motives underwent significant changes when Assyria utilised Egyptian designs, and it was these modified schemes which the Greeks developed so splendidly in their palmette and tendril ornaments.[1] It is an even clearer proof of the power of abstraction which distinguished the Mesopotamian from the Egyptian artists, that the former mastered animal form in a manner not even attempted by their great contemporary. The striking veracity with which animals are depicted in Egyptian paintings and reliefs similarly adorns the many objects of daily use which are ornamented with animal figures. But while the Egyptians succeeded, in architecture, jewellery and certain painted decorations making vegetal motives entirely subservient to decorative ends, the animal shape proved less submissive in their hands. It retained a certain degree of independence, assuming postures or simulating actions more in keeping with the habits of the living model than with the function of its image in the design. This at first produces an impression of freshness, soon replaced by a realisation of disharmony, such as is also caused by those extraordinary capitals which assume tender vegetal forms while serving to support massive architraves.[2] A similarly disturbing effect attaches to the festoons of petals and trussed living ducks which decorated the reception rooms of the private houses at Tell el Amarna,[3] and to the miniature landscapes with

[1] Riegl, *Stilfragen*; Humfry Payne, *Necrocorinthia*, pp. 9, 146. Riegl could not do full justice to the share of Phoenicia, as an intermediary between Crete and Egypt, in the creation of the palmette designs.

[2] I refer here to the naturalistic bouquets of lotus-flowers translated into stone in the tomb of Ptahshepses and at Memphis (Capart, *L'Art Égyptien*, I, *L'architecture*, Pl. 51, and Petrie, *Memphis*, I, Pl. III) and often depicted as products of the cabinet-makers' or goldsmiths' craft (Capart, *loc. cit.* Pls. 55, 76, 152), but not, of course, to the usual palm, papyrus and lotus columns, in which vegetal forms are completely adapted to the architectural purpose and become pure art forms.

[3] *F. G. Newton Memorial Volume, The Mural Painting of El-Amarneh*, edited by H. Frankfort, Pls. XVII–XX.

palms, flowers and animals modelled in the round inside vessels of precious metal,[1] or to the carved figures of trussed game or ducks, or of swimming girls, used as containers of cosmetics.[2]

In Mesopotamia, on the other hand, the shape of a living creature was so strictly subordinated to an ornamental purpose that its connection with actuality became much too distant to be disturbing. Thus animal forms were bound in rigid antithetical schemes, or intertwined, or otherwise combined with motives, or placed in attitudes which appear deliberately unnatural.

It is true, of course, that other regions have adapted animal forms to decorative purposes, but that does not diminish the unique significance in the history of art of the earliest experiments undertaken in Mesopotamia. For it is in the first place apparent that in such striking cases as the Early Chinese bronzes, or the designs of Mexican sculpture or of the North-west American Indians, one must reckon to a greater extent than most of us were hitherto prepared to admit, with the possibility of diffusion from Eastern Europe and the Middle East.[3] And in the second place a certain degree of irrelevance always adheres to comparisons with schools of art extraneous to the definite genetic relationship which holds Europe and the Near East together. And this reservation applies especially when not only general principles but also specific derivation is involved. A general principle, like the autonomy of design, may conceivably be discovered and independently applied in several localities, but we are here concerned with well-defined Near Eastern achievements and their adoption by successive generations of European artists.

Early in the seventh century B.C. Oriental art affected the young art of Greece. Its influence is especially to be noted in metal-work and vase-painting. Instead of the abstract conceptual scenes encased in panels on the geometric vases we find decorative friezes and antithetical groups.

The intimacy of the contact with the East to which these innovations are due is well demonstrated by the astonishing fact discovered by Humfry

[1] H. Schaefer, *Die altaegyptischen Prunkgefässe mit aufgesetzten Randverzuhrungen*.

[2] Examples will be found in most histories of art; the collection of ointment spoons in the British Museum has been published in *Journal of Egyptian Archaeology*, XIII, 7–13, Pls. III–IX.

[3] Professor C. G. Seligman has shown that socketed celts of a type characteristic for Central and Eastern Europe during the Late Bronze Age (1300–900 B.C.) influenced China: *Journal of the Royal Anthropological Institute*, L (1920), and *Antiquity*, IX (1937), 5–30, and the Tao-Tieh of the Chinese bronzes is shown by Godard, *Les bronzes du Luristan*, Pl. XXIII, to be explicable as a debased rendering of the lion-headed eagle Imdugud. The link between this art and the Scythian art is the T. E. Lawrence dagger-hilt in the British Museum (*British Museum Quarterly*, XII, Pl. XII, and pp. 21 f.).

Payne, that two distinct schools successively affected the great artistic centre of the seventh century, Corinth. The proto-Corinthian vases appear to be as definitely connected with "Hittite" Syrian monuments as the Corinthian vases reflect the art of Assyria.[1]

It is important to note that in this case, as in later times when Europe was stimulated by contact with the Near East, the results were not confined to the addition of certain fabulous creatures to the European repertoire, but to a renovation of the formal basis of the decorative art of the West. In the seventh century B.C. the new principles even become visible before the Oriental monsters make their appearance, though soon the vases swarm with Phoenician sphinxes, mermen, sirens, griffins, chimaerae, centaurs (Text-figs. 110–14) and all kinds of winged creatures, including Imdugud, the lion-bird (Pl. XLVII *a*). But the copying and invention of composite monsters on the Oriental pattern is incidental. The remarkable creature published by Payne (Text-fig. 114) shares with the lion of our Pl. X *d* the combination of two bodies with one head. It is, of course, a purely Greek design; but it proves, as do its Sumerian predecessor and the Etruscan and Romanesque examples (Pl. XLVII *h*), that decorative claims (in this case the need for a symmetrical motive) have gained predominance over every other consideration.

Text-fig. 110. Merman from Corinthian vase.

The effect of this contact with the East on seventh-century Greece has paradigmatical value, especially as its renewal at various later times takes place under much more complicated circumstances. We may therefore quote here Payne's description of this earliest contact between Europe and Asia:[2] "The almost immediate result of this new relation between East and West was the abandonment of most of the rules which had governed geometric decoration: its most essential positive consequence may be summarised as

[1] *Necrocorinthia*, pp. 53 f., 68, 170.

[2] From the English typescript of Payne's *Protokorinthische Vasenmalerei* (Berlin, 1933).

the power to draw with a free hand. It is surprising how quickly all traces of the tyranny of ruler and compass disappear; but it is equally remarkable how this new freedom resulted, after a scarcely perceptible interval of hesitation, in the construction of a system of forms almost as clearly defined as that of the geometric style, but very much wider in range. That is one side of the new style—a new system of forms. The second is a new ability to dispose the forms in space. The geometric artist had only one notion of decorating a surface—to replace it by another surface. He had no conception of the elementary antithesis between field and design: a surface which was

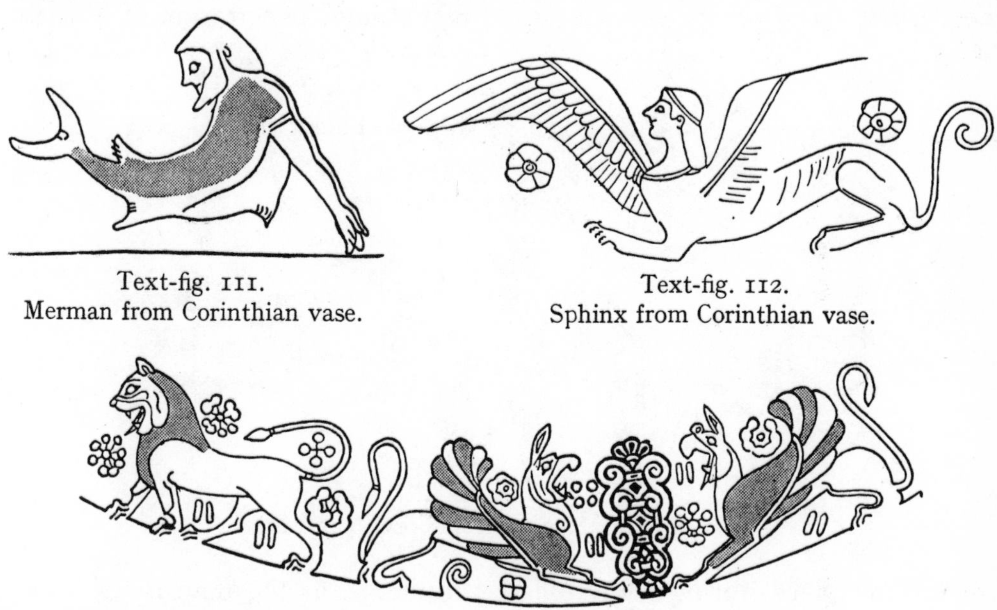

Text-fig. 111.
Merman from Corinthian vase.

Text-fig. 112.
Sphinx from Corinthian vase.

Text-fig. 113. Griffins and "Sacred Tree" from Corinthian vase.

all design and no field, one might perhaps say a *texture*, was his objective. Greek geometric decoration may indeed be claimed as an illustration of that grossly overworked phrase 'horror vacui' (though even here the words are not a fair description of the artist's psychological state). The orientalising style marks an important step forward. For all its 'filling-ornament', its love of incidental distraction, it clearly recognises the opposition of field and design; and quite early in its course it has the courage to produce effects in which the greater part of the field is left untouched.

"The new style did not come to Greece as an idea: it was a lesson learnt from imported works; thus many of the actual forms and decorative devices of oriental art appear at the same time as the new power to draw in an open field, with a free hand."

Payne has also shown that the Oriental influences did not reach Greece in the first place through Ionia, as has often been supposed, but rather through the intermediacy of Crete and Cyprus. This proves that they emanated ultimately from Phoenicia, and from the same centre of diffusion the Western Mediterranean was affected, and Etruria was saturated to such an extent with Oriental designs that their influence can be traced all through the Middle Ages and through a considerable part of the Renaissance, in the Tuscan schools of painting.[1]

It would take us too far, and necessitate a restatement of well-known fact, were we to dwell on the second period of Oriental penetration of Europe,

Text-fig. 114. Monster from Corinthian vase.

which took place during the Roman Empire. But the migrations which followed the collapse of Rome brought into Europe an extreme form of animal ornament, also derived from Mesopotamia, but independently of any development so far considered. This animal style is purely Asiatic, appearing for the first time in the "Luristan bronzes", which were produced in the mountains bordering on Mesopotamia (Text-fig. 115). The Scythians made this type of animal ornament their own, and from their homeland in the South Russian steppes it penetrated towards the east as far as China, and towards the west, first into the Celtic "La Tène" culture, and secondly, into Northern and Western Europe as a result of the migrations of Goths, Franks, Teutons and other barbarians who had become acquainted with it in Southern Russia.

Now this Scythian animal style represents an extreme of the subjection of natural form to decorative purpose which was, on the whole, avoided in

[1] Gustave Soulier, *Les influences orientales dans la peinture Toscane* (Paris, 1924).

Mesopotamia proper. Designs like our Pl. XIV*e* tend towards it, but even there, as also in Pl. XIV*h*, the natural shapes, as renderings of individual organisms, are respected, while made to serve decorative ends. This subtle equilibrium between natural form and decorative purpose is the essential quality of Mesopotamian design and the secret of its vitality. The extreme point of decorative exploitation represented by the Siberian or Chinese animal styles, or the miniatures and carved ornaments of Ireland, is perfect in itself but offers no possibilities of further development.

It is perhaps most instructive to consider the contrast with Mesopotamia in the case where it is least pronounced. Text-fig. 115 shows one of the less complicated designs for a pole-top represented amongst the "Luristan bronzes", found, as we stated, in the mountains which border Mesopotamia to the east, and showing numerous more or less distorted renderings of ancient Mesopotamian motives. In the present case the older version showed a hero between two beasts, a commonplace on Early Dynastic seals. Already on the seals, however, we found that curious monsters were developed out of this motive; but a comparison with Text-fig. 115 or with any work of the Scythian or related Asiatic animal style will demonstrate that the Mesopotamian designs retain a curiously organic character. In Pl. X*c*, for instance, the two hindquarters of a monster are joined in the manner actually observed in the case of monstrous births; the snakes are really conceived as tails, also in Pl. XI*n*, where the two lions are, moreover, clearly thought of in what one might call "terms of anatomy", namely as the legs of the standing figure. Now compare with these Mesopotamian designs the pole-top of Text-fig. 115. Here too we meet a composite creature, based on the same original pattern of a hero placed between two animals. But the arms of the central figure have coalesced with the foreparts of the lions. As a result the hero's girdle now binds the two beasts, while a human head unaccountably appears between their forepaws.

Text-fig. 115. Bronze pole-top from Luristan.

Now this example, as we have said already, is exceptionally simple. Most related works show a motley of foreparts, heads, tails, limbs of men and animals, combined into delightful but meaningless arabesques to which the allusions to organic shapes merely add piquancy.

Such violation of the organic form is almost completely absent in Mesopotamian art. But the tension incorporated in the equilibrium of the Mesopotamian schemes can at any time vitalise new combinations.

The disembodied animal style of the early medieval migrations was particularly effective in the illuminated initials and other embellishments of manuscripts (Text-fig. 116). It was unsuitable for translation into sculpture; and the same limitation applies to the works which represented for the Carolingian and early Romanesque artists the Oriental tradition. Much of this was enshrined in the art of Byzantium, partly in Hellenistic guise, partly derived afresh from Syria; Syria and Egypt moreover supplied the early churches of the West with a comparatively large proportion of their

Text-fig. 116. Illuminations from the Book of Kells.

illuminated manuscripts. But from the ninth century onwards both Byzantium and the West began to receive an increasing number of a group of Oriental productions which were the true descendants of ancient Mesopotamian art. These were the Persian metal vases, ivories, and, above all, woven silks. It has been shown that the Sassanian textiles were to a large extent manufactured in the south-western district of Persia, in Susiana,[1] where, through the Achaemenidae, Mesopotamian traditions had been particularly powerful. The conquest of Persia by the Arabs did not noticeably affect this production. Thus we find on the many costly hangings which decorated the interiors of the Romanesque cathedrals, and may have been the precursors as well as the prototypes of the stained glass windows,[2] the ancient struggle of a hero with two beasts of prey (Pl. XLVII *e*, *f*). Similar importations transmitted to the West the human-headed bull of the Assyrian

[1] Otto von Falcke, *Kunstgeschichte der Seidenweberei*.

[2] Emile Mâle, *L'Art religieux du XIIe siècle en France*, pp. 345 ff.

palace sculptures, together with a female creature of Phoenician extraction (Pl. XLVII *g*), and even Imdugud hovering above two beasts as on the Early Dynastic seals (Pl. XLVII *d*). It is true that the eagle's companions have a less ancient lineage; they go back to the griffin which first appears in Mitannian glyptic and becomes particularly popular in Assyrian times. On the other hand the beasts bite back into the wings of the bird that grasps them and the three figures are thus connected by a movement returning on itself in the best Mesopotamian fashion (Pl. XII *b*; Text-fig. 20 and p. 56). These instances could be multiplied almost indefinitely.[1] But their main value is again the revelation of the aesthetic preoccupation of Romanesque art. The sketches of Villard de Honnecourt, codifying what had been the study of a former generation, recall so closely ancient Oriental designs (compare Pl. XLVII *c* with Pl. XIV *h* and Pl. XLII *m*) as to explain by themselves why these artists found in Near Eastern works of art the solution of their problems. The combination of two bodies with one head in Pl. XLVII *h* may once more serve to summarise the tendencies of the time.

Though there can be no doubt that formal problems were in the first place responsible for the influence which Near Eastern art exercised in Europe, it would be shortsighted to overlook the fact that the creatures of Oriental imagination were also appreciated in the Middle Ages for non-aesthetic reasons. The tortured consciousness of sin, the turbulent speculations on the powers of evil, found relief in the use of ready-made forms. The naïve conjectures of minds untrammelled by scientific understanding, the sophisticated requirements of alchemists and astrologers, these and other attitudes found much of value in those works of imagination which were also dignified with an origin in the proximity of the Holy Land and which served to beautify the churches.

[1] M. Baltrušaitis has collected and studied a large number of parallels between ancient Mesopotamian and Romanesque art (*Art Sumérien, Art Roman*, Paris, 1934). Not all of them are convincing, and it is especially disturbing to see designs put side by side, and considered as resulting from the same decorative system while each of them, studied in connection with older monuments in its own immediate ancestry, may appear to illustrate the influence of other (and not always formal) factors, or to be an exception in a well-documented series. In these cases the "parenté morphologique" is but superficial. But he describes well how close similarities can have resulted from a process which in the polemics on "Diffusionism" is called Convergence, but which in our case does not start from two entirely independent sources: "Mis en contact avec les fragments d'un art ancien, le sculpteur roman a saisi par une intuition d'artiste l'ordre qui les détermine. Il l'a reconstruit et il l'a adapté à ses propres besoins." And here we find an influence of Near Eastern art on Europe which is much more extensive than the possibilities of contact, survivals, and importations can ever account for.

It is extremely difficult to determine the precise nature of each derivation. As an example we reproduce in Pl. XLVII *b* a capital from the cathedral of Nantes which illustrates, as a contemporary diatribe against animal sculptures on Romanesque cathedrals explicitly affirms,[1] a fable of Phaedrus as preserved by Boethius. The ass, having found a lyre in a field, complains: "I do not know music. If somebody else had found this lyre he would enchant listeners with heavenly harmonies."

Now we know that the ass is the only animal occurring on Mesopotamian monuments playing a harp. Besides the instance illustrated in Text-fig. 28 (p. 74) we have an inlay on a harp from Ur and a relief from Tell Halaf which preserves the motive. Did some survival in Oriental art reach France? Or did the Romanesque sculptors illustrate the fable and produce a like design? Or was the fable itself, perhaps, an explanatory tale, invented to account for such designs as appear on the seals and reliefs which we quoted and which may have been known to the Greeks although their original meaning remained obscure?

Biblical references too are apt to create a most complicated network of relationships. The account of Solomon's temple, the Prophets and Revelation contain genuine descriptions of ancient Oriental works of art. Have medieval artists worked imaginatively on these suggestions? Or have they searched for suitable designs in the Oriental art known in their time, to adapt them to the biblical text? In so doing they may well have chanced upon renderings of precisely those motives which the biblical author had also had in mind. This, for instance, would be the case where the winged centaurs (Pl. XLVII *g*) are made to illustrate the "locusts"[2] described as issuing from the bottomless pit in Revelation 9: "and the shapes of the locusts were like unto horses prepared unto battle; and on their heads were as it were crowns like gold, and their faces were as the faces of men."

But these and similar non-aesthetic grounds for the derivation of Oriental motives by the Romanesque artists are entirely inadequate when it comes to accounting for the profound influence which Near Eastern design exercised once again in Europe in the tenth–twelfth centuries A.D.

The fundamental reason lies in the solutions which the Near East has found for certain artistic problems which were precisely those besetting the craftsmen of the early Middle Ages. In Europe before that time ornamental art had been linear in character. It triumphed above all in the miniatures, and was pre-eminently anti-sculptural. A type of ornament was required

[1] Mâle, *L'Art religieux du XIIe siècle en France*, pp. 339 f.

[2] Richard Bernheimer, *Romanische Tierplastik*, p. 139.

which might be adapted to sculptural treatment, which, in other words, was suitable for a three-dimensional rendering. Such ornaments would obviously be found in an art which acknowledged the physical reality underlying its motives while using them for decorative ends. We have seen that Mesopotamian art embodies precisely this equilibrium. Its motives—even when they reached Europe in non-sculptural form, in woven stuffs or engraved in precious metals—were pre-eminently suitable to serve as a source of inspiration to the Greek and Romanesque sculptors.

To sum up, between the extremes of Egyptian "naturalism" and Central Asiatic abstraction Mesopotamian art retained a remarkably balanced position. Her animal style contains an element of tension in which the natural forms, respected in their organic structure, are nevertheless translated into the sphere of art by their complete subjection to the laws of design. In this tension, this equilibrium, lies the secret of the vitality of Mesopotamian decoration; and a position attained by the beginning of the Third Millennium before our era thus repeatedly supplied a form for the rejuvenation of European design.

I. GENERAL INDEX

CAMBRIDGE: PRINTED BY WALTER LEWIS, M.A., AT THE UNIVERSITY PRESS

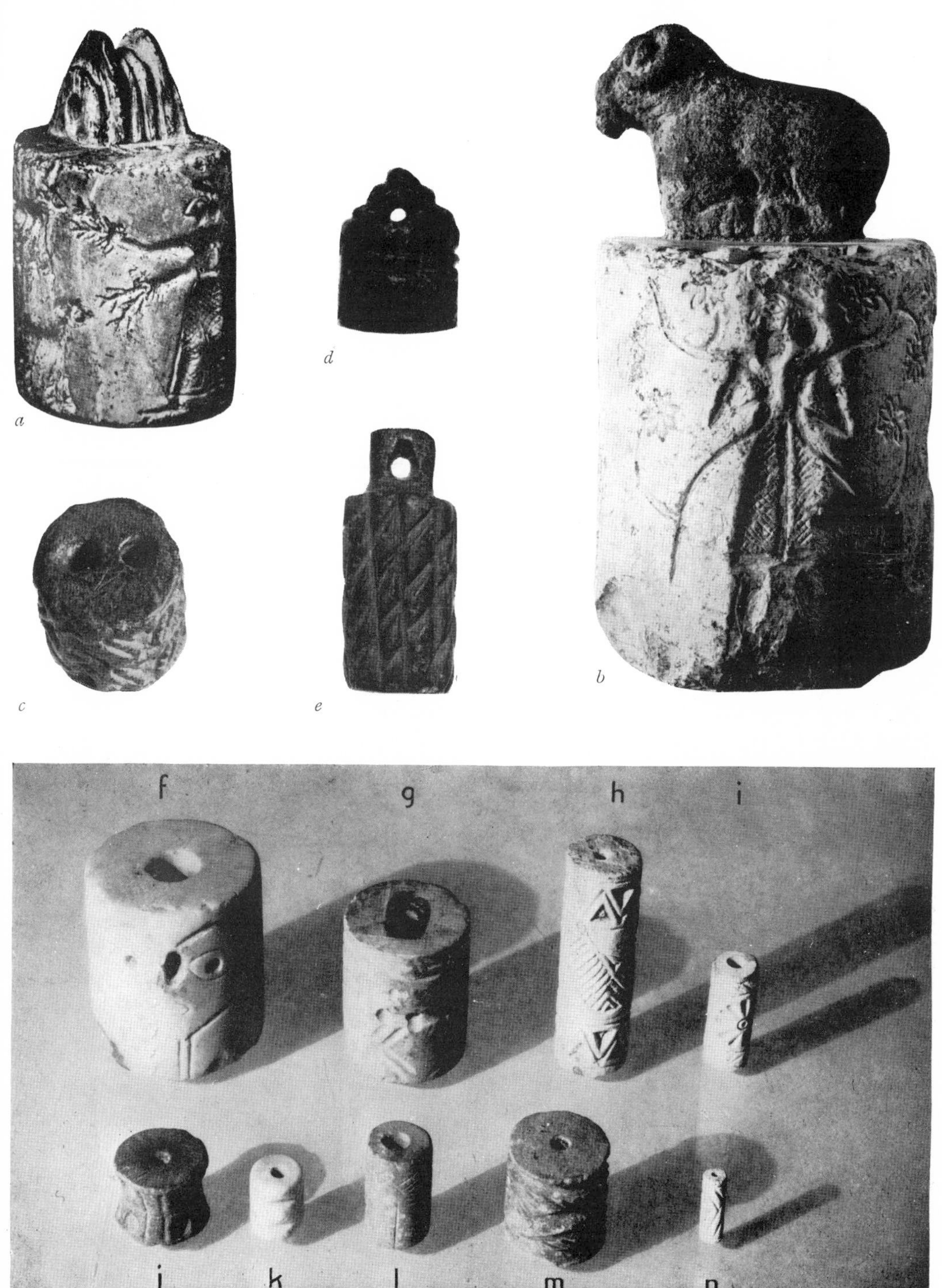

SEALS OF THE URUK AND JEMDET NASR PERIODS

CYLINDER SEALS AND IMPRESSIONS OF VARIOUS PERIODS

a

b

c

d

e

f

URUK PERIOD

URUK PERIOD

a

b

c

d

e

f

g

h

i

URUK AND JEMDET NASR PERIODS

a b c d e f g h i j

EARLIER HALF OF THE JEMDET NASR PERIOD

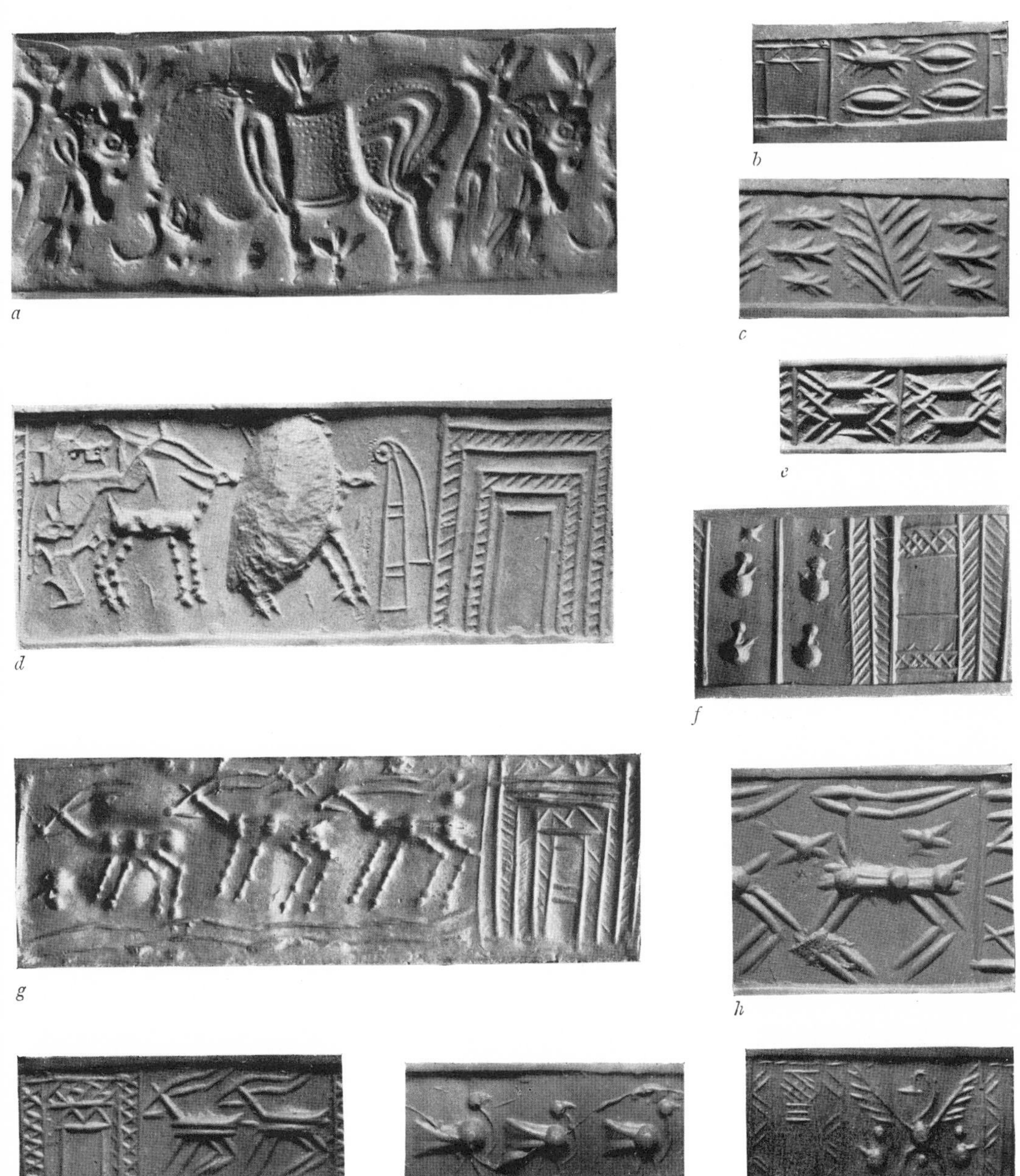

a *b* *c* *d* *e* *f* *g* *h* *i* *j* *k*

JEMDET NASR PERIOD

a

b

c

d

e

f

g

h

i

j

k

JEMDET NASR PERIOD

a *b* *c* *d* *e* *f* *g* *h*

FIRST EARLY DYNASTIC PERIOD (BROCADE STYLE)

a

b

c

d

e

f

g

h

i

j

SECOND EARLY DYNASTIC PERIOD

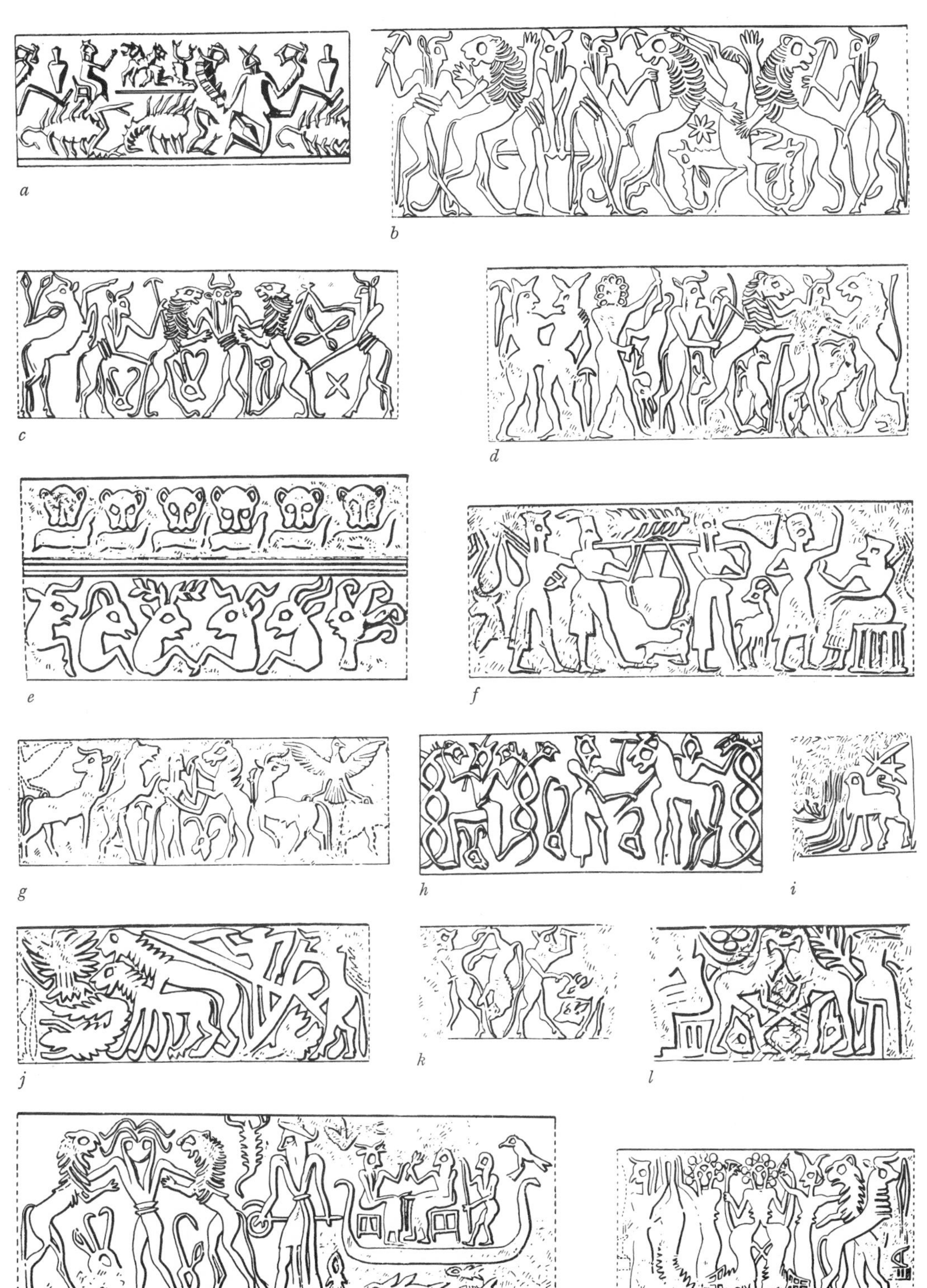

SECOND EARLY DYNASTIC PERIOD (except *e*)

a

b

c

THIRD EARLY DYNASTIC PERIOD

a

b

c

d

e

f

g

h

THIRD EARLY DYNASTIC PERIOD

a

b

c

d

f

g

e

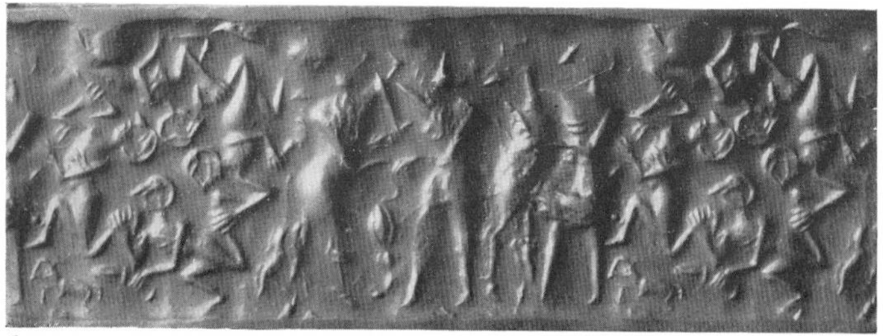
h

i

j

k

THIRD EARLY DYNASTIC PERIOD

THIRD EARLY DYNASTIC PERIOD

a

b

c

d

e

f

g

h

REIGN OF SARGON (except *h*)

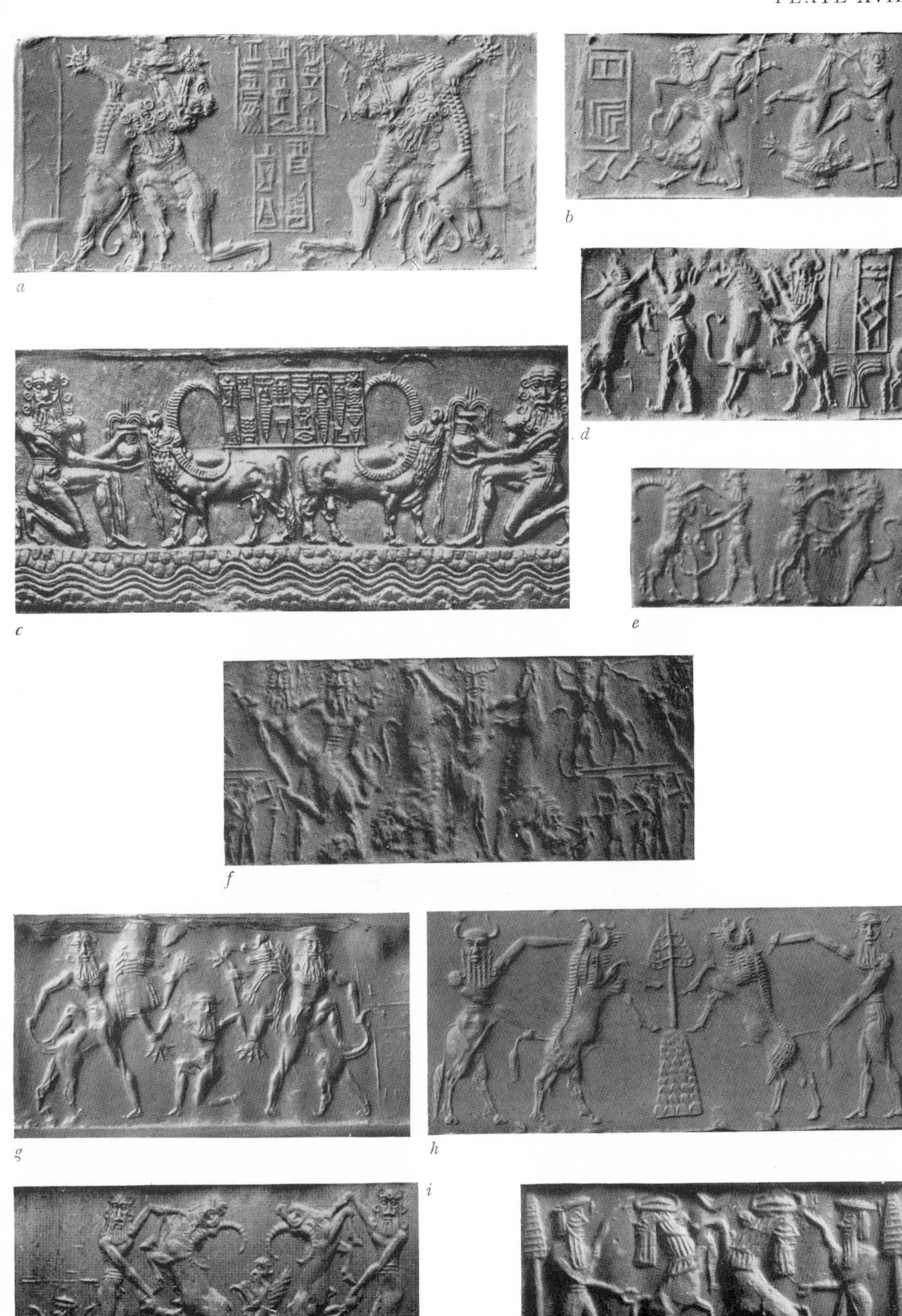

a b c d e f g h i j

DYNASTY OF AKKAD

a

b

c

d

e

f

g

h

i

j

k

DYNASTY OF AKKAD: THE SUN-GOD

a

b

c

d

e

f

DYNASTY OF AKKAD: THE SUN-GOD

DYNASTY OF AKKAD: FERTILITY GODS

a

b

c

d

e

f

g

h

i

DYNASTY OF AKKAD: FERTILITY GODS AND EA

a

b

c

d

e

f

g

h

DYNASTY OF AKKAD: VARIOUS SUBJECTS

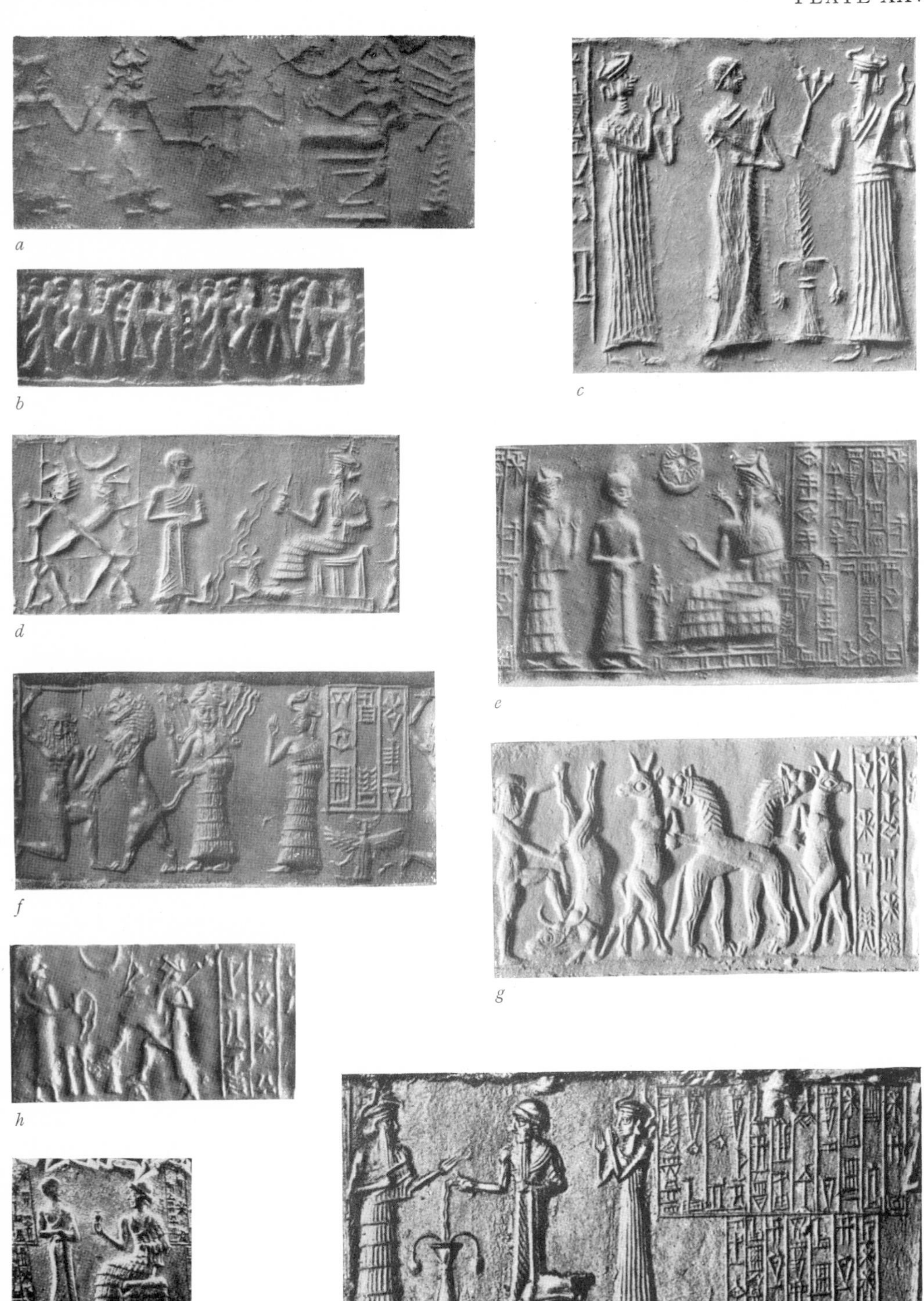

a b c d e f g h i j

AKKADIAN PERIOD (*b*), GUTI PERIOD (*a*) AND THIRD DYNASTY OF UR

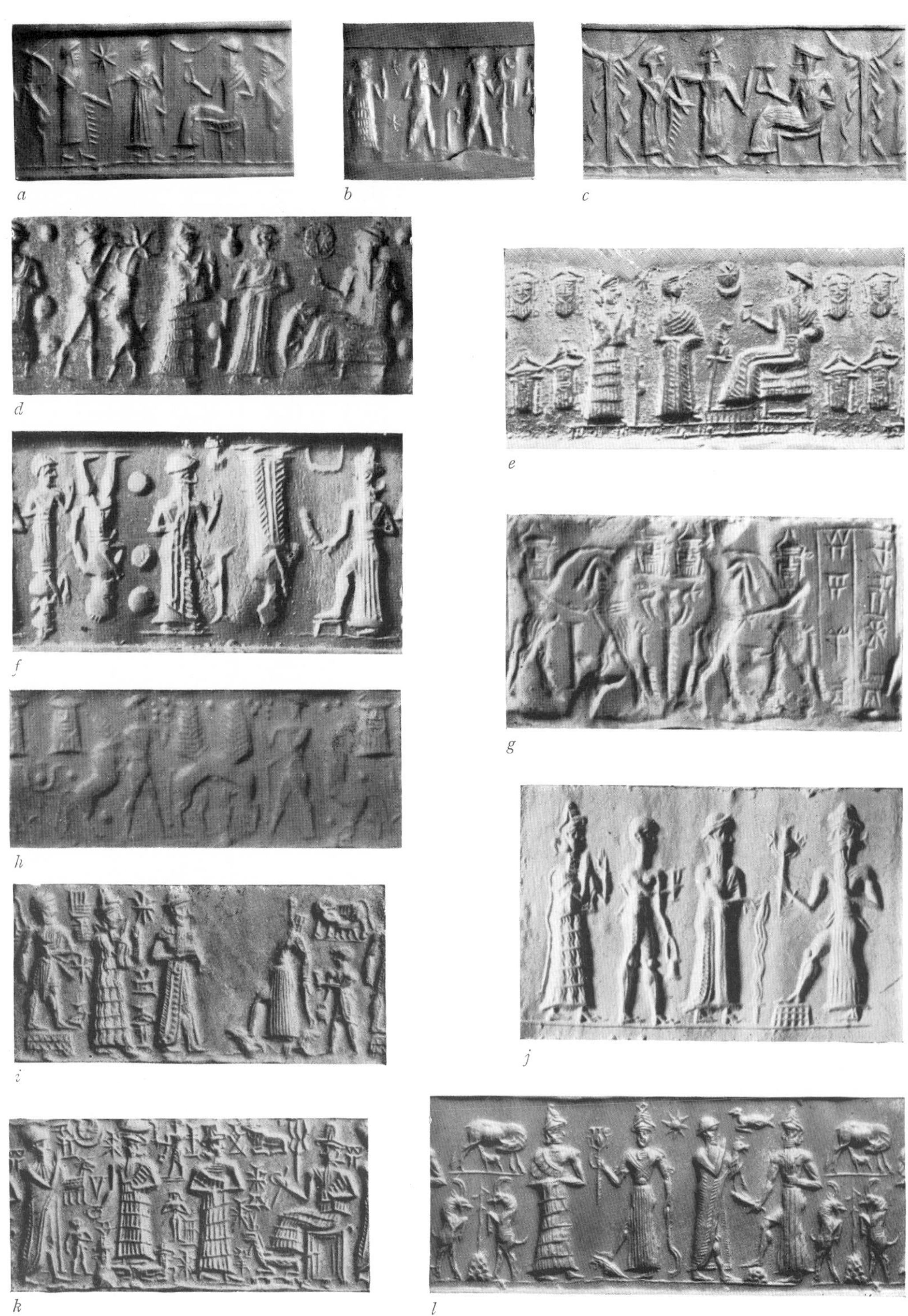

a b c d e f g h i j k l

ISIN-LARSA PERIOD (*a–c*) AND FIRST DYNASTY OF BABYLON

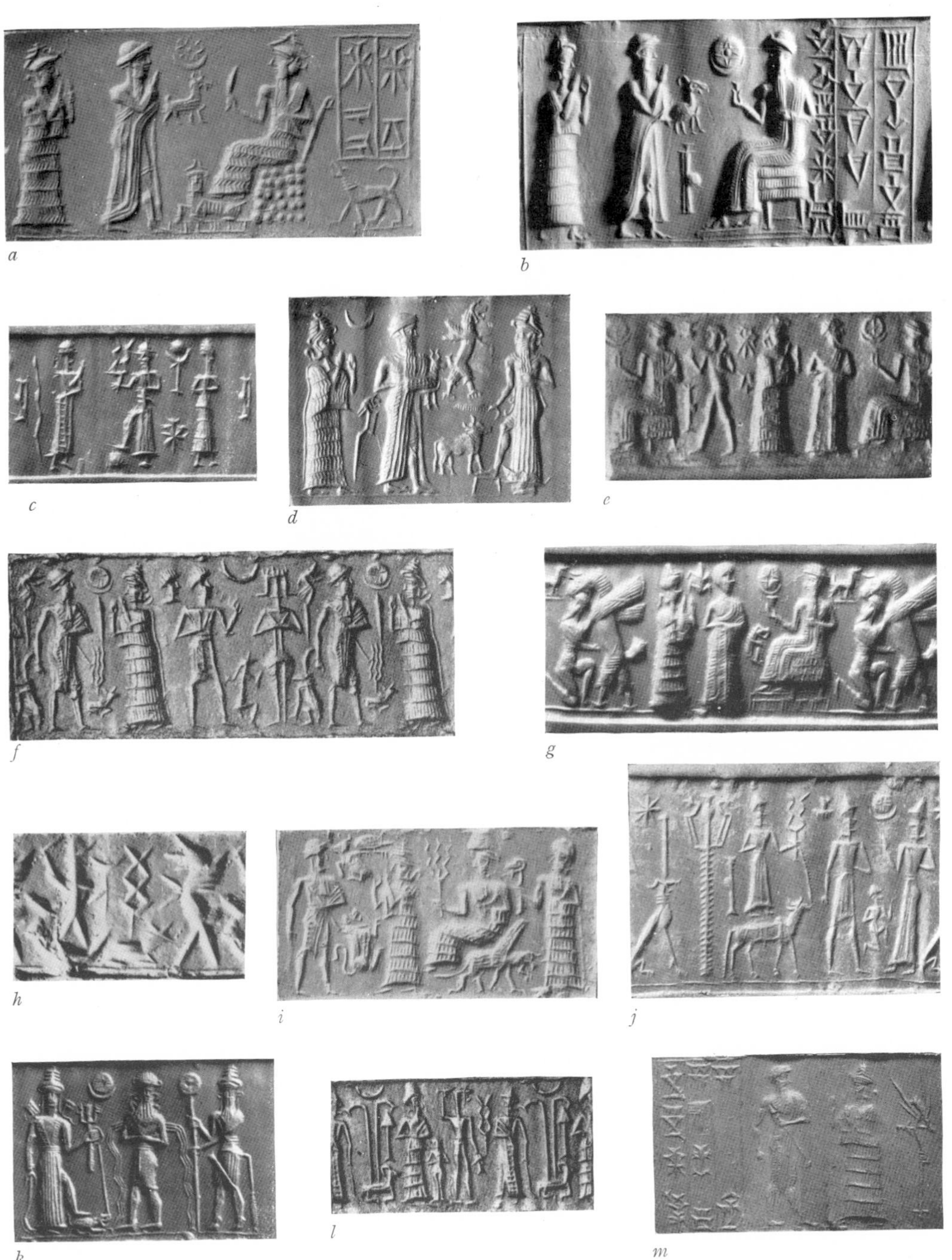

a *b* *c* *d* *e* *f* *g* *h* *i* *j* *k* *l* *m*

FIRST BABYLONIAN DYNASTY: SHAMASH AND ADAD

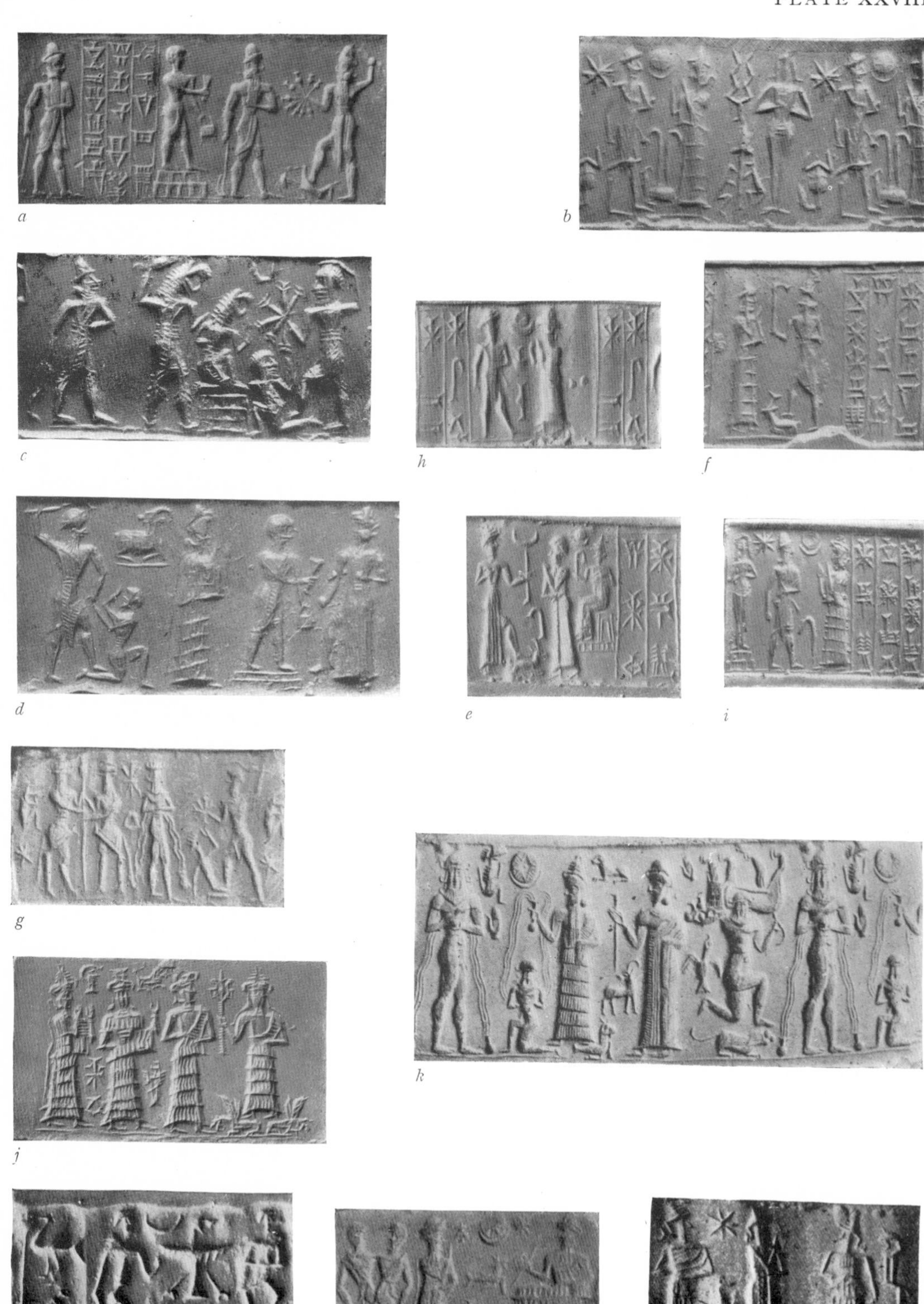

a b c h f d e i g k j l m n

FIRST DYNASTY OF BABYLON: AMURRU, MARDUK AND OTHER GODS

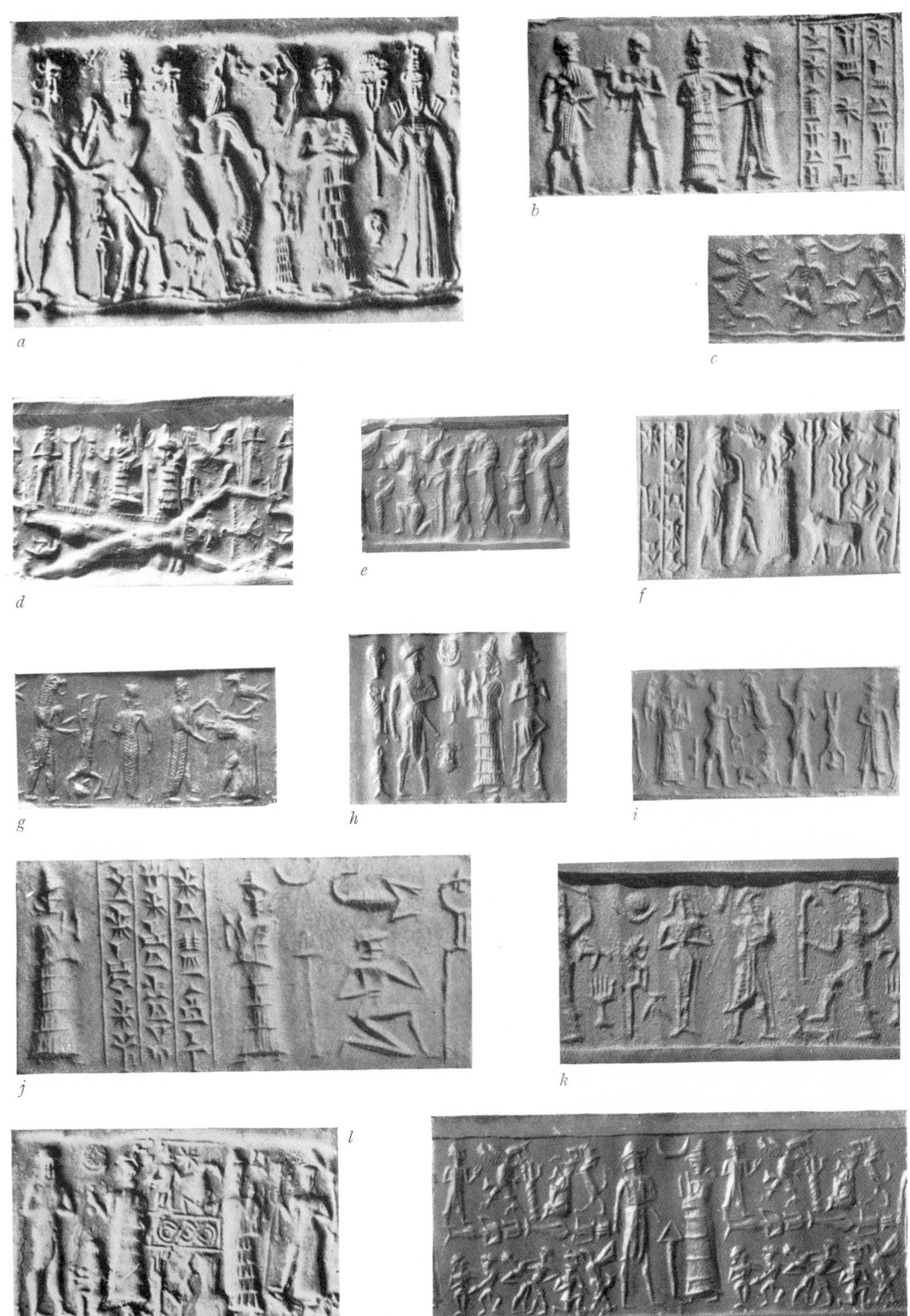

FIRST DYNASTY OF BABYLON: VARIOUS GROUPS

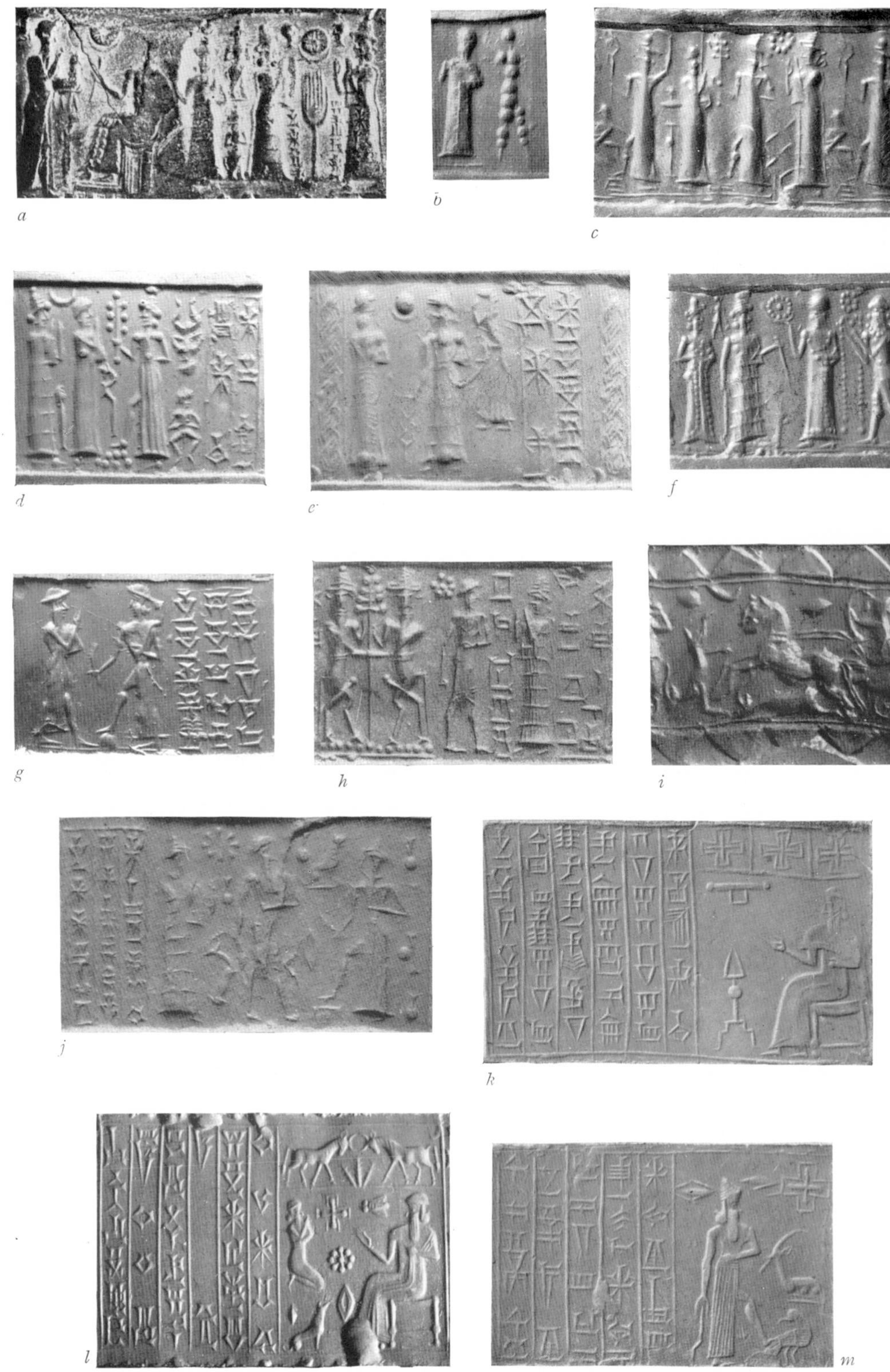

THE END OF THE FIRST BABYLONIAN DYNASTY (*c–f*) AND KASSITES (*h–m*)

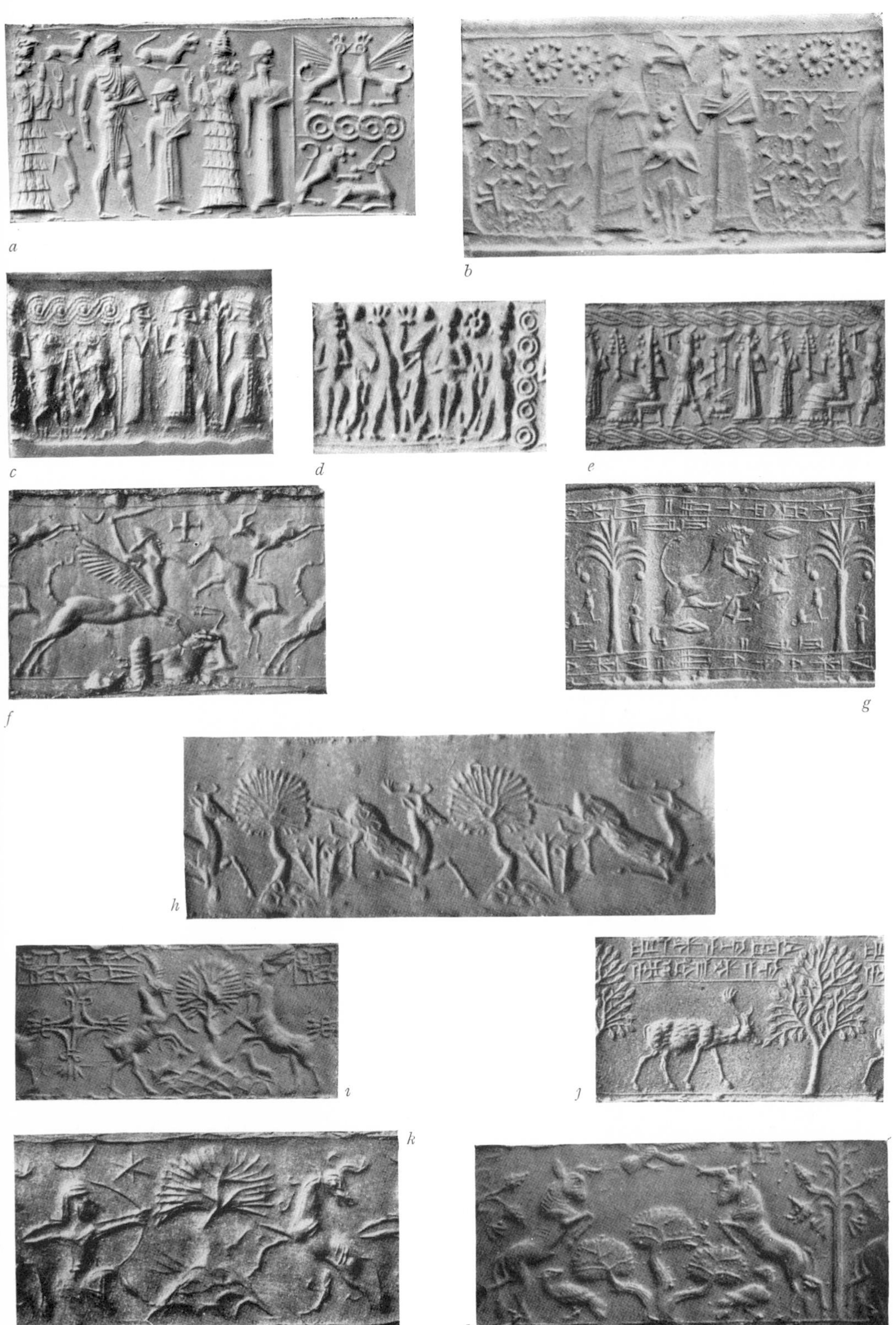

SEALS OF MITANNIAN (*a, c–e*), LATE KASSITE (*b, f, g*) AND MIDDLE ASSYRIAN (*h–l*) STYLE

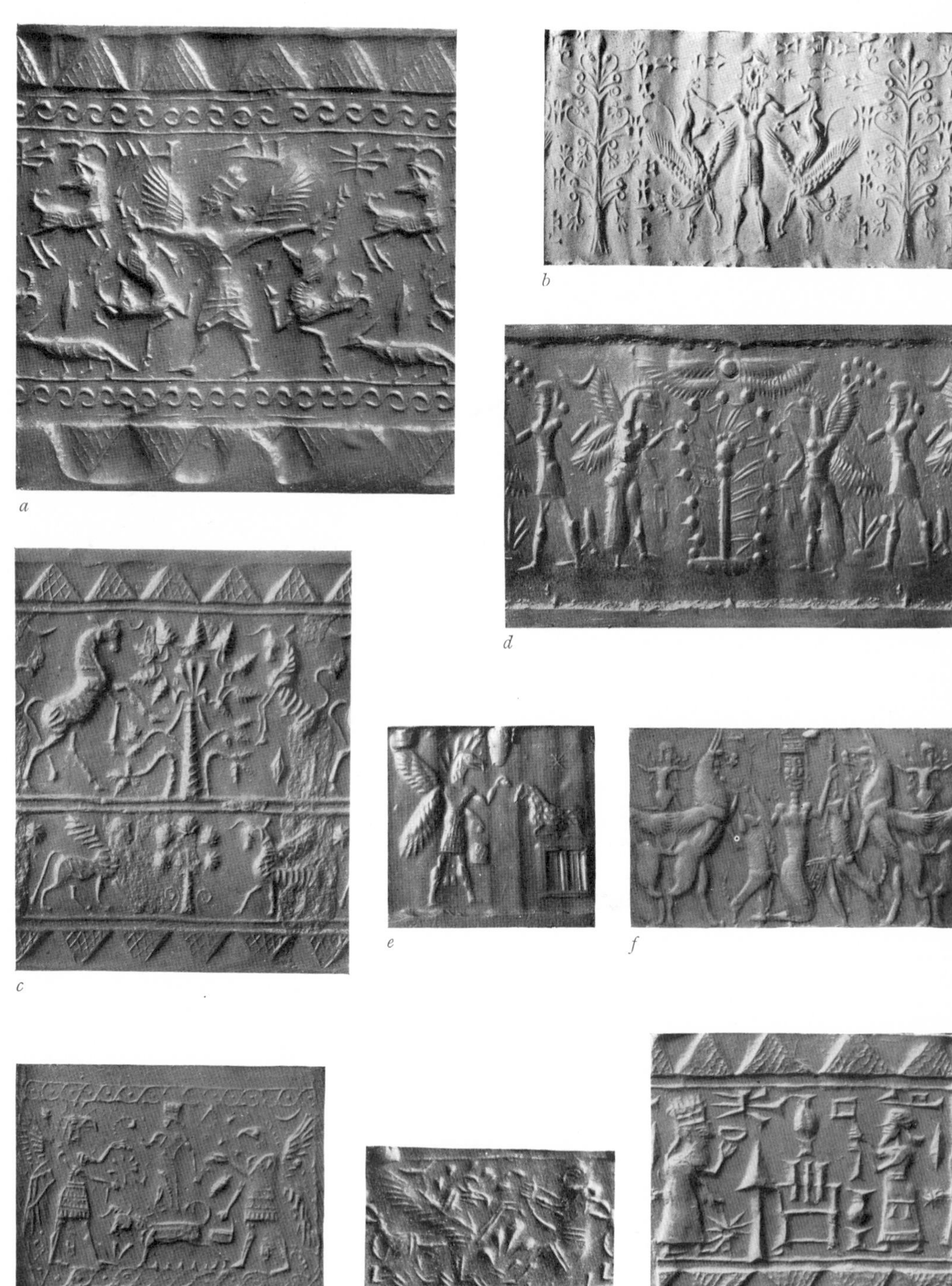

ASSYRIAN SEALS OF THE THIRTEENTH–TENTH CENTURY B.C.

a

b

c

d

e

f

g

h

i

j

k

ASSYRIAN SEALS OF THE NINTH CENTURY B.C.

a

b

c

d

e

f

g

h

i

j

ASSYRIAN SEALS OF THE NINTH AND EIGHTH CENTURIES B.C.

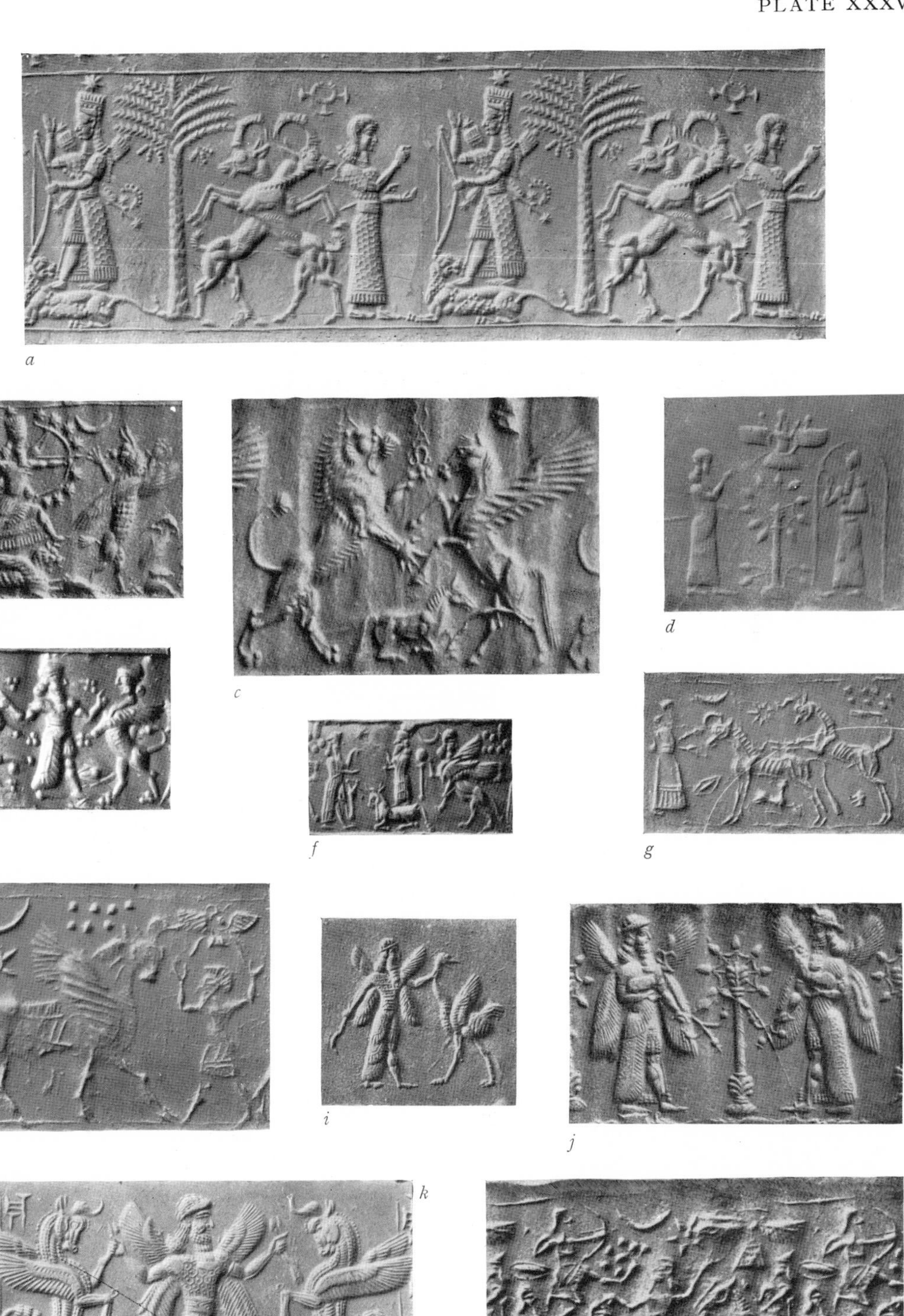

ASSYRIAN SEALS OF 750–650 B.C.

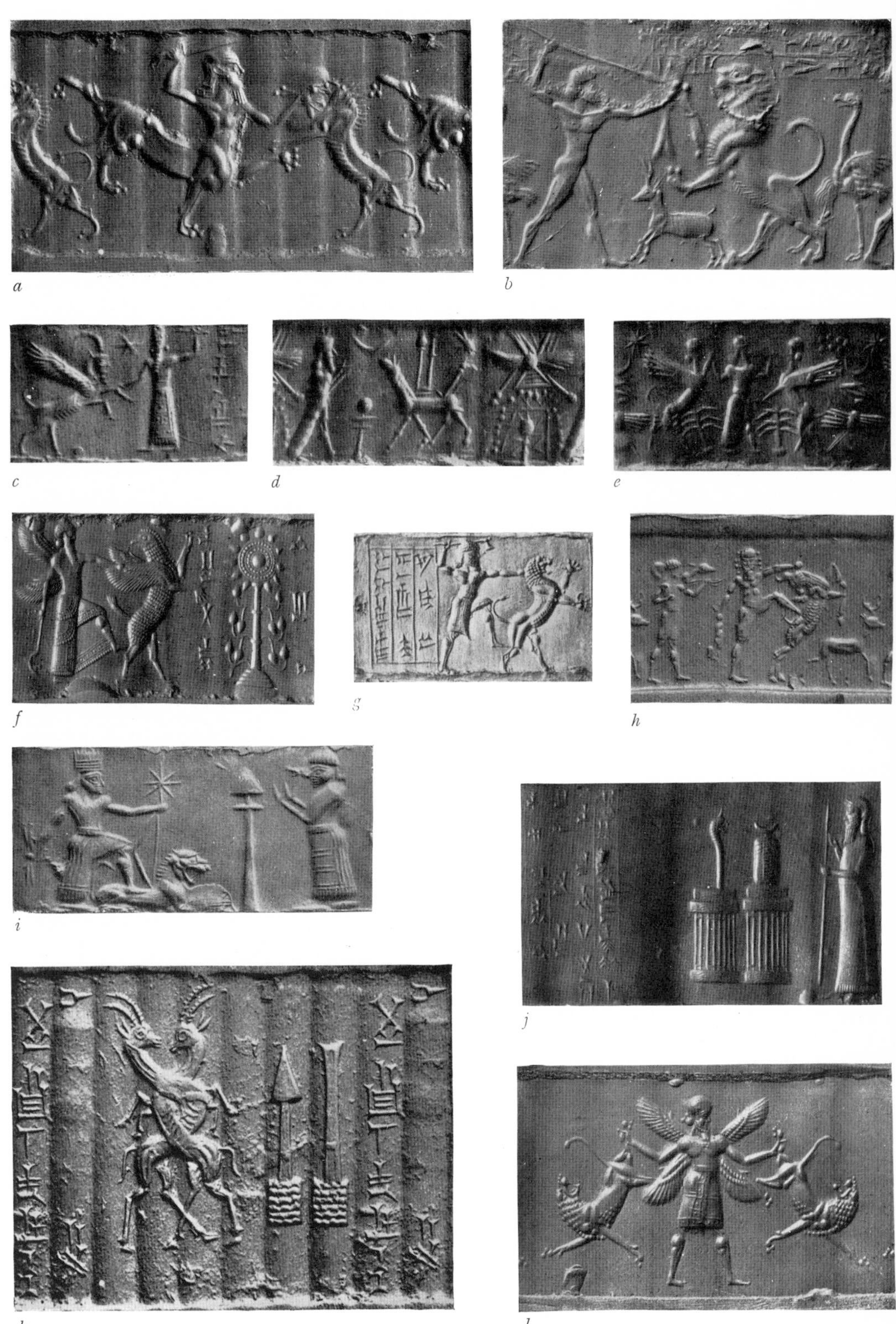

ASSYRIAN (*a, e*) AND NEO-BABYLONIAN SEALS

SEALS OF THE ACHAEMENID PERIOD

SEALS OF PERIPHERAL REGIONS: JEMDET NASR PERIOD

a *b* *c* *d* *e* *f* *g* *h* *i* *j* *k* *l* *m* *n* *o* *p* *q* *r*

SEALS OF PERIPHERAL REGIONS FROM ABOUT 2800–1800 B.C.

a *b* *c* *d* *e* *f* *g* *h* *i* *j* *k* *l* *m* *n* *o*

SEALS OF PERIPHERAL REGIONS OF ABOUT 2000 B.C.

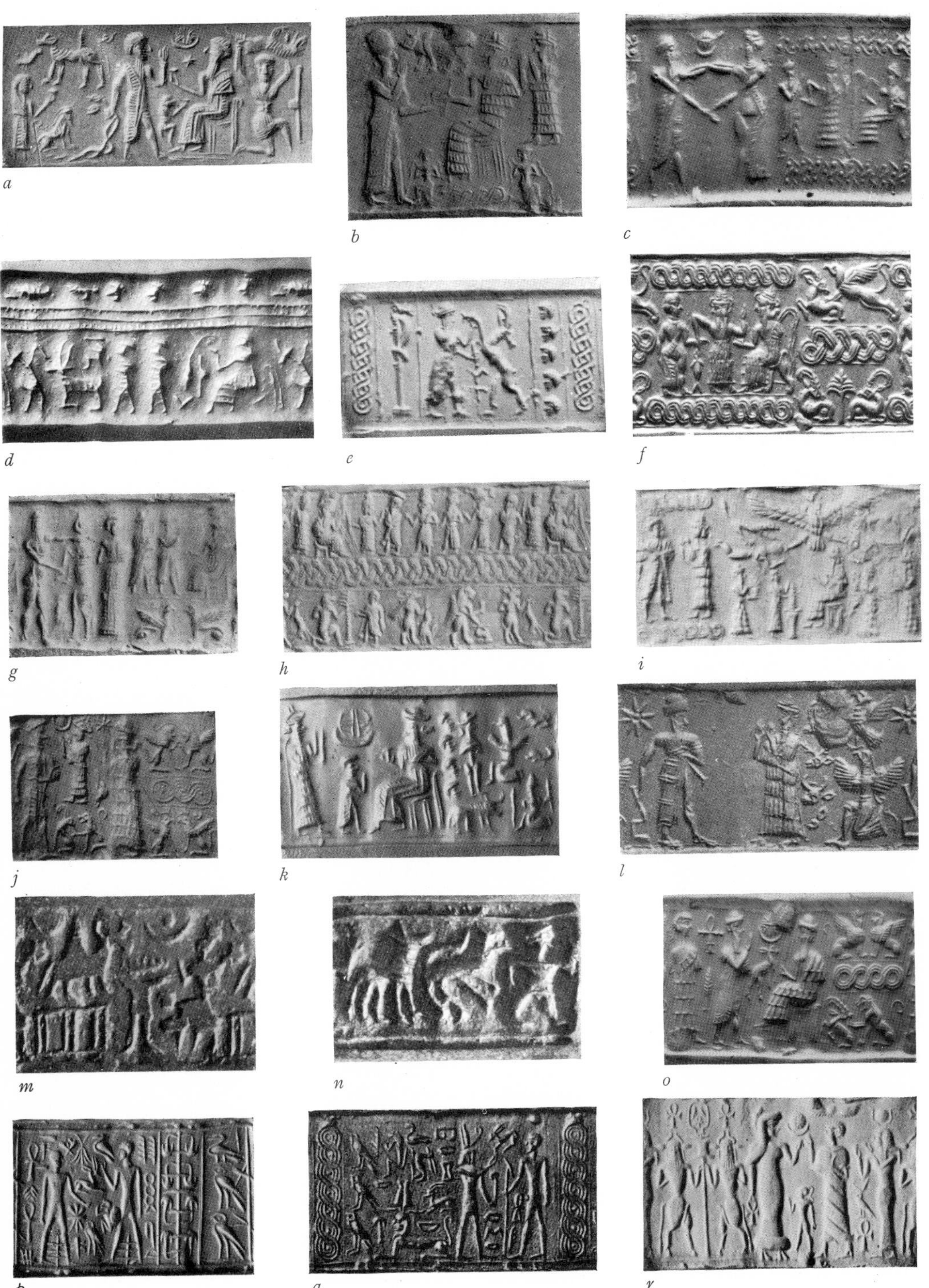

a *b* *c* *d* *e* *f* *g* *h* *i* *j* *k* *l* *m* *n* *o* *p* *q* *r*

SYRIAN SEALS OF THE FIRST GROUP AND HYKSOS CYLINDERS (*p–r*)

MITANNIAN SEALS (*a*, *b*, *o*) AND SYRIAN SEALS OF THE SECOND GROUP

MITANNIAN SEALS AND HITTITE CYLINDER (*n*, *o*)

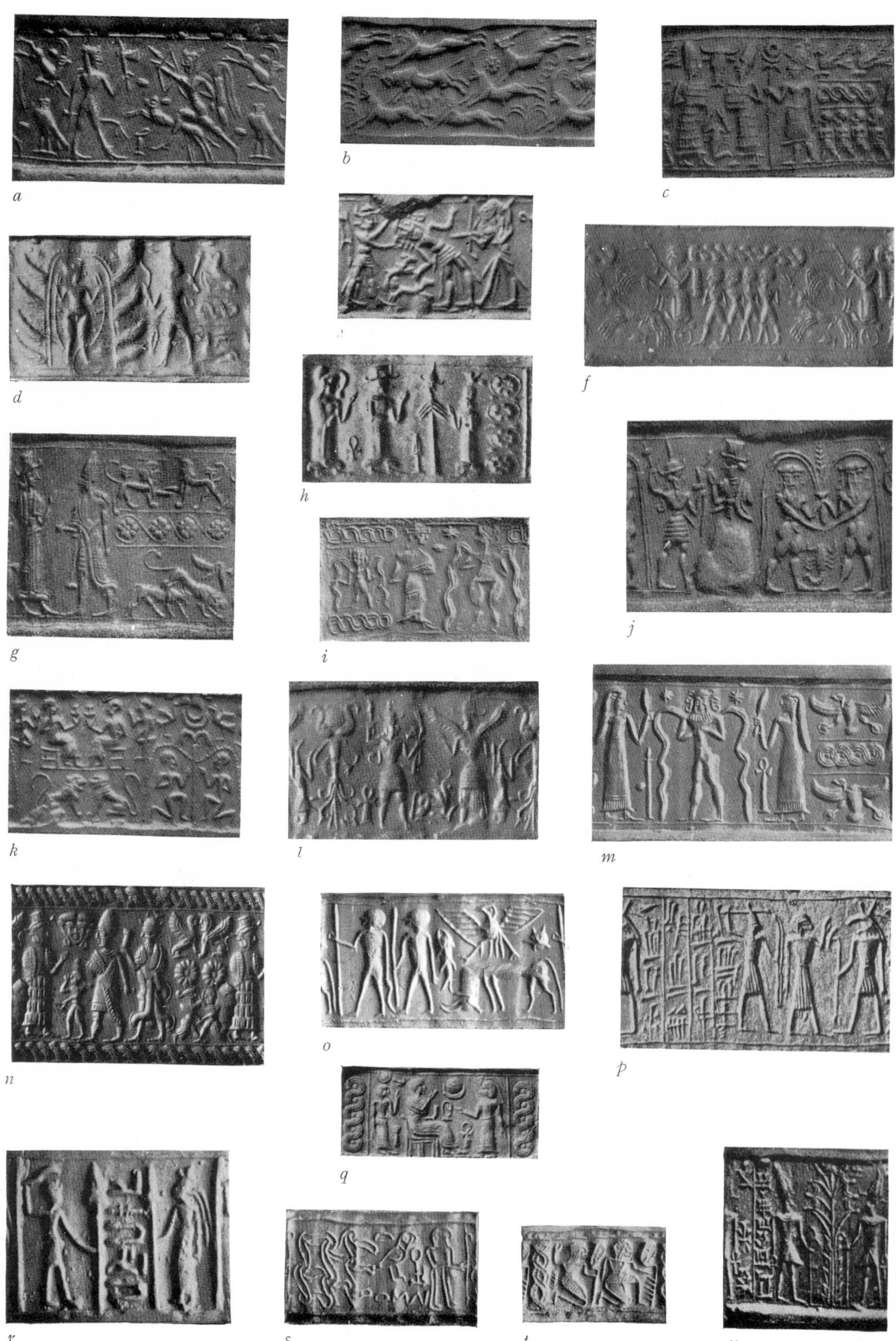

SECOND SYRIAN GROUP (*a–n*) AND PALESTINIAN SEALS

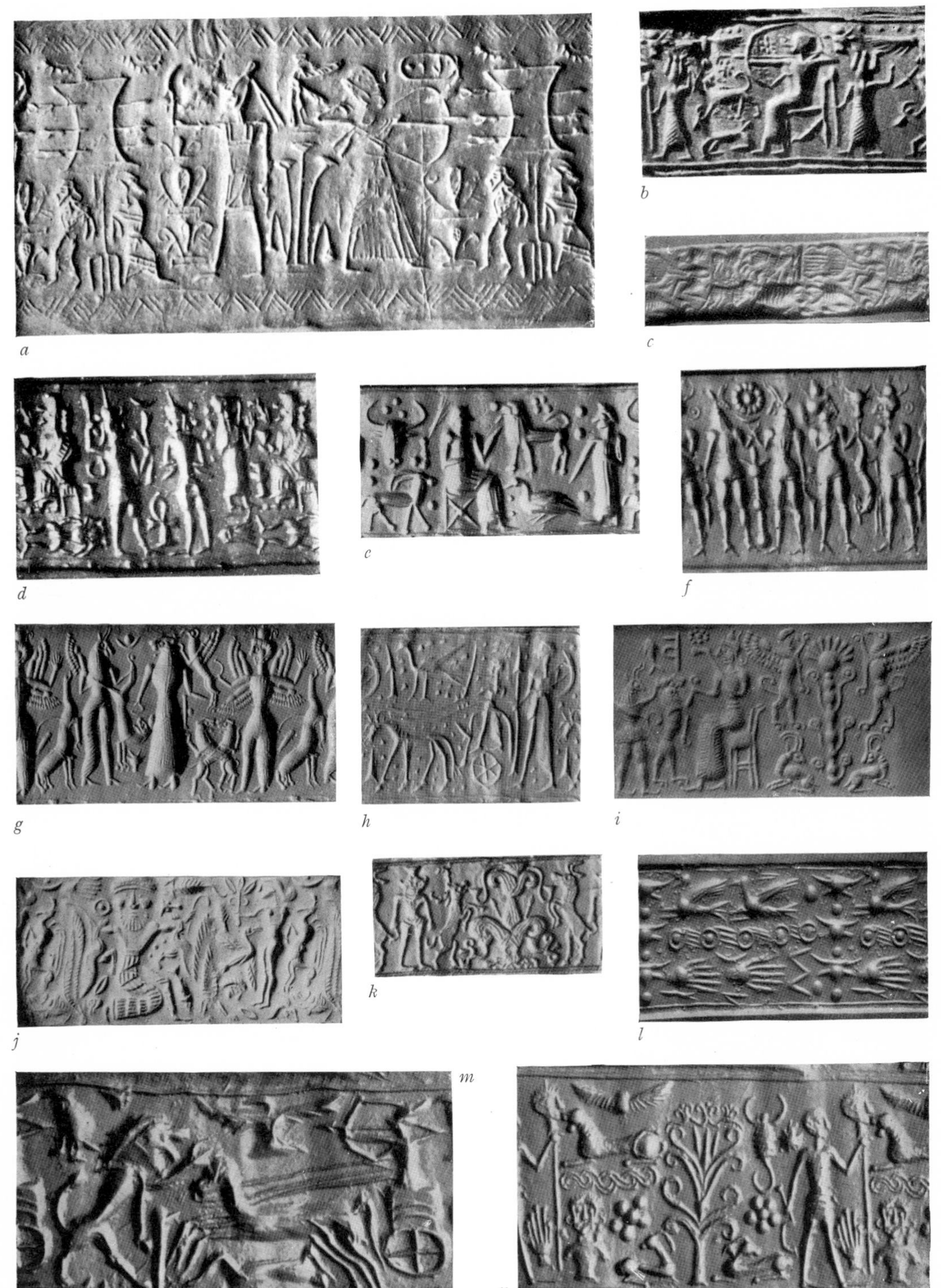

THIRD SYRIAN GROUP

EGYPTIAN AND AEGEAN CYLINDERS (*r, s, v*)

MESOPOTAMIAN MOTIVES IN EUROPEAN ART